FANCY PIG[EONS]

CONTAINING

FULL DIRECTIONS FOR THEIR BREEDING AND MANAGEMENT,

WITH

DESCRIPTIONS OF EVERY KNOWN VARIETY,

AND

ALL OTHER INFORMATION OF INTEREST OR USE TO PIGEON FANCIERS.

ILLUSTRATED.

By JAMES C. LYELL.

1881.

Copyright © 2011 Read Books Ltd.
This book is copyright and may not be
reproduced or copied in any way without
the express permission of the publisher in writing

British Library Cataloguing-in-Publication Data
A catalogue record for this book is available from
the British Library

Contents

	Page No.
The Origin of Fancy Pigeons	3
The Literature of Fancy Pigeons	8
The Pigeon House, Loft, and Aviary	23
Selection of Stock	34
Feeding, Breeding, and Management	37
Colours of Fancy Pigeons	46
Exhibiting Pigeons	51
Diseases if Pigeons	55
Varieties of Domestic Pigeons	64
Common Pigeon	66
The Nun Pigeon	68
The Helmet Pigeon	71
The Coloured headed Pigeon	72
The Spot Pigeon – The Bavette Pigeon	73
The Breast Pigeon	74
The Latz Pigeon	75
The Mane Pigeon	76
The Archangel Pigeon	77
The Ice Pigeon	81
The Miroite Pigeon	82
The Fire Pigeon	83
The Swallow Pigeon	86

The Carmelite Pigeon..87
The Stork Pigeon..88
The Magpie Pigeon...90
The Shield Pigeon – The Priest Pigeon............91
The Monk Pigeon – The Whitehead or
Moulting Pigeon..93
The White Spot Pigeon..94
The Hyacinth Pigeon..97
The Starling Pigeon..97
The Suabian Pigeon..99
The Swiss Pigeon...101
The Black-Backed Gull Pigeon........................102
The Runt Pigeon..103
The Leghorn Runt Pigeon.................................107
The Frizzled or Friesland Pigeon....................110
The Frillback Pigeon..111
The Lace Pigeon..112
The Swift Pigeon...113
The Swallow-Tailed Pigeon.............................115
The Ringbeater Pigeon......................................116
The Mahomet Pigeon...119
The Lowtan Pigeon..122
The Sherajee Pigeon..123
The Mookee Pigeon...125
The Goolee Pigeon...127

The Coral-Eyed Pigeon..................................128
The Capuchin Pigeon.....................................129
The Laugher Pigeon......................................130
The Triganica Pigeon....................................133
Indian Flying Pigeons...................................135
The Antwerp Carrier Pigeon..........................139
The Short Faced Antwerp Pigeon..................148
The Tumbler Pigeon......................................150
The Short Faced Tumbler Pigeon..................164
The German Ancient Pigeon.........................181
The Trumpeter Pigeon..................................182
The Fantail Pigeon..189
The Lace Fantail..196
The Jacobin Pigeon..198
The African Owl Pigeon................................210
The English Owl Pigeon................................217
The Whiskered Owl.......................................220
The Turbit Pigeon...223
Turkish Frilled Pigeons.................................230
The Barb Pigeon..240
The English Carrier.......................................246
The Bagdad Carrier Pigeon...........................257
The Dragoon Pigeon......................................258

Foreign Wattled Pigeons..................................269
The English Pouter..275
The Norwich Cropper.....................................291
The Pigmy Pouter...301
Foreign Cropper Pigeons................................305
Foreign Pigmy Croppers.................................317
Conclusion...321

PREFACE.

The following work on the subject of Fancy Pigeons was commenced in November, 1878, in serial form, in the pages of *The Bazaar, Exchange and Mart*. During the progress of its publication I have been brought into communication with many well-known fanciers in Europe and America, whereby I have added, as I am always endeavouring to do, to the knowledge I previously possessed on the subject. I have described, according to my promise in the Introduction, many varieties of pigeons hitherto unknown in this country; while others, which were only known to the present generation from the record of their names in our old pigeon books, have been recognised in varieties existing abroad. Enough, however, has been written to show how old and how widely spread the pigeon fancy is, and though it may ebb and flow, like all kindred pastimes, it is undoubtedly gaining ground and extending throughout the world. As John Moore, author of the "Columbarium," and father of the fancy in England says in the preface of that work: "Thus we see how the Knowledge of these Birds has been propagated and encourag'd in most Parts of the World at a very great Expence;" and I may conclude in his words, "not being insensible that I shall leave much Room for others to make great Improvements, if any shall hereafter think it worth their while to follow that Track which I have only pointed out to them."

JAMES C. LYELL.

Monifieth House, Forfarshire,
January, 1881.

FANCY PIGEONS.

INTRODUCTION.

THE pigeon fancy is a pastime which has its origin in the love of the lower forms of animal life common to men in all countries. It can be traced back in history for thousands of years, as in Anacreon's "Ode to the Carrier Pigeon," and something similar to our modern pigeon fancy existed in Rome eighteen hundred years ago, as I shall afterwards show. The breeding of choice pigeons has a history in our own literature, and has not been confined, as is imagined by some, to the lower classes of society, for Willughby, the ornithologist, who wrote over two hundred years ago, speaks of the carrier pigeons he saw in the king's aviary in St. James's Park; while in the present day, Her Majesty Queen Victoria has been pleased to furnish her aviaries with fancy pigeons from the lofts of well-known breeders. Widely distributed as is the love for these birds in Great Britain and Ireland, it is probably exceeded in other countries, especially in India, where they have long been carefully tended. Akbar, the Mogul Emperor of Delhi, either wrote, or had written for him, a book on the subject of pigeons and their varieties; and to this day the native rulers of India keep large collections of these birds. I have seen the pigeonries of the King of Oude, who is probably the owner of the greatest number of choice pigeons in the world, his stock numbering many thousands.

When carried out in its highest degree, the breeding of rare domestic pigeons may be regarded as a branch of the fine arts, as it has for its object the production of living pictures, beautiful in form and rich in colour. It is an art requiring much thought and study, and is excelled in only by such as have served a long apprenticeship to it. As an engaging pastime for their leisure hours, before and after the sterner business of life, many find relaxation, both for body and mind in keeping and breeding these birds, which, from their very nature, are universal favourites.

When skill and experience are brought to bear on pigeon breeding, as on any other kindred amusement, such as dog or cage bird breeding, it can generally be made to pay, at least, the expenses connected with it, and therefore many are not deterred from engaging in what would otherwise be beyond their reach. During the last twenty-five years the show system has developed greatly, and many who have a love for pigeons, but who have not the skill or patience necessary to produce them for themselves, are willing to give large sums for choice specimens, either to gratify their taste or to win prizes with. The breeder has a great pleasure in producing, and the purchaser in owning, such good birds, and each party helps the other. The show system has not injured our choicest varieties, in my opinion, for competition has increased the number of breeders considerably, and given them an outlet both for their show, and surplus stock, as was quite unknown before.

In the following chapters on the subject of fancy pigeons, concerning their history, literature, management, and varieties, I hope to give an account of some kinds not known, or but little known, in this country, and to treat the whole subject in as lucid a manner as possible for the benefit of young pigeon fanciers.

CHAPTER I.

THE ORIGIN OF FANCY PIGEONS.

ALTHOUGH, probably, of not much account to many who delight in keeping them, the question of how the many varieties of domestic pigeons now existing in the world originated, is deserving of some attention on my part, before commencing a detailed description of the various kinds.

Naturalists look for the original stock of all tame pigeons in some wild pigeon, and for a long time the stock dove was regarded as this original. This idea is now exploded, as the stock dove is not a bird capable of domestication. The only wild pigeon now believed capable of being the originator of our domestic pigeons is the blue rock pigeon, sub-varieties of which are found in Europe, Asia, and Africa. The British blue rock inhabits the rocks and caves on our sea coasts, and certainly the difference between this bird and a common blue flying tumbler is very little. Their colour is identical, their size almost so. The head and beak of the tumbler are somewhat different from those of the rock pigeon, and the pinions of the latter are longer and stronger, as must necessarily be the case from its mode of life. In the West of Scotland, where they keep and show common pigeons, the wild blue rock domesticated is the bird so called. At the Kilmarnock show a dozen pens of these are generally to be seen, in blues, blue chequers, and sometimes white or Albino specimens.

Some fanciers, who never in the course of their lives observed the least variation in the forms of their fancy pigeons, are of opinion that the more distinct kinds, such as pouters, carriers, jacobins, and fantails, were separate creations, and owe their origin to birds having, probably in a modified form, the peculiarities of these breeds. They have even offered silver cups, or other rewards, for the production of a new form of fancy pigeon other than a mere feather variety, in the belief that such could not be produced. But the life of a fancier, who may have kept pigeons for even sixty years, is but a little while compared to the time they have been kept in the world as domestic birds; for we know they have been carefully bred for nearly two thousand years. No other domestic animal I know of has branched out into such a variety of forms and colours, from which I infer they have been long and extensively cherished by their admirers. Every leading feature of the bird seems to have been already played upon, so that one might almost be unable to suggest any other variation than what already exists. And yet, even lately, a quite new variety of pigeon appeared, as I shall afterwards show.

I think the best argument in favour of some common ancestor for the whole of our fancy pigeons is the fact that they all breed freely together, and that they are only kept up to their best forms by the guiding hands of experienced pigeon fanciers. They constantly throw back, to some remote ancestor, stock that are unfit to go on with. The worst of these, if bred together, while they will no doubt throw young in some cases better than themselves, produce also others still further removed from the desired type, and so the breed soon gets almost unrecognisable.

Supposing the more distinct varieties of pigeons to have been separate creations, then they must certainly have been so distributed in the world as not to come into contact with each other, or they would in a short time have got intermingled. And, again, if not from a common stock, then man must have, from time to time, captured the whole original stocks, or they must have died out, for I have never yet heard of anything approaching a fancy pigeon being found in a state of nature. In fact, if able to exist in a state of nature and protect themselves from birds of prey, fancy pigeons must have been so modified in their fancy points, such as crops and fan shaped tails, as to be but little removed from what we call common pigeons.

Animals in domestication, and also in a wild state, are subject to variations. In the latter state such variations are likely soon to disappear, but in domestication the guiding hand of man fixes them on account of their originality. By pairing any curious specimen of a breed with one of the common type, the young may not prove uncommon;

but they, paired with their uncommon parent, are then apt to reproduce the desired peculiarity. In this way, I believe, every fancy pigeon, however now far removed from the blue rock, has been produced; and, judging from the following analogous case, it does not seem to take very long for nature, guided by the reason of man, to produce the greatest differences in form.

It is well known that the canary bird was first introduced into Europe about three hundred years ago. The difference between the Belgian or Lancashire coppy in form, and the lizard or cinnamon in feather, and the wild canary, as still yearly imported into this country, is as great as the difference between the pouter in form and colour and the blue rock pigeon.

Such results, in a comparatively short time, from canary breeding, have led me to suppose that were bird fanciers to persevere with goldfinches, linnets, and siskins, all of which have been bred in confinement, we should ultimately see similar variations in their forms. Variety of colour constantly occurs among them in a wild state, and such has been noticed by naturalists for 200 years.

Besides the blue rock pigeon inhabiting our coasts, others, differing from it slightly, are known to exist in Asia and Africa. All or any of these that may have been domesticated may have been progenitors of fancy pigeons. One of them, the *Columba Leuconota*, inhabiting the Himalayas, has been lately brought to this country, and was figured in the *Field* newspaper. It is marked on the head and tail like a nun, and, in addition, the wings are marked something like a swallow pigeon. But whether or not it is a true rock pigeon, capable of domestication and able to produce young with a common blue rock or tame pigeon, themselves in turn fertile, is what I cannot say, not having heard of any such experiment that may have been made having turned out successfully. This subject, however, is one more for naturalists than pigeon fanciers, who have generally their hands full with the work of keeping up, and possibly improving, the interesting forms of pigeon life handed down to them from of old.

The case of a new type of form I have referred to occurred about twenty-five years ago, and is recorded in the pages of the *Poultry Chronicle*. The bird in question was a sport from common baldpate tumblers, and a reference to the illustration which will be found in the *Chronicle*, will show where its peculiarity lay. From the crown of its head rose a crest of feathers something like what embellishes the head of the great crowned pigeon of the Eastern Archipelago. The account of the bird as given at the time by its owner, Mr. W. Woodhouse, was as follows: "This curious pigeon is alive, and in my possession. It is a pure bred baldpate, of which it has the properties—viz., clean cut, pearl-eyed, clean-thighed, and ten a side. It is the only one in the world, and is a cock bird. Several competent judges have seen it, and consider it a freak of nature; but whatever it is, it is a wonder. Several of my friends wish me to breed from it to get more, but of this I am doubtful." A few weeks after the above was published, Mr. Brent, the well-known authority on pigeons, wrote as follows in the *Poultry Chronicle*: "A month or two back Mr. James Pryer, a neighbour of mine, and a tolerable judge of pigeons, informed me he had seen something curious in that line at Sevenoaks. He described it as a common chequered dovehouse pigeon, with some rather long feathers growing from the head. Seeing Mr. Woodhouse's description of his crested baldpate, I showed him the cut, and he assured me that, so far as he could see, the pigeon in question was crested just the same. We have both made enquiries respecting the bird, but have not succeeded in discovering whence it came, or where it is gone. Mr. Woodhouse's pigeon is certainly a curiosity."

It will thus be seen that twice within a short time the said peculiarity was observed in separate breeds of pigeons. Unfortunately, Mr. Woodhouse's baldpate does not seem to have produced young like itself, or we should now be in possession of a variety quite distinct from anything that has come under my notice either here or abroad. To such sports, coming uncalled for and unexpectedly, must, I think, be referred all the strange types of pigeons now existing on the globe. The whiskered owl, whose frill is so much developed that it divides at the top and runs almost round the neck in some birds, seems also a recent introduction—at least I can find no notice of this type in any old book on the subject of fancy pigeons; but this can scarcely be called a new variety; it is rather an extraordinary development of an old one.

Of late years we have received from abroad many kinds of pigeons of the highest excellence, showing such breeding that what we had before of the same types seemed but half bred beside them. Still, no quite new or distinct forms have reached us, entirely different from what we knew of, though many distinct varieties of colour have appeared. Should any types of pigeons still unknown to us be in existence, they will likely be found in Central Asia, the interior of China, or the interior of Northern Africa. If anyone with pigeon on the brain, time, money, and daring, would penetrate to Timbuctoo, he might there find something worth bringing home with him.

CHAPTER II.

THE LITERATURE OF FANCY PIGEONS.

FROM many passages in the Old and New Testaments we learn that pigeons were domesticated among the Jews, but there is nothing in the Bible to prove conclusively that choice fancy pigeons, such as we know the Romans delighted in, were kept in Palestine.

Among the Romans, Columella, the writer on agriculture, and Pliny, the author of the "Natural History of the World," in thirty-seven books, speak very decidedly regarding fancy pigeons. An edition of Pliny's work, translated by Dr. Holland into English, was published in 1601, and, though a scarce book, can still be got. The Rev. E. S. Dixon, in his "Dovecote and Aviary" (1851), says that Columella was scandalised at the inveteracy and extravagance of the Pigeon Fancy amongst his contemporaries; and that Pliny records that before Pompey's civil war, L. Axius, a Roman knight, used to sell a single pair of pigeons for four hundred denarii, equal to nearly £13 of our money.

There are also passages from these writers showing that pigeons were used as messengers, and many passages from mediæval writers have been recently collected, proving the same use of them. Tavernier, in his "Six Voyages into Persia and the East Indies," 1677, alludes to carrying pigeons, and Mr. T. C. Burnell has recently pointed out that a like allusion may be found in "An Exact and Curious Survey of the East Indies," London, 1615; but as for any descriptions of fancy pigeons, I know nothing earlier than what the Rev. E. S. Dixon quotes from Aldrovandus, whose works on natural history were published in thirteen folio volumes, in Latin, in 1637-67.

The first English writer I know of, who alludes in any particular way to fancy pigeons, is Francis Willughby, whose "Ornithology," edited by John Ray, was published in London, first in Latin, in 1676, and afterwards in English, 1678, in folio. I have had both editions, which, as regards pigeon matters, are similar; but the latter has some additional plates of bird-catching and chapters on song birds. Two of the seventy eight plates of birds are of domestic pigeons, and very crude they are—"A cropper dove, a carrier, a jacobine, a broad-tailed shaker," &c.; all seem but half bred, and could scarcely represent the birds described in the text, such as "we saw in the King's Aviary in St. James's Park, and at Mr. Cope's, an embroiderer, in Jewin-street, London." Willughby, in English, is worth about 30s.

The earliest known English book on fancy pigeons, written by an experienced pigeon fancier, is "Columbarium, or the Pigeon House, being an Introduction to a Natural History of Tame Pigeons, by John Moore. London: printed for J. Wilford, behind the Chapter House in St. Paul's Churchyard, 1735." This book is so scarce that it is something for a pigeon fancier to say he has seen it. I should suppose that only a very limited number of copies were printed, probably for distribution among the author's friends. Mr. Moore was an apothecary "at the Pestle and Mortar in Lawrence Pountney's-lane, the first great gates on the left hand from Cannon-street, who formerly lived at the Pestle and Mortar in Abchurch-lane." He was the proprietor and inventor of a vermifuge, and Pope alludes to the same in some verses he addressed to him, which may be found in his works. These verses of Pope's were first brought to the notice of the present generation of pigeon fanciers by the Rev. Alex. Headley, Rector of Hardenhuish, Wilts, well known under the *nom de plume* of "The Wiltshire Rector" of the *Journal of Horticulture*, in that paper, on October 9th, 1866. The "Columbarium" is mentioned in Lowndes' "Bibliographer's Manual," as published at 8s., or perhaps as worth that price when he published his manual, but I have seen the notice of it in the *Gentleman's Magazine* for February, 1735, among the lately published books, "price one *shilling*." Moore only lived a short time after this, his death being mentioned in the *Gentleman's Magazine* of 1737, page 252, as follows:—"April 12. Mr. John Moore, of Abchurch-lane, the noted worm doctor. He will now shortly verify Mr. Pope's witty observations, viz.:

> 'O learned friend of Abchurch-lane,
> Who sett'st our entrails free,
> Vain is thy art, thy powder vain,
> Since worms shall eat e'en thee.'"

The "Columbarium" is a thin octavo of sixty pages. There are four copies of it in the British Museum, and one in the possession of Mr. Esquilant, of Brixton, the well-known pigeon judge, which I have seen. I know of no others; but Mr. Eaton, whose works on pigeons will be afterwards mentioned, had one which is supposed to have been burnt or otherwise destroyed. I know some fanciers who tried to obtain it after his death, but it could not be found. At page 191 of his treatise of 1858 Eaton graphically describes the discovery of this rare pigeon book. He had spent many a spare hour, as I have done, in trying to obtain it, and he at last succeeded. "The boy went down a tremendous long shop to his employer, who went and laid his hand upon a book. I saw the boy coming with a book in his hand, I thought it was something about pigeons, never thought it was Moore's work. To my astonishment and delight it was the identical work I was in search of. Having it in my hands, I thought my eyes would have darted out of the sockets of my head when I beheld the book. I thought, 'I'll be blessed if ever this book leaves my possession, whatever the price.'"

The "Columbarium" was reprinted by Eaton in his "Treatise on Pigeons," 1852 and 1858, but these are now scarce themselves. It has also been reprinted in America, and lately in England (at the *Field* office). The latter is a *verbatim et literatim* copy of the original edition of 1735, and contains a brief notice of the author by W. B. Tegetmeier, F.Z.S. An original copy would, no doubt, realise a fancy price from a pigeon enthusiast.

The next book on pigeons published in this country was "A Treatise on Domestic Pigeons, inscribed to John Mayor, Esq., London, printed for and sold by C. Barry, in Ingram-court, Fenchurch-street, 1765." This work, an octavo of 160 pages, has been called, by mistake, chiefly a reprint of Moore without acknowledgment. The author, who was an experienced pigeon fancier, says in his preface : "In regard to the model of this treatise, we do not offer it to the public as an entire new work, but have proceeded on the plan of Mr. Moore, have corrected some errors, and made many additions. And as Mr. Moore's essay is very deficient for want of cuts to convey a just idea of the different species, in order to supply that defect, we have procured engravings from the best hands, at a very great expense, in order to illustrate this work, all which are done from the life, and very masterly executed, under the inspection of the author and other fanciers." It is illustrated with thirteen full page steel or copper engravings of pigeons, and a frontispiece representing the loft, matching pen, hopper, water fountain, &c.

There are two editions of this work, one being on larger and better paper than the other, and having the plates of the almond and black mottled tumblers different. In it the almond has the words "Simpson sculpt." on it, and the mottled "Mayor delint. et sculpt." below it, so that this Mayor was perhaps the person to whom the book was inscribed. The author speaks of "a kind of standard, calculated for the better judging of almond tumblers, lately published by some of the admirers of this fancy, elegantly engraved on copper plate, at the top of which is an almond tumbler, very finely executed from life, the outlines being inimitably well performed, and by much the best I ever saw, and at so reasonable a price as 6d." A copy of this "standard" is given in Eaton's latest book at page 186. It is entitled "Ordinances, established by the Columbarian Society, at the Globe Tavern, Fleet-street, respecting the perfections and imperfections of Almond or Ermin Tumblers, 1764." The engraving of the almond tumbler on it has "Simpson sculpt" below the bird, and the large paper edition of the treatise of 1765 is, no doubt, illustrated from the same plate.

The most original part of the "Treatise on Pigeons" of 1765, is the long account of the almond tumbler, a variety no more than mentioned by Moore, but which had lately risen to great estimation in London. The Mahomet pigeon, which Willughby had described, but which Moore had evidently never seen, is also well described; but most of the book is, as the author acknowledges in his preface, "on the plan of Mr. Moore." It is not known who the author was, but a correspondent has informed me that he had a copy full of manuscript notes that he supposed to be by the author, and that on the title-page, under "Domestic Pigeons," was written "by G. T., private, C. B. F."

I have had many copies of the commoner edition of this book, but only one on large paper. The value of it depends chiefly on its condition and size of paper, as many copies are very much cut into. A really good clean copy is not dear at a guinea.

Some amusing verses on fancy pigeons will be found in Vol. 6 of the "New Foundling Hospital for Wit," published in 1784.

"The New and Complete Pigeon Fancyer, or Modern Treatise on Domestic Pigeons, by Daniel Girton, of the county of Bucks, price only 1s. 6d.," followed the 1765 book, probably as it got out of print, and to supply a felt want. This has no date. It passed through many editions, of which I have seen five, all differing somewhat in the title pages. What I take to be the earliest, is that published by Alex. Hogg, at the King's Arms, No. 16, Paternoster-row. The publishers of the later editions are Alex. Hogg and Co., H. Hogg, and J. Bailey. On the back of the title page of the first edition is an advertisement of the "New and Complete Bird Fancyer, or Bird Fancyer's Recreation and Delight," by Mr. Wm. Thompson, who afterwards, in the last editions of Girton, supplants him as the author of the "Complete Pigeon Fancier." It is, then, "By Mr. William Thompson, assisted by Mr. Daniel Girton, of the County of Bucks." The name Girton is supposed to be a *nom de plume* taken from Moore's "Columbarium," where, speaking of turbits, the author says, "I have seen a flight of them kept by one Girton, that would mount almost high as tumblers."

"Girton, *alias* Thompson," is a duodecimo, and from the type of the various editions, some being modern and others old, I fancy the publications extended from about 1780 to 1820. Some of the later editions are curtailed in the subject matter; the earliest is paged up to 140, but commences at page 13, though there are not twelve pages of preface and title. All have a folding plate, containing the figures of twelve fancy pigeons, copied in small from the treatise of 1765. The book contains but little original matter, being merely a compilation from Moore and Mayor, by which title it will be easier to designate the 1765 book, and is one of a series of handbooks published by A. Hogg and his successors, and uniform with the "Complete Bird Fancier," "Complete Farmer," and others. It can usually be purchased for 5s., or less, but uncut copies, clean as from the press, such as I have had, are worth more. The Chinese pigeon mentioned by Girton would seem, from the description, not a domestic pigeon, but a wild dove.

The next pigeon book was an entirely original one, entitled "A New and Complete Treatise on the Art of Breeding and Managing the Almond Tumbler, by an Old Fancier." Two editions are said to be in existence, dated 1802 and 1804. All I have seen are dated 1802. The first issue was "printed for the author by W. Williams, No. 15, Chancery-lane, London, price 5s., 1802," and the unsold copies were bought by Alex. Hogg and Co., and sent out with a new title page, "price 4s., in extra boards." This book is an octavo of 104 pages, with a coloured frontispiece of an almond tumbler, not, in my opinion, so good a picture of a pigeon as some of those in the treatise of 1765. The author was Mr. W. P. Windus, a solicitor in London, who was afterwards secretary of the Columbarian Society. The portrait of an almond tumbler in his book is represented as carrying its wings over its tail, but an earlier

picture of an almond will, if I remember rightly, be found in some of the sporting magazines before 1800, in which the tail is carried over the wings.

In an impression of the "Almond Tumbler" of 1802, that bears the autograph of Thomas Garle, jun., 1809, who, with his father, was long connected with the Columbarian Society, I found a very interesting document. This document was an invitation to dine with the Columbarians, to elect officers for the year, and to audit accounts, and is headed by the illustration which I have copied, and is signed by Windus. It will be observed that the almond here carries his wings below his tail, and I think it is copied from the "Sporting Magazine," above referred to. In the "Gentleman's Magazine," of 1792, at page 1152, is a notice of the marriage of Mr. Windus, and in the same volume are some interesting particulars regarding another gentleman of the same name, possibly his relative.

After this time there was no original matter on the subject of fancy pigeons published in this country till 1851. Besides the books I have mentioned, several with such titles as "The Sporting Dictionary," "Dictionary of Country Affairs," "Complete Sportsman," &c., came out from time to time from the year 1700, giving, but always at secondhand, short descriptions of fancy pigeons. I have seen many of these, but for anything they contain on the subject in hand they are scarcely worth a place in a pigeon fancier's library. One small book on "Bees, Pigeons, Rabbits, and Canary Birds," by Peter Boswell, was published about forty years ago.

In 1851 appeared the "Dovecote and Aviary," by the Rev. E. S. Dixon, who had published "Ornamental and Domestic Poultry" in 1850. The "Dovecote and Aviary" is a duodecimo, published by John Murray; but copies with a different title page, bearing the name W. S. Orr and Co., who seem to have acquired the remainders, are also to be met with. Mr. Dixon was a scholar of great research, but more of a general naturalist than particular pigeon fancier. The illustrations are either by an artist who did not understand fancy pigeons, or he had the merest wasters to copy from. Still, the book has a charm of its own, and should be on the shelves of all literary pigeon fanciers. An abridgment of the dovecote part of it, embracing, in addition, fancy rabbits, was published in 1854, under the title of "Pigeons and Rabbits," by E. Sebastian Delamer, a name said to have been assumed by the author when residing on the sea coast. It is illustrated by Mr. Harrison Weir, but the "portraitures" are not what would be considered up to the mark in these exacting days. This book must have had a great sale, for it can yet be seen on almost any bookstall all over the country; but when such passages as the following are to be found in it, it can scarcely be called a good guide for the learner :—"Those tumblers which are self-coloured or whole-coloured, *i.e.*, all black or all cinnamon coloured, in various shades, or all cream colour, are called kites;" and, again, under baldpate tumblers, "The character of the head much resembles that of the turbit and the jacobine."

This was my first book on fancy pigeons; I saw it in a bookseller's window one day when trudging home from school, and began to save up immediately for its acquisition. I soon had it by heart, and such passages as "Tumblers, saith Willughby, are small and of divers colours. They have strange motions, turning themselves backwards over their head, and show like footballs in the air," are indelibly imprinted on my memory.

In 1851, John Matthews Eaton, of London, an enthusiastic fancier of short-faced tumblers, published a treatise on the Almond tumbler. This and his other works are most quaintly written. All rules of grammar and composition are set at defiance, irrelevant matter is constantly introduced, and anecdotes, told in the most rambling style, are always cropping up; but his latest work, published in 1858, incorporating the previous ones, is certainly one of the most interesting books on fancy pigeons ever published. The greater part of the "Treatise on the Almond Tumbler" (1851), is copied from Windus, and unacknowledged, a method of publication he afterwards departed from, when he scrupulously gave every previous writer his due. He seemed to have been troubled with *cacoëthes scribendi*, saying "all the world in a fever about the forthcoming exhibition, I was desirous of bringing out something; after racking my brains (which I think, generally, is about as clear as mud in a wine glass), the idea of the almond tumbler struck me, which I brought out." This book is a thin octavo, having for a frontispiece a coloured portrait of an almond tumbler "very masterly executed," as Mayor would have said, by Mr. Dean Wostenholme, the friend of the author, a pigeon fancier himself. It is by far the best picture of a pigeon published up to that time, and I question if it has been excelled since.

Encouraged by his success, Eaton, who had obtained, after much seeking, a copy of old Moore's "Columbarium," brought out in 1852, "A Treatise on the Art of Breeding and Managing Tame, Domesticated, and Fancy Pigeons." In it he reprinted the "Columbarium," taking it as his text, and adding thereto his own notes and what he found original from Mayor and Girton. This book is uniform in size with his 1851 treatise, which is embodied in it, and has for a frontispiece the same portrait of an almond tumbler. At the same time he published a set of six life size pictures of fancy pigeons, from the pencil of his friend Mr. Dean Wostenholme. These are the pouter and carrier, almond, black mottle, baldhead, and beard tumblers. They are to be met with of different colouring, being republished as the first lot were disposed of. The pouter is a yellow in some, in others a blue, and the baldhead is blue in some and red in others. The tumblers are very fair pictures, but the pouter is sadly deficient in lines; while the carrier is a grand production, as beautiful as a new medal.

As the 1852 treatise got sold out, Eaton concentrated his efforts in the production of a larger work, which he published in 1858, under the title of "A Treatise on the Art of Breeding and Managing Tame, Domesticated, Foreign, and Fancy Pigeons." This contains all of his previous books, and is illustrated with thirty coloured pictures of pigeons, also by Mr. Wostenholme, the majority of which are not up to the mark for our day. The papers on continental fancy pigeons that had appeared in the *Poultry Chronicle*, from the pen of Mr. B. P. Brent, are included in it, and the book contains more information on the subject it treats of than any previously published; in fact, it is a compilation of the works of all previous writers. It is paged up to 200, but there are some copies that contain some extra pages of opinions of the press on the book itself. These copies seem to have been made up two years later, some of the notices being dated in 1860.

In 1860 Eaton published a second set of six coloured portraits of pigeons, like the first, from the pencil of Mr. Wostenholme. These are the white fantail, yellow jacobin, silver owl, blue turbit, black mottled trumpeter, and black barb. Specimens of some of these varieties have been introduced into this country from abroad, of late years, that put these pictures as standards to one side.

These are a list of Mr. Eaton's publications on the subject of fancy pigeons, except "A New and Improved Coloured Diagram, or a Plan of Building or Fitting up a Pigeonary, embellished with tumblers, pouters, and carriers, price 2s.," which is not of much account. It shows nesting places of different sizes to suit the different kinds.

Eaton's books are getting scarce. The largest and best, that of 1858, which contains all of the previous ones, if quite clean and perfect, is not dear at a guinea.

Moubray's treatise of breeding, rearing, and fattening of domestic poultry, a work first published about 1815, containing a little, at second hand, on the subject of fancy pigeons, ran through many editions. In 1854, the last edition, much enlarged, was published under the editorship of Mr. L. Méall and Dr. Horner. This has several coloured plates, one of which contains the figures of fancy pigeons, including the pouter and carrier, evidently copied from Eaton's large portraits of 1852. In the letterpress there are notices of the principal kinds of fancy pigeons, evidently not from the pen of a fancier. The origin of the word turbit, which seems to have puzzled previous writers, is correctly given here for the first time, I believe.

The *Poultry Chronicle*, a weekly periodical, began on the 1st of March, 1854, was continued for seventy-seven weeks, the last number being published on 15th August, 1855, when it was incorporated with the *Cottage Gardener*. Complete sets of it, generally bound in three volumes, small quarto, may be occasionally met with, at from 10s. to 20s., according to condition. It is very interesting as the first journal devoted to the poultry and pigeon fancy. Many names are mentioned in its pages unknown to the present generation, while others are still extant in the prize lists of the day. In its pages, under the heading of the "Columbary," the late Mr. Brent contributed many papers on fancy pigeons, which were republished in Eaton's largest book.

"The Pigeon Book," by B. P. Brent, is a small duodecimo of 114 pages, containing his writings in the *Poultry Chronicle*, *Cottage Gardener*, &c. It is illustrated with what the title-page calls "highly finished" engravings, but some of them are very unintelligible, and more like mediæval "icons" than modern pictures. Most of them are copied from the French work on pigeons by Boitard and Corbié, to be afterwards mentioned. The book contains much information on French and German fancy pigeons.

The modern works on fancy pigeons, by Mr. Tegetmeier and Mr. Fulton, will be familiar to all fanciers. They are handsome books, well illustrated with coloured plates, the former by Mr. Harrison Weir and the latter by Mr. J. W. Ludlow, of Birmingham. "The Practical Pigeon Keeper," by Lewis Wright, published October, 1879, is a book of 232 pages, illustrated chiefly from the same blocks as the book by Baldamus, published at Dresden in 1878, to be afterwards mentioned.

The *Poultry Review*, an extinct periodical, began on 21st June, 1873, and ended with No. 81, on 31st December, 1874, may be interesting in later years, as containing many papers on, and illustrations of, fancy pigeons.

A periodical, entitled *The Pigeon*, conducted by Mr. Thomas M. Denne, who has contributed papers on pigeons to the *Field* and other journals, over the *nom de plume* of "Carrier," existed in London from 19th February, 1876, to 28th December, 1877, when, as he says, he was obliged to whistle it down. A complete set, ninety-eight numbers, makes a thick quarto volume.

I have enumerated all the literature on the subject published in this country of which I know, excepting what may be found in such books as "Beeton's Book of Pets," the "Boy's Own Book," "Rogers' Pigeon Keeper," "Pigeons," by Hugh Piper, and such like, that are of no consequence. From its commencement till the present time, the *Field* newspaper has had a column on poultry and pigeons, where may be found many articles and illustrations on the subject, enough in themselves to form an interesting volume. *The Bazaar* (to which *The Country* has been added), *The Live Stock Journal*, *The Journal of Horticulture*, and *The Fanciers' Chronicle* have also had frequent papers on pigeons.

Besides all these, there are several foreign books on the subject. It appears Akbar, the Mogul Emperor, who reigned in Delhi nearly 300 years ago, was fond of pigeons, and that his prime minister, Abdool Furjool, wrote a treatise on them about the year 1596. I have heard mention of this when in India, but I am not aware if it is extant.

I have a quarto of thirty-two pages in Latin and German, published at Jenæ in 1706, entitled "De Jure Columbarum vom Tauben-Recht" (the Law of Pigeons or Pigeon-rights), which appears to be an argument at law on the rights of pigeon fanciers or keepers. It contains quotations from Roman and Latin writers.

"Les Pigeons de Volière et de Colombier," by Messrs. Boitard and Corbie, is an octavo book of 240 pages, published at Paris in 1824. It contains twenty-five plates of pigeons, few of which are nicely drawn. Those who have Brent's book may see the style of them, as most of his are copied from this book, and not improved in the copying. Boitard and Corbie describe twenty-four races of fancy pigeons and sub-divide them into 122 varieties. The book was published with plain plates, coloured plates, and on vellum paper with coloured plates, at 6f., 12f., and 24f. respectively. It seems to treat its subject more from a naturalist's than fancier's point of view. It is now worth considerably more than the published prices, having become scarce, as much as 15s. being sometimes asked for the edition with plain plates.

Other French works on pigeons are, Lullin, F., "L'art de distinguer, d'élever, de multiplier et d'engraisser les différentes espéces et variétés des Pigeons, de Colombier, et de Volière," avec 28 planches, Paris 1860, 12mo.; Didieux, M., "Guide d'éleveur des Pigeons, de Colombier, et de Volière, Paris ; as well as several other small handbooks.

Of German books on fancy pigeons there are a considerable number. The principal one is "Das Ganze der Taubenzucht" (the whole art of breeding pigeons), by Gottlieb Neumeister. This is now in its third edition, having been first published in 1839, I believe. The copy I have was published at Weimar in 1876, and is edited by Herr Gustav Prütz, the editor of a German bi-monthly periodical on pigeons, entitled *Columbia*, which is published at Stettin. "Das Ganze der Taubenzucht" in an oblong quarto book of about sixty closely printed pages, illustrated with seventeen coloured plates of fancy pigeons, each containing from four to fourteen separate figures. They are extremely crude as regards execution, but serve to give some idea of the numerous varieties fancied in Germany.

"Die Arten der Haustaube" (the varieties of the domestic pigeon), by the above Herr Gustav Prütz, is an octavo book, which contains all the letterpress in Neumeister's work, and a little in addition. This book is not illustrated, except by a slight woodcut of an English pouter (from Tegetmeier's "Pigeons"), on the cover. The copy I have is the third edition, published at Leipzig in 1878, and the author gives a list of German publications on the subject of pigeons, which appear to be numerous. Of these I may mention, Brehm, Chr. Ludw., "Die Naturgeschichte und Zucht der Tauben," Weimar, 1857. A new edition, by Gustav Prütz, is in the press; Carl, L., "Untersuchungen über den Schädelbau domesticirter Tauben," Pirna, 1878 ; Korth, Dr. D., "Die Taubenzucht zum Vergnügen, oder die Flug-und Hoftauben," Berlin, 1855 ; Putsche, Br., "Taubenkatechismus, mit 3 Kupfertaseln," Leipzig ; "Der Taubenfreund," 6th edition, Plauen, 1876 ; "Der Tauber oder die Geheimnisse der Tauben-und Hühnerzucht," 4th edition, Naumburg,

1860; Weber, D. A., "Der Taubenfreund, oder gründlicher Unterricht in der Taubenzucht," 2nd edition, Quedlinburg, 1850; Woltmann, J. J., "Der Taubenschlag oder die Wartung und Pflege," thirteen plates, Altona, 1876.

In 1878 there was published at Dresden a new book on poultry and pigeons, entitled "Illustrirtes Handbuch der Federviehzucht," by Dr. A. E. E. Baldamus. Vol. I. contains information on fowls, ducks, geese, &c.; and Vol. II. is chiefly on pigeons. It appears to be a compilation from Neumeister, Prütz, and Fulton. It is a large octavo of 452 pages, beautifully printed, and well illustrated with good woodcuts, copied in small from Mr. Ludlow's illustrations to Fulton's pigeon book.

The Italian publications on fancy pigeons are confined, as far as I know, to descriptions of the Modenese flying pigeons. The first book on this subject was C. Malmusi's "Dei Triganieri: cenni storici" (Historical notices of the Triganieri—technical name for the Modenese pigeon flyers). This is a rare little book; it was published in 1851 in Modena, being reprinted from the journal *l'Indicatoré Modenese*. Professor Bonizzi says regarding it, "The author has collected, from books and archives, all that can be known of the history of the Triganieri, and speaks with much learning about their origin and their sport."

In 1872, Dr. Fulvio Martinelli, published at Modena, in folio, a work of 107 pages, entitled "Memoria Sulla Collezione di Colombi nostrali," regarding which Bonizzi says, "From which title everyone would certainly expect the description of a collection of pigeons; whereas, instead, the memorial commences as if it were a general treatise on pigeons, and continues giving stupid arguments; it speaks so little and so confusedly about the Modenese pigeons, that I believe it is impossible to form an idea of them from it. I hoped then to find in it useful notices about the breeding, to see verified in it the experiments which I supposed had been made by the author with our pigeons, but I was disappointed in this expectation."

In 1872 there was published by the Societa Veneto-Trentina di Scienze Naturali, an admirable treatise on the Modenese pigeons, entitled "Le Variazioni dei Colombi Domestici, di Modena, di Paolo Bonizzi." This is paged 265-312, and illustrated with two folding coloured plates, containing in all twenty varieties of the Triganica pigeon. This treatise is the work of a scholar and fancier, and goes thoroughly into its subject.

In 1876, Professor Bonizzi published, at Modena, a quarto volume of 180 pages, entitled "I. Colombi di Modena," which is an extension of his 1872 work. In this he mentions no less than 152 different varieties of the Modena pigeon, all of which have received names from the Triganieri. This is illustrated by the same two coloured plates as above-mentioned, and by two plain plates of the pigeon house and its fittings.

On the subject of racing, messenger, or what are called homing pigeons, several books have been published. In this country Messrs. Routledge and Sons have published one entitled "The Homing Pigeon," by Mr. W. B. Tegetmeier, F.Z.S., and Messrs. Hartley and Sons, Woolwich, importers of these birds, publish another called "Homing Pigeons; their Rearing, Training, and Management," price 1s. The earliest book published abroad on this subject I know of is one I have, entitled "La Colombe, Messagère plus rapide que l'éclair, plus prompte que la nue, par Michel Sabbagh, traduit de l'Arabe en François par A. I. Silvestre de Sacy. A Paris, de l'imprimerie impériale, an. xiv. = 1805." This is a beautifully printed octavo volume of ninety-six pages, which on being opened has the Arabic on the right hand and the French translation on the left. The Belgian physician, Dr. F. Chapuis, since dead (October, 1879), published the following works: "Le Pigeon Voyageur Belge, Verviers, 1865," "Le Pigeon Voyageur Belge, de son Instinct d'Orientation" and "Le Pigeon dans les Forteresses et à Zanzibar. M. La Perre de Roo is author of "Le Pigeon Messager, ou Guide pour l'élève du Pigeon Voyageur," Paris. Other French works are: Payerne, "Note sur la Nosographie des Pigeons," Cherbourg, and Espanet, Al, "De l'Éducation des Pigeons, des Oiseaux de Luxe, de Volière et de Cage," Paris.

The German books on voyageur or homing pigeons include Lenzen, H. J., "Die Brieftaube," Dresden, 1873; Dettel, Rob., "Der Geflügelhof," 5th ed., Weimar, 1874; Du Poy de Podio "Die Brieftauben in der Kriegskunst," Leipzig, 1873; and Russ, Dr. Karl, "Die Brieftaube. Ein Hand-und Lehrbuch für ihre Verpflegung, Abrichtung, &c.," Hanover, 1877.

In Herr Prütz's list of books on pigeons in his "Die Arten der Haustaube, he mentions, Harris, E. D., "The Structure, Flight, and Habits of the Different Varieties of the Domesticated Pigeon," Boston. I have not seen this, the only book on pigeons published in America, I suppose, with the exception of the reprint of "Moore's Columbarium." The American fanciers have several periodicals that treat of pigeons and other pet stock, which are generally very well got up as regards paper and printing, but I have not found, and I can scarcely yet expect to find, in them much original matter on the subject of fancy pigeons. In their illustrations of both poultry and pigeons the influence of Mr. Ludlow, of Birmingham, is very plainly seen. I have no doubt that by and bye the American fanciers will make their mark in the breeding of fancy pigeons, as they have not grudged to expend large sums in the purchase of good stock.

In conclusion I may say that the author's edition of the "Treatise on the Almond Tumbler," 1802, was priced on the title page "seven shillings," and that this is generally altered with pen and ink to "five shillings." The remainders were bought by A. Hogg and Co., who printed a new title page for them, on which was printed "price 4s., in extra boards."

Mr. Wolstenholme, the artist, who is now over eighty years of age, wrote to me lately saying, that the set of six plates of the pouter, carrier, &c., were first published by himself, for his own account, in 1834. He sold the plates to Eaton, who republished them with his "Treatise on Pigeons," in 1852. Mr. Wolstenholme wrote me in June, 1875, "I was the inventor of surface printing in colours in the year 1847, but was not able to patent it. The prints were exhibited in the Great Exhibition of 1851 as a new mode of printing. From them all the colour printing of the present day comes, from which many have made large fortunes."

For many years I have endeavoured to obtain a copy Moore's "Columbarium," and, in searching for it, I have written hundreds of letters and spent many days wandering over London enquiring for it. After correcting these pages I am happy to be able to add that on the 5th November, 1879, I obtained an original and perfect copy of this rare book, so precious to a pigeon fancier. There are now, therefore, two copies of the "Columbarium" outside of the British Museum, Mr. Esquilant's and mine.

CHAPTER III.

THE PIGEON HOUSE, LOFT, AND AVIARY.

I SUPPOSE the majority of pigeon fanciers who commenced their pursuit when young, began by keeping a few common birds or flying tumblers in boxes fixed to some wall out of reach of cats or other enemies. This was the way I began the fancy, and some narrow escapes I had when up the ladder inspecting what was going on inside my pigeon locker; and I would strongly advise all guardians of pigeon-keeping boys who have no other means of housing their pets than in wall boxes, to see that they are not only well secured to the wall—for I have known them to give way from improper fastening—but fixed at no great distance from the ground. Keeping really good pigeons in wall boxes is almost out of the question for little control over the birds can be exercised, and sooner or later, if the young fancier means advancement in his pursuit, he must find ways and means for the better housing of his pets.

When no other means of keeping pigeons than in wall boxes is convenient, then they should be made of larch or other durable wood, and well jointed, so as to allow the wind no entrance, except from the holes at which the birds go out and in, and they ought to be fixed in the most sheltered position available. To keep pigeons in boxes facing the east or north is unnecessary cruelty; for even if a wall is so exposed, the boxes can be fastened, so that the fronts need not face the cold exposure.

The box space necessary for each pair of all small pigeons, such as tumblers and turbits, is about 12in. by 12in., and 10in. high. This is the measurement inside, and, in addition, there is the landing board, which will project about 4in. Unless each pair is provided with two such apartments, there will be little peace in the colony, for pigeons do not like to lay in their last nest. Common hardy birds generally go to nest when their young ones are about a fortnight or eighteen days old, and so there is really no accommodation for them in the old place. The plan of having two nesting places (entering from one hole) on a lower level than the landing board, but divided inside by a piece of wood, so as to keep the young ones from the sitting hen, is not a good one. The young ones will find their way over the division much sooner than they would do from one separate apartment to another; and the difficulty in cleaning out the old nests, when lower in level than the landing board, in boxes fixed at some height from the ground, is very

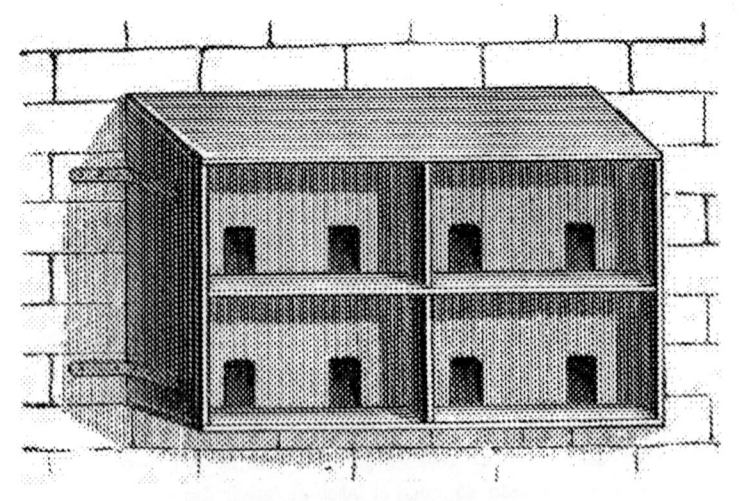

FIG. 1.—PIGEON HOUSE FOR FOUR PAIRS.

great. No scraper could do it thoroughly; even the hands of the owner could not reach all the corners, and but few could adopt such a disgusting method, as the nests of young pigeons just flown are very foul. A hinged bottom piece would certainly facilitate matters, but the wind would find its way past such an arrangement.

The inside should therefore be on the same level with the landing board, as in Fig. 1, and it will not matter much, though the landing board itself is not divided in its length between the two nests given to each pair, for although the young ones will leave the nest when about three and a half weeks old, and join their sitting parent, no bad result will follow; they will not injure the eggs; they will be much warmer at night; and by the time their successors are hatched, their parents will have driven them out, being about five weeks old, able to fly and to do for themselves. Such a pair of nests may be multiplied according to the wishes of the pigeon keeper. The roof of the whole must always have sufficient slope to carry off the rain, and should be in one piece, as wood 17in. wide can easily be got.

No one who is really interested in his pigeons will long continue to keep them in wall lockers if he can by any means avoid it, and some vacant building, shed, or loft, will be appropriated for the purpose. Such a place a fancier ought, with the assistance of a few carpenter's tools, to be able to fit up himself. Cat and rat proof he must have it, and mouse proof also, if possible, for while the former will destroy the birds themselves, the latter spoil their food.

The great majority of fancy pigeons may be allowed their liberty in the open air, with safety to their lives and positive advantage to their health, but choice pouters, carriers, short-faced tumblers, jacobins or fantails, are not so able to take care of themselves. Still, it is surprising how wary even such varieties as these become, if flown from their squeakerhood. In granting them their liberty, however, which must only be occasional, according to the weather, the owner must be entirely guided by circumstances, such as the surroundings of his place and the special character of each bird. There must always be a certain amount of risk encountered, and it is for the owner to consider whether the advantages to be gained will outweigh it. Choice pigeons no doubt live a long time in close confinement, when treated with reasonable and ordinary care, for many have no other means of keeping them. If occasional entire liberty cannot be given them, an open air flight, inclosed by wire netting, will be of great advantage. This should always be roofed in, and only open to the less exposed aspects. The larger it can be made the better; but even a very small open air flight will materially assist in keeping the birds in good health. When pigeons are kept in a room or loft, with no outside liberty, an opening, covered with wire netting, for the admittance of light and air, should be provided. It should face the south, to admit the sunlight, and have a wide board adjoining for the birds to rest on. The most domineering of them will monopolise this place as much as they can, but their domestic duties will prevent them being always there, so that all will have some advantage from it.

They may either be fed from a flat board that has a marginal edge running round it, raised about an inch, to prevent the scattering of their food, or from a self-supplying hopper. By the exercise of due care in not putting down more grain each time the birds are fed than they will eat, there need not be much waste of food. Giving them too much at a time, and then grudging to throw away any that becomes soiled is but poor economy, and a likely cause of disease among them. If a flat board is used for their feeding on, it should be well scraped each time fresh food is given, and any left over will not be lost if fowls are kept. In the breeding season, when a constant supply of food is more necessary, hoppers made of zinc or wood, such as the illustration (Fig. 2), will be

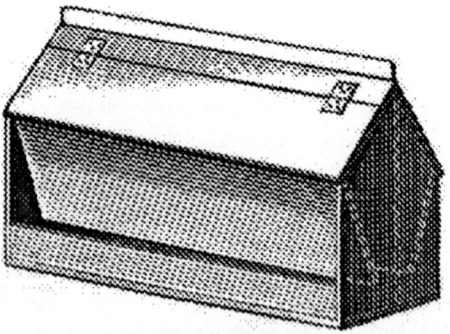

FIG. 2.—GRAIN HOPPER.

useful. They can be made of any desired length. The lid or lids, if they are intended to be divided inside, open with hinges, and should be at such an angle as will prevent the birds resting on them. A wire run along the ridge, raised an inch and a half, will keep them from settling there. As the food is eaten from the trough, the bulk inside will continue falling down, and so insure a constant supply as long as it lasts. By an inside division, dividing the hopper into two parts, two kinds or two separate mixtures of food may be supplied. Hoppers of various designs may be bought from manufacturers who make a speciality of them. One has lately been brought out in which the food is exposed by the pigeon stepping on the board in front of it, which prevents waste from mice or sparrows, their weight being insufficient to open it.

The water fountain may be bought complete, of various patterns; but a good one may be improvised by carefully punching a hole in a two gallon stone jar, near the bottom, and hermetically sealing the mouth. This, placed in a flower-pot saucer, the edge of which is higher than the orifice made in the jar, will complete the fountain. But a better kind of jar is that made of various sizes, like the illustration (Fig. 3), which, being without a bottom, can be better cleaned out. When the pigeon house has an outside flight on the ground, or when the fancier has more than one such place, supplying the birds with drinking water can be better performed from the outside. I made for myself a pattern in wood, like Fig. 4, from which I had several casts in iron taken, and I had them galvanised. These saucers are placed outside my flights, with the

FIG. 3.—WATER BOTTLE.   FIG. 4.—WATER DISH.

projecting part put through a hole cut in the wire netting. By this method, from the arrangements of my pigeonry, I can supply my birds with drinking water in half the time it would take to carry it inside.

As a specimen of a pigeonry, quite extensive enough for one man to attend to who has to do everything connected with it himself, before and after business hours, I have prepared a plan of my own place (Fig. 5), which, though not perfect by any means—for almost every day brings forth some new want—is now tolerably complete. Its arrangement may be carried out on either a greater or smaller scale by anyone, either erecting a columbarium from the beginning or adapting some existing building. P is the entrance door to the court, which measures about

80ft. by 60ft., and is surrounded by high walls. The buildings are placed against the north wall, which is about 12ft. high, and they slope down to about 7½ft. in front. The roof is slated, but about one-third of the open air flights, marked BB, CC, and DD, are roofed with glass to admit light, and they are wired in front. E is the entrance door to the whole; I adopted this plan from having often lost birds in other places, by the doors in the open air flights being left open accidentally, being blown open by the wind, or by the birds dashing past me when entering; and it may happen that not only the birds themselves may be lost in such cases, but any young ones they may have, may die for want of a suitable change to another pair being handy at the time. The room A is about

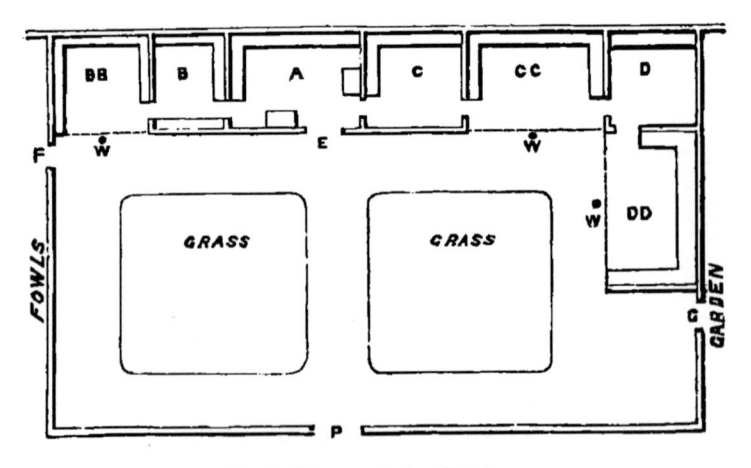

FIG. 5.—PLAN OF SMALL PIGEONRY.

16ft. long by 12ft. broad, and has a table running half round it about 2ft. broad, capable of holding ten bell-shaped wire show pens for training pouters. Below the table are two tiers of matching pens, each pair having a sliding wired frame dividing them, which, when withdrawn, enables the birds to go together. Two large corn chests for holding food are also shown, on the top of one of which are more matching pens, and the top of the other is used as a carpenter's bench, quite a necessary in such a place, and never long out of use. The rooms A, B, C, and D are lighted by roof lights, opening when required for ventilation.

B is a room about 9ft. by 12ft. for small pigeons, such as tumblers, turbits, owls, and jacobins, and is fitted with four tiers of nesting places, constructed on the principle shown in Fig. 6.

Each nest box (Fig. 6) is about 14in. long by 12in. deep, and 11in. high. A door, hinged at the bottom, covers two nests, which suffice for a pair of birds, and each nest is numbered for reference. About one-fourth of the door is cut away for entrance, and a landing board, supported by a small bracket, is fixed to it. A button screwed to the wood that divides

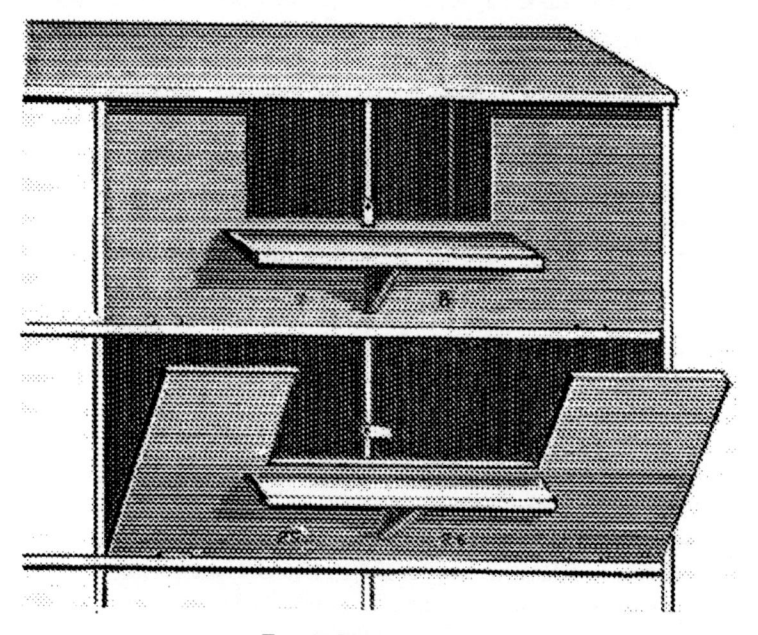

FIG. 6.—NESTING BOXES.

each pair of nests keeps the door secure, and if made so as to have no play, will never be accidentally forced up. The pair of nests numbered 7 and 8 are shown closed, and those marked 25 and 26 partly open. I find this style of nesting place answers very well for small pigeons, each pair of birds having all they require; they nest first in the one and then in the other, and by the time the young ones are able to come out they are strong enough to fly. The single landing boards have the advantage of keeping each pair entirely to themselves, and they are generally able to hold their own against all comers, as there is little room for fighting on them.

BB (Fig. 5) is the open air flight of B, and has resting boards, 3½ft. from the ground, 18in. wide, and close to the wall, running round it. When there is a space between the board and the wall it is dangerous for pouters, fantails, and such pigeons. I like the broad resting boards, as they give plenty of room for the birds passing each other. WW are the water fountains for the open air flights, placed outside, with their saucers projecting through the wire. In the front of BB there is a trap fitted with bolting wires, enabling the birds when at liberty, which they always are in good weather, to enter, but not to pass out, unless the bolting wires be tied up. C is a room 12ft. by 12ft., fitted up with three tiers of nests for pouters. Each nest is 2ft. long, 18in. deep, and 18in. high. I had them with hinged doors, something like those shown in Fig. 6, but did not find them to answer for pouters. In the winter they are quite open, and have a block of wood placed in them, for the birds to perch on. In the breeding season I cover them half in, run a piece of wood 3in. square up the centre, and the birds nest in the dark half. Like others I know, I could never be satisfied with so few birds as I could find accommodation for on the ground, so must run certain risks from the young ones falling from the higher nests, and be as careful in guarding against such mishaps as possible. D is another room, 10ft. by 12ft., fitted up with nesting places as in C, and has a flight of 18ft. long, marked DD.

There is a great advantage in having several compartments in a pigeonry, for without them it will sometimes be found almost impossible to unmatch certain pairs, when it is desirable to do so.

Earthenware nest pans of from 8in. to 10in. in diameter are used very much in England for pigeons breeding in; but in Scotland, or at least in the eastern part of it, they are not much in request. I have used them myself, but never found any advantage from them, and have long ago given them up. As a protection for the eggs I spread coarse sawdust in the nesting places to the depth of an inch. On this the birds build their own nests of straw, or I make them for them when necessary. In the breeding houses I have used sawdust over the floor, to the depth of one or two inches, and have found it very suitable. When passed through a riddle of ¼in. mesh once a week, it will last for several weeks, but should

The Pigeon House, Loft, and Aviary. 31

be renewed oftener if the place be troubled with insects. Pine sawdust soon loses the pungent smell, which helps somewhat, though not entirely, to drive away vermin.

Unless pigeon houses are often cleaned out, the smell arising from the dung soon becomes unpleasant. I clean out my own places every morning, and as, from their extent, the time required in doing so is considerable, I have been obliged to find out the most suitable tools for the purpose. These are a triangular steel scraper (Fig. 7) and a steel hand shovel (Fig. 8). The former is good for all corner places and the latter for broad surfaces, such as the floors and resting boards in the flights. When held at the proper angle, the latter removes everything

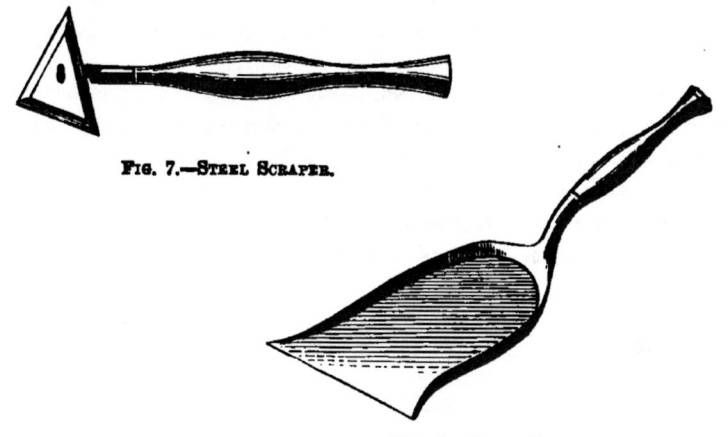

FIG. 7.—STEEL SCRAPER.

FIG. 8.—STEEL SHOVEL.

opposed to it as fast as one can walk along. It should be of the best steel and kept sharp. Those made of sheet iron wear but a short time. A stable broom, set with stiff Brazil fibre, is also necessary for sweeping all up, when the scraper and shovel have done their part, in freeing the dung from the wood. I have given up using sawdust on the floors for some time, not that I disapprove of it, but merely because I could not procure it conveniently. The labour in cleaning out the houses is as great when sawdust is used as when it is not, for the renewing and riddling of it takes up much time, and when the floors are scraped daily the dung has no time to harden and adhere to the wood, when it becomes more difficult to remove.

The best covering for the floors of outside flights is small gravel; such as can be got from sea beaches, mixed to some extent with broken shells, is very useful, the birds using much of it to aid them in digesting their food. It should be raked up now and then, and renewed when it gets soiled. A tray, containing lime from old buildings, should also be provided in the flight, and unless this be done the fancier must look for an undue proportion of soft-shelled eggs. Pigeons are very fond of salt, which can be given them in various forms. Some throw down a little common coarse salt, on a flat board, once or twice a week, or place a piece of rock salt in a corner of the flight; while others mix old lime, gravel, clay, and salt into a mass, and put it into boxes, open on one side or pierced with holes, for the birds to peck at. Recipes for making the salt cat, as it is called, may be found in the old pigeon books; but the above ingredients are all that are really required.

What has been called a great improvement in fitting up a pigeon house is an arrangement similar to a lot of hat or clothes pegs fixed to the walls for the birds to perch on. These may neither be unsuitable nor unserviceable for small active pigeons, but they are certainly dangerous for pouters, carriers, fantails, jacobins, and trumpeters of the better sort, all of which should have no resting places except their nests, or the floor of the loft.

CHAPTER IV.

SELECTION OF STOCK.

In the selection of stock the pigeon fancier has many varieties to choose from. Not only do the forms of pigeons vary much, but their plumage is diversified to an extraordinary degree, and the disposition or temper of the birds themselves varies greatly in different breeds. Most, if not all, who begin pigeon keeping early in life, commence with common kinds, with which they learn the rudiments of the fancy, and so gain the experience necessary to enable them to keep the more choice breeds with success. Of all who do so begin pigeon-keeping, however, but few follow it up in after life, either from want of the necessary accommodation being found in the places to which their destiny may lead them, or, more often, because the pursuit has no real hold on their minds. Whether the fancier begin early or late in life, it is necessary for him to spend some probationary time in mastering the rudiments of his pursuit, and to do so with expensive birds, the beauties of which he cannot probably realise, is a waste of money, unless he may have some experienced friend often at hand to direct him in their management.

As a beginning, no better pigeons than common tumblers can be put into the hands of a young fancier. They are neat and tidy in appearance, of varied and beautiful colours, and their performances in the air are a constant source of pleasure to their owners. There are few fanciers, however select their pigeons may be, who, if they can find accommodation for them, fail to keep some pairs of these engaging birds. They breed freely, are very hardy, and are serviceable feeders for other pigeons.

The pigeons that look best on the wing are those of pronounced markings, such as baldheads, turbits, and nuns. As they wheel round in their flight, the contrast between the white and coloured part of their plumage is very striking. Pouters, of what might be called a second quality, for the choicest are scarcely to be trusted at large, Norwich croppers, pigmy pouters (such as Austrians and Isobels), and pouting horsemen, or half-bred pouters and carriers, are all capital flyers and sail through the air in fine style.

The pigeons that become most familiar with their owners are pouters and fantails. It is necessary for the former to become very tame if intended to be exhibited, as, otherwise, they lose much of their beauty and chance of success in competition. On the other hand, carriers look best wild and alarmed, familiarity on their part spoiling their fine shape and statuesque appearance.

Runts, though they look quiet and sedate in the loft, are often of a spiteful disposition, making the feathers fly by the dozen from birds that happen to encroach on their preserves.

Carriers are also very vicious, and play sad havoc with each other when they fall out.

Trumpeters, such as were in England before the so called Russian ones were introduced, were noted for their quarrelsome disposition, and I have seen an unruly cock of this breed monopolise a whole loft to himself, preventing, till his removal, the least chance of success in breeding from the birds associated with him.

Owls, the Oriental frilled varieties, and turbits, the latter in a less degree, are shy and reserved in their demeanour, leaving their nests and young ones on the slightest alarm; but this will be of little consequence if the cause of their disquietude be soon removed, when they will generally return without delay to their nests.

If pigeons of varied and striking plumage be required, they may be found in archangels, almond tumblers, the eastern frilled varieties, and in many of the German toys; contrasts of colour among nuns, magpies, swallows and such kinds; while pouters, carriers, short faces, barbs, jacobins, fantails, owls, turbits, and trumpeters present abnormal conformation, and are denominated high-class pigeons, in distinction from those having little but curious colour and marking, because such conformation is more difficult to produce, and therefore thought more of when obtained in a high degree than mere feather.

But though a genuine pigeon fancier may have a preference for some particular variety, he will not be insensible to the beauties of others; and during an extended career in the fancy, he will most likely have been possessed of specimens of every kind of fancy pigeon he has been able to obtain. There is always a charm to the fancier in the acquisition of some new variety not previously possessed by him, which is taken up as a kind of extra thing, in addition to the variety on which his fancy is more permanently fixed, and as he tires of it some other novelty will take its place; for, as will be afterwards explained, it is not wise to keep many varieties at a time if it is expected to breed any of them to perfection. Each distinct kind of pigeon is a study in itself, still, in addition to the favoured kind and without detracting from the attention it may require, one or two other breeds may be introduced into the loft, when room can be afforded them, as a sort of bye-play.

In addition to the breeds that are strictly fancy pigeons, there are those known as homing or racing pigeons, in the breeding and training of which many find great enjoyment. The dragoon, long-faced beard, and skinnum were formerly used in England for this purpose, but of late the Antwerp carrier is almost exclusively employed for flying long matches. The flying fancy is a branch of the pigeon fancy by itself, and may be more properly denominated as racing, though in the management of the birds themselves there is little difference from that necessary for the generality of fancy pigeons.

CHAPTER V.

FEEDING, BREEDING, AND MANAGEMENT.

THE grain used for feeding fancy pigeons is wheat, barley, beans, peas, tares, and Indian corn, besides some other kinds. All of these are good in their way, and may be mixed together. The fancier will find that some birds prefer one kind, and some another. The grain should neither be too new, nor too old, for when used in the same year as it is grown, it is inclined to be too relaxing, and apt to scour the birds. On the other hand, old grain, that has been ill kept and perforated by worms or weevils, has lost most of its goodness, and a great part of it will be refused by the birds. Grain may be kept well for a considerable time if spread on a wooden floor to the depth of 6in. or 9in., and turned over once a week or so. The place should be free from damp, or it will become musty. Well conditioned grain keeps the birds in good health, and makes a great difference in the number of young ones reared, for any that has become too hard from age cannot be easily digested by them, and musty or worm-eaten stuff, being distasteful to them, the young ones suffer in consequence. When floor space is not available for storage of grain, it should be changed from one bin to another as often as convenient, or if kept in sacks they should be shaken up now and then, with the object of destroying moths and other insects, which will assuredly find their way amongst it if left long undisturbed.

Wheat may be used more freely in the summer than in the winter. Pigeons are fond of it, and, when given them to the extent of one fourth of their supply, it is beneficial during the breeding season.

Barley is good food for pigeons, and I have used it, to some extent,

Feeding, Breeding, and Management.

nearly all the year round; indeed, I have known of good results from pigeons fed on nothing but barley. It is generally the cheapest of all pigeon food, and cheapness is an object with many, but the birds are not fond of it.

Peas are the staple food for fancy pigeons, and the kind I use are imported into Leith from the Continent. They are much smaller than the grey field peas usually grown in this country, which are, however, the best of food, and are principally grey mottled, with some admixture of white and blue ones; occasionally they have a few rather large beans among them. They weigh about 63lb. per bushel, and cost from 35s. to 42s. per quarter, according to the market. I have read of white peas being unsuitable food for pigeons; but the very best results I have ever known in pouter breeding were from them and Indian corn mixed.

Beans are good feeding also, but the small ones, known as tick beans, are not always procurable at a reasonable price. Such as are known as Egyptian, which are of a medium size, may be got cheaply sometimes. Horse beans are rather large for the majority of pigeons, but pouters eat them readily when mixed with their other food, in small proportion.

Tares are capital feeding. They are of two kinds, home and foreign. The former, at least as grown in Scotland, are nearly as large as small peas; but have been lately at famine prices, from 80s. to 100s. a quarter. The foreign are very small, not half the size of the home kind, though quite as good for pigeons. When procurable at or under 40s. a quarter I always use them, and I have bought them as low as £7 the ton, which is only about 31s. per quarter.

Indian corn or maize is of various kinds. One sort is large and flat in the grain, and another small and round. The former is said to be the best value as food, but it is not so suitable for pigeons as the latter, which is called Hungarian, as it is inclined to stick in their throats. Maize may be generally bought at about the rate of £7 per ton, though I have known it as low as £5 10s. Considering its weight per bushel, and nutritious qualities, I believe it is the cheapest of all grain for the pigeon fancier, and it may be used in the proportion of one fourth all the year round.

I have never used buckwheat or dari; the latter is a small tare-shaped white grain from the Levant, and has been well spoken of in late years as good feeding for pigeons. Sound rice, often procurable cheaply when partly broken, is good to mix with the stock of grain. Paddy, or rice in the husk, which is like barley in appearance, though somewhat flatter, is much used in India, where I have bought it as low as 2s. per maund of 82lb. There is also a capital pigeon grain, grown in Bengal, called mollah, costing there from 3s. to 4s. per maund. This is a small round pea, about 3-16ths of an inch in diameter, blue-grey in colour, and mottled with brown spots. Mollah is first-class feeding, and might be imported into England and sold much cheaper than beans, peas, and tares, and still leave a good profit to the shipper.

Pigeons are fond of all the seeds given to cage birds, such as millet, canary, and hempseed, but they are too dear for general use, though they may be given as an occasional treat. Hempseed is very stimulating, and should be seldom given to pigeons kept in close confinement.

I have already referred to the way pigeons may be fed in lofts. When an outside flight, covered with gravel, is provided for them, the best way to feed them is to throw their food on the ground, always provided they can see to pick it up, which certain heavily wattled pigeons cannot do. For such, hoppers must be provided. Supposing a good many to be kept, this will be the most expeditious way of supplying them. Hoppers, to supply perhaps a hundred birds, must be rather numerous to prevent them constantly quarrelling over them, and more food is destroyed by feeding them from a flat board than from the ground when kept constantly supplied with clean gravel a few inches in depth. During the breeding season they should be fed early in the morning, at least, before eight o'clock; and if food can be left for them over night they will go to it much before this hour in the summer-time; but this is not absolutely necessary. Forgetting to feed them for half a day will cause the death of many young ones, not so much for want of food as from cold; for in such a case the old ones will not continue sitting on them, but leave them and hang about waiting for their food. Young pigeons, from their birth to their seventh day, cannot long survive the want of their parents' warm protection, even in the heat of summer.

The water vessels should be refilled daily, even if they hold more than a day's supply; for if allowed to run dry the same bad results follow as from want of food. They should be frequently cleaned out with boiling water, and such as have only a hole in them should have some gritty sand shaken up in them when being cleansed. If placed outside the flight and exposed to the rays of the summer sun, they must either be protected from it by a box in extra hot days, or frequently refilled with cold water, for sun-heated water is prejudicial both to the old and young ones.

As pigeons at liberty eat freely of lettuce and such green food, this may be supplied occasionally to those kept in confinement, but it is not an absolute necessity for them, and I never give them such in the winter time.

Bathing water may be allowed them twice a week, which is about as often as they will care to use it. If supplied in the loft, no vessel, however constructed, will prevent them dashing it about all round for 2ft. or 3ft., but a little saw-dust thrown upon the overflow will absorb it in a few minutes, when it may be swept up. If the bath be made with sides inclining inwards, much less water will be scattered about than when they are upright or sloping outwards.

Supposing the pigeon fancier to have his loft and its arrangements completed, and to have selected his stock of birds, the first thing he will have to do will be to pair them together. In matching them up, with the object of breeding good young ones, the general rule may be laid down that whatever faults one of the pair may possess, its mate should not possess the same. A pair of pigeons having between them the properties sufficient to constitute a perfect specimen, or something approaching to it, are likely to amalgamate, in some of their progeny, the good points they possess; and by this method are the most perfect specimens of fancy pigeons produced. But, besides the appearance of the birds themselves, that of their parents and more remote ancestors should be considered where it may be done, as pigeons, in common with other animals, throw back to their ancestral form, as much, and often more, than to their own parents. It will therefore be seen that successful pigeon breeding requires considerable study, although good pigeons are not unfrequently produced from bad stock by throwing back to better ancestors, but such chance birds are not reliable for stock purposes. It is always better that a beginner should procure his stock birds from a breeder who has proved his ability to turn out good stock of any particular variety, than to buy those of whose pedigree he can learn nothing; for there is much virtue in a good strain, and much disappointment saved by procuring such. And yet the very best of pigeons will produce plenty of young ones quite unfit to go on breeding from, as all races living in a strictly artificial state must necessarily do, so a fair amount of quality should be looked for in birds intended to commence breeding from.

Pigeons are mated together by placing them in contiguous pens, where they can see each other. When in good health they will generally show signs of becoming paired in a few days, but it is, of course, necessary to keep them from the sight of other birds, and especially of their last mates, or it will not be easy to match them up. When properly paired, it is always as well, when practicable, to place them in a loft apart from their former mates, should they have had such, for even when these are themselves rematched, and with young ones, they will occasionally be inclined to go together again, but in this respect, and in many others, pigeons show the most various dispositions. Two or three lofts save much trouble to the fancier, and he can always work his birds about in them, so as to save time in his breeding operations. When a pair show signs of becoming matched up, they may be allowed to go together for a day, when the union between them will become more fixed than if turned into the loft at once. For this purpose, matching pens have generally a sliding wired division, withdrawable at pleasure. Once or twice in my experience I have found it impossible to permanently match up a pair of pigeons. Though each would pair in the ordinary way with other birds, they invariably separated after being together a short time, seeming to have some antipathy to each other. In such a case the only plan for keeping such a pair together, should there be some special reasons for doing so, will be to place them in a room by themselves.

When all goes well, the pair will soon begin building a nest, if provided with materials for doing so, and, usually within a week, the hen will lay her first egg, very near five o'clock in the evening. She will not sit on it through the following night, but stand over it; but next day the cock will generally be in such a hurry to begin the process of incubation, that it is always better to remove the egg as laid, substituting another, so as to insure the two hatching simultaneously, for when one is hatched a day before the other, the difference in size and strength of the young ones seems to get more marked day by day, and to increase, rather than diminish. Many hens are apt to lose the power of their limbs when about to lay, and such must be carefully looked after. Others do so only at the beginning of the breeding season, when the weather proves unusually cold. Although there is no way of knowing an egg to be such as will produce a healthy young one, it may be told with almost certainty that eggs of a certain appearance will come to no good. Those that, instead of being smooth when laid, are very rough or of a honey-combed appearance towards one end, are generally bad, and though they contain the germs of a living squab it will generally die in the shell. Very small eggs have rarely a yolk in them, and very large ones have generally a double yolk. The latter almost invariably die during incubation, though instances have been known of two healthy young ones being hatched and reared from them. Good eggs have a smooth appearance, and a few hours after being laid, a round air spot, usually at one end of them, will be observed on holding them up to the light. The hen lays her second egg forty-five hours after the first, or very nearly at two o'clock on the third day, and this is an almost invariable rule when all goes well. The first egg being replaced in the nest, incubation then commences, and in seventeen complete days, more or less, according to the weather, breed, and closeness of sitting, the young are hatched.

There is a great difference in the breeding powers of hen pigeons, and those that lay oftenest during their first season without any forcing, generally breed for more seasons than such as lay only twice or thrice in their first season. When a hen lays single eggs to a nest it is generally a sign that her procreative powers are drawing to a close, or that she is being unnaturally forced.

When the eggs have been sat on for three full days, it may be determined almost surely whether they are fertile or not. When held against a strong light, the heart and blood vessels branching from it, of the embryo squab will be clearly seen in a good egg. When no such appearance is visible, the egg is bad, or, as happens occasionally, it has not been sat on closely, if fertile; but in such a case, another day should determine whether it be good or bad. In a week a good egg is quite opaque when held against the light, and becomes of a blue colour.

Should a newly laid egg get chipped by the claw of the old bird, or by other accident, so long as the skin below the shell be not broken, there is hope for it. A good thing to mend such a flaw is the marginal paper round sheets of postage stamps, a piece of which the fancier should always keep in his pocket. Early in the season, thin-shelled eggs are often laid, and such generally get broken before being sat on many days. Should the fancier find his hen pigeons laying many eggs without shells or with thin shells, it is time for him to attend to their supply of old lime and gravel. Sometimes a good egg will get very much indented a few days before it is due to hatch. So long as the skin be not broken, and it seems to get tougher day by day, the indented shell may be carefully patched up with gummed paper.

As a rule, young pigeons that require assistance from the egg are not worth the trouble in connection with them. Short-faced tumblers are an exception; but all other breeds, if possessed of the necessary strength to develop into healthy birds, should be allowed to hatch without any interference whatever.

Young pigeons when hatched are very helpless objects, but grow so fast when all goes well that a great increase in their size may be observed day by day. They are born blind and covered with a yellow down, which, however, varies much according to the colour they are to be. Silvers and yellows are hatched with hardly any down on them, and this is a good indication of these colours. Yellows of the deepest and richest tint are, however, not hatched so thinly covered as those of a washed-out or mealy hue, such as is too often the case with many of our yellow pigeons, and attention to this will be no uncertain indication of the quality of colour that will be developed in due time in a newly-hatched squab. When a week old, the young ones will be well stubbed over with feathers, which in another week will have begun to break, and give a good idea of colour and marking. If, during this time, a daily increase in size be not observed, or if one keeps getting behind the other, something is wrong; but unless the want is evidently from lack of food or warmth, nothing can be done with squabs so young. The bowels or digestive organs are out of order, and they seldom come right. The young of all small and hardy pigeons are as big as their parents at from four to five weeks old, when they will leave the nest and soon begin to feed themselves.

Feeders, such as common pigeons, Dragoons, Antwerps, and the strong and coarse specimens of fancy varieties, are used as nurses for the more choice breeds, and, although there is much misunderstanding as to the powers of even really good birds in their ability to successfully rear their own young, feeders may be advantageously made use of in many instances; but so long as good birds do perform their natural functions, as the great majority are well able to do, it is but natural to allow them to do so. Unless other eggs or young ones be given to pigeons who have been deprived of their own, they will often lay again much sooner than they would otherwise do, and when this is often repeated nothing but disaster can result in the end. Such unnaturally forced eggs are often thin-shelled, unfertile, or, if they contain birds, they very often come to nothing. Rather than allow good hens to overlay themselves, if they cannot be supplied with substitutes in eggs or young ones, they should be penned up for a time, which will give their systems the needful rest.

The usual pair of eggs laid by the hen pigeon generally result in a cock and hen, but so many instances occur of two cocks or two hens being produced in a nest that it is never safe to reckon on the sex of young ones. Certain indications of the sex of his young pigeons will soon present themselves to an experienced fancier; and, at the same time, where many young ones are bred, there will usually be one or two whose sex will puzzle the most experienced fancier for a long time.

Odd birds in a loft, be they cocks or hens, are always very troublesome. Such should always be removed to a place by themselves, or common mates procured for them, when they may be used as feeders.

Pigeons are so productive that they often increase faster than accommodation can be provided; but nothing militates more against success in rearing young ones than overcrowded lofts, which are a fertile cause of disease, and when such does set in, the best seem to die first, at least they are more missed than the worst, which is about the truth of it. When every result of an overcrowded loft is considered, such as extra expense for food, extra trouble in attendance, and the introduction of disease, it would be found to pay far better to use an unsparing hand in killing off faulty young ones, which seldom pay anything like their cost.

Many fanciers separate the cocks from the hens during the winter season, and where there is every convenience for doing so it may be a good plan. When all nesting places are laid bare of their furnishings, there is but little inducement for the birds to breed during the short days of winter. It is at least unnatural for the sexes to lose the companionship of each other during several months of the year, and they have always seemed to me to thrive much better when left together. When all facilities for breeding are removed, as the birds begin to get deep in moult, and not replaced till the beginning of spring, there will be no trouble experienced on this account, from pouters at least, though many of the small and hardy kinds of pigeons will not take advantage of such a long rest.

When feeders are employed, the eggs of the good birds may be given to the feeders, if of the same age, or if one or two days older, but it is not safe to risk any greater difference in the age of the eggs, because, if hatched before their soft meat comes on them, the feeders will not feed them as a rule. In changing young ones, let them be a few days older than those they replace, and they will have so much additional care. When young birds are well feathered it is often unsafe to change them, as the feeders begin to know the difference in their appearance, and will occasionally either not feed them or drive them out of their nest. Some feeders are very valuable, from the care they bestow on any young ones given them, and a barren hen is often best of all in this respect. An egg placed in her nest will be taken to, and, after the interval of a day it may be removed, and a fresh pair of eggs from some choice pair of birds given to her, when she and her mate will treat them as their own, and rear them successfully in many instances. Barren hens have this advantage, that they can be made to wait till their owner has a use for them. The worst of feeders is, that they look so bad among good pigeons, and on this account they should always be kept in some separate loft if possible. A place for drafting young ones into is also a great convenience, for they soon become troublesome among breeding birds.

The elements of success in breeding good fancy pigeons may be briefly summed up as follows:—Well bred stock birds, properly paired in regard to their own and their ancestral form, supplied with good food and clean water, provided with proper breeding accommodation, not overcrowded, kept clean, and tended with all reasonable care by one who has their welfare and the love of them thoroughly at heart.

CHAPTER VI.

COLOURS OF FANCY PIGEONS.

THE colour of the wild blue rock pigeon is found in nearly all domesticated fancy breeds of pigeons, and this fact is regarded as one of the proofs of their descent from it. The British blue rock pigeon differs from its congener in Asia in having a white rump, and this difference also exists in fancy pigeons of a blue colour, which are, however, always preferred to be blue rumped for the sake of uniformity. Many shades of the blue colour are found in tame pigeons, the one in most request being a rich even dark blue, neither running too dark nor smoky in hue, nor too light and silvery in tone. The neck of a blue pigeon, of the best shade of colour, is dark, and sparkles with a metallic green and purple lustre. Two black bars cross the wings, and they should be *quite* black, though, from crossing of the colours in breeding, many blue pigeons are faulty in this respect. The tail and flight feathers are much darker in shade than the shoulders, and the former are marked with black across their ends, forming, when they are outspread, a band of black. The outer tail feathers are margined with white on their outer edge as far as the black band.

The blue rock pigeon, when partially domesticated in field dovecotes, begins to alter in colour, and the wing coverts assume a dappled appearance, being chequered on each feather with black. The dovehouse pigeon, as it is called, has been considered by some a distinct variety from the blue rock; but I have always found both the clear blue and blue-chequered varieties living together in all the field dovecotes where I have observed these semi-wild pigeons. And not only in this country, but in India, where semi-wild pigeons inhabit temples, mosques, and ruined buildings, both varieties may be found living together. The blue-chequered colour, like the blue, is found in most kinds of fancy pigeons, and may be considered the origin of all the curious spangling and chequering that exist in numerous kinds of pigeons.

The first decided change in colour of the blue rock pigeon, after the chequered variety, is where the whole plumage alters to a red tint. This variation, also found in most kinds of tame pigeons, is known as mealy. The blue is replaced by a whitey-brown tint, and the neck and wing bars become dark red. When the mealy colour is improved by selection, it can be made into a very beautiful colour, as in the mealy show Antwerp. As the blue colour becomes chequered with black, so the mealy becomes chequered with red, and is called a red chequer.

These four colours, the blue, blue chequer, mealy, and red chequer, are, then, the most original and most crude colours in tame pigeons, and they are the foundation of all other colours found in pigeons.

Besides the blue and mealy colours, there is what may be considered an offshoot of the former—the silver. In this colour the body tint assumes a dun hue, and the neck and wing bars become of a darker dun. There are two show shades of silvers, known as brown barred and black barred. They bear the same relation to each other as the whole-coloured duns, found in carriers and barbs. The carrier dun is soft and ruddy while the barb dun is often very deep and merging into black. Although the dark-barred silver is called black barred, this is quite a misnomer, for real black bars on a dun tinted body colour are, I believe, incompatible with nature.

When the reddish tint of a mealy pigeon is changed to buff the neck and bars become yellow, and this colour is known in the fancy as yellow mealy, which is a soft and beautiful colour, sometimes seen in great perfection in pouters. Another barred colour found in pigeons is powdered blue, as in the Mahomet. The head, neck, and shoulders of this bird are all tipped with a frosted silver colour, the bars across its wings and tail remaining of an intense black. This colour has been engrafted on the blue owl pigeon, but only in a degree, and a variation of it is known as powdered silver.

The barred colours of pigeons, therefore, include blue with black bars, silver with dun bars, mealy with red bars, yellow mealy with yellow bars, and powdered blue, as in the Mahomet. As powdered silvers and powdered blues are found in owls, though not with such an intense powdering as in the Mahomet, powdered mealies and yellow mealies might, I think, be bred in time, if wished for. Some of the mealy show Antwerps have already much powdering on their head and neck feathers. Through inter-breeding with other colours, there are a great number of off-coloured barred pigeons, such as kite-barred blues and reddish-barred blues; but all such are undesirable, each body colour being required pure of itself, and accompanied with sound bars to suit it.

When colour fails altogether in animals, an albino or white specimen is the result, and such are found among dovecote pigeons. Albinos, when bred with coloured pigeons, produce particoloured young, and this is the foundation of all white markings in fancy pigeons. A rarer freak of nature, however, than an albino, is when the normal colour of an animal is turned into black, which is known as a melanoid. Melanoids occur in animals living in a state of nature, such as leopards, jackals, hares, and rabbits. I have not known of this natural change occurring in field dovecotes, but there can be little doubt that the black colour in tame pigeons is owing to this natural propensity, and that it is the foundation of all whole solid colours, such as red, yellow, and dun. These solid colours, to be in perfection, should be uniform all over the bird, and not fall away to a lighter shade on the rump, wings, tail, belly, thighs, or vent. They advance in value according to the difficulty of producing them, blacks and duns being easy of acquisition, compared with reds and yellows, which latter are the choicest colours in fancy pigeons. To be seen in perfection, they must be seen on a whole-feathered bird, or at least on a bird whose standard of marking does not require a white flight and tail, for the colour of these in a whole-feathered red or yellow is the crucial point in judging of their quality of colour. Black, red, and yellow of the choicest shades must be lustrous, with metallic sheen, the black being green and the red greenish-purple, in certain lights. Yellow has also an orange lustre, interspersed with light green on the neck feathers, but there are but few yellow pigeons that show such rich colour, and it requires a strong light to show it, even when present. Dun of the dark shade, as in barbs, if dark and solid, also shows a greenish lustre; but the light or dull dun, so often seen in carriers, seldom carries any lustre beyond the neck feathers. This latter shade of dun colour, which is an off colour in all high-class fancy pigeons, except carriers, often fades with the advancing year, and when the bird gets its new feathers at the moulting season it has then an ugly mottled appearance till they are all renewed; but they gradually tone down to a uniform appearance, and the same thing happens with many silver pigeons to a greater or less degree. There is a whole blue colour, without dark neck, flights, or tail, and in which the black bars are wanting. It should be uniform in shade all over the bird, and may be seen in some Indian pigeons.

In some kinds of German pigeons, the wing bars, both in barred and solid-coloured varieties, are changed to white, or are marked with white on the bar feathers, but this is a kind of marking, composed of white and colour, that will be treated in its proper place, and does not come within the scope of this chapter.

Many German and oriental pigeons are spangled or laced on the shoulders, such as hyacinths and blondinettes, but all such spangling or lacing is composed of a combination of the colours I have detailed as belonging to fancy pigeons, whether accompanied with white or not.

Some pigeons are clothed in two distinct colours, such as the archangel. This season I bred a pigeon coloured in a way that has never before come under my observation, viz., a mealy, with black shoulders, a combination of colour that I would not have believed possible, and it is nearly clean cut, like a good turbit. There is also the combined colour known as almond, or yellow spangled with black, besides many others, such as bronzed kite and golden dun. White markings on a coloured ground and coloured markings on a white ground are legion in fancy pigeons, the same constituting the claims of many to be considered as separate varieties, and each will be referred to in turn. The advance from the normal blue may be traced as follows :—

Blue with black bars.
Blue chequered with black (blue chequer).
Whole black.
Mealy with red bars, a natural change from the blue.
Mealy chequered with red (red chequer).
Whole red.
Buff with yellow bars, a natural change from the blue or mealy.
Buff chequered with yellow (yellow chequer).
Whole yellow.
Silver with dun bars, a natural change from the blue.
Silver chequered with dun (dun chequer).
Whole dun.

All the barred, chequered, and solid colours are found in some varieties of fancy pigeons, while only some of them exist in others; but wherever blue, black, red, and yellow exist, the other colours may be got if wanted, which they seldom are, being considered off colours and of little value. The black, red, and yellow, when in the most lustrous perfection, have a beauty that may be equalled but is not surpassed by the plumage of any birds whatever, but it is seldom they are seen in perfection, and then only in some varieties of fancy pigeons. It must have taken long ages of careful breeding to bring the black, red, and yellow colours to perfection.

CHAPTER VII.

EXHIBITING PIGEONS.

PIGEON shows have probably been established in England for as long a period as any shows for the exhibition and comparison of such fancy stock. The "ordinances for judging almond tumblers" date back to 1764, and it is likely that long before this time, the pigeon fanciers of the metropolis had their meetings for the comparison of their pigeons. Before the days of railways, such meetings could only take place in some large centre, near to which there were resident many breeders, and an instance of this kind may be found in Lancashire, where shows for the exhibition of gold and silver mooney fowls have existed for time out of mind. The show system of the present day has sprung up during the lifetime of the present generation, and some of the principal exhibitions draw together birds and their owners from all over the country. The chief of these meetings are the events of the year in the pigeon fancy, and determine who are the owners or breeders of the best specimens of each respective variety. Fanciers look forward to them as opportunities for meeting such as are like-minded with themselves; where they may compare their own stock with that of others; dispose of the good birds they have for sale, and purchase such others as they may be in need of themselves. A visit to at least one of the chief shows in each season is beneficial to the fancier in many ways, and may either confirm him in his good opinion of his own birds, or enlighten him as to their demerits; for it is often the case when one stays too much at home, that he insensibly contracts exaggerated ideas of his own birds, having no opportunity of seeing the progress made by others.

There are now a great number of shows held every year in this country, where prizes of more or less value are offered for the best specimens of fancy pigeons, and there can be no doubt that it is owing to this fact, that good birds have year by year increased in value, till the sum of £100 has been paid on more than one occasion for a choice specimen. Sums varying from £25 to £50, are by no means uncommon for really first-rate birds of the high-class varieties, and an occasional sale of this kind enables the breeder to realise a good equivalent for his outlay and trouble in the production of good birds. Really good pigeons are always saleable, and as the best birds are generally bred from such as are not themselves of the very highest show form, but from judicious matching up, the breeder can generally afford to pass away his best show birds, or some of them, for a consideration. On this account many of the most successful breeders of pigeons exhibit but seldom in a season, being satisfied if they make their mark at some good show, where they dispose of what they have to part with, and then concentrate their efforts for the next breeding season. Many of the best show pigeons spend their existence in a round of exhibiting, and often produce, in consequence, nothing of note. The pitcher goes often to the well, but gets broken at last, and the constant knocking about of good birds, many of which have to be of a mature age before they can attain show form, tells on them sooner or later. The damage they sustain is not done so much in going to shows as in returning from them, for when several hundreds of birds are despatched from a show to destinations north, south, east, and west, some may lie half a day at a station before being started homewards, and when they do reach their destinations alive, which is not always the case, they may have already received so much unseen injury as will sooner or later cause their death. To guard against such results, many either go with their birds to shows or send them in charge of their servants; when neither plan can be adopted some risk must be run.

Pigeons may be sent to shows in boxes or baskets. Boxes are liable to breakages, and when made extra strong and heavy are expensive in the way of carriage. Baskets are lighter, but, from their openness, are not so desirable in cold weather, unless covered with coarse canvas. Both boxes and baskets are made in compartments, capable of holding from one to a dozen birds. Fig. 9 is a box for holding two pouters, of a pattern long in use in Scotland. It measures 16in. long by

8in. wide, and 8in. deep inside. It is divided, diagonally, into two compartments, each having an inside lid, pierced with holes for ventilation. The birds are placed in it, in opposite directions, and a couple of air holes at the broad end of each compartment are sufficient to give ventilation. The inside lids are an inch below the tops of the sides, which have notches cut in them, so that when the outside lid is shut a free current of air may pass through. The air holes represented in the figure are sufficient, and none should be made in the sides of the box or in the ends where the tails of the birds are to be. What is required is sufficient ventilation to carry off the heat and breath of the birds. When this is not given, they will be taken out of a close box, even in the coldest

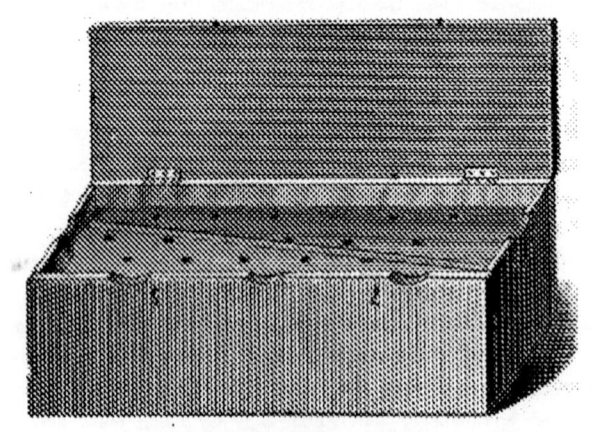

FIG. 9.—TRAVELLING BOX FOR PIGEONS.

winter weather, as wet as if soaked in water. Boxes on the same principle as shown, may be made with any number of divisions, but six are usually the greatest number, for convenience in handling. The size of each compartment may vary, according to the breed they are to be used for, but they should always be made no larger than required, for when a bird has the least extra room, it is apt to turn, or attempt to turn, when its plumage often gets much damaged.

Baskets are made exactly on the same principle as the boxes described, and are, I think, preferable on the whole. When divided into compartments by sailcloth or strong canvas, they form very good packages for pigeons. Good oblong baskets, measuring about 20in. by 12in., such as fruiterers often sell for 1s. 6d. or 2s., may be made into capital exhibition baskets by dividing them into compartments with canvas, as in Fig. 10, which is a plan for dividing such a basket into eight compartments, each 10in. by 4½in. at the wide, and 1½in. at the narrow ends, suitable for such small pigeons as turbits or owls. Jacobins are better sent in canvas than basket work divisions, and fantails should have large and lofty cloth-lined compartments to save their tails from being broken or destroyed.

The greater number of fancy pigeons may be sent to exhibitions without any preparation at home, except that in cases where the birds are of an extra wild nature some preliminary penning may be of advantage, in rendering them to some extent at home in a show pen. Some, however, and especially pouters, really require a considerable training to enable them to be shown with advantage, and this will be referred to more particularly elsewhere. Pigeons should in all cases be shown in a clean state, as many judges lay considerable stress on this point, and although a good bird can never look very bad though dirty, one equally

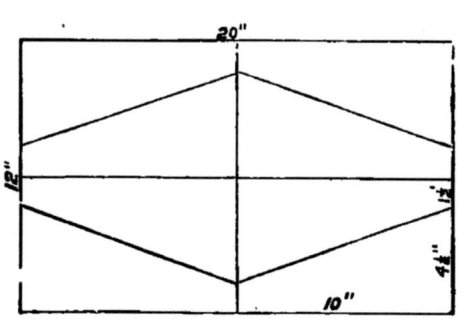

FIG. 10.—PLAN FOR PIGEON BASKET.

good in spotless plumage looks very much better. A good deal may be done for dirty birds by careful washing with soap and soft water; but washed birds have never the finish of those that do not require it. A practice that cannot be too strongly deprecated is oiling or greasing the plumage of pigeons to improve their colour. Birds so treated should never receive notice at the hands of a judge.

The best exhibition pens for pigeons are those of galvanised wire, of the beehive shape, and a good thing for strewing them with is the husk of oats, though coarse pine sawdust is better than nothing. Each pen, or at least each couple, should have water and food tins so placed that the birds can reach them without trouble. When thrown on the bottom of the pen the food gets soiled, and heavily-wattled pigeons accustomed to feed from hoppers are unable to feed from the floor.

For judging pouters, a large show pen should always be provided, as it is impossible to judge them properly otherwise; and unless exhibitors see the process of adjudication for themselves, they should be sparing of criticism afterwards, as pouters, being pigeons chiefly of shape and carriage, look very different when standing on a block, than when on their mettle in the show pen.

CHAPTER VIII.

DISEASES OF PIGEONS.

THE choicest kinds of fancy pigeons are subject to many diseases, no doubt arising in many instances from hereditary causes. Where a large stock is kept, the pens set apart for sick birds will seldom be altogether untenanted, for whether much doctoring be practised on them or not, ailing pigeons will have more chance of recovery when put in hospital than when left among the healthy birds, who often treat them very roughly. The eye of the experienced fancier soon detects a pigeon that is out of sorts, a disinclination for food or for the bath, a peculiarity in its flight or walk, and many other signs proclaim something wrong. As delay can only complicate matters, success in the treatment of a sick bird may often be attained by doing what may be done quickly. For my own part I may say that I never had much success in treating pigeons with medicines, that I have found their action very uncertain, and that about the same number of sick ones recover, in certain illnesses, whether drugged or not. For better reference I shall treat of the principal diseases fancy pigeons are liable to in alphabetical order.

Bowels, Inflammation of.—The most fatal disease of fancy pigeons is inflammation of the bowels. Nearly all have it at some period of their lives, and a large proportion before the completion of their first moult. It may almost be called the distemper of pigeons, and may be known by the huddled up appearance of the bird. The disease is sometimes so rapid in its action that in a few days the bird is reduced to nothing but skin and bone. The power of flight is soon lost, and the bird retires into a corner. When first observed, the pigeon so effected should be secluded, and have access to old lime. The best remedy I have found for this disease, which is known in the fancy as "going light," is from six to ten drops of laudanum in a teaspoonful of water, daily. Nothing seems to do the least good in many cases; but when the bird survives ten days of illness, there is always good hope of its ultimate recovery. When this disease attacks young pigeons in the nest, which it does in very many cases, there is no hope of their recovery, but I have known them, when not attacked till six weeks old, come through very severe attacks of it. The most fatal time for them, when once able to fly and do for themselves, is during their first moult, and those that pass that period without having this distemper, sometimes take it during their second year, and not unfrequently when feeding young ones. After this period, they are comparatively safe, and their systems so hardened that if they do take it they are able more easily to throw it off, though there are exceptions. I should think that among the more choice varieties of fancy pigeons something like 50 per cent. have to go through this distemper in a more or less severe form. Many do not consider a bird safe till it has passed through it in some form or other, and after safely passing through it many consider a bird about twice as valuable as it was before, so many have to succumb to its effects. Those that recover from very severe attacks may be reckoned on as good for several years. In the worst cases it is astonishing how soon they recover when they once take the turn for the better; they seem to get heavy about as fast as they got light. In this disease it is better to keep them from food for some days after seclusion, giving only water. They have generally a great desire to eat, but when it is found that the food does not pass from the crop, as it often does not, it can only do harm and hasten their death. I refer, of course, to the worst cases, each of which must be treated on its own merits, and by careful observation of the state of the crop each morning. When the food is found to pass from the crop freely, one or two days total abstinence at the commencement of the illness is all that is necessary to give the requisite rest to the inflamed or ulcerated bowels, and at the same time allow the laudanum to have its soothing effect. When the dung, from an offensive green appearance, begins to change to a more healthy state, the recovery of the bird may be reckoned on.

Canker is a disease that makes sad havoc in a loft of pigeons, when it gets established. I have generally found it make its appearance in overcrowded pigeonries, but it is undoubtedly most infectious, and may often be introduced by an infected bird, not necessarily suffering from it at the time of its introduction, but having in its system the seeds of the disease, which by the time it shows itself, makes any measures for the protection of the other birds abortive. Although foul water may not be the cause of an outbreak of canker in a loft, the water from which they drink in common has much to do with the spread of it, but beyond separating the infected birds and paying regard to cleanliness and ventilation, I cannot advise any method of retarding it when once thoroughly established in a loft, for it will run its course, and, when in a severe form, spoil a whole season's work in breeding, not disappearing till the advent of cold weather. When this disease has taken thorough root in a loft, almost every young bird of choice breed will become infected with it at from two to four weeks old, even though the feeders do not themselves have it. Few recover from it, the strain on their systems when so young being too great. Canker would sometimes seem to be the direct result from foul drinking-water and dirty food, as pigeons that are sent long distances by sea invariably become infected by it, when not kept scrupulously clean. The best guard against an outbreak of canker is strict attention to cleanliness, no overcrowding in the loft, and great care in introducing fresh birds during the breeding season. I, myself, have never had a canker epidemic among my pigeons all through a breeding season, but more than once it has appeared in my pigeonry about the end of July, and almost every young one hatched thereafter has become affected with it. It takes various forms; first in the throat, in which form it appears, to a greater or lesser extent, as lumps of cheesy looking matter, which, if only small and at the entrance of the throat, so as not to interfere with the swallowing, may be often cured by being touched with nitrate of silver or alum; but if of large extent, and deep down in the throat, so as to prevent swallowing, it causes death from starvation. Canker sometimes forms in the head, below one eye, and it will then often grow so rapidly that in a few days it will distort the head out of all proportion and cause death. I have never been able to cure this form of it. Again, the upper or under mandible is often affected and becomes swollen and distorted, preventing the squab from being fed. Painting the sores with tincture of perchloride of iron, or with glycerine and carbolic acid (six or eight of the former to one of the latter) has been advised by some; but nitrate of silver or powdered alum, according to others, is more efficacious. Canker of the beak and eye wattles of carriers and barbs may be treated in the same way, and then covered with starch or plaster of Paris; and common salt is said to be a cure for the small tumours called small pox, that sometimes appear on the wattles of carriers.

Cold in pigeons may be known by a running at the nostrils and eyes. It becomes more or less severe according to its restriction to the upper or lower air passages. More or less deposit of cankerous looking matter will take place in severe cases, but warmth and an aperient will generally effect a cure. What is known as the one-eyed cold is a more serious complaint. In this only one of the bird's eyes is effected. The lids get much swollen and close over the eye, from which, and from the nostrils and mouth as well, matter generally runs for a week or two. The inflammation is severe while it lasts, which is often for a fortnight or three weeks, but seclusion from draught, and bathing with warm water twice daily, will almost always result in cure, without the use of any medicine.

The Core.—This is a tumour that grows in or near the vent, and is not of very common occurrence. When in the vent, the bird will be seen pecking at the part, and on examination there will be found what looks like a prolapsus of that organ, wet and bloody. After a few days this will harden and dry up, and when the scab comes away the core will be with it. The core was so called by the old writers on account of its resemblance to the core of an apple. When it comes on the belly, somewhere near the vent, its presence will be unsuspected till discovered by accident. A hard lump will be felt on handling the bird, and on removing the feathers the skin will be found stretched over it like a net. On cutting the skin, the core, which is like a small shelled walnut, will come away easily, if ripe. I have not seen more than eight or ten cases of the core in thousands of pigeons.

Diarrhœa.—During the moulting season some birds will for several weeks be affected with a more or less severe diarrhœa, and pass nothing but fluid matter. The best remedy for this is a plentiful supply of old lime, and they generally recover as they get through the moult. If a bird so affected loses flesh, a change to a more binding kind of food will be of service.

Diseases of the Joints.—See "Wing Disease."

Egg Bound.—During a cold spring, or when matched up too early in the season, many hen pigeons become egg bound and lose the power of their limbs. Such should be carefully watched, as they are liable to very rough treatment from their mates and other pigeons in the loft. If, when placed on their nests, they do not pass the egg at the time of day it should come, a teaspoonful of treacle will generally do good; but a few drops of sweet oil passed into the vent with a feather will also much assist them. Some delicate hens among shortfaced tumblers are constantly affected in this way, and the result in breeding from such is so little as to be not worth the trouble in connection with them. A hen that loses the power of her limbs, from laying too early in the season, should be kept apart for a month or six weeks, to enable her to recruit her strength.

Flesh Wen.—This disease was a form of wing disease among the old writers; but apart from wens in connection with the joints, such tumours sometimes appear on the crown of the head and between the beak and eyes of pouters and other birds. They appear as small pea-shaped, movable lumps, and should be cut out before they attain large size. The skin may be opened with a sharp knife and the tumour easily pressed out, unless attached to the bone, which it sometimes is, when it must be cut away, but it is then likely to grow again.

Gizzard fallen was the old term for what is really a displacement of the bowels. Pouter hens are very subject to it after three or four years of age, and carriers and barbs also. There is no cure for it, though birds so affected will live a few months. I have never known a cock pouter with this disease, but have often seen young ones affected with it in the nest, when it has always proved fatal in my experience.

Going Light.—(See "Bowels.")

Gorging.—This is an ailment of pouters, and more especially of such as have well-developed crops, the best birds in this respect having to be carefully watched. The old cure was to pass the bird through the leg of a stocking and hang it up till the food passed off; but the same result may be attained by placing the bird in a narrow box, padded at one end to support the crop, so as to allow the food to pass into the stomach. Large cropped pouters, when allowed to feed their young, are very apt to gorge, some doing so invariably; but when this happens from their taking too much water, this may be pressed out of them by gently squeezing the crop till they disgorge it, when they will be right again in a short time. When, however, the crop is so gorged as to contain nearly as much as the weight of the whole bird, it is a bad sign, and it will then be found that neither the stocking nor box remedy will be of any use, for the stomach has lost its power of action. The crop may then be cut open, cleaned out and sewn up again, the inner and outer skins being carefully sewn separately. This operation is often successfully performed, but in many cases it is of no use, as the powers of the stomach have become impaired, and as soon as the bird is at liberty it will speedily be gorged again, nothing that is eaten passing into the stomach. From this cause many of the best pouter pigeons ever seen have died, and with those best developed in crop it will always be one of their complaints most to be feared. Besides cutting the crop open in bad cases of gorging, Moore says, "Others will tie that part of the crop in which the undigested meat lies, tight round with a string and let it rot off. This method never fails, though it spoils the shape of the crop." With a pouter considered valuable for stock, and past his best show days, a curtailment of crop is not any drawback, but rather the reverse. Charcoal capsules are useful for preventing the corruption of the food in the crop of a gorged pouter, and copaiba capsules are used to make them disgorge, and are very effective sometimes. A pouter should be attended to on showing the least signs of becoming gorged; delay is dangerous.

Insects.—Pigeons are apt to be infested with several kinds of insects. The feather louse is harmless, as far as ever I saw, and seems to be common to all pigeons. It is found chiefly about the neck feathers, and requires the natural heat of the bird to keep it alive, for on the death of a bird they may be seen crowding up towards its head, in a sort of torpid state. The pigeon louse is troublesome on all birds unable from a malformed beak to preen themselves, and when allowed to increase, for want of a little blue ointment, renders their lives truly miserable. Short-faced tumblers are as liable as any to these lice, and should be examined frequently by blowing up the feathers about the vent. A little mercurial ointment rubbed about that part, and under the wings, will kill all that come in contact with it. Ticks, I think with Mr. Brent, proceed from a flat fly that may be sometimes seen running over young pigeons, and hiding among their feathers. This fly (which is difficult to catch, and difficult to kill when caught, for it is so tough that it can scarcely be squeezed to death between the finger and thumb) is not often seen. Ticks are the largest of the insects that infest pigeon houses, and are fortunately, at least in my experience, not very common. I have never been much troubled with mites, but have known others who were, in such countless thousands, that during a whole breeding season every successive nest of young ones was covered with them, causing the death of many. I suppose they are of the same sort of vermin that trouble canary breeders. Fleas are the commonest kind of insects that infest pigeon houses, and are always present when breeding is going on, at least in my place and in many others I know of. They take up their abode under a pair as they commence to sit, and by the time the young ones are well grown, unless something has been done to destroy them, they have increased to a great extent. The most efficacious remedy for all the vermin that infest pigeon houses is bi-sulphide of carbon, a volatile stinking chemical, the use of which is almost worse than the presence of the vermin. The method of using it is to hang up a few open phials of it round the loft, when the smell it gives off is certain death to the vermin. It does not seem to affect the health of the pigeons, but the smell of it is very unpleasant, and it is very inflammable and therefore dangerous. I have tried it with success. Whitewashing the houses and flights once a year with hot lime does a great deal towards keeping down vermin; the strongest pine sawdust in my experience does very little towards that end, and my method of fighting the fleas is as follows: when making the pigeons' nests, I first lay down pine sawdust, and in the centre of it, where the birds are to sit, I place about a handful of sawdust well saturated with mineral oil (strong smelling paraffin, not the purified burning oil), I cover this, after hollowing it out, with clean sawdust, and then lay down the straw nest. This is about sufficient to keep the nest clear of fleas; but a little more of the saturated sawdust, when the young ones are half grown, will do good, if the fleas have appeared. If the young pigeons come in contact with the oily sawdust it will blister them, and the skin will come off in large pieces as it dries up; but I never found it kill them or even stop their growth. I have seen it noticed that heather cuttings make an insect proof nest, but have not tried it.

Leg weakness generally attacks young pouter pigeons early or late in the season. A bird will be going on well, and be nearly ready to quit the nest, when it will be observed to be unable to get on its legs. I have seldom known a bird so affected cured, and it is those that give promise of being extra long in limb and upstanding in carriage that are, I suppose from this desirable appearance, most liable to it. Such weakness in the limbs proceeding from some internal cause, must not, however, be mistaken for such an accident to the limb, as sometimes happens to a bird from falling from an upper nest, which is often curable by a few days of careful attention.

Moulting.—The majority of pigeons go through their annual moult without any trouble, but generally a few of them will fall into a diarrhœa during that time. When this becomes specially severe, the growth of the new feathers will sometimes suddenly stop. If the bird so affected recovers, the growth of its feathers will proceed, but many of them will be weak and unfurnished about the middle, showing where their growth was arrested, and instead of lying close to the bird's body will hang loosely, and flutter about with the wind. I have seen several cases of this, but it cannot be said to happen very often. Of course the bird so affected cannot get into proper feather before another moult. When a pigeon casts its feathers in masses, as many do, so as to be quite bare on head and neck, it should get extra protection from cold and draught till the new feathers are well grown.

Small Pox was well known to the old writers, from their description of it, but I have never known a case of it in this country. In India, however, it is a common complaint of young pigeons in the nest, and I have known seasons there when every young bird bred by myself and others, to the number of hundreds, has been attacked with it. At about a fortnight old pustules full of yellow matter would break out all over the bird, including its beak and feet. If let alone these would gradually dry up, and by the time the bird was able to fly, it would be nearly clear of them; but if broken they would bleed and grow into big sores. I think this form of small pox is quite unknown in this country now, at least I never heard any fancier say he had found it in his loft.

Spouts are fissures that form in the eye wattles of barbs and carriers, either naturally, from the skin growing into a fold, or from accident. These can never heal of themselves, but must be cut out with sharp scissors, and dressed with healing ointment. The operation is no doubt a painful one, but is compensated for by the after comfort of the bird, and the hole caused by the operation soon fills up.

Vertigo or the Megrims is an affection of the brain, causing the bird to turn its head right round, and making it fall over and flutter about. Although not an uncommon disease, I have fortunately never been much troubled with it among my pigeons. I think it is incurable, and, acting on that idea, have killed any birds so affected as soon as possible, to get them out of the way.

Wing disease is common to every variety of fancy pigeon. It can generally be detected before the bird loses all power of flight by the one-sided way in which it flies. When so observed, a bird will be found to have a swelling on some of the joints of its wings. An almost certain cure at this stage of the disease is not only to draw both primary and secondary flight feathers, but to almost strip the wing itself of all feathers except the small downy ones. The great flow of blood to the new feathers draws off the matter that would form in the swelled joint, and by the time the wing is refurnished, all signs of the swelling will have disappeared, and the bird will fly as before. Having succeeded in this way in curing scores of pigeons, I can recommend it as the best thing to do. Formerly the cure was to leech the swelling, or to wait till matter formed and then lance it; but not one bird out of a dozen will fly again after being cut about the joint, as the tendons are apt to get severed. When the same disease attacks the thigh joint it is not so easily cured, but in my experience it seldom does so as compared to the wing. The old writers divided this disease into the flesh wen and the bone wen, but the one is only an intensified form of the other. If taken in time, it may generally be cured by the method stated.

CHAPTER IX.

VARIETIES OF DOMESTIC PIGEONS.

In describing the numerous varieties of domestic pigeons with which I am acquainted, I shall commence with those least removed from the original type, from which, as I believe, all varieties descend. In this country such are named feather varieties; and in Germany they are called *Farbentauben,* or colour pigeons. Many of them have an identical conformation with the wild blue rock pigeon, and others have the addition of turned crowns or feathered legs and feet. From them I shall proceed to the intermediate class that show abnormal conformation, and which will include varieties, such as the runts, with their extraordinary size; the frizzled, frillback, and lace pigeons, with their altered formation of plumage; and the ringbeater, lowtan, and tumbler, with their peculiar flight or movements. I shall then conclude with the description of what are called high class pigeons; the favourites of the most exacting pigeon fanciers, the birds that come up but seldom to the standard of excellence laid down for them, because they have not only abnormal conformation, but carriage of body or style of movement and beauty of feather as well, and so combine in themselves such a sum of excellence, when anything like perfect, that the successful breeding of them is not only the work of men, but of clever thinking men. These last—that we call high-class pigeons—have been named by the Germans, "race" or "original" pigeons; and while many have been able to assent to the blue rock theory of descent of the feather varieties, the high-class birds are so removed from them, that some writers have considered them as separate creations. On this question, since writing the chapter on the "Origin of Fancy Pigeons," I have found in the work of Neumeister, the German writer, the following: "We shall not be very far removed from the truth in supposing that the first beginning in forming races took place by climatic influences, according to the same acting laws that produced species, but that these, by domestication, artificially conducted pairing, and continued breeding, in the course of thousands of years were raised to the highest expression of race types. Original races with perfect characteristics are not found in a free natural state; these only could be produced under the care and guardianship of man, who, as their protector, is rejoiced up to the present day by their fine and rare forms, pleasing manners, and symmetrical arrangement of colours. But that the supposition of their descent from one primitive race is justified is proved by the facility with which all the races, the common field pigeon included, can pair and produce fruitful young ones, by the strikingly great resemblance of their nature, and the inclination constantly to return to the wild blue colour and shape of the field pigeon (Columba livia). The treacherous bluish colouring which so frequently springs up in black, red, and yellow, on certain parts (rump, vent, flights, and tail), is only too well known to every attentive breeder."

These ideas are quite in accordance with what I have expressed here and elsewhere. I have already instanced the great differences existing in various races of canary birds from what we know was their original stock, and as we can fix the time that it has taken to accomplish such results with comparative accuracy, the "thousands of years" supposed necessary by Neumeister for the perfecting of "Race" pigeons may be somewhat modified, though I have no doubt that some of our varieties may have an unwritten pedigree of at least two thousand years.

CHAPTER X.

COMMON PIGEONS.

COMMON pigeons, strictly speaking, are rock or dovehouse pigeons, as found in a state of nature or in a semi-wild state. I have already referred to them elsewhere, and have only to add that in the west of Scotland they are bred by pigeon fanciers, who have a class for their favourites at the annual show held in the town of Kilmarnock.

Looking, as I have often done, at the class at this show, which generally includes over a dozen entries of blues and blue chequers, I have felt that I would rather not have the responsibility of awarding the prizes, they are so very much alike. When a breed comes to be produced as they are, for size, good shape, and purity of colour and type, they must necessarily cease to be regarded as quite common, and would more truly be designated as fancy rock or dovehouse pigeons. Common pigeons are generally understood to be those of mixed race, so interbred that it is often impossible to guess at their ancestry, and the same abound in almost every town and village in the kingdom. The old English name for them was runts, probably having the same meaning as when applied to common cattle, as Welsh runts, though a canary hen of three years of age was also called a runt. (See old dictionaries.) Moore refers to common pigeons, after describing the fancy runts: "To these we may add the common runt, which are kept purely for the dish, and generally in locker holes in inn yards or other places, and are well known to everybody; they are good feeders, and therefore good nurses for any of the more curious sorts of pigeons."

In France these common runts are known as Pigeons Mondains, and according to Boitard and Corbie, who describe them as having no special characteristics, because they assume all forms and colours, what they lose in purity they gain in the way of fecundity. When extra feather-footed, they are known as Pigeons Patu, and they describe and illustrate types of both denominations. Common runts, when selected for their gay and striking colours, are so far interesting that their young assume the most various though uneven markings, and, for my own part, I would rather breed a motley lot of such, than confine myself to some single uninteresting, though undoubtedly distinct and pure race, such as the spot pigeon.

In France a considerable trade is done in supplying the markets with hand-fed young pigeons fattened in the following way: when the birds are about three weeks old they are placed in cages containing about thirty or forty, kept in a dark place, and fed five or six times a day through a pipe with a liquid paste of buckwheat flour mixed with whole maize. They become fat in five or six days, and "it is astonishing how much delicacy they assume in such a short time."

I believe there is a limited trade for supplying the London markets with hand-fed or crammed pigeons, but the chief towns in this country are supplied almost exclusively direct from field dovecotes. Purchasers may know how to select young and tender birds by the presence of yellow down on their neck feathers. When the value of the manure from a few pairs of common pigeons, kept in an aviary, is taken into account, the value of the young ones will pay for their food. The manure may be kept in barrels, each layer of an inch in depth being covered with a similar layer of dry earth or road scrapings, which will deodorise it and make a very rich compost, worth several pounds a ton. The fine siftings of ashes will do as well as dry earth for deodorising it. I have seen capital crops from very poor soil on which such a compost has been thrown, perhaps three or four times as thickly as guano is generally spread.

CHAPTER XI.

THE NUN PIGEON.

THE nun, from its striking contrast of colours, has always held a high place among toy pigeons. It is supposed to derive its name from the arrangement of its marking, but in France it is the Jacobine, with its coloured body and white head, that is called a nun (*Nonnain*). The French call it *Pigeon Coquille Hollondais*, the Dutch shell pigeon, from its shell crown; and the Germans, *Das Nönnchen*, the little nun, to distinguish it from a somewhat similarly marked variety. Neumeister says that, although hitherto considered as belonging to the field or dovehouse type of pigeons, the nun is an undoubted tumbler in its formation, and in this I agree with him. Having been bred so long, however—it is described by Willoughby under the name of helmet—for mere markings, the tumbling propensity no longer remains.

The nun is a compact, trimly built pigeon, of upright carriage, with a tumbler's head, beak, and pearl eye, which, in the black variety, is surrounded with a narrow blackish cere. The shell, which has been miscalled a hood, should be very extensive, and resemble a cockle-shell filled with plaster of Paris, stuck, as it were, on the back of the bird's head. It should on no account take a cupped form, but, viewed in profile, be perpendicular, and so extensive that, when seen from before, it should describe three-quarters of a circle. The more even its edge, so as to form an unbroken line, the better, and although but few have it so large, it should come down below the level of the eyes, and, of course, the more it stands out from the head the better, when it resembles the glory around the head of a mediæval saint.

The nun is found of several colours, such as black, blue, dun, red,

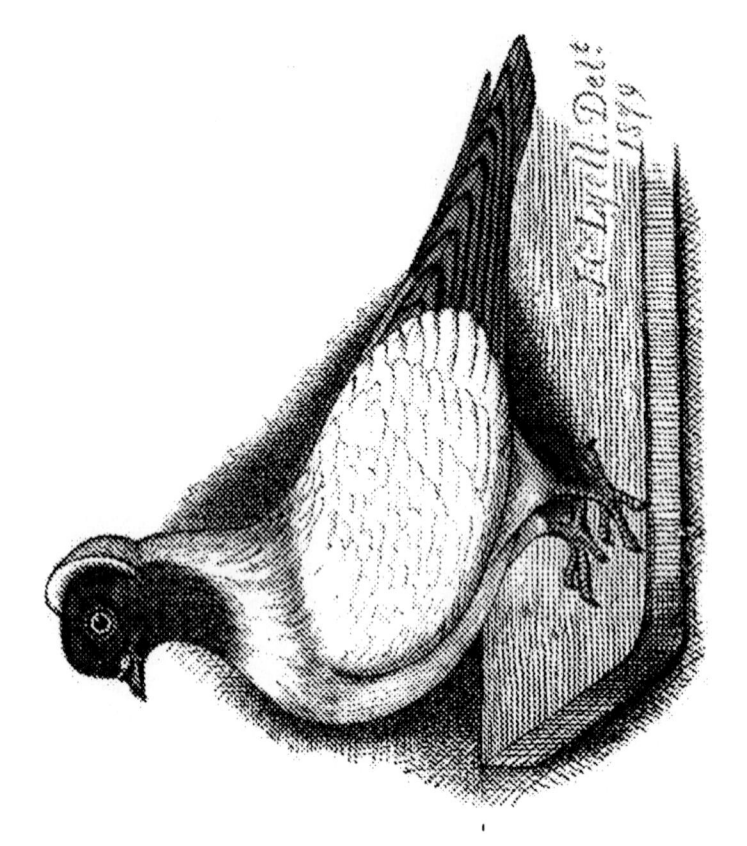

THE NUN PIGEON.

and yellow headed. From the contrast, the black is the favourite colour, and it exceeds in number all the other colours together. I shall take the black first in my description, and, although it is comparatively easy to breed this colour good, yet many nuns are to be found very off-coloured in their black. These, however, have their value in breeding, for it will be found in breeding every variety of pigeon that two birds, each of the best possible shade of colour, do not generally throw such good colour, as one of very good colour and another—not of bad colour but—slightly off in colour. I could not understand for long why this should be so, but the solution of the mystery is no doubt the fact that nature, having reached a certain pitch in artificial forms of life, is inclined to reaction.

The very best specimens of all fancy stock are often failures when mated with others equally good; while with those slightly inferior to themselves, but well come, they perpetuate their highest qualities.

The black nun, however good in colour, must not carry a light beak like other black-headed pigeons such as barbs, which are preferred white-beaked; but its beak should be as black as possible, and I may say it never is white-beaked as far as I have noticed. The head, as far back as the shell, which should stand up purely white, must be black. As the shell feathers grow with a forward inclination, and those of the crown of the head backward, the latter, where they meet the shell feathers, take an upward turn and form the support of the shell. If all the backward growing feathers of the crown are black, the shell will therefore have a black lining, which, being unwished for, causes the dodging exhibitor to cut or pluck them, and so show a clean white shell.

When the young nun is about twelve days old the head feathers will, in a good one, be black only a little way behind the middle of the crown, and those feathers which adjoin the rising shell will be white. By the time the feathers are full grown the black will then reach the shell, but not rise against it. The black head of the nun runs round the corners of the shell, so that when the bird is viewed from behind two black pointed patches are seen, and the colour runs down the sides of the neck to the breast, with a wide sweep, forming the bib, which, the bigger and more evenly cut it is, the higher the bird is valued.

The flight feathers, that is, the ten primaries, should be black. Moore only speaks of six coloured flights in the nun, but nothing under ten a side can be reckoned a standard bird now. Eight a side certainly looks a full flight when the wing is closed, but not when the bird is flying; however, eight a side with quite clean butts of the wings, is preferable to more black flights with the spurious wing and adjacent feathers coloured, a very common fault with all nuns, especially with full-flighted ones. Here, again, is plucking resorted to, but an examination of the open wing will enable the searcher to detect it, if at all extensive. The twelve tail feathers, with their upper and under coverts, must also be black and cut sharply across. Of course, there should be no black feathers over the rest of the body, nor white ones among the black markings, but a prevailing foul marking is at the knees or hocks, where the thigh feathers finish off.

The feet and legs of the black nun, when in the nest, are either quite black or heavily patched with black, but this generally wears away afterwards, though some birds retain it partly, especially those of a very rich colour. They look much better, however, with bright vermilion-coloured legs and feet. The nails of the toes should be quite black, and many a good bird has a small fault in having some of them light.

Probably, on account of the less contrast in colour, red and yellow headed nuns have not been so much considered by breeders as blacks, at least, they do not exist in such perfection, being, as a rule, very deficient both in shell and quality of colour; and it so happens that the marking of the nun encroaches on those parts of the bird which present the very greatest difficulty to the breeder of red and yellow pigeons—the tail and flights. Could red and yellow nuns be produced of such rich and lustrous colour as some kinds of pigeons display, I would consider them as very much finer examples of man's ingenuity than blacks, while, at the same time, they would lack the contrast, though the red would not be much behind even there. Red and yellow nuns have light beaks and toenails.

The illustration is from Mr. Archibald Duthie's winner at the Crystal Palace and elsewhere, one of the best of the breed I ever handled. She is a small bird, has nine and ten coloured flights, with a very finely displayed shell.

CHAPTER XII.

THE HELMET PIGEON.

THE pigeon known at present as the helmet, is a German tumbler. Neumeister describes it under the name of *Der Farbenplättige Tümmler oder die Calottentaube* (coloured crested tumbler, or calotte pigeon), and says that it has long been bred in the greatest perfection in Hamburg. The helmet is of the size of our ordinary flying tumblers, and is similarly formed in head, beak, and body. The upper mandible is coloured, the lower white; the head is black, blue, red, or yellow; the tail, with its coverts, matching the same. The line of demarcation of the helmet or coloured cap should run through the eye, as it were, and dip somewhat at the back of the head. The iris should be as pearly white as possible. The helmet is generally smooth-headed and clean-legged, but Brent mentions a variety with feathered legs and feet, and says that these are coloured from the hocks down to match the head and tail. Neumeister says that some are hooded, and that such are more valued, having an additional beauty to commend them to the breeder.

Willoughby refers to helmets as follows: "In these the head, tail, and quill feathers of the wings are always of one colour, sometimes white, sometimes black, red, yellow, or blue; the rest of the body of another, different from that, whatever it be. These are called Helme by the Low Dutch, as Aldrovandus writes, from the relation of the forementioned Dutchman."

I am inclined to think the above refers to what we now understand as nuns and baldheads, though he does not speak of the shell crests of the former; but his meagre descriptions, given principally from mere hearsay, are not always to be depended on.

Moore, after describing the nun, mentions the helmet as being similar to it, except that it has no hood, and says that it is generally gravel-eyed. This breed of helmet pigeon seems to have become extinct in England. Being evidently only a plain-headed nun, a part of that beautiful pigeon, so to speak, there is no reason why we should wish it restored.

On the introduction of the German calotte, the name helmet was no doubt given it as being quite appropriate and "to let" at the time, no other variety claiming it.

CHAPTER XIII.

THE COLOURED HEADED PIGEON.

A VARIETY closely allied to the nun and helmet in marking is the German *Farbenköpfige Taube,* or coloured headed pigeon, also known as the *bärtige* or bearded pigeon, from its bib, which is not, however, of the tumbler type in formation of head and beak. Neumeister describes them as rather larger than the common field pigeon. They are found of all the principal feathers, and the beak and toenails correspond to the colour of the markings. The black variety has the special name of the *Mohrenkopf* (Moor's head), while others are blue head, yellow head, and so on. The head is broadly hooded and the iris, Neumeister says, ought to be dark, but is generally yellow, just as when a pearl eye is demanded, it often comes dark. The whole head is coloured, the shell hood included, though it is white in his illustration, and the colour runs down the breast, forming a bib. The tail, with its coverts, is coloured, and the rest of the bird white. The feet and legs are generally smooth, but sometimes feathered. He describes an unhooded variety, which must have a narrow white stripe dividing the coloured head at the nape, finishing at the back of the head.

Boitard and Corbie describe a similar variety to the above under the name of *pigeon coquille barbu*; and still another, the *pigeon coquille Tête de Morts,* or death's head shell pigeon, which has only the head and bib black, all the rest being pure white. It has clean legs and pearl eyes.

THE BAVETTE.

CHAPTER XIV.

THE SPOT PIGEON.

THE spot has been described by every English writer, including Willoughby, and is common on the Continent. The Germans call it the *Maskentaube*, or masked pigeon; and the French *pigeon heurté*, or spot pigeon. It is of the size and make of the common field pigeon, generally smooth headed and clean legged, all white, except a spot of colour on the forehead, extending from the beak wattle to the middle of the head, either blue, black, red, or yellow, and with a coloured tail and tail coverts to correspond. The yellow variety goes by the name of *heurté Siam* in France, according to Boitard and Corbie. Some are peak headed, and a few shell hooded, in which case the feet and legs are generally feathered as well. Boitard and Corbie speak of a variety with white tails, the spot being the only coloured portion of their feathers. These are classed with the *mondains*, or common pigeons. The upper mandible of the spot is coloured in accordance with its markings, the lower white.

CHAPTER XV.

THE BAVETTE PIGEON.

THE bavette pigeon, which I have so named from its white bib, has been quite lately introduced into this country by Messrs. John Baily and Son, of Mount-street, Grosvenor-square, in whose aviaries I first saw it. As will be seen from the illustration, it is nearly the reverse of the nun, having a black shell crest, on which the white feathers of the head should not encroach. The bib should come well down on the breast, and be sharply cut. The beak is white and the iris dark hazel, though I should consider a pearl or yellow iris as a great improvement. The tail, with its coverts, is white. The legs and feet are stockinged, and white from the hooks down. The position, size, and shape of the shell crest should be as in the nun. The only body colour I have seen in this variety is black, but there are probably blues, reds, and yellows also, all of which would look well.

It is true that Dixon, in the "Dovecote and Aviary," quoting from Temminck, the ornithologist, mentions black bodied nuns with white heads under the name of *Nonnains Maurins*; but this is not the variety I am describing. The jacobin is called *Nonnain* or nun in France, and the *Nonnain Maurin* is a variety of the jacobin fully described by Boitard and Corbie.

The bavette is an exceedingly pretty pigeon, and entitled to rank high among the feather varieties. From the formation of its head and beak, which are similar to those of the spot, and not so like those of the tumbler as the nun, it must be placed among what the Germans call the field pigeons.

Since writing the above I have seen a bavette pigeon with black beak and orange irides. This, I believe, is the correct type. This variety has been shown under the absurd name of "Lightning Conductors," a name given them on account of their rapid flight.

CHAPTER XVI.

THE BREAST PIGEON.

Die Brusttaube, Farbenbrüstige Taube, der Bruster. — The breast, coloured breasted, or breaster pigeon, is a German toy of peculiar marking, belonging to the field type of pigeons, but more slenderly built, a good flyer and breeder. It is marked on the head, neck, and breast, black, blue, red, or yellow, the colour being cut across, or evenly belted before reaching the thighs. The back, wings, tail, and under part are pure white, but only after the first moult, the nest feathers being tinged with colour. A variety of the yellow ones retain yellow wing bars, but these are rare. The beak is light and the iris yellow. There are smooth headed, peak crested, and shell hooded, also smooth and feathered

THE LATZ PIGEON.

legged specimens, to be found among this breed. The black variety generally retains some colour on the white parts, from which it derives the special name of *Russtaube* or soot pigeon.

There are also breast pigeons having the said marking reversed, the head, neck, and breast being white, and the rest of the feathers coloured. It may therefore be reckoned that, with the variations of smooth and feathered legs, smooth, peaked, and shell-crested heads, the reversing of the markings, and the four principal colours, that there are no less than forty-eight variations of this breed alone, which gives some idea of how vast a number of varieties of domestic pigeons there are in the world.

Brent calls this pigeon the white Archangel, in addition to its usual name. Being found of other colours than yellow or copper, however, the name is not appropriate, and besides, the bronze breast of the Archangel goes no further than the ends of its feathers; underneath they are black.

CHAPTER XVII.

THE LATZ PIGEON.

THE German *Latz*, signifying bodice or stomacher pigeon, also called in Germany the latz shell pigeon of Holland and helmet pigeon, is of the size and type of the field pigeon, and a good flyer and breeder. Its head is adorned with a peculiar helmet or large shell hood, not found so marked in any other species. From the back of its head to half way down the back of its neck the feathers run up and to the side, forming an extensive hood. They do not lie closely and in a mass, but loosely and in disorder. The beak accords with the colour of the marking. Blues, reds, and yellows, according to Neumeister, seem to have died out, while the blacks are frequently to be found under the name *Wiener latstauben*, Vienna bodice pigeons. The head, front and sides of the neck and breast, as shown in the illustration, are coloured, giving the appearance of a coloured bodice, from which the bird derives its name. The rest of the plumage, including all the shell feathers, is white. The eye is said to have a brownish black iris, but is yellow in Neumeister's illustration, and I should consider a pearl or yellow more beautiful than a bull eye. The feet and legs are generally stockinged, though sometimes heavily feathered and hooked, or trousered, as he calls it. The latz is certainly a pretty pigeon, and would make a good addition to the aviaries of those who like birds of well contrasted markings, and likely to breed very true to them.

CHAPTER XVIII.

THE MANE PIGEON.

Die Mähnentaube oder Krausige Mohrenköpf—the mane or curly Moor head pigeon—is said by Neumeister to be probably the latz pigeon perfected by long breeding. From his description of it, they have much in common. It is rather larger than the field pigeon, broader breasted and more thick-set in make. It is said to be found chiefly in Thuringia and the Saxon Erz mountains, and is generally of black markings. Its rather thick strong beak is polished black, its eye large and black brown in the iris. The thighs, legs, and feet are heavily feathered, the claws white. The ground colour is white, except as in the latz, the head, front and sides of neck, and breast, which are black; the tail, with its coverts, are, however, also black in this variety. Its characteristic is the white waving mane on the back neck, reaching upwards, downwards, and to the sides of the neck, parting the black of the bodice marking from the white. The mane consists of thinly sown flaky feathers hanging around the neck disorderly, and in the form of a mane, not by any means close, as in the jacobin, but reaching as far down the neck as the coloured bodice does in front.

The chief difference between the latz and mane pigeons seems to lie in the greater development of loose disordered feathers at the back of the neck, the former having only a larger hood, while these feathers in the latter take the form of a waving mane. The coloured tail and greater development of leg feather are also properties of the latter; but they are evidently near relatives.

THE ARCHANGEL.

CHAPTER XIX.

THE ARCHANGEL PIGEON.

THE first mention of the archangel pigeon in English literature is in "Dixon's Dovecote and Aviary" (1851). An authentic account of its introduction into England is given by Mr. Betty, in Mr. Tegetmeier's work. The late Mr. Frank Redmond, being in Ghent in 1839, selecting some pigeons for Sir John Sebright, procured a pair of archangels. Sir John bred them for some time, and at his death the greater number went to the aviaries of the Earl of Derby, at Knowsley, at whose death they were distributed. The English name is probably derived from the vivid metallic lustre the bird carries on the back and wing feathers, similar to what painters have shown on the wings of angels. At least it does not derive its name from the town of Archangel. The German name is *gimpel,* or the bullfinch pigeon, considered as very appropriate by Neumeister, who says: "No other pigeon displays so decidedly its name by its colouring as does the bullfinch, and thus it can be distinguished at a first glance." According to him it has only been known in Germany for about fifty years, but whether this time is to be reckoned from the date of his first edition, or from the date of the copy from which I quote (1876), I am unable to say. Some authors, he says, call it a native of Southern Germany and the Tyrol, where it is common.

I find from C. Malmusi's "Historical Notices of the Triganieri," or Pigeon Flyers of Modena (1851), that, besides the present breed, the *Triganieri* of Modena, formerly trained three other kinds of pigeons for their aërial contests. "Pausing now," he writes, "in my description of the qualities of the *triganini,* I will mention that three other distinct species, or races, of pigeons were trained to flight by the Modenese *triganieri*, that is to say, the *turchetti*, *timpani*, and *singanini*; the first is distinguished by its very short beak, eyes excessively large and prominent, surrounded by a red circle, and it came originally from Turkey." Evidently the barb. "The second has the head and breast yellowish, and the wings and tail black; it is very much used in Austria, especially at Vienna, though originally coming also from Turkey." This can only apply to the archangel, though not a quite correct description of it. Professor Bonizzi, in his work on the *triganini*, after quoting the above, says : "The *timpani* are no other than the gimpel described by Neumeister." Malmusi continues : "The *singanini* are of one sole colour throughout, whatever it may be, and are distinguished by a white spot between the wings, which extends over the back and sometimes even to the neck. This race ceased to exist in Modena some years ago, and there is a tradition that it was introduced by the gipsies of Hungary in the fifteenth century; thus these birds were called *singarini* or *singanini*."

Having now traced the archangel as far as Turkey, we shall next find it in the Orient itself. When in Calcutta, in 1869, I heard of the arrival there of a pigeon fancier from the north west provinces, with a large assortment of pigeons for sale. I found among them two pairs of archangels that were acquired by a friend of mine, in whose place I saw them often afterwards. This may not be conclusive evidence that they are an Indian breed, as they might have originated in Europe and been carried East; but I am inclined to believe that the archangel is at least an Asiatic production, either Persian or Indian.

The archangel is about the size of the common field pigeon, and of the same type in formation. Its beak should be of a dark flesh tint, brown at the tip, and free of hard blue or black colour, straight and rather long. The head is long or snaky, and the eye should be of a vivid orange colour surrounded by a narrow flesh-coloured cere or wattle. Though there are plain headed and shell crested, or, at least partially shell crested birds among the breed, the correct style of head is to be peak crested, and so good in the peak are some archangels that they leave nothing to be desired in this respect. The feathers at the back of the head should all draw to a point, ending in a finely pointed crest, and the higher this peak reaches the better. I consider it is immaterial whether there is a notch below the peak dividing it from the back neck feathers, or a kind of hog mane, showing no break, so long as the peak itself is correct.

The head, neck, breast, belly, thighs, and vent feathers should be of a bronzed copper colour, burnished with metallic lustre, solid and even. But this appearance does not pervade these feathers all through, as underneath they are of a dull black, which should not, however, assert itself to the eye, though it generally does about the thigh and vent feathers. The back, wings, and rump, should be as black as possible, though generally more or less bronzed, accompanied by metallic tints of green, blue, purple, and ruby colour, which show in any light, but which in a strong or sunlight, when the bird is moving about, sparkle like coloured jewels of price. The flight feathers are bronzed black or kite-coloured, and the tail is blue black, with a black bar at the end. I have heard of black tailed archangels, but have never seen any, nor do I consider that they should be other than dark blue tailed, both on account of the greater variety in the plumage, and because, though blue-tailed, they can still show as much lustre over their feathers as any breed we have. At least in Germany, from where we got them, the standard, according to Neumeister, is the blue-barred tail. The legs and feet should be unfeathered and of a bright red, the nails dark.

Besides the above coloured archangel pigeons there are others whose whole plumage is more subdued. The copper is changed to yellow, the back and wings to a blue black, and the tail to light blue, barred with black. This variety has no lustre compared to the other. It is a natural change that occurs in breeding, and that has a value for breeding. I have bred such from two birds of standard colouring, and they may be matched to the dark variety, when they will breed both colours and others midway between.

The archangel does not assume its full colour till after its second moult, for of the twelve secondary flights but two (the two next the primaries, as in all pigeons) are changed during the first moult. The breeder has, however, a good idea of what a bird will eventually be when it leaves the nest.

There are so-called archangels, all white and all black, which may have originated from standard birds as natural sports, by way of albinism and melanism. The black variety is very pretty with its metallic lustre. Neumeister also mentions whole red and whole yellow archangels, and the following varieties:

1. Archangels with white wings, back, rump, and tail. These, if the same on their neck and breast feathering as the standard bird, viz., dark underneath on all their copper feathers may be called a variety of the archangel. If only ordinary red or yellow, the under parts of the feathers being white, they are breast pigeons. The white archangel would, however, require to be coppered back to the vent, whereas the breaster, as described, is belted across before the thighs.

2. *Spiegel gimpel*, or mirror bullfinches, are like the preceding, but with yellow wing bars. This is, perhaps, the same rare variety that he mentions as occurring among the breast pigeons.

3. Standard archangels, with white mask or forehead spot, and white upper mandible.

4. The same, with white flight feathers.

5. Standard archangels, with white head or helmet, as in the calotte pigeon, and white upper mandible.

6. The same, with white flight feathers.

7. Standard archangels, with white wing bars—a rarity.

8. Standard archangels, with double crests, or a trumpeter's rose on the forehead.

Any of these varieties would only be interesting if got without sacrificing the more important points of the archangel—its colour and lustre. The illustration is from a fine bird, winner of many prizes, lent me by Mr. John Cowe, of Aberdeen.

CHAPTER XX.

THE ICE PIGEON.

THIS variety derives its name from its beautiful lavender blue colour, considered by the German fanciers to resemble blue ice, hence its name, *die Eistaube*. It is also known by the names *mehl* and *lasurtaube*, signifying meal and azure blue pigeon. There are several varieties of the ice pigeon, the simplest form being of a beautiful clear light blue without wing bars, but with dark flights and tail bar. This form is probably the original of the others, and is known in Germany as the *hohlblaue taube*, from its resemblance to the stock dove. It is of the size of the common field pigeon, but more thick set and broader chested, shorter necked and legged. It should be heavily feathered on the legs and feet. It has a dark beak and nails, a reddish yellow iris, and is smooth-headed. The first remove from this form is that in which the colour is still more delicate and silvery, and in which the dark flights and tail bar almost disappear, and become nearly of the same tint as the body feathers. The next form of the ice pigeon, originally from Silesia, is of the same colouring as the preceding, but with white wing bars beautifully edged with black and with black tail bar. The newest and rarest form is known in Germany as the *porzelantaube*, or porcelain pigeon, and in addition to what the last-mentioned variety—the Silesian—shows, is chequered or spangled over the coverts of the wings, shoulders, upper and middle back, with narrow white spots fringed with black.

The make and shape of all these varieties are similar. They are found smooth, medium, and rough-legged, but are preferred heavily feathered. The smooth-legged chequered or spangled ones are known in this country as Ural ice, while the rough-legged spangled birds are called Siberian ice. In all varieties they vary in colour from light to dark, but the powdered lavender ground tint, as uniform as possible, is what is desired. The blacker the edging on white wing bars and spangling, the more inclined they are to run dark in the blue. The iris is always preferred to be yellow, but is often hazel in the lightest tinted birds. There are also ice pigeons whose ground tint is changed from lavender blue to a beautiful soft powdery silver. The various types should be distinct and well marked, not half way between, neither one thing nor another, that is, the spangled variety should be heavily spangled and the merely white barred should not show any incipient spangling.

CHAPTER XXI.

THE MIROITE PIGEON.

This is a French variety, described by Boitard and Corbie, and mentioned by Brent. The French writers describe them thus : " It is inconceivable that none of the authors who have written about pigeons have mentioned this race, so remarkable by the beautiful colour of its plumage. Is it because they never heard of it ? But, however, although not common, all amateurs know it, and some possess several varieties of it. Is it because they have not regarded it as a pure race ? This cannot be the reason, for these pigeons are positively a pure race, since they cannot be crossed with any other variety, however much they resemble it, without being lost. Be it as it may, these birds have the general form of the mondains (common runts), and can scarcely be distinguished, except by the striking beauty of their plumage. They never have a cere round the eyes, and are generally yellow in the iris.

"*Pigeon Miroité Rouge.*—It is the colour of the red blood of an ox, interrupted at two-thirds of an inch from the ends of the flight and tail feathers by a grey white bar, half an inch broad. The ends of these feathers are of a red colour, a little clearer than the rest of the body;

eye, yellow iris. This charming variety, of medium size, produces well, and merits, by all accounts, the care of amateurs.

"*Pigeon Miroité Jaune.*—This pretty bird only differs from the preceding by the ground of its plumage, which is yellow; moreover, it is miroité the same on the flight and tail feathers. It has the same fecundity.

"*Pigeon Petit Miroité.*—Similar to the preceding but much smaller, about the size of the rock pigeon. This charming bird is a good breeder."

Brent says the word miroité is difficult to translate. He was informed that it meant composed of three colours, of which two were blended in one. A French gentleman has informed me that miroité means flashing, *e.g.*, the neck of the blue rock pigeon is said to be miroité. This variety may therefore take its name from its great metallic lustre, or it may be a technical name derived from the blending of the colours in its tail and flight feathers. The miroité pigeons may be had in Paris. I was recently offered some by the Parisian dealer, M. Vallée.

CHAPTER XXII.

THE FIRE PIGEON.

Die feuertaube, or the fire pigeon, is a variety I have never seen. I can find no notice of it in any other work than Neumeister's, whose description is as follows:—"It reminds one very strikingly of a strong tumbler, and is of the size of the medium field pigeon. The head is unhooded, the feet smooth, the colour of the whole plumage black with an extremely bright copper red sheen. This metallic lustre is with the fire pigeon more intense than with any other species of pigeon, and not only on the neck, but spread over the whole body, with the exception of the flights and tail. In the sunshine this pigeon reflects so splendidly that it actually irradiates and then looks almost copper red. It is exceedingly rare, and seldom or never comes into the market."

As the archangel itself is not excepted in the above description, the lustre on the fire pigeon must be a sight for a pigeon fancier to behold. If not extinct, this variety must be rather scarce and secluded, as it is never offered for sale in this country, or even mentioned in the reports of shows. It would make such a splendid addition to our feather varieties, that it would be worth the while of anyone, having opportunities of acquiring the German toys, to see if some specimens of the breed can still be got.

THE SWALLOW.

CHAPTER XXIII.

THE SWALLOW PIGEON.

THE swallow pigeon, known in Germany in several varieties as the *Schwalbentaube* and in France as the *Hirondelle*, has its name from its resemblance in marking to the tern or sea swallow. The ordinary type found in this country is usually imported from Germany, and is marked like the illustration, which is taken from a bird shown successfully by Mr. Glenday, of Broughty Ferry. The swallow has a long slender beak, the upper mandible of which is coloured in accordance with the marking. The forehead rises rather abruptly, the head is flat, and coloured above an imaginary line running from the corners of the mouth through the eyes. The hood, which should be extensive and of a cupped shell form, should be all white, and not lined with coloured feathers, or the bird loses in value. The coloured feathers in the nestling must not extend back as far as the hood, or the desired marking will not be attained at maturity, as described in the nun. The eye has a dark hazel iris, and when the markings are of rich colour, as they often are, the eye cere and corners of the mouth are bright red. The neck is slender and short, the breast broad, the body broad and flat, and the legs short. The wings and flights are coloured, but the scapular and back feathers must be all white, forming a heartshaped figure on the back, the marking here being the reverse of the magpie pigeon. The legs and feet should be heavily hocked and booted, the heavier the better, as this adds to the appearance, and is in keeping with the shape of this variety. The hock feathers must be white, but all feathers below the hocks, on the legs and feet, must be coloured. The general appearance of the swallow is that of a thickset, broad, low-standing pigeon, which has caused it to be considered on the Continent as resembling the toad in shape. The common variety figured by Boitard and Corbié has no hood. The yellow marked ones, according to them, are called *Hirondelles Siam*, while the *Hirondelles Fauve Etincelé*, or sparkling fawn-coloured swallow, is described as follows: "This charming bird is extremely rare in France; it can hardly be got except in Germany, where it is not common. Its mantle is fawn coloured, agreeably scintillated with black or red," which would appear to be an almond-feathered variety. The colours of the swallow are generally good, and sometimes very rich in quality. It is found in black, red, yellow, blue, and silver, with dark bars and without bars, and in off colours.

The Silesian swallow pigeon, according to Neumeister, answers the foregoing description, except that it is marked on the head with only a frontal spot, above the beak, of the size of a pea, while some have not even this mark, but are white-headed. Besides shell-crested and plain-headed ones, a variety exists double-crested or with a rose over the beak, like a trumpeter or priest. The Silesian swallow is best obtained in the Upper Lausitz.

The Nürnberg swallow is a peculiarly feathered variety, known, according to Neumeister, from ancient times. In marking it is like the illustration, but the quality of its colours is exceedingly rich, owing to a certain fat or oil in its system, which it has in common with certain Eastern pigeons. Its plumage fits loosely, but at the same time is thick, soft, and fatty to the touch. The colours are fiery and full, the black deeper and more velvety than with all other (German) species of pigeon; the white, on the other hand, looks as if oiled, for which reason this pigeon is called in Nürnberg "the greasy fairy." All the feathers under the wings, about the thighs, and round the vent, instead of shedding their fibres in the usual way, remain merely cases filled with yellow fat or wax, or at most only shed a small portion of their extremities. I have found the same peculiarity in other pigeons, and at one time considered it a disease, instead of which I now believe it is this fat or grease in the system which gives the extraordinary metallic lustre to the few varieties of domestic pigeons that possess it. The black Nürnberg swallow has most of these grease quills, and from its beautiful green lustre is called the "velvet fairy;" next it comes the red, while the yellow and blue have not so much of this peculiar feathering.

The Silesian and Nürnberg swallows are found in the following varieties:
- Black, red, and yellow, with white wing bars.
- Blue, with white wing bars, edged with black.
- Silver, corresponding to the blues.

Scaled winged swallows. On the ends of the coloured wing coverts are small white points resembling the scales of a fish:
- Black, red, and yellow, with white scales or chequers on the coverts, in addition to white wing bars.
- Blue, with white scales, and white wing bars edged with black.
- Blue, with white black-edged scales, and white wing bars edged with black.
- Silvers, corresponding to the blues.

CHAPTER XXIV.

THE CARMELITE PIGEON.

THE carmelite described by Boitard and Corbie, whose description has been mostly copied by Brent in his book, is evidently a variety of the swallow pigeon. M. Corbie, who had the breed under his care for nearly fifty years, considers M. Fournier, who was keeper of the aviaries of the Count de Clermont, mistaken in classing them as swallows in his account of pigeons supplied to the naturalist, M. Buffon; but the only difference between the common swallow and carmelite, as figured by Boitard and Corbie, is that the latter is smaller, has a crest, and more feet feathering than the former, which is smooth-headed. The markings are the same. In all probability the carmelite of Boitard and Corbie was the Nürnberg swallow. Brent, whose illustrations are mostly copies from Boitard and Corbie, has the carmelite similar in outline to them, but he has reversed the markings, showing it to be a magpie-coloured pigeon. How he fell into this error I cannot imagine, unless he understood the word "manteau" to refer to the scapular and back feathers, instead of to the wing coverts.

In the descriptions of both swallow and carmelite, Boitard and Corbié apply the word "manteau" to the wing coverts, as reference to their letterpress and illustrations will show.

CHAPTER XXV.

THE STORK PIGEON.

Die Storch oder Schwingentaube, stork or wing pigeon of Germany, is in size and shape similar to the spot pigeon, with which it has in common the coloured spot on the brow, black, red, yellow, or blue. If the spot is small, the upper mandible may be white, but it is usually coloured if the spot is extensive. The head may be either smooth, peaked, or shell crested. The eye is hazel-coloured. The legs and feet are preferred heavily hocked and feathered, and are coloured from the knee down, the hock feathers themselves being white. The ten flight feathers in each wing should be coloured, and all the rest of the bird must be white, except the feathers of the spurious wing and a few feathers about the wing butts. These coloured feathers give the bird its name, and when the wing is closed it has a coloured margin or framing at the butts of the wings running round it, which must be regular and not too broad. When well marked, the stork is considered one of the finest feather varieties in Germany. It has been already described in a late publication, under the name of "Spot Fairy," or "Fairy Swallow," but the chief part of its marking has not been mentioned, the coloured butts of the wings having probably been considered as foul instead of fancy marks.

THE MAGPIE PIGEON.

CHAPTER XXVI.

THE MAGPIE PIGEON.

THE magpie pigeon, now a general favourite in this country on account of the telling and nicely contrasted disposition of the white and coloured parts of its plumage, is, like the helmet, a variety of German tumbler (*Der Elstertümmler*). It goes by the name of Copenhagen tumbler in the north of Germany, and is said to be found good in Hamburg. It is among the varieties regularly imported into this country from Germany, and is found in all the chief colours. Among magpies there is a considerable difference in length of face, some being like neat medium-faced flying tumblers, while others are very much run out in beak. I never heard of any fixed standard as to the beak. Some prefer it long, like the rock pigeon, while others like the tumbler type. Brent, in his writings, complains of fanciers breeding them coarse and mousey. In plate 7 of Neumeister's book are illustrations of four magpies, a black, blue, red, and yellow. They are all in shape of body and in head and beak like medium-faced flying tumblers. It is not in a certain length of face that the points of the magpie are found, and it is absurd to see one style winning at one show, then discarded as not the correct type at the next. So it would be right to fix a standard for the guidance of all, lest ultimately we may be troubled with two classes, if not three, should a school arise whose standard may be something between the two. In my opinion, the pleasant faced tumbler type, both in shape of body and in head and beak, is correct, and should be preferred, other things being equal; but it is the marking that is the chief thing in this variety.

The magpie is to be had in black, red, yellow, blue, silver, and off colours. The first three are the choice colours, blue and silver not looking so well with the arrangement of the marking. The black looks best, and no doubt gives the name to the breed. The beak should be flesh-coloured, or, at least, no more than tipped with dark colour, in blacks, reds, and yellows. The coloured portions of the plumage of a well-marked magpie pigeon include the head, neck, and breast (which must be cut straight across, or belted, just below the crop), the back and scapular feathers (forming the figure of a heart), and the rump and tail. The rest of the feathers should be white. It is no very difficult matter to get this marking good, and yet most birds require to get, and do get, their toilets made to a certain extent to make the lines of demarcation correct. The irides should in all cases be as pearly white as possible, and the best coloured birds have the eye ceres and beak reddish flesh-coloured. The black colour is often very good, and burnished with green lustre; but the red and yellow especially the red, though often what would be called very good in many varieties of fancy pigeons, is seldom in the magpie of the very best possible colour. A red that could carry a metallic lustre to the end of the tail would be much more choice and valuable than any black. The magpie must have no feathers on the legs and feet, which ought to be very bright red, and although some have a peak crest, the smooth head is preferred.

Neumeister describes another kind of magpie pigeon under the name of *Die Elstertaube, der Verkehrtflügel* (the magpie pigeon, the reversed wing), which is similar in marking to that described, except that it is white on the head where the helmet is coloured, on which white skull cap a coloured forehead spot is indispensable. The legs and feet of this variety are feathered. He says: "It is to be regretted that this really beautiful pigeon has been so much neglected that it threatens extinction. Its beautiful marking and shape would adorn every dovecote."

THE PRIEST PIGEON.

CHAPTER XXVII.

THE SHIELD PIGEON.

THIS is a German breed, which takes its name from its marking. *Die Schild oder Deckeltaube* (the shield or cover pigeon) is of two kinds, one smooth-legged, the other heavily hocked and feather-legged and footed. The latter, which is preferred, is the larger of the two, and is a low, broad-chested, thick-set pigeon, of the field type in head and beak. The eye is dark. The marking is that known as turbit or shoulder marking, and to be right, which they rarely are, they must neither have white wing butts nor foul thighs. Although pigeons of the shield type are sometimes hooded, and even double crested, these belong to a sub-variety of the trumpeter, to be afterwards mentioned; the head of the true shield is uncrested. In colour they are found black, red, yellow, blue, silver, and in mixed colours, both plain and with white wing bars. Blues of the latter kind have a black edging on the bars. The rarest are yellows, with white bars. In this breed some are spangled, marbled, or chequered on the shoulders, with two or three colours, like some of the eastern frilled and Modena pigeons.

CHAPTER XXVIII.

THE PRIEST PIGEON.

THE priest pigeon, the *Pfaffentaube* of Germany, where it is extensively bred, is now well known in this country in several of its numerous varieties. The general form of the priest is that of a stoutly-built thick-set pigeon, rather larger than the common field pigeon, with which it agrees in shape of head and beak. It is found in the following varieties:

The common priest, which is considered the original of the others, is found in black, blue, red, yellow, and in off colours, with a white upper mandible and head. The line of demarcation must run from the mouth across the eyes, and round the inside of the crest, which must be, if good, an extensive cupped shell, not lined with the white, but coloured. The irides, often dark or broken, should be light or dark yellow, according to the plumage. The legs and feet must be well covered with coloured feathers of a medium length. The colours of the common priest are often excellent, and reds have been shown of late, not inferior in colour to any red pigeons I have ever seen.

The double crested priest is found in all colours, like the preceding. The second crest, or trumpeter's rose on the forehead, falling over the nostrils, assumes various shapes, being either in the form of a flower, rayed from its centre, or a small twisted up tuft of feathers. So long as it is symmetrical, and not all to one side, any form will do, as it is not expected to be developed as in the trumpeter.

The white-stockinged priest has, in addition, the feathers of the legs and feet white, but the thigh, belly, and vent feathers must remain coloured.

The white-barred priest may have white or coloured stockings, with white wing bars, which with the blue ground colour are bordered with black. Reds and yellows so barred are rare, and cannot be got so fine in colour as in the original breed.

The white-flighted white-barred priest is like the preceding, but has the ten primaries white. The blues have received the name of blue Brunswicks in this country.

The white-flighted, barred and tailed priest is like the preceding, with a white tail, and occurs almost always in black or blue.

The starling-barred, white-flighted and tailed priest is said by Neumeister to be the most beautiful of the priests. He says, "It is exceedingly rare, and only to be met with in the districts of Hohenzollern and the Upper Neckar, and only with a black plumage and unfeathered feet." I have never seen this kind, so cannot describe it more fully.

There are also priests which have mirrored or finched flights, *i.e.*, with triangular or rounded white spots near the extremities of the flight feathers, like some blondinettes. These spots appear after the first moult, and the bar feathers are similarly marked.

CHAPTER XXIX.

THE MONK PIGEON.

THE monk pigeon (*Die Mönchtaube* of Germany) is admitted to be a relative of the priest, compared with which, however, it is larger, and broader across the chest and back. It has no hood, but it retains the leg and feet feathering of the priest. It is found in all the chief colours, marked as follows: both mandibles are white, the whole head is white, the line of demarcation running below the eyes, which should be hazel in all varieties, though this is not absolutely necessary except in the blue and black. The flight feathers and the tail, with its coverts, are white, and the legs and feet from the knee downwards. The thighs and belly should be dark, but are often partly white, which is a fault in this breed. All colours are said to be found both with and without white wing bars.

CHAPTER XXX.

THE WHITEHEAD OR MOULTING PIGEON.

THIS pigeon, which is referred to by Brent by the name of the pilferer, as a sub-variety of the priest, is known in Germany as *Die Weisskopf oder die Mäusertaube*. *Mauser*, besides meaning to filch or pilfer, also means to change feathers or cast the skin. The German gentleman who translated Neumeister's work for me renders the above title the whitehead or moulting pigeon, and the description of the breed is as follows: "The whitehead is one of the rarest coloured pigeons, and is found only in a few places in Thuringia. Its head has a beautiful broad shell hood; the upper bill is white, the iris yellow, corresponding with the ground colour of the plumage. The legs and toes are feathered. The plumage has a metallic black, red, yellow, or dark bronze lustre, which forms the principal beauty of this pigeon. It has a broad breast and a low posture. The head and tail, with its coverts, are white. These marks are not, however, of any great fixity, the head being often marked unequally, sometimes only the upper part of it being white. The feathers on the feet are sometimes foul, and a part of the back is often white. In this variety, therefore, something always remains to be wished for. With black, red, or yellow ones, a belly changing somewhat into blue is a frequent fault in beauty which ought to be watched, and, by a suitable selection in breeding, avoided. But the white-head with perfect marks is a very fine pigeon. The black and red ones are often excellent, and particularly valued. The latter displays in fine specimens a peculiarly burning red, even on the belly, under the wings, and as far as the points of the flight feathers, which is only very rarely found in other species. Sometimes this somewhat tender pigeon produces white spotted young ones, which in moulting become quite white, but again breed correctly coloured and marked ones. The moulting pigeons prefer to remain by themselves, and rarely fly farther than the neighbouring roofs." I believe that the gorgeously coloured red priests shown of late in this country were of this variety, though they had coloured tails. They carried a metallic lustre to the very extremity of the tail—a rare thing in pigeons of a red colour.

CHAPTER XXXI.

THE WHITE SPOT PIGEON.

THE white spot pigeon (*Die Weiszblässige Taube* of Germany) is the reverse in marking of the common spot pigeon. The head is unhooded, the upper mandible white, the lower coloured in accordance with the plumage. The legs and feet are smooth in some, in others feathered. The heavier the leg feathering in this breed the better they look, but it is not easy to procure them well hocked and booted, the majority being only sparsely covered.

The white spot pigeon is of the common field type in formation of head

THE WHITE SPOT PIGEON.

and beak, and its chief value lies in the quality of its colouring and accuracy of its marking. The irides are yellow or red, following the body colour. The breed occurs in the following varieties:

The common white spot, in all ground colours, with a white, regularly formed, oval spot on the forehead. The tail, with its coverts, is also white.

The white barred spot is black or blue in colour, and has, in addition to the marks of the foregoing, white, or white edged with black, wing bars. White barred reds and yellows, as in all other breeds, are rare.

The white scaled spot is black or blue. The black in addition to white spot and white tail, has the wing coverts scaled or chequered with white, the flights tipped or finched with white spots, and the bars either white or spotted with white like the flights; but the white in this variety is of a yellow or creamy cast, showing it has its origin from the Suabian pigeon. The blue, in addition to the white spot and tail, has the wing coverts chequered with white, and black bars across the wings.

The copper winged spot, or English fire pigeon, is the most beautiful of the white spot pigeons. It is thicker set, broader breasted, and shorter than the preceding varieties. It has an orange iris, and must be heavily feathered on hocks, legs, and feet. The upper mandible, according to the German standard, should be white; but Mr. Ludlow, of Birmingham, who has bred this variety extensively, prefers it dark. It has the white forehead spot, white tail and tail coverts. The head, neck, and breast, are dark blue black, lustred with green and purple hues; the under body and leg feathering should approach the same colouring as much as possible; and the flights are blue black with a bronzed kite colouring on their inner webs. The back and wing coverts or shoulders are of a burnished copper coluor, but only after the first moult, the nestling feathers, as in other lustrous pigeons, being very dull compared with the matured plumage. Mr. Ludlow says the fire pigeon is one of the varieties that show a sexual difference in their colouring, the hens having their copper feathers distinctly tipped with black, which the cocks do not have; whether this difference exists all through the breed, or only in one strain of it, I am not aware, but Neumeister makes no mention of it. It is a matter of taste which of the two appearances is most pleasing. The copper wing is not found with white wing bars.

CHAPTER XXXII.

THE HYACINTH PIGEON.

THE hyacinth pigeon stands at the head of a French breed which is found in various colourings, and which are all included under the name of *Pigeons Maillés*, mailed, armoured, or speckled pigeons. They are large, smooth headed and clean legged pigeons, and have been classed by French naturalists with the pouters, as they have the power of slightly inflating their crops. I knew a fancier who bred them extensively, and his would have been correctly described as middle sized runts with a slight dash of the pouter. They are classed as follows :

Pigeon Maillé Jacinthe.—Speckled hyacinth pigeon. The shoulders as in a turbit, or the *manteau* in French, of clear blue, chequered or spangled in a particular pattern with white and black, or a black and blue bar on all the feathers, the outer side of the blue bar having a white spot or spangle. The ten flight feathers of each wing pure white. The head, neck, breast, belly, and tail dark purple blue, the tail barred with black.

Pigeon Maillé Jacinthe Plein, is a little less in size than the preceding, but similar in colouring, except that it has dark blue instead of white flights.

The following varieties are found both with white flights, and *plein*, or with dark flights.

Pigeon Maillé Couleur de Feu, red or flame coloured, similar to the hyacinth, but with red instead of white spangles.

Pigeon Maillé Noyer, coloured like walnut wood, or inclining to yellow in the spangles.

Pigeon Maillé Pécher, or peach coloured in the spangles.

The *Noyer* is considered as a cross between the *Jacinthe* and *Couleur de Feu* ; and the *Pécher*, as a cross between the *Jacinthe* and *Noyer*. Each variety is, however, established, and breeds true, according to Boitard and Corbie.

All I have seen of these varieties were of the dark flighted kinds. They have been promiscuously named Hyacinths, Victorias and Porcelains in our pigeon literature; but the above description is that of undoubted authorities, the white spangled ones alone being entitled to the name of Hyacinths. The white flighted varieties appear to be larger than the *plein*, and to have somewhat more of the pouter in them, and I think I can recognize them in Moore's "Columbarium" as follows :

"The Parisian Powter. This pigeon was originally bred at *Paris* and from thence brought to *Brussels*, whence it was transmitted to us; it has all the Nature of a Powter, but is generally long crop'd and not very large, it is short bodied, short leg'd, and thick in the girt; what is chiefly admir'd in this Bird is its Feather, which is indeed very beautiful and peculiar only to it self, resembling a fine piece of *Irish* stitch, being chequer'd with various Colours in every Feather, except the flight which is white; the more red it has intermix'd with the other Colours the more valuable it is. Some are Gravel ey'd, and some bull ey'd, but it is equally indifferent which eye it has." If for "every feather" we read the wing coverts—which are the only feathers, except the flights and tail, that can possibly be spangled in pigeons in the above way— Moore's description of the Parisian Pouter, the Parazence Pouter of the treatise of 1765, agrees with that of the sub-varieties of the *Pigeon Maillé Jacinthe*, or Hyacinth.

CHAPTER XXXIII.

THE STARLING PIGEON.

THE starling pigeon is a Continental variety, and in Germany it goes by the name of *Der Staarenhals*, or the starling neck. It is in size, shape, and in style of head and beak, similar to the common field or dovecote pigeon. The legs and feet are sometimes feathered, but generally smooth;

and the head, though usually uncrested, has sometimes a turn crown. The irides are red and the beak and nails black. Although the starling pigeon is found in several colours, the black variety is that most esteemed, and it should be of a deep satin black, with a purple metallic lustre, and strongly pigeon necked. On the breast there should be a crescent of white, which, the evener it is cut, the more the bird is valued. This crescent is produced by the feathers forming it being tipped with white, which accordingly comes only to perfection on completion of the first moult. Two white bars cross the wings, which, with the crescent, are in the nest feathers usually of a rusty red or kite colour. With age the starling often loses its marking to a great extent, the crescent becoming large and shapeless, the ends of its flights becoming grizzled with white, and its head grey or spotted with white. The white crescent and wing bars on the lustrous black ground, being all the marking desired, such a standard is not easy to maintain in all the progeny, which often result in birds either too dark or too light. Blue and red starling necks, though also obtainable in Germany, are not considered so beautiful. The crescent on the breast, not being, as in the English pouter, composed of white, but only of white tipped dark feathers, I believe this kind of marking on a really sound red is hardly attainable, any more than white wing bars on sound reds and yellows, and that such a red as can be got with these marks combined, fails to look well.

Neumeister says of the starling, "By reason of its particularly recommendable qualities for fielding, it is absolutely to be preferred to all other fancy pigeons that have to find most of their food. It has almost always at the same time young ones and eggs side by side, and seeks its food in any weather, summer or winter, so long as the ground is not covered with snow. For breeders of the finer species of pigeons it is highly valuable, inasmuch as it feeds almost all the young ones of other pairs running after it for food. It is the only kind that during the so called famine months, knows how to provide its young ones with the necessary food and bring them up. It is particularly distinguished by its diligent roaming, possesses all the qualities of an excellent field pigeon, and generally serves as a guide to the others in the field."

The starling neck is also known in Germany as the *Trauertaube* or mourning pigeon, a very appropriate name for the little fellow in his black coat and white bands.

THE SUABIAN PIGEON.

The French starling pigeon described by Boitard and Corbie, is stocking legged and turn crowned, and marked as the German. They only mention the black variety, and on account of its crest, place it among the *pigeons coquilles*, hence its name, *pigeon coquille étourneau*.

Brent speaks of a crested variety of the starling that has, in addition to the ordinary marks of the breed, the upper mandible and head white, as in the priest pigeon. This may probably be the starling barred priest I have already referred to, but Brent makes no mention of the white flights and tail.

CHAPTER XXXIV.

THE SUABIAN PIGEON.

THE Suabian pigeon, which is a German breed, is known also in France. Neumeister has classed it, not very correctly I think, among the priest pigeons, under the name of *Die gestaarte Silberschuppige Pfaffentaube*, the starling silver scaled priest pigeon, and says that it comes from Suabia. Boitard and Corbie class it among the *Pigeons Coquilles*, and call it the *Pigeon Coquille Souabe*. I think there can be little doubt that the Suabian was produced from the starling pigeon, by breeding together such as came too light in colour, till at length the desired marking was fixed. When in perfection, the Suabian is certainly one of the most beautifully feathered toys in creation, and a striking example of the ingenuity displayed by careful breeders of that most universally cherished bird, the domestic pigeon. In make of head and beak, and in shape of body, the Suabian, like the starling, is of the common type, but it is not considered such a good breeder or so hardy. It is found both smooth and feather legged, and both smooth-headed and turn-crowned; but the smooth-legged ones, with a good peak crest, are considered the originals, and look smartest. The ground colour of the Suabian should be of a good metallic black; but it is generally of a dull dim black. On the head and neck the feathers should be all tipped with a creamy white, interspersed with lustrous apple green and red tints, and on the breast the white must be so intensified as to take the form of a crescent or half moon, as in the starling. The back and scapular feathers and wing coverts should be spangled or chequered with black on their creamy white extremities, and the pattern this spangling assumes is of different kinds. It may either be in a triangular form, or the feathers may be laced round with black, though I have never seen the latter form so perfect as in the illustration in Tegetmeier's Pigeon Book; but as the Eastern blondinette pigeons can be bred beautifully and regularly laced on the wing coverts, the same style of marking may yet be produced in the Suabian. The primaries or flight feathers should be black, with creamy white oval spots near their extremities; and although it is rare to get specimens marked in a similar way on the principal tail feathers, no bird can be considered perfect without this. The lower back, belly, vent and thighs, should also be as black as possible, and in theory these parts should show the starling marking as well, but it will be found that this can only be attained by an excess of marking on the neck and wing coverts. To produce the happy medium in marking, and have birds with neither too little nor too much of it, is the difficult point to attain in the Suabian, and as its marking is of such an artificial character, it is no easy matter to breed it true. It is only after the first moult that its beauties become apparent, the nestling being of a rusty red, as in the starling, and not even then does it attain its full beauty, as the secondary flights are not fully moulted in its first year, but in its second. With age it often becomes blotched and irregular in spangling, like other pigeons of variegated feather. The beak and toe nails should be black, and the irides orange or red. Brent mentions a sub-variety with white upper mandible and head, like the priest, and Neumeister one with white flights and tail, both of which I consider quite out of keeping with the character of the breed.

Besides the black grounded Suabian, there is another form in which the ground colour is of a ruddy brown or chocolate hue. These have been called Porcelains, which name has also been applied to a sub-variety of the hyacinth; but it would be better to allow them to be known as brown-spangled Suabians. This sub-variety should possess the same characteristics as the other, and the more decided and pronounced it is in its ground colour the better. Many specimens are neither one thing nor another in their ground tint, and all such, unless for any special quality

THE SWISS PIGEON.

of spangling, which may be of value in breeding, are comparatively worthless in point of beauty and for show purposes.

CHAPTER XXXV.

THE SWISS PIGEON.

THIS variety is the *Schweisertaube* of Germany, where it also goes by the name of moon, crescent, and badge of honour pigeon. In Boitard and Corbie's work, it is called *Pigeon Suisse*. It is of the common type in head, beak, and body, is smooth-headed, and should be heavily hooked and feather-legged and footed. The irides are yellow or orange, and the beak and nails correspond with the colour of the markings. There are three principal colours in this breed, viz., the red, yellow, and black barred. The ground colour of all should be of a satiny white tint, shaded off into a very clear light mealy, buff, or blue according to the colour of the marks; the first having red or rich brown wing bars and breastplate, which must be a clean cut half-moon, as in the illustration; the second has similar yellow markings, and the third a crescent of the colour of the neck of a blue pigeon, and black wing bars, and tail bar. The red and yellow marked ones correspond with the red and yellow mealy colours, which do not of course have a dark bar at the end of the tail. The crescent or breastplate should in all be well lustred, and when its points meet at the back of the neck it is ring-necked, which is a great defect. Neumeister says: "The fledged young ones have no crescent marks on the breast, it only becomes visible after the first moulting. The more the ground colour approaches to pure white, and the darker and narrower at the same time the wing bars are, the more highly is the pigeon valued. It is quite a particular species and loses all value by cross breeding. In the South of Germany and in Switzerland it is often found without wing bars, with smooth feet and a yellowish crescent; although very heavily feathered feet seem to be peculiar to this race. Among the Swiss pigeons the starling neck is sometimes reckoned, also the whole coloured pigeon with no crescent, but with white wing bars, which resembles it very much. The red and yellow Swiss pigeons with dark eyes and crescent, originating from suitable pairing with the blue starling neck, although they occur very seldom, are a beautiful variety, which are paid large prices for by amateurs. The Swiss pigeon is in general not common, and is only found in Saxony, Thuringia, and Silesia."

Boitard and Corbié, in their chapter on the *Pigeons Suisses*, include several varieties which appear to me to have no connection with them, such as the *Pigeon Suisse bai doré ou bis doré*. Their description and illustration of this variety make it out to be more like the hyacinth: "Ce pigeon ressemble un peu au maillé feu," they say. Brent has reproduced the illustration of this pigeon on page 64 of his book (third edition), where it serves as a portrait of the porcelain pigeon, a subvariety of the hyacinth. I fancy that after reading that it resembled the fire-coloured *Pigeon maillé* a little, he thought it would do well to represent it.

CHAPTER XXXVI.

THE BLACK-BACKED GULL PIGEON.

I HAVE never seen this variety, which has only been described by Brent, so far as I can find. He says: "Of this variety I have seen a few specimens in London, called also the great China gull; but as to their origin I know nothing. In appearance they were much larger than the common kinds, approaching in form that of the Spanish runts, smooth-headed and clean-footed. The scapular feathers and the wings, with the exception of the extreme or the marginal pinion feathers, were black; the marginal flight feathers and the rest of the plumage being white, thus bearing a marked resemblance to the large black-backed gulls (*Larus marinus*) so common on our coasts. I believe there are also some stuffed specimens of this variety in the British Museum."

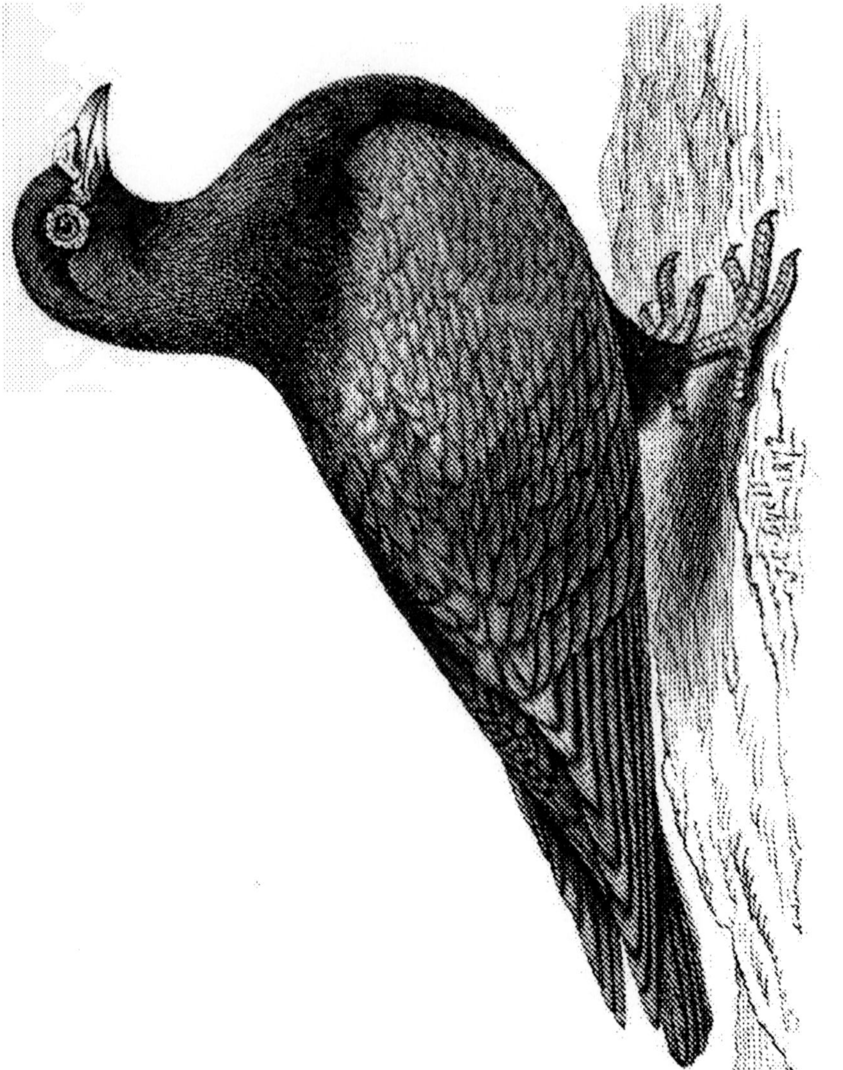

CHAPTER XXXVII.

THE RUNT PIGEON.

As explained before, the name of runt was formerly applied generally to all common pigeons in England, and it is no doubt often still so used; but pigeon fanciers now use the name to designate the variety of gigantic pigeons which Moore and subsequent authors wrote of as the Spanish runt. I should suppose that the name was given on account of the breed having but little to distinguish it, in general conformation, from the common pigeon, that they were looked upon when first introduced into England as the common pigeons of the place they came from, and that the name is not, as supposed by Willughby, a corruption of the Italian *Tronfo*, or of anything else. The runt would appear to be of an ancient race. Dixon says :—" But the point respecting runts which most deserves the notice of speculative naturalists is their extreme antiquity. The notices of them in Pliny and other nearly contemporary writers are but modern records ; for Dr. Buckland enumerates the bones of the pigeon among the remains in the cave at Kirkdale, and figures a bone, which he says approaches closely to the Spanish runt, which is one of the largest of the pigeon tribe. Ever since the classic period, these birds have been celebrated among the poultry produce of the shores of the Mediterranean."

The runt would therefore appear to have been distributed throughout Europe from Italy, and the name it bears in France, from where we get the best, is *Pigeon Romain*, which points to a like origin for the breed. The general colours of the runt are blue and silver, but there are many others, in some of which the breed can claim a high position as a fancy pigeon. The blue and silver have, perhaps, reached the greatest weights, and are probably the original colours. In appearance runts are like huge common pigeons, smooth-headed and smooth-legged, but having a rather heavy eye and beak wattle as they get old. The irides are generally orange in the blues and lighter in the silvers, and the eyes lie deep in the head, which, when viewed from before appears narrow and pinched, considering the size, of the bird. As to size, a matured pair of birds (cock and hen) weighing less than 4lb. are considered small, and 5lb. may be considered the maximum, although I have not heard of any being quite so heavy. From 4lb. 12oz. to 4lb. 15oz. has been often reached by show birds.

The illustration is from the cock of a pair of red runts I got from Messrs. Baily and Son, who imported them from France. Although in general shape and carriage of body they resemble the blue variety, they at once proclaim themselves of a different race. The irides are pure white, and form a very striking feature in them. The eye wattle is heavy in front and pinched behind, and, with the beak wattle, is of as bright a red as in the barb. The under mandible is much broader than the upper, even when shrunk in matured birds; while with young ones in the nest this point is so developed that it gives them a very strange appearance. In colour they are of a rich, deep, burning red, glossy with metallic lustre, and within very little of the best red I have ever seen in any domestic pigeons. I have also had yellow runts of the same race as these reds, and as good for their colour, but they were mottled in the way the short-faced mottled tumbler ought to be marked, that is, rose pinioned on each wing, and handkerchief backed. The marking was just about as accurate as it could be painted in a picture. I am astonished, therefore, that considering all these fine properties of colour, marking, real pearl eyes, and large size, anyone should write of the runt as having only the one point of size. In France these fancy runts are to be had in black, red, and yellow, both self-coloured and mottled. Pure whites with pearl eyes are, I believe, the rarest. They are all very bad fliers, and although good breeders, the young are somewhat delicate and difficult to rear. The fancy coloured ones do not reach the great size of the blues and silvers, and from 4lb. to 4¼lb. a pair is a good weight for them. Being powerful pigeons, runts should not be kept with small varieties. When to great strength a spiteful disposition is joined, as it often is with them, they become rather dangerous to other pigeons.

Boitard and Corbie mention several varieties of the *Pigeons Romains* distinct in colour and marking, some of the most beautiful being described as follows:

Pigeon Romain Mantelé.—All red except the shoulders or mantle, as in a turbit, which is white. Brent mentions them under the name of *Tigre rouge*. The white mantle probably appears only after the first moult.

Pigeon Romain Marcanu.—Always black or dun (*minime*), the head having a mixture of white feathers, giving it a grey appearance; irides pearl.

Pigeon Romain Gris Piqueté. — One of the largest of the race; irides yellow; plumage grey, chequered with black over the body, *à piquetures plus rapprochées sur la gorge*; feet lightly stockinged.

Pigeon Romain Minime Caillouté.—Its colour is dun or tan, with the edge of the feathers of the mantle and throat of a pale hue, drawing to a clear fire colour; smooth legs and feet; pearl eyes. It is very productive.

Pigeon Romain Soupe-de-lait.—The smallest of the race. It has a thickish membrane on the nostrils, a cere round the eyes, and yellow irides. Its feet are bare; its plumage is the colour of *café-au-lait*, with two bars of a deeper colour on the wings. This very pretty pigeon has also the essential quality of being tolerably productive.

Pigeon Romain Argenté.—Head *fond* white, mixed with a clear slate colour; neck and throat bluish black, reflecting green and metallic; the mantle of a bluish grey tinted with white, each feather darker at the base, with a light white border. Flights of a blackish grey, barred with clear grey; tail slate colour, with a black bar; pearl eyes. This superb bird is generally very productive.

The Montauban pigeon is a variety of the runt, but not so heavy, though a large bird. It is chiefly black or white, but sometimes blue, brown, and mottled. It has a large shell crest, which should extend from ear to ear, and the legs are generally feathered.

Brent says that the largest pigeons he ever saw were some white ones, with long feathers on the feet, that came from Belgium, and were called Norwegians. He says, "As I cannot give their exact size and weight, I forbear to state my ideas."

Moore says: "There are other sorts of runts, as the Roman runt, which is so big and heavy, it can hardly fly, and the Smyrna runt, which is middle-sized and feather-footed." These words are repeated by Mayor and Girtin. I think it probable that the title "Roman" was merely the retention of the French name for some importations of *Pigeons Romains*. There is nothing in the "Columbarium" to indicate that the Roman runt was of the Leghorn type.

Eaton says of runts, "I knew a pair sold for £25." They were likely something out of the common. At present they are not in great request, and it is a mistake to imagine that because they are large, they are worth keeping from an agricultural point of view. Three pairs of common tumblers would weigh about the same as a pair of large runts, and certainly not consume more food. I think the tumblers would produce twice or thrice the weight of young ones in a year that the runts would do in this country. Although Eaton's note regarding runts is printed under Moore's account of the Leghorn runt, the information he gives regarding them refers to the Spanish runt (*Pigeon Romain*), not to the cock tailed or Leghorn runt.

I have seen some very fine runts in India, in the possession of the Ex-King of Oude. He had almond feathered, and blue grizzled ones of great size, the latter the *Pigeon Romain Argenté*, I fancy, and I understand they were procured for him from France by Mr. Jamrach, who some ten years ago took many of them to Calcutta.

THE LEGHORN RUNT.

CHAPTER XXXVIII.

THE LEGHORN RUNT PIGEON.

THE Leghorn runt is a bird of quite an original type, and no doubt got the name of runt because it approached or equalled in size the Spanish runt. The peculiarity of this race of pigeons is to stand very high off the ground on long unfeathered legs, to be short in the back, broad in the breast and body, to have a short erect tail, and a long swan neck, like the letter "S." The beak is thick and rather short, and they have but little eye wattle.

Pigeons of this type of a large size were known in Moore's time; but whether those he wrote about, and those to which the author of the "Treatise" (1765) refers when he says, at page 110, "I have had a hen of the Leghorn breed that weighed two pounds two ounces, avoirdupoise weight," were of such a pronounced type as my illustration, is what I am not at all sure of.

I believe that pigeons of the Leghorn type have been distributed throughout Europe from the shores of the Mediterranean. If they originally came from the East they are not to be met with there now, so far as I have seen. In Germany, pigeons of this group go by the name of *Hühnertauben*, that is, fowl or gallinaceous pigeons, a name given them on account of their short, erect, henlike tails. From their long legs and abnormally short tails, they are the only pigeons which, when taken in the hand, as pigeon fanciers handle a pigeon, have the feet projecting beyond the tail. The flights are carried in three different ways, crossed over the tail, meeting the tail on each side, or their extremities touching each other below the tail. The last mode is the only correct one, and is in keeping with the whole shape of the bird.

In this country, pigeons of the Leghorn type have been shown under the name of Burmese, or Florentines. The former name is quite erroneous and misleading I think. Messrs. Baily and Son call them in their price lists Florentine, Maltese, or Dodo pigeons, and varieties of the race are known abroad by the first two names. Those I have seen were either black, or black mottled with white on the head, neck, and wing coverts. The following varieties of this race of pigeons are mentioned by Neumeister.

Die Malthesertaube, the Maltese pigeon, is of the size of a small English bantam fowl, with a smooth head, somewhat long and tapering, a truncate beak, strong nasal skin, deep set eyes, fleshy red eyelids, a somewhat projecting crop, broad back, round arched breast, small short wings, strong smooth red legs and feet, and a very short tail, standing up straight over the pinions of the wings, and seeming as if cut off short with scissors. The lower part of the body behind, is, as with the domestic fowl, thickly provided with down. The whole form is globular, almost as broad as it is long, and very high legged. The gallinaceous pigeon has a turned-up rump, like the peacock pigeon (fantail). It takes long steps, and its bearing, gait, and the movements of its head, are like the hen. It propagates well, and brings up young ones all the year round, except during the moulting season. The plumage is, with the pure original race, self-coloured white, next to it comes the whole-coloured blue. With other coloured ones, as black and brown, its characteristics are weakened. They are chiefly found in the neighbourhood of Linz.

Judging from Neumeister's illustration of the Maltese pigeon, it would appear to weigh something like three pounds per pair. He figures a variety called the *Kleine Maltheser*, or little Maltese, which appears little bigger than a common tumbler.

Die Florentiner oder Piemontesertaube, the Florentine or Piedmont pigeon, is a peculiarly marked variety, which I have chosen for my illustration. The head and neck, the wing coverts and flights, and the tail are coloured. The back and scapular feathers are white. This marking is also found with a slight difference in other pigeons, such as the Modena flying pigeon and the Turkish domino. The Florentine is described as being about the size of an English bantam hen, similar in characteristics to the Maltese, and generally of blue markings. Neumeister mentions the Modena flying pigeon as a variety of the Florentine, and it may have been so produced; but although the Modenese pigeon sometimes carries the tail raised, it ought to be horizontal, and it is now a very different looking bird from the Florentine.

Die Hühnerschecke taube, the hen-speckled pigeon, resembles the Maltese in its general points, but is seldom so round in build. The head is fine, the wax-coloured, somewhat strong beak, is of the usual length, the neck and legs are somewhat shorter than the Maltese, and it seldom carries its tail so upright. It has often fourteen feathers in the tail; the inner side of the leg is sometimes provided with short feathers; the ground colour is white, with black, red, yellow, and blue speckles of a very intense colour.

Ungar'sche taube, the Hungarian pigeon, is described as follows: By perseverance and chance there has risen from the Florentine the so much liked, beautifully marked, and expensive Hungarian pigeon. It occurs almost only in Austrian Hungary. The nearer it approaches the Maltese in form the better. The colouring of its plumage is beautiful, the black deep and velvety, with metallic sheen, the red and yellow fiery and sated, the blue clear. The mark is the so-called "band" mark which is peculiar to this pigeon. This white band or stripe begins at the nostrils about the breadth of a straw, widens as it goes back, dividing the colouring of the head, and disappears at the nape of the neck, which is white down to the shoulders. The colour, therefore, runs over each eye, turns down by the ears, and forms a deep pear-shaped bib on the breast. Viewed in profile, the front of the neck is coloured, the back of it white. The whole of the wing coverts and scapular feathers, the flights, the tail and its coverts, are coloured.

Der Monteneur pigeon is the last of this race mentioned by Neumeister, and I think it is the most likely of any to be the Leghorn runt of Moore, as it is said to excel both the *Romain* and *Montauban* in size. Its description is the following: "A formerly pretty well known, but for long very rare pigeon, which by its gigantic size more resembles a hen than a pigeon. Body and breast strong, provided with a rather short tail, it proves somewhat clumsy in flight, while it moves easily on the ground with its unfeathered rather high legs. The long neck is with the cocks very strong, and the crop when cooing a little more inflated than with common pigeons. In size the Monteneur excels both the

Roman and Montauban pigeons, has shorter wings and tail than these, and reminds one more of a domestic fowl than a pigeon. The colour is generally blue dappled or red. In the North of Germany these pigeons were formerly much bred in Griefswald, Stralsund, and Colberg, but seem now to have become quite extinct there."

CHAPTER XXXIX.

THE FRIZZLED OR FRIESLAND PIGEON.

THE frizzled pigeon, or Friesland runt, as it was formerly called, is not a runt of the large kind, but a bird of the size and shape of a common pigeon. Moore writes of it as follows: "This pigeon comes from Friesland, and is one of the larger Sort of middle siz'd Runts; its feathers stand all reverted, and I can't see for what it can be admir'd, except for it's Ugliness." So far Mr. Moore, whose successors, Mayor and Girton, follow on the same string with variations, both adding that these pigeons were, in their time, very scarce in England. The Friesland runt—which name I merely use because it was formerly so called, and because it matters little what name it goes by so long as it is not that of another pigeon—must have become extinct in England; but of late it has reappeared from abroad. It is known as the *Lockentaube* in Germany, where it is said to be rare, and Neumeister says it comes from Hungary. It is smooth-headed and usually stocking-legged, without much feathering on the toes. In colour it is generally blue or mealy, but I have seen turbit marked ones, with bronzed black shoulders. Its feathering is analogous to that of the frizzled fowls or Sebastopol geese, that is, reverted, making it appear to have been out in a storm. This appearance is owing to the concave surface of the feathers, more especially those of the wing coverts and back, being outward instead of inward, or next the body, as in other pigeons. On its re-introduction into England, where it has not been very uncommon for some years back, and where it has done some winning in the "Any other variety" classes, it was called by the name of another pigeon, one of an opposite character

THE FRIESLAND.

to it, the frillback. This was the more inexcusable, as the frillback was not extinct in England. If any pigeon requires a new name it is this one; being neither a runt nor a frillback, it may be appropriately named the frizzled pigeon.

CHAPTER XL.

THE FRILLBACK PIGEON.

THE first mention of this curious bird was in the "Treatise on Pigeons," dedicated to John Mayor, published in 1765. As the description is very good, concise, and clear, I reproduce it. "The frillback is something less in size than a dragoon, and in shape like the common runt; their colour generally (if not always) white; and what is chiefly remarkable in them is, the turn of their feathers, which appear as if everyone distinctly had been raised at the extremity with a small round pointed instrument, in such manner as to form a small cavity in each of them." The frillback, which is the German *Strupp oder Perltaube*, bristle or pearl pigeon, is said to be a native of the Netherlands, and Brent met with it in Saxony. It is of the size of the common field pigeon, and described as always pure white in colour, with an orange or gravelly red iris. I believe this variety is always white, and I have never seen it of any other feather. They are turn crowned and smooth legged. Their peculiar appearance is caused by the ends of their feathers, more especially those of the wing coverts and secondaries, being goffered or crimped, as if by a pair of curling tongs, as Brent describes it. This appearance is often seen in a less degree on hard feathered pigeons like dragoons. As Brent says, the frillback must not be confused with the Friesland runt, with which it has nothing whatever in common.

CHAPTER XLI.

THE LACE PIGEON.

THE lace pigeon is another variety, distinguished, like the frizzled and frillback pigeons, by the peculiar formation of its feathers. It has its prototype in the silky fowl of China and Japan, which early travellers called a fowl bearing hair or wool on its body instead of feathers. This pigeon was unknown to Moore, and was first described in our pigeon literature in the Treatise, where a very good plate of it may be seen. It is described as white in colour, turn crowned, and valued on account of its scarcity, and the peculiarity of its feathers, "the fibres, or web of which, appear disunited from each other throughout their whole plumage, and not in the least connected, as in common with all other pigeons, where they form a smooth close feather."

The lace pigeon, which is known in France as the *Pigeon Soie* (silky pigeon), and in Germany as the *Seidenhaartaube* (silken-haired pigeon), is of much the same size and bearing as the common field pigeon. It is almost always pure white in colour, and generally smooth headed. It has its name from its peculiar feathering, the fibres of all its feathers having no adhesion, but being disunited and appearing as if every second one had been cut out. The wing coverts, and quill and tail feathers, with their long fringed rays, have given it its English name of lace pigeon. It is not so hairy or woolly in appearance as the silky fowl, but more like the produce of that fowl when crossed with a common one. Its legs and feet are either quite smooth or slightly feathered; its irides are dark hazel. Being unable to fly, it must be kept in confinement, and under special conditions. However interesting as an object of curiosity, it presents little variation in its form or feather, and consequently it will be always rather uncommon. It has the power of somewhat reproducing its peculiarity when crossed with other pigeons, and the French have a half bred looking fantail, called the *pigeon trembleur paon de soie*, from which the Scotch lace fantail, to be afterwards noticed, has been perfected.

The frizzled, frillback, and lace pigeons, are examples of natural sports perfected by selection. If lost, breeders could not recover them, but would have to wait till nature provided them with a new beginning on which to work. As they exist, they can be kept up, in a fair degree of quality, with but little trouble as compared to many kinds that are called mere feather varieties, fine specimens of which are consequently much more valuable than they are. If fancy pigeons were separate creations, and not descended from a common origin, I wonder how the lace pigeon existed till taken in charge by pigeon fanciers.

CHAPTER XLII.

THE SWIFT PIGEON.

THIS pigeon, which is of Eastern origin, was first described in Fulton's book of pigeons, by Mr. Ludlow, who says that it is an Indian pigeon, but that it has been cultivated in Cairo and Alexandria, whence the best specimens have been imported into England, hence its name, the Egyptian swift. I never met with it in Bengal, nor heard fanciers there speak of such a variety; but I believe there are many distinct breeds of pigeons ▆▆▆ng in Hindostan, especially in the north west, still unknown to us, and the swift may be among them. This variety of the domestic pigeon has its name from the swift or hawk swallow, on account of its abnormally long flight feathers. Though a bird of ordinary size, it has the appearance of being larger than it is, from the fact of its feathers being long and loose. In this respect it resembles other kinds, such as the trumpeter and jacobin. The wing coverts, on account of their length, incline downwards. Both the flight and tail feathers are excessively long, the former being carried crossed above the latter, and measuring as much as 32¼in. from tip to tip, when out-stretched, according to Mr. Ludlow, who also says that the tail primaries measure 7⅜in. between tips of quill and fibre. As a comparison, I measured an ordinary sized flying tumbler cock in the same way, and his out-stretched wings covered 27in., while one of his tail primaries was 5¼in. The flight and tail of the swift, therefore, extend some 2¼in.

I

beyond those of similarly sized pigeons. To see how these measurements would compare with those of the pouter, I measured a blue pied cock of 19½in. in feather, and found that his out-stretched wings covered 37in., and that one of his tail feathers was no less that 8₁⁷₆in. in length. The swift stands low on unfeathered legs, is smooth-headed, and is represented by Mr. Ludlow as an owl-headed, gulleted pigeon, with a narrow flesh-coloured eye cere and yellow iris. In colour there are said to be blues, chequers, almond feathered ones, both dark and light, mottles, and some are of a chocolate colour, heavily shot with yellow on the neck and wing coverts, which latter is the colour he has chosen for his illustration, and which might be called an exaggeration of the golden dun found in short-faced tumblers. As represented by Mr. Ludlow it is a very beautiful colour, and one not found so pronounced in any other variety I know of.

Instead of being an advantage to the swift in flight, its long wings are an impediment to it, as the feathers are thin and weak in texture. Like the hawk swallow it rises from the ground with difficulty, but, unlike it, it cannot make use of its long wings when once in the air. I once, when my age could be told by a single figure, caught a swift swallow in a garret, which I played with on the grass for some time, as it never attempted to fly away; but happening to throw it slightly from the ground, it went off like a shot from a bow.

Mr. Ludlow says the swift is hardy and long lived, one cock, an old one on his arrival in Birmingham, in 1864, having lived till 1875. Regarding the age of fancy pigeons generally, there was lately a notice in the *Field* newspaper of the death of a white trumpeter, belonging to Mr. Oates, formerly an exhibitor of this breed, at the age of 22 years, which is the same age as the pigeon Willughby (1676) refers to in the following passage:—"Albertus sets the twentieth year for the term of a pigeon's life. As for tame pigeons (saith Aldrovandus), a certain man of good credit told me that he had heard from his father, who was much delighted in pigeons and other birds, that he had kept a pigeon two and twenty years, and that all that time it constantly bred, excepting the last six months, which time, having left its mate, it had chosen a single life. Aristotle assigns forty years to the life of a pigeon. Adrov. Ornithol. tom 2, page 370."

The oldest pigeon I ever had was a common flying tumbler, red in colour, which was fifteen years old, and in good condition. I have known of a pouter cock breeding well when twelve years old; but it would cheapen the price of fine pigeons if they all lived so long.

CHAPTER XLIII.

THE SWALLOW-TAILED PIGEON.

I HAVE never seen the variety of domestic pigeon that has a forked tail like the common house swallow, and no pigeon fancier, either here or abroad, seems to have described it from actual observation. The existence of such a breed seems to depend on what has been said by Bechstein, the German naturalist, from whom Brent, who is the only fancier who mentions it, has gathered the following: "Die taube mit Schwalbenschwanz.—Bechstein, in his 'Natural History of Germany,' describes this variety as occasionally to be found among the collections of pigeon fanciers, and says they are blue, chequered, or black mottled, the outer feathers of the tail being much prolonged, or forked like that of the chimney swallow, from which circumstance they derive their name." And Brent adds, "a pigeon fancying acquaintance informed me that he once had a pair of swallow-tailed baldheads, which he purchased in Manchester; so I conclude this variety is also to be met with in England, though I have not seen it. Some of the wild pigeons or doves of foreign countries have long wedge-shaped tails, but such a formation of tail I have never seen or heard of among our domestic pigeons."

Considering other variations in domestic pigeons, a forked tail is not an unlikely deviation; but as no home or foreign fancier has described the swallow-tailed pigeon from actual observation, and as it would be easy to add the word tail to the word swallow, especially in the mind of a naturalist, I think Bechstein's description must be regarded as apocryphal till we know more on the subject. Could we once fix the swallow-tail on the domestic pigeon, a natural variation might subsequently take place, by which the long outer tail feathers would take an outward horizontal curl, and so resemble the tail of the black grouse. I have seen in the nest tail of more than one pigeon, a decidedly swallow tailed formation, but this appearance was always lost when the feathers were changed at the first moulting. Regarding the swallow-tailed baldheads from Manchester, mentioned by Brent's acquaintance, I cannot accept the account of them; but a pair may have existed having a modified formation of the forked tail in their nest feathers.

CHAPTER XLIV.

THE RINGBEATER PIGEON.

UNDER the names of smiter, finnikin, and turner, our former writers on pigeons have described varieties agreeing more or less with the French *Pigeon Tournant*, and German *Ringschläger*, or ringbeater. Willughby says of smiters, "These do not only shake their wings as they fly; but also flying round about in a ring, especially over their Females, clap them so strongly, that they make a greater sound than two battledores or other boards struck one against another, whence it comes to pass that their quil-feathers are almost always broken and shattered; and sometimes so bad, that they cannot fly." He describes the turner merely as "having a tuft hanging down backward from their Head, parted like a horse's mane," and the finnikin "like the precedent *i.e.*, the Turner) but less."

Moore describes no smiter, but his finnikin "is in Make and Shape very like a common Runt, and much about the same Size. The crown of its head is turned much after the manner of a snake's head; it is gravel-eyed, and has a tuft of feathers on the hinder part of the crown, which runs down its neck not unlike a horse's mane; it is clean footed and legged, and always black or blue pied. When it is salacious, it rises over its hen and turns round three or four times, flapping its wings, then reverses and turns as many the other way."

The turner, he says, "is in many respects like the finnikin, except that when it is salacious and plays to the female it turns only one way, whereas the other turns both; it has no tuft on the hinder part of the head, neither is it snake-headed."

Brent says he only saw one pair of ringbeaters, which were at a pigeon dealer's in Coblentz. They were common-looking birds with peaked crowns, and red and white plumage. Their peculiar movement and circling flight were described to him, and he noticed that the vanes were beaten off the ends of their flight feathers.

Boitard and Corbie describe the *Pigeons-Tournans* as stronger than tumblers, stocking-legged, generally blue cheqered, red, or pearl white in colour, marked with a pure white horse-shoe mark on the back. "Whatever may be the space they are shut up in, they ascend to the ceiling, then descend, describing circles, first to right then to left, absolutely like a bird of prey, which hovers and then chases from high in the air." They say amateurs have discarded them on account of their quarrelsome and jealous disposition, which causes much mischief in the aviary.

The *Pigeon Lillois Claquart*, or Lille clapper, is a variety of the Lille pouter, which they say has been confounded with the turner. "It makes a noise with its wings when commencing to fly, like a clapper; hence its name." This is a usual thing with half-bred pouters, and I have often seen such kept as decoys for stray pigeons.

Brent could find nothing in the German authors regarding the ringbeater; but in the last edition of Neumeister I find the best description of this curious breed, from which it appears they may now be got not only with all their peculiarities of flight, but bred to feather as well. He says— or rather Herr Gustav Prütz, editor of the last edition says—"The excellent pigeon fancier, Führer, describes this pigeon, quite unknown in the North of Germany, in the following way : The ringbeater is a pigeon only yet appearing on the lower Rhine, and here and there in Westphalia, of stately size, strong figure, and good bearing. The head is covered with a pointed hood ; the forehead of middle height, the beak light coloured, the irides according to the plumage, the eyelids bright flesh coloured, the neck robust, breast and back proportionately broad, the legs and feet smooth." He describes a peculiarity in the primary wing feathers, which I understand to be that the fifth from the outside is very much shorter than the fourth, so that when the wing is extended the four longest feathers seem to have grown away from the others, and are not in the usual gradation. "The plumage is close fitting, and marked in all colours as follows: The whole head is white, the line of marking being the breadth of two straws below the eyes; the tail with its covert and six flights a side are white." I am not sure from the description whether this variety is white or coloured on belly and thighs. Their flight is described thus: "The characteristic of these pigeons is their flight; it is true they never fly farther than from roof to roof, but not for a single yard without flapping their wings together, so that it sounds afar; this is particularly done by the cock when courting his hen. A good beater must beat a ring round her from five to six times, *i.e.*, flying around in a circle right and left, making a loud noise by beating his wings together. The hen beats likewise but less strongly; both beat most in spring. In autumn their flights are so much beaten down that they cannot fly; and they easily meet with accidents. Their quite ragged pinions are then sometimes pulled out, which does not hurt them when done only once in a year. Those are most valuable which flap much and yet preserve their pinions well. The young ones begin to flap as soon as fledged. The ringbeater is a healthy very lively and quarrelsome pigeon, causing much disturbance in the loft, and unfitted to live with other pigeons. It is also very fruitful, and it is a matter of wonder that it is not more spread. Besides good ringbeating, we require in this pigeon a considerable size of body, fine bright colours, and pure markings. The price of purely marked black and yellow ones is several marks a pair; the red, mostly bad in colour, are cheaper."

The ringbeater is a pigeon that would be valued by many in this country, where it was formerly not uncommon. It is the same bird that Willughby wrote of as the smiter, and which Moore calls the finnikin; though evidently now bred for colour and marking as well as ringbeating. It was no doubt produced by selection from such as had its peculiar flight in a modified degree. In a loft of tumblers, some lively cock will often be found having a good deal of the above description in his flight.

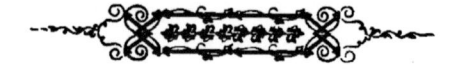

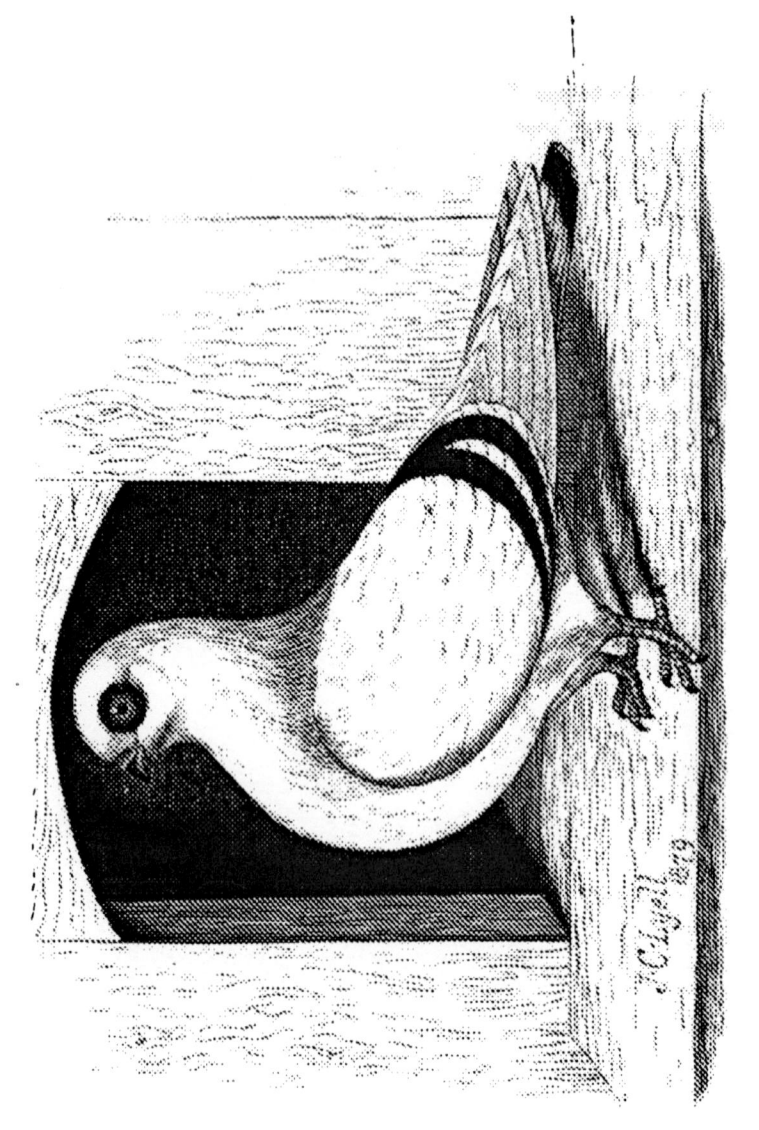

THE MAHOMET PIGEON.

CHAPTER XLV.

THE MAHOMET PIGEON.

THE Mahomet, formerly known in England as the mawmet, was first described by Willughby in 1676, who says: "Mawmets, called (as I take it) from Mahomet, perchance because brought out of Turkey, notable for their great black eyes, else like to the Barbaries." Willughby must either have seen such pigeons or had his description of them from others. When Moore wrote his book some sixty years later, he knew of no pigeons "notable for their great black eyes," but he describes the Mahomet as "no more in Reality than a white Barb, which makes the red tuberous Flesh round the Eyes look very beautiful." In the preface to the "Treatise on Pigeons" (1765), the author admits that his book is "on the plan of Mr. Moore," but says that he has corrected some of his errors and made many additions. After mentioning Moore's description of the Mahomet, he proceeds : " So far Mr. Moore ; but it is the opinion of many fanciers that the Bird called a mahomet is nearly of a cream colour, with bars cross the wings as black as ebony, the feathers very particular, being of two colours ; the upper part, or surface of them, appearing of a cream, and underneath a kind of sooty colour, nearly approaching to black ; as are likewise the flue-feathers, and even the skin, which I never observed in any other Pigeons but these ; its size much like that of a turbit, with a fine gullet, and in lieu of a frill ; the feathers rather appear like a seam ; the head is short and inclined to be thick ; hath an orange-eye, and a small naked circle of black flesh round the same ; and a beak something resembling that of a bullfinch, with a small black wattle on it."

In the pages of the *Poultry Chronicle* (1854–55) will be found a discussion on the Mahomet pigeon. Mr. W. Woodhouse, who had been breeding and showing crested, three-quarter bred white barbs, as Mahomets, informed fanciers in his letter to that journal, on 13th December, 1854, how he bred them. Brent would not accept these birds as Mahomets, for he had shortly before, when writing of them, quoted the above description of the true breed from the treatise, and had actually seen a pair in London. He says, " This is one of the varieties of fancy pigeons with which I have but a very slight acquaintance, having only once seen a pair at a London dealer's, and their appearance gave me the idea of a cross between an owl and a barb pigeon; nevertheless, their seam and black wattle, cere, and skin, I consider sufficient distinctive peculiarities to give them a place among fancy pigeons as a separate variety."

I shall again refer to the appearance in London, about this time, of this pair of true Mahomet pigeons when I come to write of the powdered English owl.

About the year 1868, Mr. Boyd, of Edinburgh, brought home with him from Constantinople, a pair of Mahomets. They became the property of Mr. James Wallace, of Glasgow, who showed them there, in 1869, as Damascenes. The hen lived but a short time, and the cock came into my possession in 1878, but he was then past breeding, and he shortly afterwards met his death from an accident. Of those I have seen, only a few pairs altogether, he was the most pronounced in type, and most in accordance with the description of 1765.

In shape and size of body, the Mahomet is not unlike the barb, and were it not that its beak and eye wattles are nearly black, instead of red, it might naturally be supposed to be of the barb race. The head is full and round, the beak short and thick, but not hooked; the irides are bright orange or deep yellow, and the beak and eye wattles, though almost black, are covered, when in health, with a powder that makes them of a beautiful blue colour. In colour this pigeon is of the most lovely light blue, frosted all over as if with powder, except on the wing bars, flights, and tail. The bars should remain, as in the old description, as black as ebony; the flights are of a medium tint, darker than shown in the illustration, as is the tail, except that it has the jet black bar at its extremity. The lower part of the neck is lustrous with hues of very light green and purple. The beak and nails are black, the feet and legs bright red, sometimes stockinged, but I much prefer them smooth. Although of such a beautiful light blue, or what is called a French white tint on the surface, the neck and body feathers are dark bluish black underneath when exposed; but this must not assert itself when the bird is at liberty. This beautiful colouring is not confined entirely to the Mahomet, as the same feather, or nearly so, may be found among the ice pigeons, but what makes the former of such an original type is the dark eye wattles. It would almost seem to be related to the owl race of pigeons as well, as it has a very pronounced gullet and seam, or division down the breast, though no actual frill.

This distinction, and the shape of its head, make it a likely cross for the blue owl, which I know was tried with success in the case of the one I had; but I shall refer to this again.

It is a pity that the Mahomet is so scarce, for although it has not in its composition what would make it, even though plentiful, only to be seen of high quality now and then, as the pouter or turbit, it would be a beautiful and telling variety in an aviary of different kinds, and likely to breed very true to its characteristics. I know the one I had was often picked out by strangers as the most beautiful pigeon in my place.

The Mahomet shows the powdered blue colour in the very highest degree, and it has the power of reproducing its colour to a great extent when crossed with a blue or silver pigeon.

CHAPTER XLVI.

THE LOWTAN PIGEON.

THE lowtan pigeon is indeed a curiosity among pigeons. It is a native of India, and has never been brought to this country so far as I know. It was quite unknown here, until some letters regarding it, from Indian correspondents, were published in the *Field* newspaper. These may be found in Tegetmeier's book, and they give a good account of it. I knew the lowtan very well in Bengal, and have seen many of them. In size they were the same as the common field pigeon, and all I have seen were pure white with a turn crown, neither peak nor shell headed, but something between the two. Their eyes were dark hazel, their legs and feet unfeathered, and in general appearance they were nothing more than sixpenny common pigeons. To make the lowtan perform, it is laid hold of across the back, held horizontally, and shaken smartly from side to side three or four times. This seems to put it into a fit, for on laying it on the ground it immediately turns head over tail till exhausted, but it is generally picked up after fluttering about for a short time, as there is a belief that it would die if left alone, though this is not the case. Whether the lowtan suffers pain or not when made to roll about, I cannot say, but if it does, it soon recovers, for on being taken up during its fluttering fit, it becomes quiet, and when let fly it will at once play up to its mate, if a cock, or commence to eat as if nothing had happened. There is no variety in its exhibition, which is rather unpleasing after being seen once or twice, and those who keep lowtans seldom put them through their manœuvres.

One of the correspondents referred to, writing from Madras, mentions two varieties of the lowtan, one being the *Kulmee* or high caste kind, that would roll about on being merely touched on the head or peak, while the other kind, the *Sadhee* or common lowtan, required to be shaken as I have described, before it would perform. He says that in the book on pigeons written for Akbar by Abdool Furjool, about 1596, both varieties are mentioned.

The other correspondent, writing from Rohilcund, had kept the common lowtans for two years, and on inquiring for the high caste or *Choteen* lowtan—so called because they were said to roll on the *Chotes* or turncrown being touched—he procured four specimens, all of which rolled on being struck on the back of the head with the forefinger. One of them was similar to his common lowtans, another similar in appearance, but turbit marked, being white with dark shoulders, and the other two had "great long legs feathered to the toes."

I never happened to see any of the kind that performed on being merely touched, nor other than pure white ones.

CHAPTER XLVII.

THE SHERAJEE PIGEON.

THE Sherajee, so named in Bengal, but called Sherazie in Northern India, is a favourite pigeon in Hindostan. The name is no doubt derived from the city of Sheraz, in Persia, where it might have originated. This pigeon is in shape and size very similar to the tight-feathered trumpeters, common in this country before the so-called Russians were introduced. The head and beak of the Sherajee are of the common type, the latter neither short nor long and thin; and birds of good colour have always a reddish tinge on the eye ceres, beak wattles, and edges of the mouth. The irides are dark hazel colour, the head unhooded, and the legs and feet feathered; long toe feathers spreading out on each side being much admired. The marking of the Sherajee is peculiar to itself, nothing similar to it being found in any other variety I know of. The upper mandible is coloured, except with those colours that are generally accompanied by a flesh-coloured beak, and the marking, commencing at the beak wattle, runs over the head and down the back of the neck, till it meets the back and wings. Looked at in profile, the marking should show a clean division down the side of the neck; from behind the neck appears all coloured, and from before all white. The back, wings, and flight feathers are also coloured, the rest of the plumage being pure white.

A rarer variety of the Sherajee is that known as the mottled. The breast of this variety must be well mottled over with single feathers, no two of which ought to touch each other. This is a kind of mottling peculiar to Indian fancy pigeons, being the reverse of what is required in this country, where standard mottling is always composed of single white feathers on a coloured ground. The mottled Sherajee, when anything like perfect, becomes a very valuable pigeon, and is often sold at so much the mottle, and I was told on good and satisfactory authority that as much as 1000 rupees had been paid for a fine bird of this breed. While a few coloured feathers on the breast of the Sherajee only spoil what might otherwise be a good plain-breasted bird, when the number reaches to about thirty single well separated mottles, the value is reckoned something in the same way as that of the diamond, by squaring the number of feathers and multiplying by a price. After all, 1000 rupees, formerly equal to about £100 sterling, is no more than has been paid in this country for a carrier, and Indian potentates are known to be as keen in acquiring the objects of their fancy as people of any other country.

The Sherajee can only be seen good in the collections of experienced pigeon fanciers, though no bird is more common in the places in Calcutta where pigeon shops abound. I have seen them in black, red, yellow, and dun, also in blue and silver, both barred and barless, and in many off colours. Those found in the bazaars for sale are almost invariably of black marking, and generally either bare or only half feathered on the legs.

Some five or six hundred large vessels leave Calcutta for Great Britain every year, and few of them without some live stock on board as pets, for sailors are very fond of a monkey, parrot, or pair of birds to amuse themselves with on the long voyage. In this way many black Sherajee pigeons, such as can be bought for 2s. or 3s. a pair, have reached this country, and probably they have been coming for the last 200 years or more; but the earliest mention of this breed I know of in our literature, is in the *Poultry Chronicle* vol. 3, page 443, in the report of Prescot Show, in Lancashire, on the 4th July, 1855, as follows: "The

Mookee. *Goolee.* *Sherajee.*

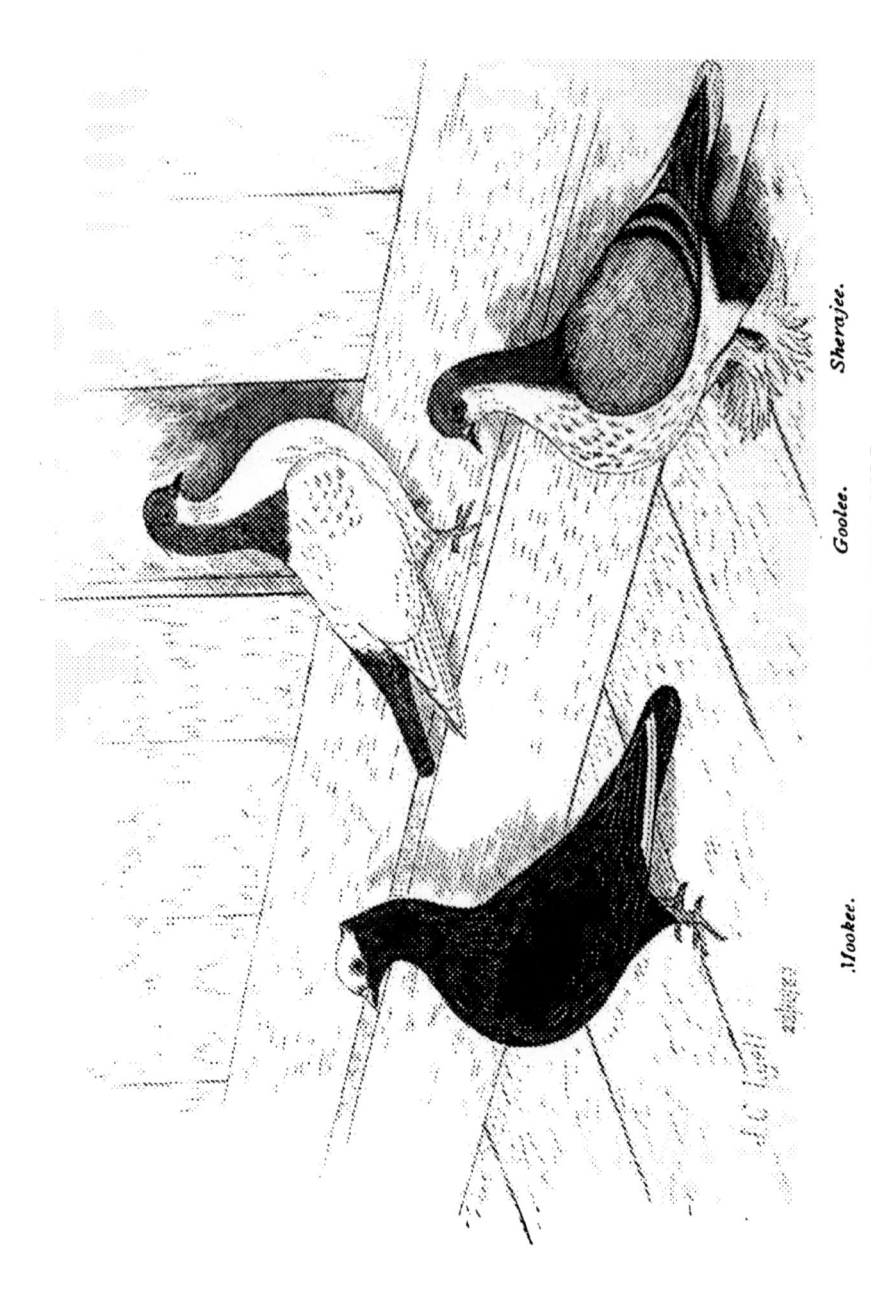

INDIAN FANCY PIGEONS.

pigeons seemed to be the subject of universal interest. Among these were two pens, quite new (and distinct as to variety), and which we believe have never hitherto been shown at any public competition. We allude to birds entered as 'Tailors,' why so called we know not, but are informed the original parent birds were imported from the Canadas (under that name) at an immense expense, by the late Earl of Derby, for the Knowsley aviary." And then follows the description of them; agreeing with what I have given of the Sherajee, except as to mottled breast and feathered feet, which shows them to have been merely sailors' pigeons, though called "tailors," and no doubt they were bought in Liverpool from some East India vessel, the Canadas not having any such stock to part with. Again, at page 491 of the same volume, they are referred to by Mr. Brent as follows: "I beg to second Mr. Eaton's appeal to pigeon fanciers, and hope they will support the Anerley show; and trust to see some of the rare varieties there, such as laughers, silk fantails, taylors, and others."

In Brent's pigeon book, and in Eaton's 1858 treatise, the name of "tailor" is dropped, and that of Lahore or martin substituted, the former being given because Brent had found they came from that city, and the latter on account of their resemblance in marking to the martin or window swallow (*Hirundo urbica*).

CHAPTER XLVIII.

THE MOOKEE PIGEON.

THIS is another Indian pigeon, of pure and distinct race, that has not been unknown in British seaports, having a connection with the East Indies during the past twenty or thirty years; but which has not been recognised as the narrow-tailed shaker of Willughby's "Ornithology," published in London in 1676. Willughby says of this kind: "Narrow or close tailed shaking pigeons—*Anglicè*, narrow-tailed shakers. These agree with the precedent (broad-tailed shakers) in shaking, but differ in the narrowness of their tails, as the name imports. They are said also to vary in colour. This kind we have not as yet seen, nor have we more to say of it." Willughby had this information, without doubt, from some pigeon fancier who knew the breed, though he does not name his authority, as he elsewhere names Mr. Cope, of Jewin-street.

When Moore wrote his "Columbarium," about sixty years later, he described the narrow-tailed shaker, the last kind he mentions in his book, as follows: "This Pigeon is reckon'd by some a distinct Species, tho' I am apt to believe it is only a bastard breed between the foregoing (the broad-tail'd shaker) and some other Bird. Its neck is shorter and thicker, its back longer, the Feathers of its Tail are not so much spread out, but fall as it were double, lying over one another, and the Tail generally lops very much." And thus, from Moore onwards, every writer described the narrow-tailed shaker as a crossbred fantail, as no doubt the bird above described was, Moore never having seen the true breed. But it will be observed that Moore says, "This pigeon is reckon'd by some a distinct species." No pigeon fancier would reckon a crossbred fantail as a distinct species, so there were, even in Moore's time, some who either had known or had been told about the true narrow-tailed shaker, which is the Indian Mookee, a pigeon having the tremulous shaking neck of the fantail, and a close narrow tail with the normal number of twelve feathers.

The head of the Mookee is flat, showing no stop, and is all drawn to a point; it also is invariably peaked behind. The irides are dark hazel in colour. The upper mandible is white, and the lower follows the plumage. The whole head is white, above a line running across the eyes. The two longest flight feathers should be white, and all the rest of the bird coloured. The head often comes foul or unequally cut, and the flights often foul. Three, or even four, a side, are better than unequal flights, but two a side are considered the standard. The curious thing about the Mookee is the tremulous shaking of the neck, which is never absent, and which is most constant when the bird is salacious. It is singular to see the cock driving the hen to nest: his head and neck shake continually backward and forward, but he never loses his balance. The tail is carried horizontally and close, as in most pigeons.

I have seen all colours in this breed, as in the Sherajee, but the great majority are black. Blues with black bars, barless blues, and duns, are next in order of number, while reds and yellows are comparatively scarce, though they were to be seen in the possession of several Calcutta fanciers ten years ago.

Putting aside the curious markings, it is obvious that the Mookee is not a bastard fantail, for, united to a close tail of twelve feathers, it has all the shaking of ordinary fantails; and it is known that in crossing the fantail, its tremulous neck motion is lost long before the tail is reduced to twelve feathers. It is as probable that extra tail feathers in the Mookee resulted in the broad-tailed shaker, as that it was bred down from the fantail. No one can say now how either variety was produced, and to experiment on the subject would be wasting time that might be better employed, as we have both varieties ready made to our hands.

The Mookee is a good breeder and feeder. It is a long-lived pigeon. One dun cock that I sent to Dundee, from Calcutta, old when he left, lived for ten years afterwards.

CHAPTER XLIX.

THE GOOLEE PIGEON.

THE Goolee is a small pigeon, not much larger than the short faced-tumbler. It was in the possession of a Mr. Wood, in Calcutta, one of four brothers, all pigeon fanciers, that I first saw a good collection of Goolees, and what at once struck me was their close resemblance in shape and carriage to our short-faced tumblers. The Goolee has a spindle beak, like that of our small clean-legged flying tumblers, and an abruptly rising forehead, showing a decided stop. Were the best of them to be subjected to treatment from the skull improvers, that our late books on pigeons make a point of illustrating for the benefit of unthinking people, the result would be birds differing little from short-faces, except in colour. The benighted heathens, however, do not use such instruments, for they only value properties that can be bred in their pigeons. But this may be the result of simple ignorance, for I know well that if they once thought any additional value would accrue from a made skull, they would not, any more than many among us, ever consider the cruelty there is in shaping the heads of tender pigeons.

The upper mandible of the Goolee is coloured, the lower white, but reds and yellows have generally light beaks. The marking of the head and neck is the same as in the Sherajee. The irides are usually dark, but a white or orange iris would, I think, be more pleasing. The tail, with its coverts, is also coloured. This marking is found in all solid colours, and when the colours are rich and lustrous, as they often are, the eye ceres and corners of the mouth are of a decidedly reddish hue. The rest of the plumage is all white, except in a rarer variety, known as the mottled Goolee. The mottled variety, to be right, must have a rose-pinion of coloured feathers on the wing coverts; when this rose-pinion is composed of well separated feathers, the effect is very pleasing. Some of the mottled Goolees are of three colours, such as dark dun on head, neck, and tail, yellow mottled shoulders, and white ground. I have seen them of this rare combination of colours, and I believe other three coloured varieties exist, such as black marked ones, with red mottled shoulders. The Goolee is clean legged, walks on tip-toe when proud, trails its wings, and has the carriage of a good almond tumbler. There are in Bengal as many degrees in quality in this variety as there are here between the best short-faces and common flying tumblers. The choicest birds can only be seen in the possession of experienced breeders, and are never offered for sale in the bazaars. The Goolee shares with the Sherajee the position of chief favourite among Calcutta pigeon fanciers, some preferring the former, others the latter. Fine specimens of both kinds fetch long prices.

CHAPTER L.

THE CORAL-EYED PIGEON.

THE Coral eye is a variety of the domestic pigeon well known in Bengal. I have seen these birds in the possession of different fanciers in Calcutta, among whom they went by the above name; and I believe their Hindostanee designation has the same meaning. In size and shape the coral eye pigeon resembles a strong English owl pigeon, but its head and beak are more of the common type, the latter not long and spindly, but of moderate length and thickness. It is neither turn crowned nor feather-legged, and always, as far as I have seen, whole coloured blue, with the usual black wing bars. What constitutes this pigeon of pure and distinct race is the colour of its irides, which are large in size, and bolting like the choice African owl. In colour they are of a vivid ruby red, of the hue known among jewel merchants as "pigeon's blood." I have seen nothing nearly approaching them in any other breed of pigeon, for they are like big beads of living fire sparkling in the head of the bird, and so pronounced that they tell at the distance of several yards. This pigeon breeds true, but loses all value if crossed with another variety. It is an instance of the manifold variations that exist in that universal favourite the domestic pigeon. I once described this pigeon in the *Journal of Horticulture* some years ago, before which I am not aware that it was ever mentioned in this country.

CHAPTER LI.

THE CAPUCHIN PIGEON.

A PIGEON under this name was described by Moore, who says that it is in shape and make very like the jacobin, but something larger in body, longer in beak, with a tolerable hood, but no chain, though in feather and other properties the same. He says, "Some will assert it to be a distinct Species, but I am more inclinable to imagine it is only a bastard breed from a Jacobine and another Pigeon; however thus far I am sure, that a Jack and another will breed a Bird so like it, as will puzzle the Authors of this Assertion to distinguish it, from what they call their separate Species."

Remembering what Moore has said of the Mahomet and narrow-tailed shaker, I doubt if his half-bred jacobin was really what some fanciers asserted to be the true Capuchin. Moore evidently knew the motto, *viam aut inveniam aut faciam*, and it puzzles me to hear of any fancier asserting a half-bred jacobin to be a distinct species; however, if there was a pure race, as described, known as the Capuchin then, we do not know it now; for its description cannot apply to the bird we now class under that name.

The Capuchin was first imported into England and first described in Fulton's book by my friend Mr. H. P. Caridia, of Birmingham. It is a native of one locality of Asia Minor, he says, and those I have seen are certainly of pure and distinct race. The head is round and full in front, the beak short and fine, the iris pure white and surrounded by a thin purple-black cere, and the beak and toe nails are black. The plumage is a rich metallic black, sparkling with lustre, the tail with its coverts alone being white. Mr. Caridia says there are also similiarly marked blues and whole coloured whites. The Capuchin gets its name from an extensive close fitting hood on the back of its head, which comes down a very short distance on each side of its neck. It carries the flights low, generally below the tail. It is thin necked, broad chested, and has much of the shape and carriage of the shortfaced tumbler. It is said to be a good flyer, breeder, and feeder.

I have heard some say that this pigeon is the original of our jacobins, which I consider an hallucination. Its black eye cere alone points to a separate origin, but I believe the third or fourth cross from it and the jacobin has resulted in very fair specimens of the latter breed, which I can easily imagine would be the case. I could fancy it to have originated from the jacobin and the Mahomet, but this is mere speculation. The breed as it stands may be many centuries old.

CHAPTER LII.

THE LAUGHER PIGEON.

THE Laugher is a breed of pigeon that has been known in this country, off and on, since Moore's time. It seems to have died out and been reimported several times. From all accounts it has almost nothing to distinguish it in general appearance from the common pigeon. Brent mentions two stocks of these birds he knew of. The first closely resembled blue chequered dovehouse pigeons, but were rather smaller and had very slightly feathered legs, the only difference he could notice being a slight fulness at back of the neck behind the head, and the edge of the eyelids being inclined to red. The cock of a pair he had was dark chequered, the hen the same, but pied with white. The other stock, which was imported from India, he was told, and which were taken thence by Mahometans who had been on a pilgrimage to Mecca, were of the same dovehouse form, but with narrow peaked crowns, and in colour of a light haggle, or something between a grizzle and a gay mottle. A pair lately described, that belonged to Mr. Betty, were little bigger than African owls, rather long in flight and tail, blue rumped, clean legged, and of a dark blue chequer. Moore says "It is red mottled; and some tell me they have seen blues. They are said to come from the holy Land, near Jerusalem." It seems, therefore, that the laugher is of different colours, sometimes peaked, and sometimes slightly feathered on the legs. Their peculiar voice is what makes them a distinct breed, and Moore describes it thus: "When the Cock plays to his Hen, he has a hoarse Coo, not unlike the Guggling of a Bottle of Water, when pour'd out, and then makes a Noise, which very much imitates a soft Laughter, and from thence this Bird has its Name."

Mr. Betty's pair were described in the *Live Stock Journal* in February, 1878, as "singing pigeons." "The notes were very soft, between cooing and drumming, clear, audible throughout the room, and were continued for about half a minute . . . The hen often, but not invariably, sings an accompaniment in a lower key."

I have a pair of the same race of pigeons that came, I was told, from Egypt. They are white, with peaked crowns, hog manes, well feathered legs, orange irides, brownish tinged beaks, and are both ticked with red on the head and throat. They are thickly made, low-standing pigeons, above the average size, and more like the trumpeter breed than the foregoing descriptions. The cock laughs and drums for from ten to thirty seconds when salacious, his notes being both musical and pleasant to listen to. The hen responds in a more subdued voice, and both shake their wings with a tremulous motion when their concert is going on.

CHAPTER LIII.

THE TRIGANICA PIGEON.

In the city of Modena, the sport of pigeon-flying has been in vogue from time immemorial. Those who are devoted to this sport are called Triganieri, and the bird they employ is known as the Triganica, or Triganina pigeon. Historical evidence carries the sport back to the year 1327, the date of the Modenese statute, *De Columbis non capiendis nec trappola tenenda.* In the same statute, reformed in 1547, the word Triganieros, used only in Modena, is first found. In the Latin poem *De Aucupio Coternicum,* by the Modenese, Seraphino Salvarani, published in 1678, there is a fine description of the method in which the Triganieri carry on their aërial warfare. Tasso has alluded to them as

> . . . A company of loose livers,
> Given up to gaming and making pigeons fly,
> Which were called Triganieri,
> Natural enemies to the Bacchettoni,

the latter being "certain people who go about by day kissing little pictures painted on boards, and in the evening assemble together to use the scourge on their bare backs." About the time that Moore wrote his "Columbarium," Dr. Domenico Vandelli was writing a description of the sport carried on with pigeons by the Triganieri, which differed but little from that in vogue at the present day. The dovecotes are on the roofs of the houses, and they are surrounded by stepped platforms, on which the Triganieri stand, directing the flight of their pigeons by the waving of a little flag at the end of a pole. The flag, some grain of which the birds are fond, and the shrill whistle of the owner, instead of which a cornet was used in olden times, are all the means used for directing them. The object of the sport is the pleasure of making them fly as required, and the capture of birds belonging to enemies. Some of the phrases used will illustrate the methods employed.

THE TRIGANICA, OR MODENA PIGEON.

Guastare, is to let loose for flight one or more pigeons for the first time.

Sparare, is to let loose for flight, and to send round in circles, the pigeons already trained.

Mischiare, is to join together and confuse in one single band the various flying bands which belong to several Triganieri, taught to do this by a signal given them by their respective masters.

Strappare, is the sudden division and separation of the united bands, at the whistle of any Triganiere, who thus calls back his band to his own roof, when they are all united together.

Scavezzare, is the signal which the Triganiere makes with his flag to his band, when he observes, mingled with his own birds, one or more strange pigeons, which they can more easily surround and bring to his dovecote.

Avvujare, is to induce a band, into which some strange pigeons have been brought, to fly backwards and forwards in long-continued flights around the dovecote, in order to seize a favourable opportunity of making them all descend together.

Trattare, or *Gustare*, is the giving of grain to the pigeons when they have descended, as a reward for having been obedient in their flight to the signals of the Triganiere.

Tirar giù niente, is the recalling of the flock of pigeons by their master when they do not obey his signals, without giving them food, the better to incite them to obedience.

Andare indietro spalla, is to feign to send the pigeons to mingle with others, and when they have almost mingled, to call them back suddenly, with the probability of some of the pigeons of the other bands returning with them.

Dare la mano, is the act of taking up the strange pigeons which have perched on the platform with the pigeons of the Triganiere.

When Vandelli wrote, the sport was carried on in four ways. First, on the terms of good friendship, in which a reciprocal restitution of captives was made without compensation. Second, on the terms of fair battle, by the redemption of the captives at a price agreed upon by the combatants. Third, on declared war, when the pigeons were taken with impunity, and with no obligation on the part of the captor to restore them. And fourth, on war to the last drop of blood, when the captive was immediately hung from the platform in full sight of the dovecote of the adversary, or there was attached to its tail a little bottle of gunpowder, in which a fuse was placed, and then, when the enemy sent out his pigeons, the captive was let loose after the fuse had been fired, so that when it arrived in the midst of the flight the bottle burst, and many of the pigeons near were killed or wounded.

In the present day, however, such cruel reprisals are not in use, and the sport is generally carried à lira, or on the terms of the redemption of captives at the rate of a Modenese lira.

I am indebted to the Italian books I have mentioned for the foregoing information on the Triganieri, and chiefly to Malmusi's "Dei Triganieri," 1851.

The Triganica pigeon, which is of comparatively modern origin—other varieties, as described under the Archangel pigeon, having been previously used for the sport—is said by Neumeister to be a variety of the *Hühnertauben*, under which classification he describes it. The marking is certainly very similar to that of the *Florentiner*, but the Triganica pigeon is now only a medium-sized bird, and though many of them carry their tails somewhat erect, they ought to carry them horizontally. This variety certainly shows some relationship to the Leghorn runt race in being high on the legs, short in the flights and tail, and in being marked much the same as the *Florentiner*, but its shape is in every respect modified, and other elements have without doubt entered into its composition. The illustration is from a bird lent me by Mr. Ivatts, of Dublin, which was very little larger than a common flying tumbler.

There are no less than 152 colours in this variety, all of which have received names from the Triganieri, and these may be found in Professor Bonizzi's "I Colombi di Modena." Seventy-six of these are what are called *schietti*, or pure colours, that is, the pigeons are all coloured without any entirely white feathers, and the other seventy-six are the corresponding *gazzi*, or magpies of these colours, that is, pied with white, like the illustration. Some of the most beautiful colours are, black with the wing coverts chequered with red, which I have attempted to show in the illustration. Black, with the wing coverts heavily tipped with red, so that the whole shoulder, as in a turbit, is red, the head, flights, and tail being jet black. The same with yellow chequered or whole yellow shoulders. Dun head, flights and tail, the shoulders buff, but tipped with bright yellow. The same with solid yellow shoulders. Blue magpies, with red or yellow wing bars, black barred blues being of no value. Light blue, of a uniform tint, without any wing bars. Black and white grizzles, in which every coloured feather should show black and white. Blue and white grizzles. Three coloured birds, in which every feather should show black, red and white. Oddities, having one wing of one colour, and the other of another colour. I have lately seen some good Triganica pigeons in the possession of Mr. O. Neef, of Forest Hill, from whom I have obtained a pair of light silvery blue magpies, marbled on the shoulders with dark blue, and with yellow wing bars.

These pigeons are bred by many fanciers, who have neither time nor inclination for the sport as practised by the Triganieri proper. Some of the colours are rare, and only in the hands of their producers, who are so jealous of parting with them that they will rather destroy their surplus stock than let the breed out of their hands. The magpies present the same difficulties in breeding as other pied pigeons, coloured feathers in the parts that should be white, and *vice versâ*, troubling the breeders in Modena as much as they do us in our pied varieties; so that a perfectly marked pigeon is a rarity, and is consequently considered valuable.

CHAPTER LIV.

INDIAN FLYING PIGEONS.

IN passing through the streets of large cities in Northern India, from an hour before sunset till dark, an observer may see many people on the flat roofs of the houses, directing the flight of large flocks of pigeons by means of flags attached to long bamboo poles. This sport is carried on with great energy in the city of Delhi, where I have seen immense numbers of pigeons flown in this way. In Calcutta also, anyone who may be passing through the native parts of the city, near sunset, will see the same sport carried on by numerous pigeon flyers. Garden Reach (the southern suburb of Calcutta) was formerly the residence of many of the principal merchants and civil servants, whose palatial houses, standing in their compounds of from two to twenty acres of ground, are now chiefly owned by the ex-king of Oude, a State prisoner there, who has gradually bought up a great many of them, and surrounded them by a high wall. When passing up the Hooghly river I often saw flights of pigeons that seemed to number thousands, flying, to all appearance, under command, over the king's grounds; but, as it was impossible to gain admittance to the place, I could never get a closer inspection of them, till observing in the newspapers one day that certain people would be admitted, I hastened to avail myself of the opportunity. The ex-king of Oude has what is said to be the largest private collection of rare birds and animals in the world, on which he has spent an immense sum of money, and of which he is very fond. It would be out of place here to describe the beautifully laid out grounds, the lovely plants, the rare animals, the marble-margined tanks or ponds, surrounded by gilded railings, and full of rare aquatic birds, and the houses fitted up as aviaries, and full of the most gorgeously feathered birds; so I shall confine myself to a description of the four great flights of pigeons which are kept in four of the houses in the king's grounds. These flights are said to number about a thousand in each, and are composed of only one breed, the native name of which I forget. This variety is a medium-sized, very hard-feathered, smooth-headed, bare-legged, boldly upstanding, rather long-faced pigeon, not unlike the cross between a dragoon and tumbler. It is invariably pied in colour, the head and neck, as far as in the Triganica or nun pigeons, being usually coloured. The rest of the plumage is white, on which irregular patches of colour, differing in different individuals, may be found. It is difficult to find any two exactly alike in marking. The four large flocks are of four colours, one being black pied, and the others red, yellow, and blue pied. The houses these flocks are kept in were formerly dwelling houses, in the upper rooms of which, I was told the pigeons were bred. The keeper of each flight has a long bamboo, to which is attached a small flag, and a jar of seed, something like millet in appearance. He must also be an adept in being able to utter a shrill whistle, by placing his first and second fingers between his lips. It will therefore be seen that the *modus operandi* of directing the pigeons is exactly the same as in use in Modena. The flight I observed first was composed of blue pieds, whose keeper drove them out of the lower hall of the house, in which they were, with his bamboo. They all settled on a large rack, such as is fitted up in greenhouses for placing the pots on, which stood in front of the house. He then gave his shrill whistle, waved his flag, and the whole flock rose into the air. The other flights were up at the same time, and it was a fine sight to see them intermingling, separating, and wheeling round in their flight; the dense masses casting shadows on the ground like passing clouds, and the whizzing of their many wings being pleasant to hear. After they had flown for some time, I asked the keeper to bring them down, and I could then see how quick they were, for the moment he dropped his flag and put his hand into the seed jar, they stopped in their flight, hung in the air for a moment, and then came down to the ground at my feet with a rush. The keeper went in amongst them and picked up one, which he shook from side to side and then tossed into the air. It was a yellow pied, from one of the other flights.

It is probable that pigeon flying carried on in this way has travelled westward from Asia. The Italian books make mention of a similar practice being common in Moscow. It is well known that the Taj Mahal at Agra, and other fine buildings that are the glory of the East, were designed by Italian architects, and nothing is more likely than that some of the Italians who were in India from two to three hundred years ago may have been pigeon fanciers, and taken the sport home with them. There is even some resemblance in the respective breeds used for the sport in Italy and India. The Modenese statutes of 1327 and 1547 prohibit the snaring of pigeons by nets or strings, but they do not prove conclusively that this sport was in use then. Some of the Venetians may have originated the sport in the fifteenth century. The Venetians had intimate business relations with India 400 years ago, and their coins are still plentiful there. I have bought Venetian ducats in India, where they are valued for their purity, and hoarded up with the gold Mohurs of Akbar. The sport may have reached Italy from Turkey or the Levant, for I have no doubt it is carried on in Persia, Turkish Arabia, and Asia Minor, with little or no difference from that of Hindostan.

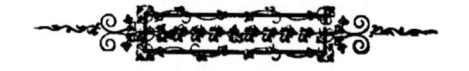

CHAPTER LV.

THE ANTWERP CARRIER PIGEON.

THE well-known love of pigeons generally for their homes, has been taken advantage of from the earliest ages by making use of them as messengers. The flying fancier can point to Anacreon's "Ode to the Carrier Pigeon," written twenty-five centuries ago, as a proof of the existence of his fancy in early times :

> Tell me why, my sweetest dove,
> Thus your humid pinions move?
> *   *   *   *
> Curious stranger! I belong
> To the bard of Teian song;
> With his mandate now I fly
> To the nymph of azure eye.

Throughout history there are records of the use of carrier pigeons as messengers to and from beleaguered cities ; from the amphitheatre, to tell the result of the sports or combats; from caravans, to announce their setting out or arrival. Many passages from mediæval writers have recently been brought to light regarding their employment, and if in modern times the telegraph has superseded them in Europe as swift carriers of news, railways have afforded such facile means of training them, that probably at no other period of the world's history, have such immense numbers of these birds been kept by sweepstakes and other fliers, as at the present time.

The subject itself being without the scope of my scheme, my remarks on it will be more general than particular. A reference to my chapter on the literature connected with pigeons will show that many books have been published here and abroad on this subject, which is of such a special character, and outside the pigeon fancy proper, that an exhaustive treatise it would occupy more space here than could be found for it ; and, er all, it would be chiefly a compilation from what has been already published, as I do not pretend to have studied the subject otherwise than in a general and but slightly experimental way.

The pigeons formerly used in this country as messengers were mainly of carrier descent, such as horsemen, dragoons, skinnums—the cross of the first two with tumblers—and long-faced beards, which no doubt were merely beard-marked skinnums, and bred in the same way, but for marking especially. All such have been for long known amongst us as homing pigeons, and were so referred to by Moore in his "Columbarium," where, at page 5, in describing the construction of the "Trap or Airy," he says: "Others build them very wide and lofty, designing them to give Room and Air to Pigeons of the homing Sort." Again, at page 32, under the Horseman, "This Practice is of admirable Service to 'em, when they come to be train'd for the homing Part"; and elsewhere, when writing of the "Powting Horseman."

On the Continent the pigeon now chiefly used for match flying is the Antwerp carrier, or Belgian voyageur, which has been bred from a judicious mixture of several long and high flying varieties. The first of these, a pigeon that can itself do long distances, is the smerle of Liege, which is quoted in Mr. Tegetmeier's book as capable, when matured, of doing 500 miles in twelve hours, in fine weather. The smerle is the opposite in appearance of the dragoon type, being arched and broad in skull, with a short thick beak, and with evident appearance of owl descent, some of them even showing the frilled breast. The next is the continental cumulet, a pigeon noted for the length of time it can keep on the wing. I have seen it mentioned that these pigeons have flown as long as thirteen hours at a stretch, the distance covered during that time being probably several hundred miles. They are of various colours, but blacks and reds, with white tails or white flights, or with both, are known as varieties, while pure whites, ticked with red on the head and neck, are also a well-known race, distinguished in France as the *Pigeon volant cou-rouge*. The cumulet is much alike in size and shape to the common clean legged flying tumbler. It is rather longer in beak; it has a pure white iris, which is larger than usual in pigeons, the pupil being small and contracted. The third ingredient of the composite bird, now known as the Antwerp carrier, is the English dragoon, known in Belgium as the Bec-Anglais; and the fusion of these three varieties has taken place during the present century, and a race of pigeons has been established, remarkable for their power of flying long distances in quick time. The cross of the dragoon with the smerle or cumulet is called a demi-bec, and the cross of the dragoon-smerle with the cumulet, or dragoon-cumulet with the smerle, a Quart-bec. The Quart-bec, bred over again to the smerle or cumulet, takes after its progenitors, so that among the best pigeons there are various types of skull, some after the owl strain, while others are more run out in head and beak. The chief colours found in the Antwerp are blue, blue-chequer, mealy, and red chequer, and these colours pied to some extent with white. These colours are the most natural, being what are found among semi-wild pigeons, and in process of time have doubtless asserted themselves as the hardiest and fittest for the severe work they have to perform.

Coming now to the consideration of the wonderful performances of Antwerps in returning distances of 500 miles and more, there is no doubt that training has much to do with it, that great numbers of them are lost in the severe training they get, and that the percentage of birds that would return from a first toss of 400 miles would be but small. Still, they have been known to return to their domicile from such a distance, without any previous training, and therefore there remains something still unexplained in connection with them, which may never be satisfactorily elucidated. Dogs, cats, and other animals have been known to return immense distances when taken from home—they have been sent by sea and have returned by land; but then we hear of such incidents when they happen, and of those who do not so distinguish themselves we never hear.

Some years ago Mr. James Huie, of Glasgow, the well-known pouter fancier, a writer whose diction and style of composition have caused many to wish that he had written otherwise than only fugitively on fancy pigeons, contributed the following article on the Antwerp carrier to the *Journal of Horticulture*:

"POWER OF WING AND COMPASS.

" I hear a voice you cannot hear,
  Which bids me not to stay;
  I see a hand you cannot see,
  Which beckons me away.

" There has been much interesting writing on the powers of the carrier pigeon, the length and rapidity of their flights and modes of training, along with speculations as to their guide for their homeward course. The latter points to the theory of this bird flying by sight alone. I find that the Rev. E. S. Dixon, in his very interesting work, 'The Dovecote and Aviary,' takes this same view; and though I always hesitate to place my opinion against that of such men of letters as Mr. Dixon, still on this point (the guide of the carrier on the wing) I beg most respectfully to differ. It is pretty well known that I am not an Antwerp-carrier fancier, and do not encourage the Antwerp as a bird that ought to be in the fancy, for several reasons which I shall not discuss at present. But Antwerps I keep for two purposes: first, as feeders for my young pouters, and second for table use. For both these purposes I find them most suitable. First, then, as to the power of wing possessed by this bird. I do not think this point is yet fully developed in this country; but so far as my personal experience goes I shall give it. The plain narrative I think may answer the purpose best. It may be interesting, and I hope will not weary readers.

"Several years ago, when in Manchester, I called on Mr. W. Millward, bird dealer, from whom I had all my Belgian canaries. He had lately arrived from the Continent, and brought with him a stock of Antwerp carriers, which he then found to be most unprofitable. Not having before seen such birds, which I could be sure of having been imported, I purchased three pairs. The stock consisted of mostly blues, some mealies, and some nameless colours; but all were self-coloured, and all showing a cross of the owl, a slight division of the feathers on the breast. Some of them had the breast feathers slightly turned, indicating the frill. They were wild as newly caught hawks, and strong enough to carry before them a pane of window glass, as one of them did when in my possession. After much care and caution I found them to be hardy birds, breeders almost the year round—indeed, I am never without some few young ones. During the season, when early light, they take two flights per day, the cocks and unoccupied hens at about 7 a.m., the hens and unoccupied cocks about 1 p.m. The flock invariably fly southward, and are away for about an hour and a half each time. I have seen them fully ten miles south still holding in that direction. When first noticed on their return they are always at a very great height; but should it be blowing hard (the weather seems of little consequence to them) they often return from the northward, having no doubt been carried to the east or west beyond their home. Three years passed, when a friend came on a visit from Ledbury, Herefordshire. This friend saw my Antwerps, and expressed a wish for a pair or two to breed for table use. After his leaving for home I caught three pairs all bred in my loft (Antwerp loft, for with them I have nothing else). They were put into a box (not a basket or cage), and addressed to a mutual friend in Manchester, as they could not reach Ledbury in one day from Glasgow. They reached Manchester in the evening, were re-booked for Ledbury next morning, and reached their destination that evening; but until then were not taken out of the box in which I had placed them. Before sending the birds away I pulled the flight feathers out of the right wing of each bird, and my instructions were, 'Keep them confined with such a netting as will let them see the locality, till they have each a nest of young ones, and are sitting upon their second eggs.' Those instructions were rigidly adhered to. One night the netting was removed according to instructions, and the birds were at liberty next morning. A man was set to watch. The cocks took sundry short flights, and by and by relieved their mates occupied in incubation; the hens came out, and at once took wing. The date now I cannot give precisely—let me call it the 18th of July. On the morning of the 20th I had a letter from my friend, dated the day before (the 19th), saying, 'The birds were yesterday morning let out, but two of them have not returned. I am afraid they are lost.' While in the act of reading my friend's letter, my man who attends to those birds came into my office saying, 'I think two of Mr. ——'s birds are back.' Scarcely believing him, I went out into the yard, and there certainly were two of the hens I had sent to Ledbury.

"Now, I can tell to a mile the distance between Glasgow and Ledbury, Herefordshire, by railway; but I will let our readers measure the distance as the crow flies, and decide whether or not this is a very long flight. Mark, first, those birds had never been trained; second, they had never been in the hands of anyone till caught by me, when I pulled the flight feathers from one wing of each bird. These birds would leave their cote at Ledbury about 10 or 11 a.m. on the 18th, and as I did not know what day or week they were to be set at liberty, of course I did not expect them, and at all events I certainly did not expect they would at any time return to Glasgow on the wing. For all I know they may have reached on the evening of the 18th or during the day of the 19th. Two months after this I gave a pair to a friend in Paisley—a pair of young ones. They had only been two days outside the loft, and never had left it beyond a hundred yards. They were taken away squeakers, and confined with a netting in front for three weeks. When let out they were at their birthplace in ten or twelve minutes. It is only seven miles to Paisley by road. Those birds had never been flown."

That some pigeons, especially those of certain breeds, both from a strong natural and inherited love of home, will return from long distances without any previous training, is therefore an established fact. But at the same time little dependence could be placed on even the best bred flying pigeons without training. They must, therefore, be flown first from a short distance, and gradually by increased stages till perfect at their work, during which process of training many of them are of course lost. It has been recommended by writers on this subject that birds in their first year should not be flown above a hundred miles from home, and not over two hundred miles in their second year, as they are not fully matured till over two years of age.

It is an established fact that pedigree in homing birds is of the first consequence, so that those entering on this pursuit should by all means endeavour to procure stock from fliers of repute. If the best homers could be selected by appearance there would be no need to go farther. It is well known that some of the best have had little in their looks to recommend them.

At some shows prizes are offered "for the likeliest pigeons for flying purposes." Showing these birds in this way is a mere farce, and is only encouraged so long as it proves profitable. Such classes will be discontinued when the aggregate entry money falls below the prizes offered. As a fancy pigeon the homer has no value, as a feeder it may be worth from twelve to eighteenpence, as a flier it may be worth £20. I could understand an exhibition of winners of races, but not of the best-looking homers; for two pigeons may be very much alike, and while one of them has nothing in its breeding or performance to recommend it, the other may be the fiftieth in descent from ancestors, each one of which was celebrated as a homer, and be itself equal to any of them.

On the Continent the flying fancy is much followed. It is said that Belgium has 150 clubs or societies for the cultivation of the voyageur pigeon. Herr Prütz, in his *Die arten der Haustaube*, gives a list of 250 German societies for the same purpose. In this country this fancy is increasing and rising in public estimation, many gentlemen and respectable people being devoted to it. The use of the voyageur for war purposes has been recognised on the Continent, and government studs of them have been established in France, Germany, and other countries. The principal foreign flying matches take place in July, and extend over distances of from 200 to 500 miles. Twice have races been organised from Rome to Belgium, a distance of some 900 miles, but with so little success, both as to time and the percentage of returns, that it is now recognised that this long fly can only be attained at too great a sacrifice.

The most absurd stories regarding carrier pigeons are often circulated in the newspapers—such as the return of some sent to the Arctic regions to their home in Ayrshire, the flight of others across the Atlantic Ocean, and the capture of others at sea with stamps on their wings showing them to have been employed during the siege of Paris, which happened seven or eight years before their capture, since which event their flight feathers must have been renewed annually. It seems impossible to kill these fables, and they crop up at regular intervals. One or more carriers were captured at sea during the siege of Paris, and were shown at exhibitions of pigeons as objects of interest. Since then the story has been re-published repeatedly as a late event, and it will probably continue to be published in time to come as it comes under the observation of those who do not understand the way in which pigeons are used as messengers.

Where prizes for homing pigeons are offered at shows, the following remarks on judging them, by Mr. W. B. Tegetmeier, who is probably the highest authority on the subject, will be found of value. He says:

"The classes for homing Antwerps, which are now common at many shows, offer considerable difficulty to those who have to award the prizes, unless, indeed, as not very often happens, they are practically acquainted with the breed.

"When the judge is not in this position the birds selected are usually of the short-faced Birmingham type; and I have seen at Bingley Hall and elsewhere prizes given to a set of bad show birds, the best of which would have been lost at twenty or thirty miles, even if they could have been trained that distance. It should be borne in mind that the properties of a homing pigeon lie in the wing more than in the head, and a judge who simply looks at a pen and decides the prizes upon the appearance of the birds, proves that he knows nothing whatever about the subject on which he undertakes to decide.

"At the exhibition of the birds that won in the late (1876) race to Brussels from the Alexandra Palace, several distinct types were recognisable. Some of the birds were rather light and fine in the head, whilst others were heavy, thicker in head, and stouter in body. Although the lighter birds are generally regarded as flying well in fine weather and for short distances, the stouter are usually regarded as the standard type.

"Of the three engravings which accompany this article, the first (Fig. 1)

Fig. 1.

represents, life size, a head, which may be regarded as that of a very handsome Belgian voyageur cock. It may be taken as that of the bird which Mons. Ch. Mills and Mr. C. L. Sutherland—both practical men—gave me the first prize for at the Alexandra poultry show, 1875. But it was not drawn from that bird, but from a cock I obtained of Mons. Ch. Mills. The bird has all the properties that I desire to see in the head of a flying pigeon. A full developed brain case, showing a large brain and such a structure of head as indicates strength and endurance, and he is

L

without any tendency to the absurd exaggeration of any fancy point. Of course no really practical judge would give a prize in a homing class even to such a bird unless he were in first rate condition, with his plumage hard and firm, the flight feathers broad and overlapping, and the bones of the wing well clothed with powerful muscles. To prove that this bird is as good as he looks, I may give his history. He was hatched early in 1874 from a bird of Mons. Ch. Mills, that was one of the first winners in the great annual national match from Marseilles, in the south of France, to Belgium—a 500 miles race. The same year, as a young bird, he flew

FIG. 2.

from St. Quentin and Creil (about 200 miles), and in 1875 he again flew from St. Quentin, taking first prize; also from Paris, Orleans, and was a winner in the race from London—200 miles.

"At my request Mons. Ch. Mills sent him over to show at the Alexandra poultry show, 19th Oct., 1875, and I induced him—very reluctantly, I am afraid—to part with him. The bird was necessarily useless to me to fly, for, on liberation, he would doubtless have returned to Brussels, as I have had birds do after two years' confinement in

England, but I kept him to breed from, and his early progeny are very good indeed.

"So good is the bird in appearance that I have repeatedly refused the offer of £5 for him merely as a stock bird.

"Fig. 2 represents a homing Antwerp belonging to me to which the judges gave the silver cup at the Crystal Palace poultry show in 1875. The bird was certainly a handsome one, but not, in my opinion, equal to the former, even in looks; he was purely Belgian bred, and was a good homer, having flown about 100 miles in previous years. In 1876 I entered him in a private race from Brussels, but—the truth must be told —I have never seen him since he was let off in that pleasant city on the morning of the 20th July, and was lost, although his companion in the race, not half as good looking, is walking about before my eyes.

"I have now shown what is regarded as the most esteemed type of Belgian birds—viz., as regards cocks, for the hens are generally less stout in the head and beak; and I may state that the sketches are executed with the most extreme accuracy, not only as regards the form, but also as to the expression of the birds. Mr. T. W. Wood, one of the most accurate of natural history draughtsmen, devoted very great care to their delineation, and I may state that the drawings are not altered to suit my views of what a good homer should be, but show the birds exactly as they are.

FIG. 3.

"I now wish to show what is not an uncommon view of a homing bird amongst some amateurs. The outline sketch (Fig. 3) is traced with the closest accuracy from one of the drawings of Mr. Ludlow, of Birmingham, published in the "New York Pet, Stock, and Poultry Bulletin." The drawing represented, with all Mr. Ludlow's skill, an indifferent Birmingham show Antwerp, with pert upright carriage, short stubby beak, large eyes, small head and brain, and is no more like a Belgian voyageur than I to Hercules. Such a bird could not fly fifty miles, and would not fly five.

"I have visited over and over again the lofts of the Belgian amateurs; I have owned and still own hundreds of these birds; I have had thousands pass through my hands; but in all Belgium I never saw a bird approaching the form that is apparently regarded by Mr. Ludlow and the Birmingham fanciers as that of a Belgian voyageur.

"The exhibition of the right sort of birds is very much promoted by their liberation after being judged in the pens, the prizes being withheld if the birds are not returned at a given time. It is true some of the birds may live close to the show, and have their flying powers very slightly tested, but really good flyers are certain to be sent for the selection of the judge, and the shortfaced show birds will be kept at home.

"The liberation clause should always be qualified with the stipulation 'weather permitting,' for it would be a serious matter if, during the worst flying months of the year, a flight of really good birds should be liberated in a fog or in hazy weather when they could not see their way home. For, in spite of all the nonsense written about flying by instinct, all practical men know that a bird flies by sight. I have lost some of the best birds I ever possessed from trying to fly them across London on a foggy day."

CHAPTER LVI.

THE SHORT-FACED ANTWERP PIGEON.

THIS pigeon has been produced principally from the smerle of Liege, one of the varieties from which the Belgian voyageur descends, as mentioned in my last chapter. According to Fulton, who ought to know, some breeders have made use of the barb in breeding it. Its chief properties lie in its head, which must be capacious, and present in profile an unbroken curve from the nape to the point of the beak. The beak itself ought to be thick and short, the under mandible approaching the upper in consistency as much as possible, and fitting close to it, or, as fanciers say, boxed. Any gullet is objectionable, and detracts from the appearance and value of this variety in the opinion of its admirers. Viewed in front, the head ought also to be round from eye to eye. The irides should be orange or blood red in colour, light or pearl eyes being faulty. The eyes must be prominent or bolting, and be surrounded with a fair but not excessive amount of wattle. Like other pigeons of this type of head, the beak wattle thickens with age; it should be of considerable substance, lying well spread on each side, and by the time the bird arrives at maturity—some three or four years—it should have filled up all inequalities in the curve of the head, and if it stands out a little beyond the curve it is not considered any fault in a good bird. Mere shortness of face, therefore, is no desideratum in this bird, but rather the reverse, for room is required for the forehead behind the beak wattle to fill out, and this is the point which gives a finish to a good bird and makes it massive in skull. For this reason, the name *short-faced* Antwerp has been objected to as inappropriate; but as that of *exhibition* Antwerp, which has been subsituted, applies equally to other varieties of the breed, the long-faced and medium-faced, both of them regularly exhibited, I prefer to keep the first title, both because the bird has been known for long as the short-faced Antwerp, and because it actually is so compared with the others.

The short-faced Antwerp should be a large pigeon, bold in appearance, upstanding, and tight feathered. The choicest colour is the mealy, almost always now called silver-dun, which is a good-sounding name, but there is certainly no silver in this colour, neither is there any dun. The mealy colour may be said to have been bred to perfection in this pigeon. The cocks are sometimes finely powdered on the head and upper neck, while the lower neck, breast, and wing bars are of a rich brown or red; but it is difficult to get the same colour in the hens, which are generally dark headed. Next comes the red-chequer, both dark and light; the blue-chequer, also of various shades, and the black-barred blue, the original colour of wild pigeons. These are the chief colours, valued, I believe, in the order named. Then come silvers, preferred with bars of as dark a dun as possible; dun-chequers, called silver-chequers; yellow-mealies, called creamies; and, lastly, blacks, which are sooty or blue-black, showing bars of a deeper black.

My opinion of the short-faced Antwerp is in accordance with that of a great many men who are the mainstays of the pigeon fancy. I cannot admit that it has one original point in its composition entitling it to be called an original variety, and all the diagrams and illustrations published of it only confirm this opinion. The chief difference between it and the owl is said to be that the latter is essentially a short-faced pigeon, which the Antwerp ought not to be. No doubt all the owl tribe are known as short-faced frilled pigeons; but they would quite as correctly be called blunt-faced, for mere shortness of face is not any desideratum in them, as it takes away room for the filling up of the forehead behind the beak wattle. This, when well developed, gives them, above all else, a look of quality, just as it does the Antwerp.

The short-faced Antwerp may be difficult to breed good, according to the standard laid down for it; but, when bred as good as can be, it is no more than a pigeon with some owl points in its head, and, for the most part, clothed in the mere off colours of fancy pigeons. I think the encouragement it gets tends to foster low art in pigeon breeding, wastes time and trouble that might be much better employed, and that there is no result, from an artistic point of view, in its production. Many fanciers, whose judgment of pigeons is acknowledged to be sound, agree with me in this opinion.

CHAPTER LVII.

THE TUMBLER PIGEON.

THE above heading causes the almost forgotten past to be remembered. Visions of bygone celebrities, that were known by such names as the red mottle, the blue hen, the red breaster, Hay's white cock, and such like, crowd up from the days of the springtime of life. I recall the feat of my little blue tumbler which, when heading against a strong wind, and neither making nor losing any headway, turned clean over forty times within the minute, in the same aërial space. The pennies that ought to have been spent on biscuits to appease the mid-day appetite, were hoarded up till such a sum was accumulated as would cause some well-known performer to change ownership; and then there was joy in fetching it home, and the basket was opened many times on the way for "another look." I fancy there are more tumbler pigeons kept in this country than of all other kinds put together, and that the accumulation of genuine pleasure derived by their owners from them exceeds that from all other kinds. Many a fancier has begun with tumblers, and but few refuse to provide a place for their first favourites, into whatever other channels their fancy may roam.

The tumbler derives its name from its inherited propensity of turning over backwards in its flight. What causes the tumbler to turn in this way is not known, though many theories have been propounded to account for it. Some well bred birds never attain to it, while others carry it to such an excess that they cannot rise from the ground a couple of feet. These then become known as ground tumblers. They often resume flying and tumbling in the air, and again become grounders. House tumblers are such as can rise from the ground, but which often tumble in their flight across a room. They do not, however, always perform when required to do so. Air tumblers sometimes become so proficient and systematic in their performances, that they change hands for ten shillings each and upwards among poor men. Such birds will sometimes go off tumbling and fall in value to the normal price of a shilling, and after remaining very ordinary ones for a year or two, suddenly become good ones again, and rise in value in proportion. Many a good tumbler has never given a turn till two or three years old, and some can never get more than half over in their attempts to turn. I certainly think, that in the case of ordinary tumblers, tumbling is a real pleasure to them, and that they do it voluntarily; but that the habit grows on some birds to such an extent, that they either cannot rise from the ground, or if in mid air they lose command of themselves occasionally, and, striking against some projection, so destroy themselves.

There are many styles of tumbling, and the one most generally admired is that in which the bird turns over once at a time and often, but without losing way in its flight. At the same time, those that rise and fall in the air by alternate soaring and rolling, each roll being composed of several backward turns, are also liked by many people. Some birds make the most extraordinary motions in the air, turning at right angles in their flight, and throw themselves about so rapidly that the eye can scarcely follow their turns. High-flying tumblers generally tumble only when ascending or descending; but they sometimes go so high, in fact, quite out of sight, that it is impossible to follow them in their movements. I have watched them on a clear day till they seemed no bigger than mites, and then lost them altogether. Tumblers when allowed unlimited freedom become lazy and unwilling to fly, and they seldom fly in concert. Some remaining on the housetops are seen by those in the air, and this tends to bring them down sooner than they might otherwise come.

Great care and much trouble is necessary in getting up a good flight of tumblers ; birds that will not rise must be weeded out, and to insure success they must be flown only at stated times. The morning is the best time, before they are fed ; and after they return to their loft, they should be confined till late in the afternoon or till next morning, according to the wishes of their owner. To fly tumblers systematically is indeed a separate branch of the pigeon fancy, which is only excelled in by such as lay themselves out for it. I have known fanciers, including myself, buy the best soaring birds that money could buy, and I have seen them gradually deteriorate, for want of the necessary attention being bestowed on them. As to the time a flight of good tumblers will fly, from two to four hours is not uncommon, and I have seen it mentioned that no less than eleven hours have been done in a match. I am not acquainted, however, with the rules for conducting such matches, whether the birds must keep flying voluntarily, or whether their owner is allowed to prevent them settling if he can. Tumblers require special training for flying time matches. Parched peas are considered the best feeding for them, as they take long to digest, and assist in keeping up their strength during the time they keep on the wing. Without such special food they would become faint in a few hours.

The tumbler is spread in great variety throughout Europe and Asia. It has long been known in this country, and is described by Willughby (1678). He says : " These are small and of divers colours. They have strange motions, turning themselves backwards over their heads, and show like footballs in the air." The ordinary tumbler of this country is a small pigeon, thin in the neck, full in the breast, of medium length in flights and tail, short legged, and free of leg and foot feather. The head is round and free from sharp angles, and the forehead of middle height. The beak should be short and thin, or what is known as a spindle beak. The beak and eye wattle should be as small and unpronounced as possible. The eye should be white or pearl coloured in the iris, but is usually of a red pearl, not nearly so white as in the Continental cumulet. There are, however, many yellow, red, and hazel eyed birds, as good performers as ever flew; but I am describing the tumbler as it ought to be when shown, and as it is in many lofts where kept only to be flown, for good-looking birds, that are good performers as well, may be got by selection from the immense numbers kept in every large town. I have seen good clean legged tumblers with shell crests, and also peak-headed ones. I once bred several peaked yellow whole feathers from a pair of smooth-headed ones. I could only account for this variation as a natural sport.

The tumbler may be got in all the principal colours, such as whole blue, silver, black, red, yellow, dun, and white; and in such infinite variety of mottles, grizzles, and splashes, that it would be no difficult matter to put up a hundred matched pairs, any one of which might easily be distinguished from the rest. Birds are matched together for their excellence in tumbling, no matter what colour they are, and they therefore produce a great variety of curiously coloured and marked offspring. It is generally from tumblers so matched up for their powers of tumbling, that the house and ground tumblers are produced, and, accordingly, many of them have little in their appearance, from a fancy point of view, to recommend them in the way of feather. Such are out of place in the show pen, however, for which the colours must be pure and good to enable them to compete successfully.

Show tumblers are sub-divided—at Kilmarnock, for instance, where they have long been favourites, and where they have an extensive classification—into self colours, mottles, baldheads, and beards. I am of opinion that foreign elements have been in some cases introduced into the breeding of the self colours and mottles to give colour, and that few of the pretty birds to be seen at shows would be of much account in a flight; but there is this to be said of showing tumblers, that independently of performance in the air, they are worth show recognition from a fancy point of view, while the Antwerp carrier or voyageur pigeon of Belgium is not. The show tumbler should have, in the first place, all the character in shape of head, beak, and body of the best type of the real performing tumbler, and on no account have about the head, even a suspicion of any cross with the short-faced tumbler. Many people erroneously think, or used to think, that the half or quarter bred short-face, being neater in head, is better for the show pen; but this absurd idea is on the wane, if not altogether eradicated. There is a medium between shortness and too great length of face, and between too thick and too thin a beak for the show tumbler. I have known a quarter-bred barb win all through a season as a common black tumbler. The barb cross gave colour, pearl eyes, and a white beak; but the latter was too thick, and there was too much beak and eye wattle to deceive me. The reddish tinge on beak and eye wattle was no conclusive proof of the cross, because this accompanies fine colour in black, red, and yellow, and I have had the very best performers so coloured in the eye wattles. The black, red, and yellow ought to be as sound, and accompanied with as much metallic lustre, as possible. Glossy blacks may be seen, but I have never seen reds and yellows within many shades of the colour to be seen in many foreign pigeons. These colours not being in the breed, therefore, in their best possible tints, any crosses with other varieties which do possess them, must inevitably result in the loss of the tumbling propensity, however much all the appearance of the pure tumbler may be retained; but as the tumbling propensity is of no moment, and cannot be tested in the show pen, shape and feather are all that are looked for in the tumbler as a show pigeon.

As some races of tumblers of the best quality, as regards performances in the air, and which have been kept to feather to a certain extent, I may mention the red mottles, not marked so exactly as the show mottles (to be afterwards mentioned), but being mottled over the whole wing coverts, and often with white feathers in the neck, tail, and flights; black and yellow mottles of the same character; blacks with white flight feathers, white beaks, and reddish eye wattle; whites ticked on the neck with red; and, lastly, almond feathered ones. I have known fanciers confine themselves to some of these breeds, and by careful selection of such as were good flyers and performers, establish flights which would breed very true to feather.

I may here mention a well-known variety of the flying tumbler, known as the Macclesfield tippler, which must only make single turns in its flight. Some of these birds are very fine flyers, and so rapid in their tumbling that the eye can scarcely follow them. I believe the tippler is of various colours, but there is one especial marking which I have seen many of, that is, white, with dark head, flights, and tail. The marking is generally kity-black, the flight feathers showing sometimes black, brown, and white. The marking of the head is not cut off

THE ALMOND TUMBLER.

sharply, like that of the nun, but gradually disappears in mottling, and there are more or less grizzled feathers on the neck, breast, and body. This variety breeds true to these characteristics, but with some variation in darkness of points.

In addition to such tumblers as I have described, Moore mentions the Dutch tumbler as "much of the same make, but larger, often featherleg'd, and more jowlter-headed with a thin Flesh or Skin round the Eye, not unlike a very sheer Dragoon; some People don't esteem them upon this Account, tho' I have known very good ones of the *Dutch* breed, not any Ways inferior to what they call the *English*. Others have remarkt that they are apt to tumble too much, and to lose Ground, that is, sink beneath the rest of the Flight, which is a very great Fault, but I have observ'd the same by the *English*, and am apt to believe that most of the extraordinary Feathers have been produc'd by mixing with the *Dutch* breed; for it is generally observ'd that the *English* Tumblers are chiefly black, blue, or white." This is a good description of what are now known as Birmingham rollers, many of which are much larger and coarser pigeons than the neat, trim, clean-legged tumblers.

Rollers are of many colours, such as whole feathers; mottles; saddles, marked exactly the same as the magpie; white sides marked the reverse of the turbit when through the moult, but self-coloured as nestlings; badges, which are all coloured except with some white sprinkling about the head, white flights, and white leg-feathering from the hocks down; grizzles, of various shades, and oddities of all kinds of uneven markings. Rollers may be smooth or feather-legged. Many are heavily-hocked, with feathers on the feet 3in. to 4in. long. They are much fancied in Birmingham and the midland counties, where great numbers of them are kept, and when bred for good shape, colour, and markings, they realise considerable prices for show purposes. I have seen tumblers imported from the Continent with much of the character of these pigeons.

THE MOTTLED TUMBLER.

Mottled flying tumblers for the show pen are either black, red, or yellow, though I have occasionally seen duns. The mottling of these birds should either be a rose pinion on the shoulders, composed of single white feathers, no two of which should be in contact or run together, or the same marking accompanied by what is known as a handkerchief back, which is a V-shaped figure on the back between the shoulders, also composed, when right, of single separated white feathers; while the mottling of the rose pinion is on the wing coverts, the handkerchief back is on the scapular feathers. Some admire the rose wing alone, others the compound marking. The chief defect in mottles is an excess of white feathers, and when these are not absolutely in patches, weeding can transform a bird nearly right into perfection. Removing a few superfluous white feathers is not so difficult as supplying some to a wing rather undermarked; but there are men who will stick at nothing to win somehow, and I have known of a self-coloured bird transformed into a perfect mottle, the white feathers being pasted in. A bird so treated succeeded in winning first prize in a class of mottles at a late Scotch show. There can be no doubt that no pigeon has its toilet made to a greater extent than the show mottle, and that if absolute perfection has been seen, it has been but rarely.

In breeding mottles, the best plan is to learn first how the pigeons to be mated have been bred, for as many generations back as can be found out. If they should have descended through some generations of nearly perfectly marked birds, they ought to breed many such themselves; but, as the general plan is to mate a self-coloured bird, bred in most cases from a mottle and a self-colour, to a mottle bred in the same way, self-colours and mottles are produced from such mating. Self-colours, therefore, are part of the mottle breeder's stock, and represent more than they appear to do. To put a self-coloured to a gay bird is not the plan that experience has taught as most likely to produce the right marking, for the produce is ever inclined to run too gay. And yet, if the self-colour and mottle matching results in an undue proportion of under marked birds, one rather overmarked must be thrown in occasionally. To attain success in mottle breeding, a fancier cannot know too much of the pedigree of his stock birds, and the longer he has the strain the better he should be able to produce good ones.

The young mottle does not leave the nest as it appears after its first moult, but entirely self-coloured. If a bird has even a few grizzled feathers about it as a nestling, it often becomes too white after moulting. It is during its first autumnal moult, therefore, that its beauties become apparent, and that is the time when eager eyes are on the watch

THE BEARD TUMBLER.

for a coming wonder. Many flying tumblers which are self-coloured as nestlings become more than half white during their first moult. The mottled flying tumbler is not nearly so difficult to breed good as the short-faced mottle; but yet it is difficult enough to breed, and if the majority of birds seen at shows were penned unweeded they would be found very mismarked. Foul feathers in the neck and breast are very prevalent, but it is easy to remove many such without the possibility of detection, and, therefore, many fanciers who admire the mottle, prefer rather to spend their time over pigeons not so easily manufactured for the show pen.

BALDHEAD AND BEARD TUMBLERS.

When Moore, in his description of the tumbler, said, "This Pigeon affords a very great Variety of Colours in its Plumage, as blacks, blues, whites, reds, yellows, Duns, Silvers, and, in short, a pleasant mixture of all these Colours with the white," it is probable that he included baldheads and beards as "pleasant mixtures." To the author of the treatise (1765), however, is due the first account of these favourite varieties of the tumbler, and his report of them, which is one of the original pieces in his book, is as follows : "The bald-pated tumblers, which are of various colours in their body, as blacks, blues, &c., with a clean white head, a pearl eye, white flight and white tail, are esteemed good flyers, and are very pretty, even when flying in the air, for the contrast of the feather appears at that distance when the weather is clear and fine; but the blue ones are reputed to rise higher than any other colour. There are also some called blue or black-bearded, that is, either of those colours having a long white spot from the under jaw and cheek, a little way down the throat, and regularly shaped, which has a pretty effect as an ornament; and if they run clean in the flight and tail, as before mentioned in the bald-pated ones, they are accounted handsome."

Baldheads are found in black, blue, silver, red, and yellow, and in off colours, as chequers and mealies. The correct marking is as follows: Both mandibles should be white; and the whole head above a line running about $\frac{1}{8}$in. under the eyes, should also be white. The line should be cut straight and sharp. This marking is called "high cut," in opposition to the white extending any further down the neck, which is called "low cut;" and if the line of demarcation is uneven, or if the white in any case dips down in patches, the bird is said to be slobbered. The baldhead must have pearl eyes, though many otherwise good ones are spoilt by having one or both eyes bull, or dark hazel in colour. This, however, in a flying baldhead is an intolerable fault for the show pen, and the oftener bull-eyed birds are bred from the greater the proportion of young ones so affected will be produced. The primary flights should be white, and as they almost invariably number ten in each wing, the correct marking in the baldhead is spoken of as ten a side. White to the turn of the flight would be the more correct standard, as a bird with only nine primaries a side would be foul flighted if it had ten white feathers a side, for the tenth white feather would in that case be a secondary, all of which must be coloured. Next, if the bird be lifted up by its wings, it should be all white below them, including the rump and tail, with its upper and under coverts. If it has any coloured feathers on thighs or vent, it is foul thighed or vented, both very great faults. If the colour of the breast does not finish off in a straight sharp line, about an inch before the thighs—evenly belted, as it is called—it is faulty. In shape of head, beak, and body, and in size and carriage, the baldhead is similar to the small clean-legged flying tumbler. I have never seen any with feathered legs, and I am not aware if such exist.

The baldhead is a good flyer, and a favourite pigeon with many on account of its beauty, both when seen close or in the air. It is sometimes a good tumbler, but not so generally as the common tumblers first described, for, having in many cases been bred for feather or for high flying alone, the tumbling propensity has not been so carefully cultivated; at the same time, I have had and seen many really first class tumbling baldheads.

I have never seen any almond feathered common baldheads, but they might be produced in time by crossing with the common almond tumbler. I have seen yellows with a few black ticks through the hackle, but I think fanciers are agreed that the almond feather is not suitable in any pigeon with white markings, such as the baldhead or pouter, and that, however well it might look in its early beauty, it would not compare with black, red, and yellow in their best tints, when it began to darken with age.

The beard tumbler, like the preceding, is found in black, blue, silver, red, and yellow. The ordinary variety of flying tumbling beard is similar in size, &c., to the common baldhead and other tumblers. It is always clean legged, as far as I have noticed. Its correct marking is the following: The upper mandible should be coloured, though reds and yellows may have it white, and the lower in all cases white. The beard, from which the bird has its name, is a dash of white extending from eye to eye across the throat. Commencing below the eye as a point, it widens to about half an inch below the beak, and it should be exactly alike on each cheek. This is the marking as described in the treatise before mentioned, but another style of beard, known as the pepper-faced or peppered beard, has this dash of white, sprinkled with coloured feathers. I think this is an undesirable marking, though it was liked by many in days gone by. There are also beards with a coloured line down the throat, dividing the white into two parts. In addition to the white beard, the flights should be white to the turn, and the tail with its coverts, upper and under, should be white; all else should be coloured. I am aware that it is not easy to get beards entirely dark thighed, with ten white flights a side; but that is no reason why the standard should be reduced. Such birds have been seen, and are all the more valuable because scarce. It is considered that seven or eight a side is good enough for a dark-thighed bird, but I have had a strain of tumblers with far less white about them than the beard—viz., blacks, all coloured except the primary flights, which were white, and they bred true. And when beards are once got full-flighted and dark-thighed they will breed true after a time, though it may be difficult to fix such marking without trouble. Standards of excellence in pigeons should be standards difficult of attainment, and they should also be artistically beautiful and original to entitle them to support. Although the beard ought not to be entirely dark-thighed, there is always some white where the feathers finish off at the hocks, but the less of this the better. The beard ought to have pearl eyes, and as the whole head above the eyes is coloured, this is not a difficult point to maintain.

In blue beards the hens are always smoky in colour, and I have never seen any of a good bright blue. This fault appears to be in the breed, as it is in some other breeds of blue-marked pigeons. It might possibly be eradicated by crossing blue beard cocks with good coloured whole blue hens; but such experiments take years to complete, and when the result is so remote and the reward uncertain, who will be at the trouble of it, neglecting what might truly be reckoned more important work in the fancy? Black, blue, and silver beards of the common flying tumbler type were, when I kept them in my boyhood, capital flyers and tumblers.

The long-faced beard is a pigeon marked the same as the common one, but a much larger bird, and measuring from 1¼in. to 1½in. in face, *i.e.*, from the centre of the eye to the point of the beak, or even more. I am not aware if it ever tumbles, but I believe generally not. It was most likely produced from the beard and dragoon, and carefully bred for marking, length of face, and absence of wattle. It was formerly much used as a match flyer and messenger, being capable of doing over 100 miles. I think it must have been produced in London, for I never read of it in any foreign pigeon book. I have only seen blacks and blues of this variety, and the latter are often good in colour in both sexes, which is probably some slight proof of its dragoon descent.

A flight of balds and beards, assorted in colour, is a pretty sight. In clear weather the white markings tell well against the coloured body at a considerable height in the air. To make them fly high and well together, however, they require all the attention necessary in raising a flight of tumblers, and they must not be allowed continual liberty, otherwise they will give little satisfaction as high flyers.

For those who employ feeders for all small high-class pigeons they answer every requirement, being careful nurses and breeders the year through, except in the depth of winter; and when they are kept for this purpose alone they are all the better for unlimited freedom, as in country places they gather much green food and other things serviceable in the rearing of young birds, which they could not procure if kept confined.

Foreign Tumblers.

The tumbler is as great a favourite abroad as with us, and it is distributed everywhere on the continent of Europe in great variety. In my youthful days, and probably still, though I never now watch the arrival of Baltic traders as I then did, vessels from Russia often brought to Dundee what we used to call Riga tumblers. They were self-coloured blacks, reds, and yellows, of large size, with heavily feathered legs and feet, the quills on the latter often 4in. in length, and with a large shell crest. Indeed, they were very similar in shape and size to the trumpeter as we then had it, and they only wanted the rose on the forehead to complete their trumpeter appearance. They were good in colour and good performers. I have not seen any of them for several years, and I am unaware if they are still to the fore in this country.

Neumeister, on plate 7 of his book, figures nine tumblers. Two of them, a red and yellow, are *Calottentauben*, which I have already described as the helmet. Four others, black, red, yellow, and blue, are *Elstertümmlertauben*, described by me under the magpie. Another is a yellow wholefeather, and the remaining two are a pair of beards, a red and a black. These beards are marked differently from ours, having only the white beard and white flights, the tail and all else being coloured. His description of them is as follows:—"*Der farbigweisspiessige Tümmler* (the coloured, white-spotted tumbler). This variety has under the bill mostly a white beard of the size of a pea" (not so in the illustration, however, but a beard from eye to eye); "the six or eight pinions are white, and if the tail is coloured, there must be no white feathers below the rump. However, if the tail is white, this pigeon goes by the name of white tail; if head and tail are white, it is called whitehead tumbler." I have seen yellow whole feathered, stocking-legged German tumblers, in no way different in size and appearance from British ones, but with what Neumeister calls a swan's neck. After the cock played up to his hen there was a tremulous quivering motion in their necks, similar to that in the fantail and mookee, but different in degree, not being so heaving and prolonged, but quicker and sooner over. These were shown me by Mr. O. Neef, of Forest Hill, who also had some beautiful silver magpie tumblers, with stocking legs. On their coloured breasts, however, they had a small crescent-shaped mark of white. These tumblers, both yellows and silver magpies, had nothing to distinguish them in head and beak from ordinary British flying tumblers, but Mr. Neef had also the wonderful and highly bred German tumblers, known as Ancients (Altstämmer), which bear the same relation to ordinary tumblers as our short-faces do, though they are very different from them in head and beak; but they require a separate description, being, like our short-faces, a race far removed from ordinary tumblers.

Neumeister likewise mentions the following: "As excellent flying pigeons are especially to be mentioned the Berlin, the Prague dappled, the Magdeburg, the Dantzig highflyer, the Vienna riser, the white

Stralsund, the Hallerstadt, the Vienna Gamsel, the Dutch Flüchter (among which are the so-called chimney sweepers), the Hanoverian (soloflier), and the Brunswick white-pointed beard tumblers, which latter, castrated, occur frequently as flying pigeons, and have proved excellent as such. The castration must not take place too prematurely."

I suppose castrating tumblers is quite unknown in this country. A bird treated in this way will, of course, always be of service for the training of the young birds, having no parental duties to perform, and this is no doubt the purpose in view. It was something new to me to read the above, as I had never known of this practice in all my experience before.

Besides all these, Herr Prütz, in his "Die Arten der Haustaube," describes still another tumbler, as follows: "As exceedingly interesting we mention here the brander, one of the few three-coloured pigeons. The whole body is copper brown, only at the ends of the wings and the tail the original black colour appears. Where the copper brown has remained rather dark on the body, the black colour likewise is more predominant on the ends of the wings and tail, *videlicet*, both then appear more black than brown. The legs are smooth, the eyes pearl-coloured. The brander is principally bred in Copenhagen, formerly in great numbers in Rostock, and is very much to be recommended as a flying pigeon." This is a literal translation, but it is not clear to me, from it, how the brander is a three-coloured pigeon. Copper brown, with more or less black on the flights and tail, seems to indicate two distinct colours only.

There is no great variety of the tumbler race mentioned by Boitard and Corbie. While the British and German names for these birds are alike, the French call the common tumbler, *Pigeon Culbutant Pantomime*, "because that also by their fantastical movements they imitate in some manner the grotesque gestures and leaps of certain mountebanks." They affirm that "in 1817 the English bought in France all that they could find for sale." They describe a variety called the *Culbutant Savoyard*, which is similar to the common kind in form, but which has a plumage "streaked, or rather daubed over, with white, grey, fawn, and black." This seems to be a light almond or almond splash.

A distinct variety of the tumbler has been lately introduced into this country from Turkey by Mr. H. P. Caridia, of Birmingham, under the name of the Turkish or oriental roller. Besides being said to possess all the qualities of a first-rate flier and performer, it is of an original forma-

Satinette.   Blondinette.   Turbiteen.   Visor.
Domino.

TURBIT FANCY PIGEONS.

tion. They were first described and illustrated by Mr. J. W. Ludlow, of Birmingham, in the *Fanciers' Gazette* of 20th June, 1874. They are longer in head and beak than our tumblers, the head being flatter, and wanting the high forehead, and the beak thicker and stronger. The neck is rather short, as are the legs. The back is hollow, and the tail is carried rather elevated and over the flights. The tail is the most peculiar feature in their formation, it being long and composed of from fourteen to twenty-two feathers, the average being about sixteen. These feathers have no approach or resemblance to a fantail, but lie one over the other in two divisions, showing a slight division or split between them. As is common with other varieties having an abnormal number of tail feathers, a double feather growing from one quill is often seen in this breed. They also want the oil gland above the tail. They are of many colours, such as black, white, dun, and almond splash, the blacks being well lustred, and with white black-tipped beaks—as is usual with good-coloured blacks among British tumblers. I have not had any of these rollers myself, but Mr. Ludlow, from whose description I have gathered the above, asserts that they are capital performers and fliers.

CHAPTER LVIII.

THE SHORT-FACED TUMBLER PIGEON.

THE ALMOND.

SOON after the death of John Moore, author of the "Columbarium," a variety of tumbler called the Almond became in great estimation in London, and supplanted the pouter and carrier in the lofts of many breeders. We are enabled to trace its history with some degree of accuracy. There is no doubt that its cultivation began before Moore wrote, as will be seen from the following passage in his book, where he says, in writing of tumblers: "But amongst all, there is Mixture of three Colours, vulgarly call'd an Almond, perhaps from the quantity of Almond colour'd Feathers that are found in the Hackle: Others call it an Ermine, I suppose from the black Spots that are generally in it; however I am sensible the Name is not compatible to the Term so call'd in Heraldry, which is only white spotted with black; yet as the Gentlemen of the Fancy have assign'd this Name to this mottley Colour, I shan't quarrel with them about a Term: if the three Colours run thro' the Feathers of the Flight and Tail, it is reckon'd a very good Almond, or Ermine, and is much valued.

"N.B.—An ermine Tumbler never comes to the full Beauty of its Feather, till it has twice molted off, and when it grows very old will decline, till it runs away to a down-right Mottle or other Colour."

The almond tumbler was therefore very much valued, when the three colours ran through the flights and tail, as early as 1735; and a standard had by that time been established for it in regard to feather. But it seems unlikely, if it was then anything else than an almond feathered common tumbler, that Moore would have omitted to describe its peculiarities of head, beak, and carriage. It seems probable, therefore, that at this date it had not altered much in size and shape from the common tumblers, among which he described it as a variety.

Thirty years afterwards, the almond tumbler had made great progress in London, for it is described by the author of the treatise of 1765 at length, and as then distinct in character from the common tumblers. It was then "a very small Pigeon, with a short body, short legs, a full chest, a thin neck, a very short and spindle beak, and a round button head, and the iris of the eye a bright pearl colour." But the illustration which accompanied this description was disappointing, as it represented a pigeon of a much commoner type compared to the modern short-faced tumbler, than some of the other illustrations were, compared to their modern representatives. The author had, however, become enamoured of the almond, and considered that the title of the King of Pigeons, conferred by former fanciers on the carrier, would with greater propriety be conferred on the new favourite. Some of the reasons he gives for this opinion are its exceeding beauty and diversity of plumage, its increasing value—twenty guineas having been paid for five pairs, and those not of the best—and the ease with which it could be bred, compared with the pouter and carrier. Then, after dilating through four pages over the difficulties of pouter breeding, he adds, "The above, and many other inconveniences too tedious to mention attending the pouter, and no trouble at all (comparatively speaking) attending the other, easily accounts for the preference given to the almond tumbler," which requires "no attendance while breeding, provided you supply them with meat and water, and throw them a little straw." Considering that he himself quotes a sale of pouters by auction, where the prices realised were as high as sixteen guineas a pair, and that Moore had known eight guineas refused for a single pouter, the price of the almond tumblers—two guineas each—was nothing great; but then he says they were not the best, and probably some of the lot of five pairs were worth much more than the average price of the lot.

The fancy for the almond tumbler was now established, and the year before (1764), a standard had been published setting forth the perfections and imperfections of the bird. This was entitled "Ordinances, established by the Columbarian Society," and was headed by a picture of an almond, "elegantly engraved on copperplate." The almond went on increasing in popularity after this, and the knowledge of its name, at least, became widely known, so that people who would not have recognised it though they had seen it, had heard of the celebrated almond tumbler.

The *Sporting Magazine*, soon after its commencement in 1792, had a portrait of a choice specimen, and in 1802 a monograph on the breed was published in London by "An Old Fancier." The author was Mr. W. P. Windus, a solicitor, a member and afterwards the president of the Columbarian Society. An engraved circular, dated 1813, headed by a picture of an almond and signed by him, calling a meeting of the society, is in my possession. His treatise was the first book ever published on a single variety of the domestic pigeon, and it goes thoroughly into its subject. We learn from it that though it had been necessary to limit the length of face, from the point of the beak to the iris or inner circle of the eye, to seven-eighths of an inch, it was usual, when he wrote, to see birds scarcely six-eighths in face, so that a great improvement had been made.

In 1851, Mr. Eaton, an enthusiastic fancier of the almond tumbler, published another monograph on the breed, so that this pigeon has been twice honoured above all other fancy varieties. Mr. Eaton's book is an unacknowledged reprint of the 1802 one, with additions, describing the almond as it was in his day, and this brings us down to modern times.

Although it is expressly stated by the author of the treatise (1765), that "This beautiful and very valuable species were originally produced from the common tumblers, being properly matched so as to intermix the feather, viz., blacks, black-grisles, black-splash'd, yellows, whites, duns, &c., and are always attainable if you are endowed with patience sufficient for the tedious process, which requires a length of time," I have to submit, that as regards the almond feather alone, it is not confined to the tumbler. He himself mentions an almond barb and an almond narrow-tailed shaker, which was purchased by a certain nobleman, and I have seen almond runts and almond feathered pigeons in India, besides a very good commencement for this colour in a yellow ground, broken to some extent with black, in turbits and jacobins. The oriental roller is also to be got of a light almond. The short-faced tumbler, however, independent of colour, is a different matter, and how it was produced is a question worth some attention. Not to admit the possibility of its origin from the common tumbler alone, would be a denial of all I have advanced when writing of the origin of fancy pigeons; but certain facts having presented themselves to me in my experience and observation of pigeons, I have acquired the belief that the short-faced tumbler is a composite breed, and was derived from the common tumbler and some other varieties. When in India, the love of pigeons which has possessed me since I could crawl, caused me to associate with pigeon fanciers there; and when I saw a race of birds (the Goolees), having all the shape and carriage of the short-faced tumblers, of much the same size and of the same style of head, it struck me, that as the Mookee had been described by Willughby in 1676, the Goolee might also have been in England at that time, and have helped to found the breed of short-faces.

About two years ago, being in London, I met Mr. Jayne, of Croydon, one of the principal breeders of almond tumblers, and as he invited me to see his stud of birds, I gladly availed myself of the opportunity. After seeing his stock, I asked him if he believed that the short-faced tumbler had been bred from the common tumbler and nothing else. He replied that it was the result of crosses between the tumbler and other varieties, that the African owl had been used in producing it, and that his friend, the late Mr. Morey, was the only man he ever knew who could give its true history. Eaton, in his 1858 book, at page 187, says, "the late Mr. Harry Edward Morey, chairman of the City Columbarian Society, and an excellent old fancier, used to say, however low his stud of birds was reduced, he had never been without pigeons for the last sixty years." The combined evidence of Mr. Jayne and Mr. Morey, therefore, goes back to the last century, and it is probable enough that Mr. Morey had spoken, in his youth, to men who had been pigeon fanciers before the treatise of 1765 was ever designed, and that was about the time the almond tumbler became of consequence in the fancy. Since speaking with Mr. Jayne on this subject, I found in the *Field* newspaper of Oct. 19, 1872, a report of an address he delivered to the members of the National Peristeronic Society, when he was president. His subject was "The Almond Tumbler," and I quote the following sentences: "You are aware my only hobby has been a short-faced pigeon, and of all the varieties none can equal, in my idea, the almond tumbler; if for no other reason, I should admire it as a purely English manufactured pigeon. How often and how deeply have I lamented that I allowed to escape the knowledge of this beautiful bird possessed by my esteemed companion, the late Mr. Morey. He was the only person that I ever heard give a description of the thirty-two crosses by which this almond tumbler was produced."

Without having seen Mr. Jayne and conversed with him on the subject, I should not have known what to understand by the thirty-two crosses he refers to—whether they were merely crosses of different coloured tumblers to produce the almond feather, or of other breeds of fancy pigeons as well, to produce the short-faced tumbler. The latter is what he meant, and as the knowledge Mr. Morey possessed is lost, all I can say is that there is good evidence for my belief, that the short-face has something more in its composition than the common tumbler.

The pictures of the almond tumbler in the Treatises of 1765, 1802, and 1851 show the gradual improvements made in eighty-six years. I do not put much stress on the wings being carried over the tail in those of 1765 and 1802, as they might have been so represented on account of trailing wings being considered faulty. Windus says, regarding carriage: "The bird should stand low, with a fine, prominent, and full, or, as the Fanciers term it, a square chest, which is thrown up considerably by the bird's elevating himself on tiptoe, and thereby depressing his tail, so that the point of it touches the flooring of the area, penn, or whatever place he stands upon." And yet a picture of an almond carrying his tail off the ground and over his trailing wings had appeared about ten years before he wrote this, and his own circular, dated 1813, in my possession, is headed by the picture on page 13 of his book, so that he evidently altered his opinion from that expressed above.

As interesting to the fancier of short-faces, on account of the light it throws on the materials used about eighty years ago for breeding almonds, I here give a copy of a little handbill in my possession, which is probably unique. I found it, with the circular signed by Windus, in a copy of the 1802 treatise, which has the autograph of Thos. Garle, jun., 7th Feb. 1809. The reward offered would imply that the pigeons were valuable. Though the bill is undated, the type shows it to have been issued not later than 1810. The old letter s, like f, is used, while the modern s is used in the treatise of 1802, but as old type might have been employed for such purposes after it had been laid aside for books, I give the date as above, though it might have been much earlier.

Fifteen Guineas
REWARD.

WHEREAS the DOVE-HOUSE of MR. PARR, of *Bethnal-Green*, was on FRIDAY Night, the 13th inst., BROKE OPEN, and the following
TWELVE TUMBLER PIGEONS
Stole therein:

A very fine Feathered ALMOND COCK, small Size, remarkable bright Pearl Eyes, fine Beak, the end of upper Bill rather Brown, owing to the Canker when young.

A Rich ALMOND COCK, large size, a little White on the Back of his Neck, no Yellow in his Tail except a little in the middle of one Feather, a Brown mark on one side of his Neck in front.
A Rich ALMOND COCK, small short Body, good Shape, Pearl Eyes, and fine Beak.
A Broad-Chested SPLASH COCK, stands low, bold Head, Pearl Eyes, fine Beak which droops at the Point, stocking Leg'd.
Another SPLASH COCK, small round Head, Pearl Eyes, short straight Beak
A Soft Ground HEN, round Head, good Shape, a few rich Dun Feathers about her Neck and Flights, stocking Leg'd, a little broken Eyed.
A DUN HEN, fine Pearl Eyes, straight Beak, rather thin Face.
An ALMOND HEN, strong Ground, a few Kite Feathers in her Left Flight, bright Pearl Eyes, and fine straight Beak.
A remarkable clear BLACK SPLASH COCK, Pearl Eyes, round Head, a little coarse in Beak & Wattle.
A large dark SPLASH COCK, lofty round Head, broken Eyes, short down Beak.
A soft ground ALMOND COCK, dull pearl Eyes.
Also a RED COCK, his right Wing only two thirds grown.
Whoever will discover the Offender or Offenders, shall on Recovery of the said Pigeons. receive FIVE GUINEAS, and in Proportion for any Part thereof; and on Conviction, a further Reward of TEN GUINEAS to be paid by Mr. PARR, No. 103, *Holborn-Hill*.
Or if any Person will give Mr. PARR a Hint respecting the said Robbery, his Name shall be kept secret, and fully satisfied for such Information.

It will have been noticed that Mr. Jayne mentioned the African owl as a progenitor of the short-faced tumbler. The first pair of these beautiful pigeons known to the present generation were exhibited within the past twenty-five years, but that they were known in this country in the last century I quite believe, and Mr. Jayne had, no doubt, very good reasons for his statement, Mr. Morey probably having mentioned such birds as part of the composition of the short-face.

Having, therefore, considered at some length the history of the short-faced tumbler, so far as I have been able to trace it, I now come to a consideration of the bird as it exists. The almond feathered short-face first demands my attention, both because it has always been considered the representative of its race, and because it best answers the standard of perfection laid down. It has always been a matter of speculation, from Moore downwards, why this pigeon got the name of *almond* tumbler, and it has generally been supposed that it was so called from the almond nut coloured feathers which compose its ground tint. The nut itself, as also the shell, both inside and outside, in all stages from ripe to rotten, have been fixed on by authorities as "the reason why." I could never see why only one of the colours in this bird should give it its name, and think that a whole feathered yellow pigeon would be more appropriately called an almond. I incline to the belief that the name is not derived from either the nut or its shell, but that, as suggested by Brent, the word almond is a corruption of *Allemand*, the French word signifying German, and that almond feathered pigeons of some sort, brought from France under the name of *Allemand* pigeons, originated the name. Such coloured French tumbler pigeons are described by Boitard and Corbie in 1824, as the *Pigeon culbutant Savoyard*, as I have already mentioned.

Taking the almond as the representation of all the short-faced tumblers, it may be described as a very small pigeon, only larger than the African owl, and it is generally said to have five properties of feather, carriage, head, beak, and eye.

Feather.—A standard almond is one having its twelve primary tail feathers, and its primary flights, whether nine or ten a side, composed of the three colours, black, red, and yellow. A bird of nine a side, all standard feathers, is preferable, in my opinion, to one with ten a side having only nine in each wing standard feathers, because it is full flighted ; but if the bird with ten a side had only the shortest flight in each wing out in colour, it would be much nearer perfection than if any of its other flights were wrong in colour. There are, however, so many other properties in the almond, that it is unlikely that such close competition will often arise but where it is a case of showing standard birds only, the whole of the flight feathers, whether nine or ten a side, must show the three colours. The ground colour of the almond should be of as deep and rich a yellow as can be got ; but it is generally either mealy and spotty in colour, or of a reddish yellow, which can neither be called red nor yellow, like unpolished mahogany wood. As the most difficult thing is to produce the bright yellow ground, which, indeed, has been seen but seldom, it is the point of most consequence ; in fact, however good in head and beak a bird may be, it is not a real almond if it has not the ground colour. If the bird does not come out of the nest of a good ground colour on back, wings, and rump, it can never attain to it later in life. The ground colour being right, it must be pencilled over with black, of as intense a deepness as possible, not in any particular pattern, but to show well as a whole. This pencilling ought to increase with the autumnal moults till the bird is from two to three years of age, when it comes to its best, after which it gets annually darker, till it becomes more black than yellow, and the tail and flights lose their standard character through absence of white. Even then the bird is beautiful, though past its best from a standard point of view. In the Treatise (1765) the author says, at page 57, "I have had some in my collection that have had few feathers in them but what have contained the three colours that constitute the almond or ermine, viz., black, white, and yellow, variously and richly interspersed." This has been often quoted as to mean that the three colours should run through all the feathers of the almond; but no white must appear elsewhere than in flights and tail at any period of the bird's existence. When the ground colour is only a yellow tinged with white, it is called an almond splash, and to breed from such is to go backwards, and is like breeding from bad coloured pigeons of any sort. The almond tumbler is one of the varieties which show a sexual difference in colouring, the hens for the most part being weaker in their ground colour than the cocks, though there are exceptions, and wanting the black pencilling evenly distributed over the body. There is generally less break in the feather, and the black is seldom of so deep a tint. A really good hen takes longer to come to perfection than a cock, and consequently remains longer in feather. There is also no such thing as a standard feathered hen in flights and tail, or, at least, such is of the greatest rarity.

Carriage.—The shape and carriage of the almond is the next property to be mentioned. The breast ought to be broad and prominent, the neck short and thin, the back hollow, the rump rather full, and the tail carried above the flights, which should touch the ground, but not drag on it. The head should be thrown back, and the bird should walk on tiptoe on short unfeathered legs. Nothing is more attractive than excellent carriage in an almond, and it is a sign of good blood; for, however fine a bird may be in its other properties, it never can look well without good carriage. Shape and carriage have been called one and the same thing; but a bird may have all the necessary conformation, and yet lack that spirit and vivaciousness which enables it to carry itself properly. The almond shows best when salacious, and when driving his hen to nest.

Beak.—Two distinct forms of beak are seen in short-faces, and that which is most generally admired, and which I admire, is what is known as the goldfinch beak, which is formed like that of the well-known song bird. The goldfinch beak, from its shape, is generally longer, and more inclined to keep growing at the point than the other form of beak, which more resembles a grain of barley, dipping a little at the end. The goldfinch form is, however, so distinct from the beak of any other variety of pigeon, that, in my opinion, it is the most worthy of encouragement; but whichever style of beak the short-face may have, it must be straight out from its head, with neither an upward nor downward inclination, and as short and as fine as possible. The beak wattle should be small and delicate in appearance, any coarseness being considered a great fault. The portrait of an almond by Wolstenholme, in Eaton's books, shows the perfect beak.

Head.—The head ought to be very lofty, broad, and overhanging the beak if it can be got. Though the skull itself may not do so, the feathers growing out from the forehead sometimes give it that appearance in a fine bird, which then has a deep stop or indentation at the root of the beak. The head itself ought to be round from all points of view, and when the cheek feathers are puffed out, or muffed, as it is called, it adds wonderfully to the natty appearance of the short-face.

Eye.—The iris ought to be white or pearl coloured and surrounded by a fine and narrow eye wattle, of which the less there is the better. A full and prominent eye adds greatly to the appearance. The faults of eye are a reddish pearl, a dusky or clouded iris, and a broken eye, which looks very bad and spoils the appearance of any bird.

As the almond feather is a composite one, made up of various colours, it is preserved by the judicious crossing of its various sub-varieties, such as kites, duns, agates, and wholefeathers. Kites are of various shades, from such as are almost black, with only the primaries bronzed with yellow, to such as have the yellow cast on their feathers more or less all over them, especially on the breast. Duns also show the yellow on their neck and breast feathers when rich in colour, and are then called golden duns. Duns are almost invariably hens, and when bred from two well-grounded almonds, are useful for matching with a rich almond. Agates are such as are red or yellow, splashed or mottled with white. They are of various markings, some showing a preponderance of colour, and others of white. Wholefeathers are either red or yellow, and when sound in colour through flights and tail (which is sometimes seen in reds and very rarely in yellows), they are both valuable for almond breeding and for themselves, as they are the choicest of the sub-varieties of the almond. Black splashes, or what might be called black agates, appear to have been formerly used in almond breeding; but this colour seems to have been bred entirely out of our modern birds, which is perhaps the cause of the black pencilling in our almonds being usually of a kitey or dun black; and on this account a cross of a good black mottle or mottle-bred black might be of advantage. Even the darkest kites always show a smoky tail barred at the end with darker colour, and however much such birds may assist in breaking the feather in almond breeding, they cannot impart the desired velvety black colour. Red and yellow wholefeathers, grizzled with white in flights and tail, or agate wholefeathers, as they have been called, are merely unsound reds and yellows, weak in strength of colour. All these sub-varieties of the almond are used in almond breeding, and they are matched with almonds according to the way they are themselves bred. Although it is not unusual to breed almonds together occasionally, such breeding, from richly-grounded ones, often results in young ones entirely or almost white, with what are called bladder eyes, almost or quite blind. When such a result happens, the pair must be dismatched at once, and some of the off colours used. I have seen a pair of almonds produce all the colours I have mentioned except blacks and black splashes, so it will easily be seen that there is much uncertainty in the production of this beautiful pigeon, and that it is a study in itself. When I was young in the fancy I thought the almond tumbler the finest and the most beautiful of all pigeons, and I was never weary of admiring my first pair, which were Spitalfields bred birds, and which cost me a sum of £5. It is over twenty years ago since then, but I well remember that I bred five birds from them during their first season (two almond cocks, an almond hen, and two golden dun hens), which realised me £12, and pigeons were cheaper in those days than of late years.

Since the secret, so well kept for so long, and which was in reality a trade secret, of manufacturing the heads of short-faced tumblers, was given to the world in Fulton's book of pigeons, the almond fancy has declined; but after a time it will rise again, when the importance attached to the head of the bird gives way to its other beautiful properties. There is enough in the natural short-faced tumbler in all its varieties to entitle it to the position of a very high class pigeon. The shaping of the skull, which is begun when the squab is a few days old and continued during its growth in the nest, is done by pressing with a wooden instrument, shaped for the purpose, or with the thumb nail, at the root of its beak, and so forcing the bone back into the head, which gives breadth, height, and a deep stop. This is a cruel process, which kills many in the doing, and which renders the lives of those that survive it for the most part miserable. No pigeon is so much troubled with vermin as the short-face, as it is wholly unable, with its tiny beak, to free itself from them; and when the beak is distorted in the shaping of the skull, as it often is, it is then quite unfit to keep itself free from parasites. The signs to know a made-faced bird are, first, when it is up-faced, which is never natural; and if the lower mandible protrudes beyond the upper at the point, it may be taken as certain that the operator has been at work. Wry beaks are, no doubt, often produced naturally in short-faces, but there is something about a natural wry beak different from one which is the effect of shaping the skull. The natural wry beak, though crossing at the point, generally fits closely further back, which is not the case with the other. As I have seen many short-faces of high quality which I know were never tampered with when young, I would not condemn the whole race, as some do, because manipulated birds may sometimes get away undetected; but I would hold for absolute disqualification of all birds which clearly showed they had been tampered with, because the whole system of making heads is a swindle, and only done to obtain money under false pretences.

Many a man has gone into the short-faced fancy, and finding he could never produce birds anything like so good as those he began with, for the simple reason that they were unnatural, has given it up in bewilderment; or, learning how the thing was done, he has become a modeller himself, and then cheated others as he was cheated himself. The decline in this fancy is principally on account of the unsatisfactoriness of merely producing quality in pigeons by hand. Honest men wish to *breed* quality, not to *make* it with a wooden spoon. I think it may be safely said, that when a bird does not show that something has been done to it, there has been so little done that it may be allowed to pass as natural; but when the skull has been forced in, the upper mandible is always displaced to a certain extent, and a bird showing this should invariably be passed over. The under mandible may be turned up, but it cannot be forced back. I think that it depends on the judges whether the short-faced fancy is to decline still further, or whether it is to rise again. The short-face itself is naturally a charming pigeon, beautiful in all its standard colourings and original in many ways; but it has occupied a higher position in the fancy than it was entitled to, probably on account of being a native production. It may be safely left to find its own level.

Since writing the foregoing, there has come into my possession a set of eight life-size oil paintings of fancy pigeons, one of which is an almond tumbler. From a careful study of them, I conclude they are the work of a faithful and conscientious artist, and if not older than Moore's "Columbarium," they are at least older than the treatise of 1765. As I shall have to notice several of them later on, I shall defer stating my reasons for fixing their age at present. The almond represents a common tumbler in shape and general style, carrying its wings over its tail. It is a rich feathered bird, showing white in its flight feathers. I may also here mention that two of the set represent varieties I have already written of —the nun and helmet. The nun is a black, full flighted as far as shown, having the eight primaries in sight, coloured. It has a very deep bib, a very full shell, and a pure white iris. The helmet is a red, of the kind Moore mentions, marked as the nun with coloured flights, smooth headed, and with a red pearl iris. The pictures are evidently portraits, as many little faults are represented, which would have been left out had the artist meant to depict perfect birds.

The Mottle.

As already pointed out, from the "Treatise on Pigeons" of 1765, and from the old handbill, black splashes and black grizzles were formerly sub-varieties of the short-faced almond tumbler. These gradually settled down into a separate variety, and are referred to at page 64 of that book, as follows : "There was also a prize last season for black mottled tumblers, whose properties should agree with those of the almond tumbler, except the feather, which should be a black ground, the body mottled with white, with a black tail and flight ; and when they are in perfection they are an excessively pretty fancy, and very valuable. There is also another very pretty fancy, equal at least, if not superior to the black mottled—viz., the yellow mottled tumbler, whose properties likewise agree with the almond tumbler, except the feather, which should be a yellow ground, the body mottled with white, and a yellow flight and tail. Either of these two last mentioned fancies are extremely useful (provided they answer in their other properties) to intermix occasionally with the almond." The illustration of the mottle accompanying the remarks represents a long-legged common-looking type of tumbler, with a black flight and tail, and white body, over which are dotted about thirty-four well separated black feathers. I scarcely think it represents the author's intentions, as he expressly says, "a black ground, the body mottled with white." The mottle may, however, be said to have been then in its infancy, and a standard more difficult of attainment would soon be aimed at. The present standard is the same as mentioned for the mottled flying tumbler, viz., a self-coloured pigeon with a rose pinion of single well separated white feathers on the shoulder, either with or without the V-shaped handkerchief back, but with it for choice. This standard of feather, accompanying good short-face properties of head, back, eye, and carriage, makes up one of the most difficult standards in fancy pigeons to breed at all good. When a fancier, with such experience of short-faced tumblers as Mr. Fulton, has said that he has only seen a few pairs of mottles that could even be trimmed into something like perfection, and that the nearest approach to a perfect bird he ever knew of had to be weeded on both breast and shoulders, it will be seen how much remains to be done for the short-faced mottle; whoever follows after this fancy, then, has not only to contend against made heads, as in the almond, but also against trimming, which can do but little for the latter, and so he sets himself a difficult task. Perhaps, there have been but few long-faced mottles ever produced anything like perfectly marked; but there are certain inherent faults of marking in the short-faced mottle, as it exists, which makes it harder to produce than the long-faced. There still exists, however, what may be called the remnants of a good strain of black mottles, in which the ground colour is good, but which are much inclined to a blaze of white on the forehead, and to orange instead of white eyes. Both are great faults, and a white eyed bird has only to be seen by the side of a yellow or orange eyed one to show how very much better it looks. From the amount of colour in the mottle there is but little to contend with in the way of broken eyes, as in the almond. In head and beak, though sometimes passable, they are never so broad nor so lofty as the best almonds, while in carriage they are sometimes very good indeed, which is a great set-off to their appearance. In breeding black mottles the blaze face should be avoided, however good they may otherwise be, and it might be eradicated in time, as in black pied pouters, which nearly always had it twenty years ago.

About eight years ago, I bought two pairs of black mottles from the late Mr. James Ford, of London, who then had a good strain of them. Two of them were very fairly marked, and the others were mottle-bred black wholefeathers of the same strain. As the mottles were quite free of blaze on the forehead, I managed to keep it out of the great proportion of the produce; but the orange eye, which one of the whole feathers had, was difficult to alter, the best marked young ones generally coming with it. I found that a bird which had any white on it as a nestling became too gay when it moulted off, and that when a bird moulted something like what a mottle ought to be, it came out of the nest all black. There was, therefore, no distinguishing between what were to become fair mottles or remain wholefeathers till after the first moult. Dun mottles are occasionally bred from blacks, and they are useful for breeding back to blacks, but dun being an off-colour, few care for them.

Red and yellow mottles would each be more difficult to keep good in colour than blacks; but I am not aware that any long standing strain of either is in existence. In almond breeding, both red and yellow agates are often produced well marked to the mottle standard. These, however, have generally a weak, washed-out colour in flight and tail feathers, and white rumps as well; but it is from the judicious breeding of such with red and yellow wholefeathers and agate wholefeathers, that a strain of red and yellow mottles might be produced. Such red and yellow mottles as were in existence when the fancy for them was at its best, were doubtless produced in this way.

Considering the difficulty there is in producing short-faced mottles, and remembering the fact that none have ever been seen naturally perfect in marking, it is a question if the standard of feather for them is not too high. A standard that would allow of white feathers on the head, neck, breast, wings, and back; but retaining the entirely dark flights, tail, rump, and under body, would be a pleasing one. There would also be great difficulty in keeping the white feathers separate, as they are always inclined to run together.

THE BLUE.

There is another whole-feathered short-faced tumbler now seldom seen—viz., the blue. It was formerly bred to great perfection in London. Eaton, who has a picture of one in his treatise of 1858, says: "I cannot by any possibility let the opportunity pass, without noticing the observations and great admiration the venerable and much-respected old Fanciers bestow upon the amazingly pretty little compact sky or powder blue whole-feather, with its black bars, black as ebony; the short-faced head and beak, with its other properties—the pretty little blue tumbler. Whenever they have the opportunity to see one, I have almost fancied they would have gone into fits, in observing a good one with its five splendid properties—head, beak, eye, carriage or shape, and feather. It appeared to me almost to make them boys again; it has as great or greater an effect upon them as going to the mill to be ground young again. Unfortunately, it is seldom you have the opportunity to see one; they are very scarce at this time (1858)."

It was soon after this time, in 1862, that I saw in the possession of Mr. Fulton, who then lived in Deptford, a very fine pair of short-faced blue tumblers. I have often spoken to him about them since, and I believe such good birds as they were are not now in existence. Though probably made faced, they were broad and lofty in skull, with splendid colour and fine carriage.

BALDHEADS AND BEARDS.

Short-faced baldheads of good quality are now extremely scarce. They have always been rare, but formerly there were at least some very fair ones in blacks, blues, and silvers. Blacks are scarcest at the present time, and it is now nearly twenty years since I have seen a good pair of that colour, which were sent by Mr. Fulton to a gentleman in Scotland. They were good in colour, head, and eye, but low cut. During the past ten or fifteen years, short-faced balds have been represented chiefly by the strain of Mr. Woodhouse, who has shown blues and silvers, with which he has carried off most of the prizes at the principal shows, where classes were given for balds. Red and yellow balds have lately been shown of very fair colour and quality, and I understand they were produced from a cross with the almond and its sub-varieties. They were bred by Mr. Burchett, a London fancier, who sold off a year or two ago, when they were distributed among the breeders of this very beautiful and interesting variety. The standard of feather for the short-faced is the same as for the long-faced bald; but there are very few, if any, really well marked ones in existence, which combine high shortfaced properties of head, beak, eye, and carriage. Compared to the best almonds they are far behind, and all I have seen, which I knew to be untampered with about the head, could only be called pleasant faced at the best. I have, however, seen of late several of each colour—excepting the blacks, which seem nowhere at present— manufactured into very passable ones. I say manufactured,

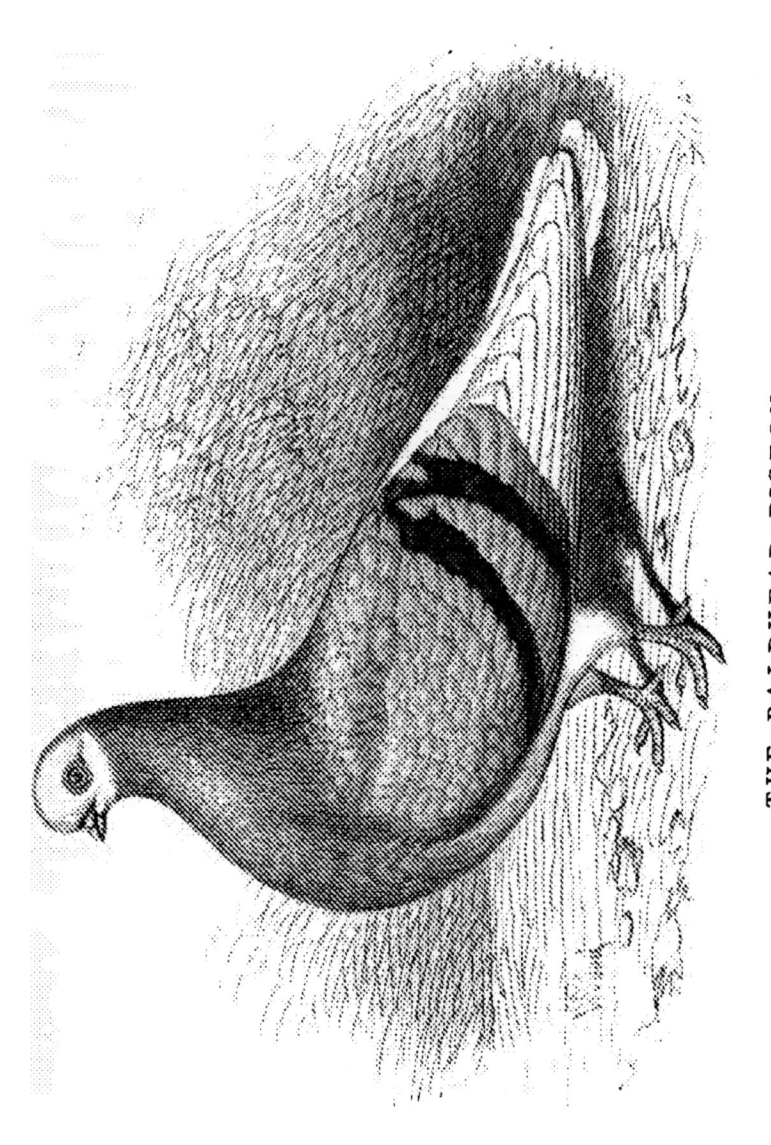

THE BALDHEAD PIGEON.

because it was plain from their appearance that they had been tampered with, and the young ones they produced showed it clearly. Beards are even of lower quality, as judged by the short-faced standard than balds, and the only colours in existence at all good are the blues and silvers. Mr. Woodhouse has bred some of the best. As for black, red, and yellow really short-faced beards, I have never seen any. Beards ought to be marked exactly the same as the flying ones.

All short-faced tumblers of high quality have a difficulty in shedding their flight and tail feathers during their moult. The feathers will grow to their complete length without bursting from their sheaths, and if allowed to do so their fibres will rot. The upper skin of the feather should be scraped off with the thumb nail as it continues to grow, and the inside core of the feather carefully removed. By this means the feathers may be preserved good.

It is difficult to see what is to be the future of the short-faced tumbler in all its varieties. From what I know of human nature, I do not expect that the making or shaping of skulls will stop short of the millennium, whenever that happy time may come. I know, however, that a great many men will not compete with such practices, so I suppose the short-face will be left to those whom it may concern. If judges would lay stress on feather, carriage, fineness and style of beak, and eye, insisting on the beak being natural, and ignoring the least sign of a shaped head, it would be the means of raising the short-face in general estimation. It has undoubtedly fallen from its high position, but being naturally a high class pigeon it deserves justice. What its true position among fancy pigeons is, must be left to individual fancy; in my opinion it was ranked too high in being placed alongside of the pouter and carrier, or even immediately after them.

CHAPTER LIX.

THE GERMAN ANCIENT PIGEON.

THE German *Altstämmer*, or ancient, is a very beautiful variety, which bears something of the same relation to certain German breeds of common tumblers that our short-faced almonds, mottles, and baldheads do to our common flying tumblers. And as our short-faces were certainly produced in London, so the high class ancient was produced in Berlin, the metropolis of Germany. It is to Mr. O. Noef, of Forest Hill, a member of the National Peristeronic Society, that we are indebted for introducing the ancient—rare in its native place—into this country. He informed me that his father was formerly one of the fanciers and breeders of this pigeon, the origin of which is unknown; but which, from its name, is considered a very old variety, and which was for long confined to Berlin, though now bred also in Stettin. It is only incidentally mentioned in the latest edition of Neumeister's "Das Ganze der Taubenzucht," edited by Prütz (1876); but more fully described in "Die Arten der Haustaube," by Prütz (1878). It is there said to be found in all whole colours, except blue. He says: "There are self-coloured black, red, yellow, and white; black, red, and yellow with white wings; also mottled, and as a very much admired kind, the magpie coloured." The magpie marked ancients, in black, red, and yellow, as I saw them lately in the possession of Mr. Neef, are medium sized pigeons, larger than our short-faces, smooth headed, and stocking legged. The head is broad and rather flat, the forehead very broad and well ribbed up, the beak very short and thick, and nearly as broad at the base as it is long. The beak wattle is moderate but not rough, the eye wattle bright red, and as large as a silver fourpenny piece, round and flat, not standing out like a barb's. The eye is prominent and of a clear pearl colour. The carriage is very upright, the head thrown back, the breast prominent and broad, the flights well up over the tail, the flights and tail rather short, the legs moderately long, and the thighs visible in profile. The size and general outline is very similar to that of the Turkish satinettes and turbiteens. The marking is exactly the same as that of the common magpie pigeon, except that on the breast there is a white crescent or half moon mark, which measures from an inch to an inch and a-half between the horns. To breed this little beauty mark good is a difficulty. The colours of those I saw were fine; but the red and yellow were not of the best possible tints, such as is occasionally seen in certain varieties of pigeons. In addition to all the aforesaid properties which go to make up a good short-faced ancient, it ought to have the trembling neck described before, as possessed by the common ancient; but I believe it is rare to see this in the high class breed.

The origin of the short-faced ancient is said to be unknown, but I think it is easy to make a good guess at it. Our short-faced tumblers were doubtless founded chiefly on our common tumblers, as the various colours and markings in them show; but what gave them their principal fancy points of shape, carriage, and form of head, is not so easy to determine, unless it was the Indian Goolee. In Germany, there are common tumblers similar in all respects to what we have, but with trembling necks; and others magpie marked with the white crescent on the breast. These varieties were evidently the foundation of the ancient, and its round head, full broad forehead, and large red eye wattle, were as evidently derived from the barb. A well-known author on pigeons, with whom I have talked the matter over, agrees with me in this idea.

The short-faced ancient has as many fancy properties of form and feather in its composition as the short-faced tumbler, though it has been founded on quite different lines of ideal beauty. Its beak should be short, straight, and thick; but any stop or indentation behind the wattle —which causes all the mischief in our short-faces, because it tempts people to make, instead of to breed it—is no point of beauty in the ancient.

Herr Prütz says: "The principal breeder of the ancient, who possesses some in all its varieties, is Herr E. Bredow, of Westend, Stettin, the only place where they are bred in large numbers. It is not to be wondered at that a high price is paid for them—a pair very often fetching 100 marks —when it is considered how difficult it is to breed them, and what care and pains have to be taken to bring the young ones through the moult."

CHAPTER LX.

THE TRUMPETER PIGEON.

THE trumpeter pigeon has been known in this country at least since Moore's time, and it is common on the Continent of Europe. In France it is called the *pigeon tambour glou-glou*, and in Germany, the *trommeltaube*, or drummer. Its various names are therefore all derived from its voice, which, not being reckoned of any consequence in the show pen, may be left unnoticed till I describe the form and feather of this wonderful pigeon. Until soon after the year 1865, when some very high class trumpeters were imported into this country, the breed appears to have remained almost stationary since Moore described it. The earliest picture of a trumpeter I know of, is that in the treatise of 1765, which, indeed, represents a very poor black mottle, with black flights and tail, and white body, over which is sprinkled about thirty-five black feathers. It has black thighs and leg feathering, but is bare toed. The author, who copied his description of the breed from Moore, says, " they are generally pearl-eyed, black mottled, very feather-footed and legged, turn crowned like the nun, and sometimes like a finnikin, but much larger, which are reckoned the better sort as being more melodious."

It would be of no advantage to minutely describe the trumpeter as we had it before 1865, because the central Asian breed, which was imported shortly after that date, put it entirely into the shade. The best we used to have were blacks, black mottles, and whites; though duns, reds, and yellows were occasionally to be met with, and I once bred a very good blue mottle. The new breed coming here *viâ* Russia received the name of Russian trumpeter, which is what the Germans call such birds as we formerly had, because they are found in their greatest beauty in the neighbourhood of Moscow. The new trumpeter is, however, not a native of Russia, but of Bokhara in Central Asia, and its appearance in

THE TRUMPETER.

Europe was no doubt the effect of the Russian conquests in the East during late years. At the same time, choice trumpeters may have existed for a long while in the interior of Russia, but if they have, I doubt not but that they originally came from Asia. Finding these choice birds described by Neumeister and Prütz as *Bucharische trommeltauben*, I inquired of several German gentlemen the meaning of the name, whether it signified Bucharest or Bokhara, but no one could decide. About a year ago, however, when corresponding with Mr. Charles Jamrach, of London, regarding some of these pigeons brought here by a Russian, he informed me that the man actually brought them all the way from Bokhara, with other live stock. So I think it is conclusive that they are a Central Asian breed which has only lately reached us in its purity, all previous importations of trumpeters having either been inferior, or allowed by Europeans to decline in quality; while, on the other hand, it is possible that when European fanciers did nothing to raise the character of what they had the Bokharians may have improved theirs from stock similar to what we had before.

The trumpeter is certainly a very high class original pigeon, but for some reason not a general favourite, though no one will deny that it has many beautiful properties. The reason that it is not more generally fancied and bred, is doubtless the fact that it has nothing in its conformation very abnormal, such as the pouter, carrier, or turbit, all of which present great difficulty in breeding towards an ideal standard, while its peculiarities are almost entirely those of feathering, of such a fixed type, that it presents little scope for competition. Were as many fanciers to employ their time in breeding trumpeters as pouters, there would be twenty of the former for one of the latter approaching perfection. Fanciers know this, and therefore the trumpeter is left in a few hands, regarded more as a curiosity than as a fanciers' pigeon. Supposing, with all its fine properties, the short-faced mottled tumblers' standard of feather were to be fixed for the trumpeter, it would then present difficulties which any fancier might be proud in overcoming, but this standard is not only full of difficulties, as already explained, but it is a standard open above all others to fraud. The Germans have long since bred trumpeters to turbit and other markings, though in doing so they have lost quality in the more important points of the breed. Brent and others have written of the difficulty there is in preserving the voice and rose of the trumpeter when it is crossed; but though it doubtless takes a long time to recover either, it can be done, as in the case of the Altenburg trumpeter, which I shall afterwards describe, and which is superior in voice to the pure breed itself. Could all the peculiarities of the breed be well retained, in addition to well defined specific markings, such as white with coloured shoulders, the trumpeter would rank higher in the fancy than at present, when many care not how badly their birds may be mottled, or even splashed, so long as they are good in rose and other points. The fancy points of the trumpeter are rose, crest, eye, leg and foot feather, colour and marking, quality of feather, size, shape and carriage, and voice.

Rose is the first property of the trumpeter, and is what makes it distinct from all other pigeons. The priest and other varieties which possess it, do so only in a modified degree, and are supposed to have derived it from this pigeon. The rose is formed by the feathers on the crown of the head growing out from a centre in regular form, like a carnation. In a good bird it will be large enough to form a complete covering to the head, hiding the eyes, reaching nearly to the shell crest, and covering the beak wattle, but not the point of the beak. All the feathers forming the rose should lie well down without any irregularity, and the more circular and even it is at its edges the better.

Crest is an extensive shell hood, reaching round the back of the head almost from eye to eye, and finishing off at its extremities with an ornamental turn of the same formation as the rose. The crest ought to be of a cupped form, reaching over the head, but though wanted as firm and compact as possible, is always more or less loose in texture from the nature of the bird's feather. The feathers forming the crest, and those supporting it, can be moved by the bird at will, and the crest is therefore seen more loose at times than at others.

Eye.—Though described by the old writers as pearl eyed, the trumpeter was generally red or orange-coloured in the irides immediately before the introduction of the Bokhara breed. The latter have generally fine pearl eyes, regarding which Prütz says, "The fine pearl eyes betray the noble race which exacts admiration from every fancier."

Leg and Foot Feather.—The legs and feet should be heavily hocked and feathered, and in this property the former birds excelled the first importations of the Asian race; but the latter, from the silkiness of their feather, were more liable to have their long toe feathers broken, which partly accounted for the want of them. Their toe feathers want the strength of those of the old tight plumaged birds, and seldom reach their natural length without damage. I have noticed that birds bred from good imported ones, when inclined to closeness of plumage, which is faulty, grow stronger toe feathers. It is almost impossible to preserve these feathers unbroken, for any length of time after the moult. An examination of the feet will always show what strength of feather the bird is there naturally furnished with, though the feathers may be broken off short.

Colour and Marking.—The Bokhara Trumpeters are chiefly blacks, and blacks mottled or splashed in some way with white, though both duns and dun mottles have been imported. The beak is almost always white, and is a pleasing feature in the breed, as it looks well just appearing from under the rose. The bird I sketched my illustration from was a very fine dun mottle, with a strong red cast through its dun feathers. It was not marked as I have drawn it, but was almost half white with dark flights and tail. As a standard to breed from, I think the marking shown in the illustration, which is the same as is wanted in the short-faced mottled tumbler, is preferable to any gayer marking; but so long as the white is disposed in single feathers, a bird mottled on the head and neck, as well as on the wing coverts and back, looks very well if the tail, flights, under parts, and leg and foot feather remain black. Many trumpeters are nearly white, but I have not seen any of the highest class entirely so.

Some are all black except the head and upper neck, which sometimes remain nearly white; and if the rose alone could be got white, or even lightly grizzled, the rest of the bird remaining black, it would look very well, and such a marking might in time become fixed if bred for. I understand from the Rev. T. B. C. Williams, who was lately travelling on the Continent, that blood red trumpeters of the highest class are in existence. He informed me that he saw a pair of them in Paris, and an idea of their rarity and value may be learned from the fact, that the price asked for them was £130. He described them as fine in colour and well lustred. I have no doubt that there must be yellows as well. I would not grudge going a hundred miles to see either. I have never bred any of the new trumpeters, but my experience with the former kind, both here and in India, with English ones, showed me that they alter very much in feather during their first moult; after which I always found them to moult without further change. A bird which moulted into a fair mottle, always came out of the nest entirely black, or with only a few grizzled feathers on the wing coverts. If there was much white on a nestling, it generally got very gay, and some would become half white when almost black in the nest. I never saw a bird get darker during its first moult.

Quality of Feather.—The choice trumpeter should be long and loose in feather, the flights should reach beyond the tail, and all the feathers should be soft and silky in texture.

Size.—The actual size of the trumpeter should be above the average of fancy pigeons, the larger the better, as if rose, &c., are in proportion, large size adds to its appearance.

Shape and Carriage.—The appearance of a good bird is that of a very low standing, broad-set, short-necked pigeon, almost close to the ground, unable to see about it, except in a downward direction; it gropes about from place to place and is fond of retiring into corners, where it drums to its mate.

Voice.—One of the chief pleasures in keeping trumpeters is to hear their pleasant notes. They are, with their sub-varieties and the laughers, the musicians of the Columbarium. I would think little of a bird, however good in fancy points, if quite deficient in voice; and, although it cannot be taken into account in judging at a show, it should be carefully cultivated in the loft. Many of the old breed were capital drummers and kept up a constant concert in their lofts; but many of the new ones are very deficient in vocal powers, which is perhaps the reason they left their native place. I knew of one, not long ago, which had no more voice than a common tumbler, if it had as much. The trumpeter's voice does not seem to have been cultivated so well in this country as in Germany. From Neumeister and Prütz I find what constitutes a good drummer there—"Excited by anger or love, its voice falls directly, or from the usual cooing—which, however, must rarely be heard in a good drum pigeon—suddenly into that rolling, quivering, deep hollow drumming; at the same time—mostly sitting still—moving the beak, puffing up its crop a little—the less the better—moving to and fro the front part of its body, and trembling with its wings. For correct drumming there are required a good beginning, a distinctly marked delivery, alternate rising and falling of the sound, shaking, and sustaining. The more frequently, and especially the more sustainedly without stopping, it drums in good style, the more valuable is the pigeon. There are cocks which, with quite short interruptions, drum away for ten minutes, and make themselves heard the whole day, especially in spring, or if they get a good supply of hempseed. Even when eating they drum away, and by a number of good ones a dunning noise is produced. The principal sounds come rolling out of the mouth like the beating of a drum, the lower mandible at the same time moving up and down. The sounds become by turns stronger and weaker, and die off till they can scarcely be heard. The more subdued sounds form a monotone rolling, which is produced in the interior without movement of the beak, and thus appearing to come from another bird altogether. There is no difference in the sounds whether the crop be full or empty. The hen also drums, less frequently, however, and with less force and perseverance."

It is usual, during the breeding season, to clip the trumpeter's rose, not only to allow it to see better, but because it gets clagged with food when feeding its young ones.

In Germany there is a sub-variety of the trumpeter, marked like the Shield pigeons, or exactly as a turbit ought to be marked, all white with coloured shoulders. Neumeister figures them on plate 10 of his book under the name of *Bastard Trommeltauben*. They are represented with well feathered feet, but with smaller rose and crest than the pure trumpeters on the same plate. The black and blue have white wing bars, the red and yellow are solid shouldered. In Tegetmeier's book there is a picture of a pair of these pigeons with red shoulders and white wing bars, called Letz pigeons, under which name the author says they had been exhibited at English shows. There was probably some mistake in the naming of them—perhaps the Latz was meant—at least, I cannot find the name in any German book. Brent says, in the "Poultry Chronicle," that "*lats-chige*"—rough slippered—is a German provincial name for the trumpeter.

Neumeister also figures another sub-variety, the reverse in marking of the preceding, viz., all red and yellow with white shoulders. These probably come out of the nest self-coloured, and moult white sided, like tumblers and runts. Boitard and Corbie describe some varieties of the trumpeter, which M. Corbie brought from Germany, the breed having become scarce in France at the time they wrote. These are the above red and yellow white sides, whole blacks with white wing bars, grey headed blacks, blues with white heads, flights, and tails, and similar blues, with the addition of yellow wing bars. Some of these were probably Priest pigeons.

The Altenburg trumpeter is a German race, regarding which Neumeister, says, "Its home is the district of Altenburg, where of old it originated from a mixture of the Russian drummer with the blue rock pigeon." It appears sometimes to have the rose and crest of the trumpeter, sometimes neither, and sometimes only one of these ornaments. His illustration of it represents a pigeon with a small rose on the forehead, but no crest at the back of the head. It has feathered legs and feet. "It is of an insignificant exterior and bad bearing. The eye is pearl-coloured, the legs sometimes smooth and sometimes feathered, the toes generally bare. The plumage is full and rather loose, self-coloured, mostly dull or dirty blue, gray, or pale blue, in different gradations, with brownish-black or dirty white wing bars. There are also others of a pale yellow, with brownish-yellow wing bars. The ability of drumming is the only characteristic of the Altenburg drummer, whose voice contrasts very favourably with the Russian, by a longer sustained clearness, height, flexibility, and variation. The hen is especially distinguished by her melodious voice. In hardiness and breeding powers it is at least equal to the Russian; however, it is not fond of flying, nor is it easily tamed."

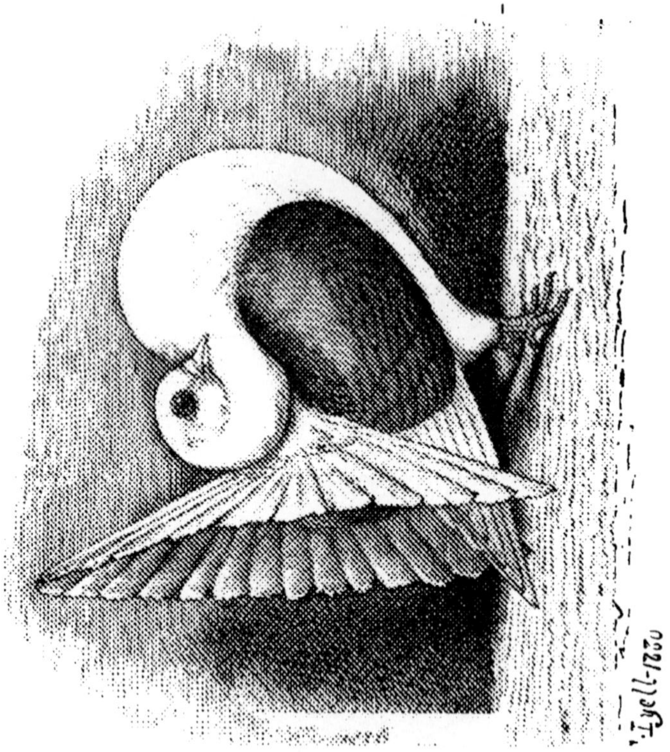

CHAPTER LXI.

THE FANTAIL PIGEON.

WRITERS on pigeons, both British and foreign, agree that Hindostan was the birthplace of the fantail pigeon. It is certainly there where it is found in the greatest numbers. That such a curious and beautiful domestic bird would be early taken by traders from where it originated into distant lands, there can be no doubt; but it is impossible to fix any time for its arrival in Europe. The Romans, in all probability, would have it from India, if it existed there 2000 years ago. I often think that there must be old manuscripts existing that would be of great interest to pigeon fanciers, and some day or other old lore on the subject of our domestic pigeons may come to light when least expected. In Calcutta the fantail is the commonest variety found for sale, and I think I am well within the mark in saying that from 200 to 300 pairs of them annually leave that city, in vessels bound to the different ports connected with it by trade. Fantails have existed for at least two centuries in England, as we find from Willughby, who refers to them as "Broad tail'd Shakers—called Shakers because they do almost constantly shake or wag their heads and necks up and down. Broad tailed, from the great number of feathers they have in their tails; they say not fewer than twenty-six. When they walk up and down, they do for the most part hold their tails erect, like a hen or Turkey Cock. These also vary much in Colour." It is also necessary, for the better understanding of what I shall have to say, to quote Moore's description, who also terms the bird the broad tailed shaker. "This Pigeon has a beautiful long thin Neck, which bends like the Neck of a Swan, leaning towards the Back; it has a frequent tremulous Motion, or shaking in the Neck, especially when salacious, which is the Reason they are called Shakers. It has a full Breast, a very short Back, and a Tail consisting

of a great Number of Feathers, seldom less than four-and-twenty
it spreads in a very elegant Manner, like the Tail of a Turke
and throws it up so much that the Head and Tail frequentl;
They are called by some Fan-Tails, and I once saw one that h
and-thirty Feathers in its Tail; but when they have so many F
it is apt to make them lop their Tails, and not let it meet wit
Head, which is a very great Fault. They are most commonly al
tho' I have seen both black, blue, red, and yellow Pieds, but th
ones have generally the best Carriage in their Tail and Head ;
are two Sorts of these broad tail'd Shakers, the one having a Nec
longer and more slender than the other; but the longest Neck is t
beautiful and the most esteem'd."

If the chief varieties of fancy pigeons, excepting the native br
the pouter, and carrier, did exist in anything like perfection in :
time, they must have declined in quality during the following o
for it is during the lifetime of the present generation that th
trumpeter, fantail, jacobin, owl, and turbit have been improved,
every case by the introduction of foreign blood. So that our c
be well termed the renaissance of the fancy. Moore mentions tw
ties of the fantail, but the long-necked, tremulous, short-backed
seems to have died out in England, along with good quality in the
the above-mentioned kinds.

The Indian fantail, as found in Calcutta, is usually entirely
with a large well-spread tail, a long back, and without much tr
motion in the neck. It is rare to get them both smooth headed a
of leg feather, as most have a peak-crested head or grouse-fe
legs, while some have both. The Indian fanciers are fond of
small brass bangles on the legs of their fantails. This they d
they are in the nest, so that they cannot fall off when full grown
bangles being hollow and open at the edges, have small metal b
into them. Their edges are then brought closely together, and as t
walk about a tinkling sound is produced. The tail feathers of 1
in India are sometimes cut off short, and peacock's feathers int
into the hollow stumps. If well done this has a pretty effect. A
entirely white fantails, whole blues, and ash-coloured or barless b
the commonest. The latter are nearly even in colour all over. I
fancier in Calcutta who had a breed of glossy green lustred blacl

peaked heads and feathered legs. I knew of whole reds and yellows in India, but never saw any. They belonged to a doctor in the Government service at Dinapore, and at his death were advertised for sale, but before I could secure them, as I intended doing, they were bought by a native gentleman. I heard that fine coloured reds and yellows could be got in the north west provinces of India.

Moore mentions having seen black, blue, red, and yellow pieds. Three of the old paintings of pigeons in my possession, already referred to, are of fantails. The best is a completely turbit-marked or saddle-backed yellow, while the other two are almond-feathered. The latter have low cut white heads and bibs, and are partly white in the tail. The author of the treatise mentions an almond narrow-tailed shaker, which was purchased by a certain nobleman. My two paintings of almonds represent more than narrow-tailed shakers, but they do not come up to the yellow saddle back, which is a very good fantail. The red and yellow pieds must have become extinct in England, but black and blue pieds still exist, I believe. They also existed in Scotland fifty years ago, and were found in Dundee and its neighbourhood. From forty to fifty years ago there was imported into Dundee—from where is not certain, though a fancier there, Mr. David M'Intosh, who remembers the bird well, asserts that it came from India—a well-marked black saddle-back shaker hen of high quality, which was the originator of the breed known as Dundee saddle-backed fantails. This hen, crossed with the then existing breed of black and blue pieds, produced a race of pied broad-tailed shakers of the greatest excellence, which have unfortunately become very scarce. A fancier named Mudie, who was lame, and went by the name of "Cripple Mudie," had the strain forty years ago, and he bred many excellent specimens of red and black-sided ones. He possessed the original hen, which, when mated with a black splashed cock, produced one or more red pieds, which were the progenitors of the red-marked ones now nearly extinct. From recent inquiries I have made, I believe this to be the true account of the origin of these birds. The original black-saddled hen was first secured by a Mr. Alexander Dow, who told me only a day or two ago (March, 1880) that he sold her to the said Mudie. One of the first pigeons I ever possessed, was a red saddle-backed fantail. This was thirty years ago, and about ten years afterwards I had another red-sided cock of extraordinary style. The latter could never breed while I had it, but when it became three or four years of age it began to breed. It was then in the possession of a fancier named Mure, in Glasgow, and I believe its descendants are still to the fore in the west of Scotland. The reason the coloured-sided birds became so scarce about Dundee was, that pure white ones became the fashion. To obtain these, crossing with whites was resorted to, but splashed and saddle marked ones continued for long, and still continue to come, even when breeding whites together, on account of the coloured strain there is in them. As far as I ever saw, the Dundee saddle-backs were seldom marked quite so accurately as a turbit, but had generally more or less coloured feathers in the head, neck, and breast, and sometimes in the tail. And the few good ones still in existence are marked more or less in the same way, though they do not appear so at shows. Careful breeding would, however, do much to rectify this, if even only a few persevering fanciers were to turn their thoughts to the breed. I know one or two who are directing their attention to saddle-backs, and hope they will be successful.

There is no doubt in my mind that the bird or birds which made the Dundee breed of fantails, came from India, because I had one of the same style in Calcutta. It was a red saddle-back cock, and the exact counterpart of the one I sold to the Glasgow fancier some twenty years ago. I bought it in the Tiretta Bazaar, Calcutta, about ten years since, and it was the only one of the wonderful shaking breed I ever saw there. Not following up its history at the time, I never learned where it came from; but on my return to this country I wrote to a friend in India who could procure me similar birds if they were to be got, and he told me they were very scarce, but that he knew of them. He died shortly afterwards, however, and I have not been able to learn more about them. The bird in question lived but a short time. It was not clean cut, but had a mottled neck and breast, like the old Dundee birds.

Twenty years ago, when shows began to get common in this country, white fantails of a large size, with little action, loose in feather, and with immense tails, which were sometimes carried right over their backs, concealing them entirely, were often exhibited. Scotch fanciers, whose ideas of a fantail were all towards high style of carriage, could not endure these non-shakers, which, though called English fantails, were, I believe, if the truth were told, nothing but imported Calcutta birds or their immediate descendants. The battle for precedence between the two breeds—for they are distinct breeds—then commenced, and it has ended in a compromise. English fantail fanciers have crossed their large motionless birds with the small Scotch shaking breed, and Scotch fanciers have bred for tail, so that both can now meet on the show bench with more equality than formerly. For my own part I like one or two of the old breed of small, round, compact, close-feathered, dancing birds, which I never tire of admiring, as they are ever on the move. At the same time, they are seldom seen with the tails necessary for show birds, to breed which is the difficulty. They breed very true, although they have often been crossed to make them entirely white, and, except for the size, shape, and carriage of tail, they can so easily be bred good, that they present little scope for competition.

I shall now describe what I consider constitutes a perfect fantail, the properties of which may be reckoned to consist of size, make and shape, carriage, tail, and feather.

Size.—Other things being equal, I prefer the fantail as small as possible. I weighed a cock and hen, matured birds, of the Dundee shaking breed, and they were 12oz. and 10oz. respectively. The hen was extra small, the cock of an average size.

Make and Shape.—Taking size into account, all the fantails I have ever seen, excepting one pair, were of the same formation in head and beak, viz., the common type. Cocks, from their sex, look rather coarser than hens. The head is long, narrow, and flat, the beak long and slender. The beak wattle should be small, and there should be no eye wattle. Smooth legs are necessary in the show fantail, and nearly all fanciers prefer smooth heads. When the head is crested, the crest is generally a neat peak, and I never saw a shell crested one. I do not dislike a peak crest on a good fantail, though it necessarily takes from the rounded outline of the head and neck. I once saw a pair of white fantails with rather round heads and shorter and thicker beaks than usual, but they were not good birds otherwise. I believe they were imported from the Continent. Except for the flights, tail, and legs, the shape of the fantail should be as round, compact, and close feathered as possible. It should look like a pigeon pressed into the shape of a ball. A peculiarity generally found in the best shakers is the split breast, an indentation running up the middle of it, which is most apparent in birds headed blacks, blues with white heads, flights, and tails, and similar blues, with the addition of yellow wing bars. Some of these were probably Priest pigeons.

The Altenburg trumpeter is a German race, regarding which Neumeister, says, "Its home is the district of Altenburg, where of old it originated from a mixture of the Russian drummer with the blue rock pigeon." It appears sometimes to have the rose and crest of the trumpeter, sometimes neither, and sometimes only one of these ornaments. His illustration of it represents a pigeon with a small rose on the forehead, but no crest at the back of the head. It has feathered legs and feet. "It is of an insignificant exterior and bad bearing. The eye is pearl-coloured, the legs sometimes smooth and sometimes feathered, the toes generally bare. The plumage is full and rather loose, self-coloured, mostly dull or dirty blue, gray, or pale blue, in different gradations, with brownish-black or dirty white wing bars. There are also others of a pale yellow, with brownish-yellow wing bars. The ability of drumming is the only characteristic of the Altenburg drummer, whose voice contrasts very favourably with the Russian, by a longer sustained clearness, height, flexibility, and variation. The hen is especially distinguished by her melodious voice. In hardiness and breeding powers it is at least equal to the Russian; however, it is not fond of flying, nor is it easily tamed."

have seen them with the tail coloured as well. The German and French names for the fantail, are *Pfautaube*, and *Pigeon trembleur paon*, both signifying peacock pigeon.

CHAPTER LXII.

THE LACE FANTAIL.

THE lace fantail, so called from its feathering being similar to that of the lace pigeon already referred to, is known in Germany as the *Seiden Pfautaube*, and in France as the *pigeon trembleur paon de Soie*, names signifying silken fantail. I believe it is generally white. It was probably produced from the fantail and lace pigeon. Mr. Ure, of Dundee, who bred them for many years, began with what might be called a narrow tailed or half-bred looking white one. From it—I believe he had only the one bird—and his Dundee shaking fantails, he raised a strain of lace fantails, which are now well established and widely distributed. The late Mr. James Wallace, of Glasgow, had some of this strain, and although in general they were only ordinary birds as fantails, he had one, about three years ago, which was a first class bird, both in carriage and tail, in fact by far the best I ever saw. He told me that he had not always bred lace-feathered birds together since he began with them, but had occasionally crossed with an ordinarily feathered white fantail, for style. The lace feather is therefore not only easy to maintain, but is easily transmitted to another variety. The lace fantail is unable to fly, and must therefore be kept in confinement.

After describing this pigeon, Boitard and Corbie have the following: "*Pigeon trembleur de la Guyane.*—This superb variety has the tail large and displayed like the peacock, and has been brought from Guiana, from which it takes its name. The ground of its plumage is of a dull white; the wings are blue, shaded with a sort of bright eyes and rays of black bars. All the races of small pigeons crossed with the lace fantail produce laced pigeons of all forms and colours, but especially if the latter is bred with a pigeon with black barred wings, their young will have fringed bars of various colours imitating tapering fringes, and producing a very agreeable effect." This would appear to be a coloured-winged lace fantail with a fancifully derived name, just as they name certain colours in other varieties "Siam." It seems unlikely that any special variety should hail from Guiana.

CHAPTER LXIII.

THE JACOBIN PIGEON.

DURING the past few years there has been considerable controversy over this variety, which is one of the choicest in the whole fancy. Such controversy was nothing new, for although it turned on a fresh question regarding what constitutes the true breed, our first writer of note on pigeons—John Moore, himself—clearly indicates that there were differences of opinion in his day about this pigeon. Subsequent writers, mostly imitators of Moore, continued denouncing the jacobins of their time as not the true breed, and there has been no rest for its breeders, as first one, and then another writer, felt called on to declaim in no measured terms against their ideal. As it is in a multitude of witnesses that the truth may be expected to be found, ultimate good is bound to come out of healthy discussion. I will give my ideas on the questions forming the chief differences of opinion later on, and commence with an account of what is known of the jacobin from books. Brent says it is mentioned by Aldrovandus in his second volume of "Ornithology," as the *Columba Cypria cucullata*. Willughby, who was indebted to Aldrovandus for a good deal of what he wrote on pigeons, says: "*Jacobines*, called by the Low Dutch Cappers, because, on the hinder part of the head or nape of the neck, certain feathers reflected upward encompass the head behind, almost after the fashion of a monk's hood when he puts it back to uncover his head. These are called Cyprus pigeons by Aldrovand, and there are of them rough-footed. Aldrovandus hath set forth three or four, either species or accidental varieties of this kind. Their bill is short, the irides of their eyes of a pearl colour, and the head (as Mr. Cope told us) is all white." It is to be noted that there were bald-headed jacobins before 1676, according to what Mr. Cope, the pouter fancier of Jewin-street, told Willughby.

Moore, of course, gives a good account of the jacobin, which was then,

THE JACOBIN PIGEON.

as now, called the jack, for shortness. It was then, "if true, the smallest of all Pigeons, and the smaller still the better"; and he adds, "there are but very few now to be found in *England* compleat." I think it unlikely that Moore ever saw such good jacobins as are in existence at the present time, after recording that "the Feathers of this Chain ought to be long and close, so that if you strain the Neck a little, by taking hold of the Bill, the two sides will lap over each other in some of the best." The very best in his time, therefore, required the above treatment before their chains would cross in front. Nowadays, many jacobins exist whose chains lap over naturally, not only without straining the neck by "taking hold of the Bill," but without cutting out a piece of the skin of the throat, as "Mayor" says (1765), was practised for the same purpose. Moore describes a pigeon known as a ruff, "larger than the true original Jacobine, tho' in shape and make much the same. It has a longer Beak, the Irides of the Eyes in some are of a Pearl Colour, in others of a Gravel Colour, the Feathers of its Hood and Chain are much longer, tho' the Chain does not come down so low to the Shoulders of the Wings, neither are they so close and compact as the others, but are apt to blow about by every blast of Wind, fall more backward off the Head, and lie in a rough confus'd Manner, whence the Pigeon has its Name." "The Strain of Jacobines has been much vitiated by matching them to this Pigeon, in Order to improve their Chain by the Length of the Ruff's Feathers, but instead of this, the Jack is bred larger, longer-beakt, looser in its Hood and Chain, and in short worsted in all its original Properties."

The account of the jacobin in the Treatise of 1765 contains very little in addition to that of Moore, whose ideas are retained, though his language is altered. The ruff is also described, and its use in jacobin breeding condemned. Yellow jacobins had the preference over the other colours. The portrait or illustration in that book, representing the breed, is however, very good considering all things, and is the earliest fancier's picture of a jacobin I know of; Willughby's of 1676, and another of 1734, lately copied into the *Live Stock Journal*, not being worth consideration. The following passage from the Treatise, page 117, points to another picture of a jacobin as existing, but I have not yet met with it: "The following being in itself so uncommon, and a fact, I cannot help taking notice of it: a person the other day passing through

Fleet-street, seeing a print of this Bird" (the jacobin) "at a shop window, stopped to make his observations thereon, and having well viewed it, he went in and purchased it, declaring to the seller that he never saw a stronger likeness in his life; and as for the wig, it was exactly the same he always wore. For he imagined it altogether a caricatura of one of his intimate acquaintance; and the person of whom he bought it, did not think it necessary at that time to undeceive him."

The picture of a jacobin in the Treatise represents a very round-headed, short-beaked, rather down-faced, apparently high-cut bird, with the broad eye wattle of a good jacobin. It is entirely dark thighed and vented, and full flighted as far as seen. The chain feathers are long, but do not meet in front as they ought to do. The mane is clearly brought out, but is not so even at its ridge as many modern birds have it. We know that the short-faced tumbler had not reached a high degree of quality when the author wrote, and, as he says, "the true jack is a very small Bird, very little bigger than a tumbler"; we know that, whatever its size was when Moore wrote, it was by no means the smallest of pigeons thirty years afterwards. The fact is, all the small varieties of pigeons produce extra small stock occasionally, and although small size is admired in many varieties, quality in the properties that go to make them excellent ought not to be, and is not, sacrificed for size.

One of my set of eight old paintings of pigeons is a self-coloured jacobin, with feathered legs and bare feet. It is a gravel-eyed, short and open chained, large bird, not worth consideration from a fancier's point of view. Although I was able to rub off the varnish from the other seven pictures, I could make nothing of this one; but from what I can make out, it represents a blue with black bars.

There is not much difference in modern opinion regarding what a jacobin pigeon ought to be, excepting on the property called the mane. Some say the mane is wrong, and that a breed existed having a clean division of the feathers all round the back of the neck, which was the true breed. If this is correct I have never seen it, and, moreover, I do not believe it is natural for the feathers of the jacobin to grow in this way. I have formed this opinion from the observation of great numbers of the breed, both British and foreign, not poor half-bred looking things, known in country places, and by mere keepers of pigeons, as ruffs, but what were fairly good jacobins. The feathers at the back of the neck in the jacobin, trumpeter, and some other varieties, can be moved by them at will, so that they assume different positions at different times. The jacobin in the Treatise is certainly a maned bird, and Brent wrote in the *Poultry Chronicle* of 20th September, 1854, when describing the jacobin: "At the lower part of the chain the feathers turn out all round, and expose a centre spot of white down." Exactly so; the rose is the centre of chain, tippet, and mane. The following is what the German author, Neumeister, says: "The feathery ruff runs along the sides of the neck, down over the angles of the wings, reaches upwards over a part of the crown, like a cowl, forming the mane (mähne) towards the back part of the neck. This feathery ruff is parted along the sides of the neck towards the front, the back, and the top." From all the foregoing, nothing could be more clear than that the mane is not a modern property of the jacobin. I am inclined to believe, that the mere assertion that it was modern has been the cause of most of the late disturbance, some fanciers being so conservative that they oppose on principle all new ideas. Be that as it may, let the perfect, or something like perfect, maneless jacobin be brought out if it can be produced, and there will not be two opinions regarding its claim to be called a high-class pigeon. I do not, however, expect to see it, not believing it to be natural.

Another hallucination regarding the jacobin, is, that its head and beak, or its marking, were derived from the bald-headed tumbler. It was a short-faced bird before the short-faced tumbler was in existence. It would be something like a hundred years after Willughby described it, before a short-faced baldhead was produced. The baldhead is first described, in 1765, among common tumblers. Is it for its marking that it is a relative of the tumbler? Then why not choose the German monk, priest, ringbeater, or even the old bald-headed German pouter, for its ancestor, not to mention the Indian mookee and plenty more? I do not know how Aldrovand's picture of a jacobin is marked, if it figured in his book, but I know from Willughby, that Mr. Cope told him the jacobin was bald-headed in 1676. To say that it derived its marking from the tumbler, is about on a par with what a "judge" once said to me at a show, when I asked him why he had entirely passed some very good baldheads in a class of flying tumblers. "Give a prize to these things," said he; "why, they're bred from jacobins." I could only sigh as I turned away, for I quite lost the power of speech. In comparing the pictures of the jacobin and almond tumbler in the Treatise, the former is all we want in head and beak, the latter a mere long-faced common tumbler. Nothing could be more erroneous than to say, as Brent and others have said, that a short-faced baldhead with a jacobin's hood and chain would be the perfect jacobin. It might be a pretty pigeon, but it would be the very opposite of a jacobin in many ways.

The properties of the jacobin are size, shape, carriage, head, beak, eye, legs and feet, quality of feather, hood, chain, tippet, rose, mane, colour, and marking. It must not be inferred that I consider them valuable in the order named. I shall merely describe what I consider a perfect bird, and no bird can be considered very good which is not fairly well up in all points. The same remarks must be held to apply to my descriptions of all other varieties.

Size.—There is considerable difference in size among jacobins. When other things are equal, the smaller pigeon is to be preferred. By equal, I mean equal in proportion to size.

Shape.—The neck ought to be long. This is a grand property, the effect of which can easily be seen by comparing different birds together. The body ought to be long and narrow in girth. A well-bred jacobin, which weighs the same or even rather more than a pigeon of another variety, will easily force its way through the bars of a cage which will effectually confine the latter. I have seen this illustrated in the case of a very small African owl and jacobin, the latter being much the heavier pigeon of the two, which gives a good idea of the difference in shape between the two varieties.

Carriage.—A jacobin of the best type, whose head is well smothered in hood and chain, is unable to see well about it. Such birds have a groping way of going about, and endeavour by stretching their necks to see over those chain feathers which obscure their vision. Some of the longest-chained birds are, consequently, all the better for being clipped about the eyes during the breeding season, like the best trumpeters. The real carriage of the jacobin is seen when the cock is driving the hen to nest. The head is carried well up, and the chain will then lap over in front, if it ever will.

Head.—The head very broad across the crown, and well rounded off over the eyes. There should be a little tuft of feathers projecting over each eye like two small horns; but this is only seen in broad-skulled, short-faced birds, and not always in them. They are quite a peculiarity of the breed. The forehead must be broad and prominent, well rounded in profile from the crown to the beak wattle, and not showing a stop as in the short-faced tumbler. A narrow skull, and run out or mousey head, is a great fault.

Beak.—This should be short and rather thick at its base, but coming to a fine point with a downward inclination. The true beak is differently formed from that of the owl tribe, not being so blunt and thick at the tip, and the beak wattle should be fine and smooth. Any gullet is faulty, though it is sometimes found in good birds.

Eye.—The irides should be of a pure pearly white colour, but have often a reddish tinge round their outer circles. Clouded or dusky pearl, yellow, red, broken, and entirely dark or bull eyes, are all found in jacobins, and are all to be avoided. Bad as a bull eye looks, it can often be bred out easier than a yellow one, if it has not existed to any great extent in the strain. The eye wattle ought to be broad, and of a bright red colour. I have seen the wattle almost, if not quite, a quarter of an inch in breadth. In richness of colour, it follows the quality of colour in the feather. Bad blacks, reds, or yellows, do not have a deep red eye wattle, though a strawberry bred from a rich black and red may, and such a wattle on a strawberry would indicate that it was of a good-coloured strain. I look on the broad bright red eye wattle as a great attraction in an otherwise good bird.

Legs and Feet.—Although the jacobin may be got with feathered legs, such a variety having existed for centuries, being mentioned by Aldrovandus, Willughby, and Moore, our standard permits only smooth legs and feet, which should be small, neat, and bright red in colour.

Quality of Feather.—The feathers should be soft and silky, of great length, and making the bird appear larger and heavier than it should prove on being handled. The flights should extend considerably beyond the tail, as much as an inch when the bird is in the hand, though usually not to such an extent when it is at liberty, but the longer they are the better.

Hood.—The hood is the property of utmost consequence in the jacobin. It is formed by the feathers round the back of the head and upper neck all growing forward. The feathers of the head do not, in a good bird, turn up where they meet the forward growing hood, and so fall into the sweep of it, as they would prevent it lying close; but the hood forces itself through these feathers in a succession of regular steps, and every feather forming the hood should grow towards the beak. Sometimes the feathers on one side will grow towards the other, and so form a twisted hood, more or less faulty. The head feathers will often prove too strong for the hood, and cause it to stick up, which spoils the bird; and there are altogether so many difficulties in getting a perfectly formed hood, that one naturally perfect, which requires no faking whatever, is half the battle in producing a good pigeon of this variety. Supposing the formation of the hood to be right, its position is next to be considered: some commence low down on the nape, and cannot in consequence come far enough forward. Such a hood, often plastered down at the back of the head, is not what is wanted; it ought to grow well forward at the back of the head, and it will then, in a long-feathered bird, get as far as the middle of the head, over the eyes; should lie close, but not as if pasted to the head, a slight space between it and the crown being well liked. It ought also to be regular in its outline, and not be split or divided in its centre, as many are, but be compact, well filled up, and look like a feathered cap reaching over the head to protect it.

Chain.—The chain or frill is the continuation of the forward-growing hood feathers down each side of the neck. The first difficulty with a good chain is the cheek feathers or whiskers growing out against it and causing irregularity in its shape, to obviate which they are often weeded out. The chain should come down on each side of the neck as far as possible, and, without "taking hold of the Bill," should at least meet in front, hiding the beak; so that in a first-rate bird the crown of its head is alone visible, both beak and eyes being hidden in feathers. An open throat is faulty, according to its extent. In birds whose chains lap over, it is not by one side lying right over the other, but by the two sides meeting and forcing their way through each other, which, of course, causes a certain irregularity that cannot be avoided. Otherwise, the whole outline of hood and chain ought to be as even as possible. The feathers forming the hood and chain should present a smooth surface, each one lying in order, and this is the difficulty with very long-feathered birds; the shorter-feathered ones, with half an inch or more of open throat, being much easier to produce good in this respect.

It will now be seen how a long neck adds to the appearance of the jacobin, and how it gives room for a display of chain. Let a short-necked one be never so good in hood and chain, it looks very mean beside an equally well furnished long-necked one. The ends of the chain must turn beautifully round at the bottom, and so commence the tippet.

Tippet.—This is formed by the feathers growing backwards over the shoulders and back. It ought to be full and convex in shape all round, and the longer and fuller in feather a bird is, the better it will be in this property.

Rose.—Opposed to the theory that the perfect jacobin should have a clean division of the feathers at the back of its neck, part growing forward to form the hood and chain, and part backward to form the tippet, is the fact, that on each side of the neck the feathers grow out all round from a centre, as on the head of the trumpeter. The formation of the rose may be well seen in a young bird as it gradually feathers in the nest. When about three weeks old, the young one which will become good when matured, has a perfectly formed rose on each side of its neck, the feathers at the top of which become the mane. At maturity, the rose should appear as an oval-shaped spot of white down, hollow in the centre, in those colours which have a white under-down to the feather, as red and yellow. In blacks, the downy part of the feather is not white, but of a medium tint; but, although the black cannot therefore have such a contrast in colour between the chain and rose, the formation of the latter should be correct. The formation of hood, chain, tippet, and mane may be all very good, and yet the rose may be faulty from an awkward feather or two standing up in the centre of it, the removal of which causes all to look well.

Mane.—The feathers forming the mane have no connection with those of the hood, but grow from low down on each side of the neck, being those which take an upward direction from the centre, known as the rose. They ought to fall in with the sweep of the hood and tippet, filling up the cavity which, but for them, would exist. A good mane is difficult to get, as, instead of its ridge being sharp and even, one of the sides forming it often presses down the other, causing a twisted mane; or each side may force itself through the other at some part, and so spoil the hogged appearance it ought to have. And the feathers forming the mane are also movable by the bird at will, so that what may be a good mane at one time, is, at another, only a mass of rough feathers. The outline of the hood and mane should form part of a circle, and the deeper in feather a jacobin is from ridge of mane to bottom of chain, and the broader from front of chain to tippet, the better, for all of which a long neck is of the greatest consequence. The great difficulty is to get the whole formation even in its outline, and firm in texture as well, for, the feathers being long, soft, and silky, they are generally inclined to be loose.

Colour.—The chief colours of the jacobin are red, yellow, and black, and for the most part they are of good quality. Before the introduction of certain foreign pigeons, jacobins were indeed regarded as sometimes perfect in colour; but I have never seen any with the same lustre and fatty quills about the under body, as I have referred to when writing of the swallow, and which the Smyrna turbiteens have in perfection. The red, yellow, and black, which is the order in which jacobins exist at present as regards quality in properties, are, however, generally good, and sometimes very good in colour, though not absolutely perfect when compared with turbiteens. The thigh and vent feathers ought to be as lustrous as the wing coverts, though they often fall away in reds and yellows to a half tint, and sometimes to a mere grey, which is an indication of bad colour elsewhere. The nearer the thigh and vent feathers approach the colour of the wing coverts, the better will be the colour throughout. There are blue and silver jacobins, but, so far, they do not approach the red, yellow, and black, in quality. Mottles also exist, and they are an old variety, being mentioned by Moore. Mottles are chiefly reds, and, while retaining the white head, flights, and tail, they should be marked as much as possible with single coloured feathers over a white ground. Pure whites are favourites, and present a difficulty in regard to pearl eyes, being inclined, like other pure white pigeons, to be hazel or broken in the irides. When whites have a coloured feather or two in the hood or chain, the pearl eye generally accompanies them; and as it is impossible to detect the removal of a few feathers, what appear to be white jacobins at shows are not always so in reality. In off-colours, the chief are the strawberry or sandy, of various shades; duns; red and yellow chequers; an occasional red or yellow mealy, with distinct wing bars; and the very dark chequer or bad black, which, while often of a fair black on the wing coverts, is of blue grey on the thighs and vent. These are all the result of crossing the black, red, and yellow, or the produce of sound colours and such as themselves. The first cross of black and red in all varieties of pigeons, even in those of superlative colour, often results in a strawberry, which is accordingly useful in breeding back to these colours, and especially to the black. It altogether depends, however, on how the strawberry itself may have been bred, whether or not it may be a good match for some of the solid colours, its indiscriminate use being calculated to spoil good colours. I have known a pair of red jacobins produce red, yellow, black, and dun young ones in one season. This was on account of the way they were bred, the cock being from a red and black, and the hen from a red and a yellow.

Marking.—The jacobin, in common with many other varieties of fancy pigeons, none of which have any connection with it, except that, as I believe, they all descended originally from a common origin, is marked in the way called bald headed. It has been so for at least two hundred years. Many instances occur to me of bald-headed pigeons being produced from a self-coloured bird when mated with a pure white. The first pair of pigeons I ever possessed, which I bought for sixpence while they were still unhatched, and which I saw in the nest day by day as they feathered, were a pair of baldheads—a blue and a red—and were bred from a whole-coloured red cock and white hen. They were common pigeons of mixed race, and they certainly may have had baldhead tumbler blood in them, but I think it unlikely. The young ones had very low-cut, slobbered necks, and I merely mention them to show that a coloured bird, mated to a pure white, often breeds coloured young ones with white points. As I write there is a similar instance in my pigeon house. A pure white peak-headed cock common pigeon, with an appearance of fantail blood, mated with a whole dun tumbler hen, used as feeders, have a pair of their own young ones ready to fly, their eggs not having been changed. One is a blue baldhead and the other a dun baldhead, such another pair as those I began the fancy with, thirty years ago, when aged seven. Again, when passing through Leadenhall Market one summer, I saw a cage containing two or three dozen of blue and blue chequered dovehouse pigeons, among which was one with clean white head and flights. I looked at it particularly, and felt certain it was of the same race as the rest. It was, most likely, the produce of a blue and a white, or albino, such as may be found in almost any field dovecote. In fact, a coloured body with white points may be found in many domestic animals, such as horses, dogs, and rabbits, and was doubtless originally produced from the cross of self-colours with albinos. I merely mention all this because some people refer the marking of the jacobin to the bald-headed tumbler, while nothing is more certain than that it could have been produced without any admixture of alien blood.

The head of the jacobin ought to be white, above a line running from the mouth across the eyes. Both mandibles are white in rich-coloured reds and yellows; but a high-cut black has often the lower mandible coloured, or partly so. There is a natural line between the eyes and mouth, which serves as a guide for marking; at the same time a few of the short feathers below this line are generally white, or, if not, a few of those above it are sometimes coloured, for it is difficult to get the marking quite exact. When the white comes below the eyes, or any way down the throat, the bird is low-cut, certainly no great eyesore in a first-class bird, which will never show it unless its chain be opened out. But the high-cut marking is what is desired. The flight feathers should be white to the turn, and the tail with its coverts also white. All else should be coloured, though even in the darkest thighed and vented birds there is generally some white where the thigh feathers finish off at the hocks. When this can only be detected by handling it is no great fault. It was for some time a very difficult matter to get full-flighted, high-cut, dark-thighed birds, because so many were low-cut and white-thighed; but during the last few years there has been an immense progress made in the desired marking. I have seen jacobins imported from the Continent beautifully marked, though not to be compared with our own in the more important points of the breed; at the same time, I believe foreign blood has been used here, during the past twenty years, in bringing the jacobin to its present high quality.

Formerly, the carrier, pouter, and short-faced tumbler were the only varieties regarded in this country as high-class pigeons. The jacobin, turbit, &c., were toys. Ideas have changed, and the jacobin is now regarded as a very high class pigeon. Not only is it full of properties difficult to breed, but it is one of the most beautiful pigeons known, and a general favourite. I dislike placing the different varieties of pigeons in any order of merit, and will only say that, in my opinion, it ranks among the first four, leaving other fanciers to please themselves.

The jacobin is known in France as the *Pigeon Nonnain*, or *Pigeon Nonnain Capucin*. A variety mentioned by Boitard and Corbie as the *Nonnain Maurin* is described as follows: "It is black, with the head, tail, and flight white. It is of a size above the ordinary nuns" (*Nonnains, i.e.*, jacobins), "approaching to that of pouters. It has, like the latter, the habit of inflating its throat a little. It has an elegant form, and the ruff of feathers raised gracefully, but it is not very productive." Dixon, in his "Dovecote and Aviary," quoting from Temminck, mistakes this variety for a nun, the name having misled him. In France nuns are styled *Pigeons Coquilles*—shell-headed pigeons.

In Germany, the jacobin is chiefly known as the *Perückentaube*, or wig pigeon, of which there are several sub-varieties. I have seen self-coloured blacks, all colours of bald-headed with feathered legs, also most of the baldhead colours with both feathered legs and rose on the forehead, like a priest pigeon. None of these equal our birds in quality, and the last named, being evidently derived from a cross with the sub-varieties of the trumpeter, have thick bodies, and are looked on in Germany, according to Prütz, as the cause of the true breed having become "worsted in all its properties," as old Moore said, when writing of the ruff.

CHAPTER LXIV.

THE AFRICAN OWL PIGEON.

The African owl pigeon may be taken as the chief representative of the race of frill-breasted, gulleted, round-headed, down-faced pigeons, because it comes nearest to the ideal standard of perfection which fanciers have agreed upon as being the correct type of the whole family in its various sub-varieties. This race of pigeons is not only one of the most original, but it is one of the most beautiful and engaging, its varieties being general favourites. Some of the countries bordering on the Mediterranean Sea would seem to be the home of this family of pigeons, as those we had in this country, or from France and Germany, before the introduction of Tunis owls and Turkish frilled pigeons, were very much inferior in many respects. There is only a meagre account of them in our early literature. Willughby says : " Turbits, of the meaning and original of which name I must confess myself to be ignorant : they have a very short thick Bill, like that of a Bullfinch ; the crown of their head is flat and depressed ; the feathers on the Breast reflected both ways. They are about the bigness of the Jacobines, or a little bigger. I take these to be the Candy or Indian doves of Aldrovand, tom. 2, pp. 477-478, the Low Dutch Cortbeke." A naturalist, describing the turbit at the present time, might give a similar description, the head being "flat and depressed" in the great majority. From the following account of the turbit and owl, by Moore, the description of the latter being the first notice by name there is of it, it will be seen how much he was indebted to Willughby, who wrote about sixty years before him :

"*The Turbit.*—The Reason, why this Pigeon is so nam'd by the *English*, I cannot by any Means account for ; the low *Dutch* call it *Cort-beke* or *Short-bill* upon the Account of the Shortness of its Beak. It is a small Pigeon very little bigger than a Jacobine, its Beak is very short like a

THE AFRICAN OWL.

Partridge, and the shorter the better; it has a round button Head, and the Feathers on the Breast open and reflect both Ways, standing out almost like a Fringe or the Frill of a modern Shirt; this is call'd the Purle, and the more of it the Bird has, the more it is admir'd. As for the Feather, their Tail and Back of the Wings ought to be of one entire Colour, as blue, black, red, yellow, dun and sometimes chequer'd; the flight Feathers and all the rest of the Body shou'd be white. They are a very pretty light Pigeon, and if us'd to fly when young, some of them make very good flyers. I have seen a Flight of them kept by one *Girton* that wou'd mount almost high as Tumblers. There are of this Sort all white, black, and blue, which by a Mistake are often call'd and taken for Owls."

"*The Owl.*—This Pigeon is in make and Shape like the former, except that the upper Chap of its Beak is hookt over like an Owl's from whence it has its Name. Its Plumage is always entirely white, blue, or black."

Moore also mentions, when writing of the disease called the vertigo: "I once had a Turbit, of the Owl Kind, taken with it in a violent Manner."

There is no mention of the gullet or crest in this description; the head, however, is said to be *round*, and it was not the shoulder marking alone that constituted a turbit, as it might be self-coloured. The difference between the turbit and owl seemed to be only in the beak.

On reading the descriptions of the turbit and owl in the Treatise of 1765, which are very much more extensive than Moore's, it would appear that either some recent importations of finer owls had been made, or that breeders had effected great improvements on the old stock. The illustrations accompanying the descriptions differ very little in their outlines; both are plain headed, exactly alike in beak, that of the owl not being hooked, the chief difference lying in the turbit's head being very round, while the owl is rather flat-crowned. The author says: "The owl is, according to Mr. Moore, a small Pigeon, very little larger than a jacobine, which might be their size in his time; but at present they are brought to such perfection, that they are hardly, if anything, larger than a very small tumbler. . . . Its plumage is always of one entire colour, as white, a fine sky-blue, black, and yellow, &c., except some that are chequered. The blue ones should have black bars cross the wings; and the lighter they are in colour, particularly in the hackle, the more they are valued." He mentions the gullet "reaching down from the beak to the frill," both in the owl and turbit, and that the latter, when red and yellow, had white, not coloured tails. For about a hundred years after the preceding was written, or till about 1860, there seems to have been no improvement made in pigeons of the owl tribe in England; I rather think they must have lost quality from neglect. Mr. Jayne says the African owl was used as part of the composition of the short-faced tumbler, but the record of how and when is lost. Mr. Fulton says in his book that a Dundee fancier had African owls in 1838, and that they were brought to this country by his brother. From what I was told by the said fancier years ago, I could never believe the pigeons in question were African owls. In 1838 he would be about twenty years of age, and his elder brother, who was not a seafaring man, having occasion to make a voyage to the Baltic, brought home with him some coloured-tailed white owls, regarding which a Danish gentleman said that he doubted if they were up to the standard of an English turbit. No one seeming to care for some that he had imported, he returned them.

So much for the pigeons imported into Dundee in 1838. They were doubtless the coloured-tailed white owls, which Messrs. Baily and Son have often imported and sold as Meeves, I believe, and which bear about the same relation to African owls that skinnums do to carriers.

Only lately there was a notice of this breed in the *Fanciers' Chronicle*. It was about the year 1858, that the first pair of African owls known to the present generation of British pigeon fanciers, was imported into this country. They were exhibited at the Crystal Palace show by their importer, Mr. E. V. Harcourt, and the description of them in *The Field* newspaper of 22nd January, 1858, is the following: "Owls (all colours) well represented; but the best pair of owls in the show was certainly a pair of whites, in the class for other varieties, under the name of 'Boos' pigeons from Tunis." Since then thousands of these beautiful pigeons have been imported from the North of Africa, chiefly, I believe, from Tunis. The late Mr. John Baily, jun., who, with his father, did a large business in exporting and importing fancy pigeons, informed me that these beautiful birds were bred, he understood, about the mosques in Tunis, and allowed to pair together as they liked. If this is so, they must certainly be the only variety there, or the breed could not be kept pure. As far as I know, no experienced fancier has yet visited Tunis, so we have but little information regarding these birds, and can only judge of them as they appear. How they originated or came to be located in Tunis is a mystery. The great proportion of those brought to this country are quite worthless in comparison with the select few in each shipment, so that Mr. Baily told me that latterly it did not pay to import them, as, when the one or two good ones had been picked out, the rest were unsaleable. From the careless treatment they generally get on the voyage, as well as from the fact that a great proportion of them arrive in their nest feathers, canker and other diseases of the head and throat are very prevalent among those that come to this country, so that I have known only some ten or fifteen per cent. of a lot survive the first month of their residence here. They are very delicate pigeons, but when acclimatised are fairly hardy and good breeders. I have bred them both here and in India, where they do very well.

In detailing the properties of the African or Tunisian owl, I may say that the nearer all the frill-breasted gulleted pigeons approach its ideal standard of conformation, the better they are. Some fanciers agree with me, others do not. Under each variety I shall describe the various differences of feather, size, &c., which constitute them separate breeds.

Size.—The African owl is the smallest domestic pigeon known. A good pair will weigh about a pound, and hens are sometimes found not over seven ounces in weight. The smaller they are the more they are valued, if good in the various properties which constitute the breed.

Shape.—Short in neck, broad-chested, short in flights and tail, the legs long enough to make the thighs visible in profile, the back rather hollow, and the rump rather full.

Carriage very erect, the head carried well up, and the chest full and prominent.

Head as round as possible, both from the nape to the beak wattle, and from eye to eye. The prevailing fault in the head is more or less flatness on the crown, and there is often a prominence at the back, which is undesirable. The forehead very broad; the cheeks full.

Beak, short and thick; the upper mandible as much as possible in the same curve as the head, so that from the nape to the point of the beak a half circle should be described. The under mandible should approach the upper in consistency as much as possible, and fit closely to it, or, in the language of pigeon fanciers, the beak should be "boxed." The only difference between the owl and turbit, according to Moore, was in the beak, the upper mandible of the former being "hookt over like an owl's, from whence it has its name." The upper mandible in all pigeons is inclined to overlap the under more or less, and in the race under review it sometimes does so very considerably, from the formation of the head and beak; but I have found that when it does, it is generally owing to a weak under mandible, while I have also found that birds so formed are much troubled with vermin, being unable to keep themselves free from them, like short-faced tumblers, whose beaks have been distorted in the process of head shaping. The upper mandible of a pigeon has no independent motion, and is not jointed like that of a parrot, which can move its upper beak at will, so that, though much hooked, it can lay hold of anything small. The best under mandibled African owls I have seen were not much hooked in the upper beak. The picture of an owl in the Treatise of 1765 does not represent a bird with a hooked beak, nor has Mr. Ludlow in Mr. Fulton's book represented any of this family of pigeons so. The mandibles may never be completely boxed, but the nearer they are so, the better in my opinion. The mouth should be wide and deep in the head.

Eye should be large, prominent or bolting, and placed in the centre of the head. The irides are hazel or "bull" in whites, and orange or yellow in coloured birds.

Beak and eye wattles vary considerably in birds of the same family. A moderate amount is natural, and therefore allowable. The beak wattle thickens with age, and so long as it does not stand out much beyond the curve of the skull, it cannot be objected to. Neither the beak nor eye wattles should be rough and lumpy, otherwise they give coarseness to owls and their varieties.

Gullet is a thin transparent skin filling up the hollow of the throat, commencing on the under mandible as far forward as the feathers grow, and reaching, in a good bird, to the top of the frill. This property can be seen whenever a bird is hatched, if the beak be gently raised. It is about the last part of a bird to be covered with feathers, and I may say here that pigeons of the owl tribe feather differently from all other pigeons, the sides of the breast feathering before the frill makes its appearance, and the centre of the breast remaining bare for about three weeks from the date of birth. The longer and deeper the gullet is, the better, and if it is not present in a bird when hatched it never comes later. With age it generally thickens at its junction with the lower mandible, forming there a little lump, which is, in fact, a jew-wattle. This gives a fulness to a bird's appearance, but it cannot be got on a young one. Gullet, to a more or less extent, is seen sometimes in various kinds of pigeons; but the owl tribe and Mahomet are the only races in which it is regarded as necessary. In them it is a beautiful property, giving them that breadth across the neck in profile which adds so much to their appearance, and without which they fail to look well.

Frill is the property in which the African owl is most deficient. Great numbers have been imported entirely wanting in this necessary adornment, while the most have far too little of it. Such frills as the wonderful whiskered owls have are never seen on African owls. The frill ought to spread out on each side of the breast, the more of which it covers the better, and it is formed by the feathers composing it growing out in all directions. It ought not to lie in any particular position, but stand out from the breast roughly, as I have attempted to show in my drawing. The more confusedly the feathers forming it grow the better it looks. Where it joins the gullet it ought to divide and spread to right and left, and so form the figure of a cross. Hence this race is sometimes called "cross" pigeon in Germany (*Kreus-taube*). None of the owl tribe, with the exception of the whiskered owl, to be afterwards described, are yet complete in this beautiful property, and when they will be it is impossible even to guess, for their standard of perfection is one so complex and difficult of attainment, that to have all of it fairly good, is as hard a task as the whole fancy presents, excepting the standard of no variety whatever.

Legs and feet small and neat, bright red in colour, and free of feathers from the hocks down.

Colour, self coloured white, blue, and black. It will be noticed that Moore has mentioned these colours as those of the owl, and that other colours were not mentioned till thirty years later. The majority of African owls as imported are whites, and black and blue pieds, whole blues and blacks being, however, not uncommon. The number of splashed birds that come would favour the idea, from their appearance, that no regard is paid to the matching of them for colour. The only apparent regular marking is white, with black or blue tail; but nothing comes oftener from a pure white and whole blue or black than such marking. From the fact of my having bred pure white, whole blue, and black and blue splashes, from a black tailed white cock and blue tailed white hen, I think that if Mr. Baily was not well informed when he told me how these pigeons are bred in Tunis, very little regard to colour must be given in matching them. No reds nor yellows have been brought here, so far as I know, nor even mealies, the origin of these colours; but I would expect to find an occasional mealy were I to visit the native place of these pigeons, as such a natural variation is very likely to have been produced. I once had a blue hen, an imported bird, from Messrs. Baily, with most of the frill white. I consider this marking a very suitable one for the coloured owl, and I am inclined to think that the bird I had was not a mere chance production, for I find notice of the same marking in Neumeister's book among the frilled pigeons, all of which, whether self coloured or turbit marked, go by the name of Mövchen (seagulls) in Germany, so that the blue shouldered variety seems to have given the name to the entire family. The blue Tunis owl is often of a good deep sound colour, with jet black bars, and is also frequently of a smoky tint, the evident result of having been crossed with the black. The black is generally of a dull colour, showing bars of a darker hue, and is never of such intensity and accompanied with such lustre as is seen in other varieties. I should imagine there are blue chequers among these pigeons, but I have not seen any. The colours of the African owl, as far as known here, are, therefore, the original blue, and albinos, and melanoids, as found in most, if not all domestic animals, and black and blue splashes. But although the artificial colours, the result of extended breeding on the part of fanciers, are unknown in this breed, its form is sometimes found in such perfection that, with the exception of more frill, it may be said to be as complete a pigeon as we know of.

Small size being a desideratum in the Tunis owl, and the hen in all kinds of pigeons being less than the cock, the former generally comes nearer perfection than the latter for this reason; but what gives a better idea than anything else of the high state of breeding found in this variety, is, that the hens are equal to the cocks in all that goes to make a perfect bird—a most rare thing to find in other varieties of frilled and gulleted pigeons. I have an idea that red and yellow African owls may yet appear, for the interior of Tunis is not as yet much known

THE ENGLISH OWL.

to Europeans; and I cannot but believe that if, as Mr. Baily told me, exporters have to employ a man about the mosques to catch such fine birds as we have already received, others, showing still more of the breeders' skill, must be in existence in the hands of fanciers.

The Germans have named the Tunis owls *Ægyptische Mövchen* (Egyptian sea gulls).

CHAPTER LXV.

THE ENGLISH OWL PIGEON.

THE English owl, as it existed at the time the African variety was introduced, could not be found so good in owl properties as at present, so that the difference between the two varieties was then more marked than it is now. The improvement has been effected by crossing with the Tunis breed. There are not two standards for owls as regards shape of head and beak, gullet, frill, &c. The difference between the two varieties consists only of size and greater variety of colour.

Size.—The English owl is wanted as large as possible, so that it may present a contrast with the African, as the pouter does with the pigmy pouter. To gain size, it is said that crossing with the short-faced Antwerp, which is of owl descent, has been resorted to, and that the barb has been used to give breadth of skull. I have seen English owls with more beak and eye wattle than the pure breed could, in my opinion, have, and which, instead of having had their value enhanced thereby, ought to have been disqualified when exhibited, or at least ignored. I believe a reaction has lately set in against excessively wattled owls.

Colour.—The English owl is self coloured, and exists in white, black, red, yellow, dun, blue, silver, and in various off colours, as mealies and chequers. Splashed owls are not regarded, except it may be locally, or as stock birds. The blues and silvers are chiefly fancied and bred, and the best English owls are of these colours. The blue should be of a deep, sound, rich colour, even in tone, with broad black wing and tail bars, and dark hackle, lustrous with green and purple hues. The silver should be of a light creamy dun body colour, with very dark dun wing and tail bars, merging into black, and with lustrous dun hackle. White rumps in both are faulty, but cannot be regarded in blue and silver pigeons as of the same degree of magnitude that they would in the solid colours. The chief defects are indistinctness and bad colour of wing bars, ticked or slightly chequered wing coverts, sometimes showing indications of a third bar, and too light body colour and hackle, through crossing with the powdered blues and silvers; which latter, as varieties of the blues and silvers, require special mention, as they have a history of their own.

As the author of the "Treatise on Pigeons" (1765) says, regarding blue owls, "the lighter they are in colour, particularly in the hackle, the more they are valued," a distinction not recorded by Moore thirty years previously, and, as the true Mahomet pigeon, unknown to Moore, was well described by the author of the above quotation, I have thought that it had been made use of in his time to produce the colour known as powdered blue, as it certainly has of late years. The powdered blue and silver English owls of our day were, however, bred in London about the year 1855, according to a letter extant in the *Live Stock Journal* of 1878, signed Harrison Weir, who states therein that they were produced by himself and the late Matthew Wicking. When requested by me, in the same publication, to state how they were bred, if it was no secret, Mr. Weir made no sign. I have considered that the appearance in London of a pair of true Mahomets about the year 1850, as mentioned by Brent, had some connection with the powdered owls which appeared soon afterwards. That they sported from common blues is very unlikely; but from the long mousy faces and freedom from gullet of any I ever saw, they might have been bred from the German ice pigeon, which has much of the same colouring as the Mahomet. The late Mr. James Wallace of Glasgow, with the Mahomet pigeon already mentioned by me, and a blue English owl, bred beautifully powdered birds, wanting the frill, which he recovered by the next cross of these half breds with blue owls, though at the expense of some colour. These quarter bred Mahomets were equal in powder and better owls than any of Mr. Weir's breed I ever saw. Some mystery seemed to be made out of the production of the powdered owl in London; but there is really no mystery in the matter, for, even if it was not produced as I say, similar coloured and better owls can be so produced. That the same kind of owl existed in the last century seems likely, and in the year 1824, Boitard and Corbie published the following in Paris, "*Pigeon Cravate Anglais; columba turbita anglica; En anglais, Turbit pigeon.* . . . plumage entirely amethyst blue with black bars on the wings. This pretty variety is very pure, for it cannot be crossed with another variety without entirely losing its colour." Like the German writers, Boitard and Corbie do not distinguish between owls and turbits—all are *Pigeons à Cravate*. The above, though called the turbit, cannot read as referring to a turbit marked pigeon; such marking, with blue and other coloured *Manteaux*, they also describe. I understand it to mean a self coloured very light blue pigeon, that could not bear crossing without losing its peculiar colour, which is the characteristic of the English powdered owl. It may be that the French had, in 1824, such pigeons as are described in our Treatise of 1765, which they called *Cravate Anglais*, and that from them were descended the London powdered owls of late years.

So long as the powdered owl was considered of an original colour it was worth while preserving; but, as it is, at its best, only half powdered in comparison with the Mahomet, I see no reason why any special value should be put on it, more especially as it is inferior in owl properties to the best blues and silvers. The colour in perfection should be the same as that of the Mahomet in the blue, and the silver should bear the relation to it that the common silver does to the common blue, the same as in the ice pigeons. As for red and yellow English owls, they are inferior to the blues and silvers, probably on account of no African owls of these colours ever having reached us with which to improve them. I have seen and had red and yellow owls of good colour, however, and they probably represented the breed as it existed in England when the Treatise of 1765 was written. Twenty years ago I had one pair of yellow mottled owls, marked nearly as exactly as the show mottled tumbler ought to be. I received them from Glasgow, but they were imported from the continent, I believe. Whole coloured owls, excepting the wing bars, which are white, are mentioned by the German writers; also white ones with coloured tails, and coloured ones with white tails.

The standard of the owl requires a smooth head, as a crest, and especially a peak crest, from its formation, takes much from the roundness of the head. Still, peak crested owls are not uncommon, and I have known very good ones bred from the best blue English owls. Self coloured, peak crested, black, red, and yellow owls are sometimes called whole coloured, or solid turbits; but the name turbit is usually, and ought only to be, applied to white frilled pigeons with coloured shoulders.

The English owl being wanted large, the hen generally fails in this respect from looking so well as the cock, for the same reason as in the African breed she often excels him; but in conformation also, she is generally, as in all other frilled races except the African, much inferior, so that good hens are rare.

The English owl is a variety which is now widely spread and greatly fancied, so that choice specimens are very valuable. There is little doubt that it owes all its quality to the African breed, and that but for it, it would not be what it is. There were no such English owls as exist now twenty years ago, and much still remains to be done with them, for until both cocks and hens that will bear comparison with the little foreigners, in all but size, are produced, they cannot be said to have reached their best state.

Hitherto, the supply of African owls from Tunis has not failed; but should it do so, it is a question if they would continue to exist in this country for any length of time, on account of the delicacy of the breed. If they could not be kept up here, unless by constant importations, it is an additional reason why the large English owl should be cultivated.

CHAPTER LXVI.

THE WHISKERED OWL.

This beautiful variety is of a medium size, between the African and English owls. Those I have seen were whole blue in colour, with the usual black wing and tail bars. In head, beak, gullet, and general owl properties they could only be called passable, and could not be compared with the African variety. In frill, however, they were extraordinary, their breasts being covered with it from butt to butt of wings.

The frill also reached up below the throat, and dividing to right and left, was continued almost round the neck. I understand that in some of them it actually goes quite round the neck. These pigeons are called Chinese gulls in Germany (*Chinesische Mövchen*), and the only account of them I have found is by Neumeister and Prütz, as follows:

"The Chinese gull is somewhat larger, but not so finely built as the Egyptian gull (Tunis owl). The beautifully arched head is smooth and not so angular, but rounder; the strong bill, somewhat crooked in front, is a little longer, in the form of a parrot's beak, with which bird this pigeon has much resemblance in many respects, as, namely, in bearing, neck, and eyes. The eye is large, the iris orange coloured and very lively. The breast is full, the neck short and powerful, the pinions reach to twelve millim. from the end of the tail. Feet and toes are short and smooth. The *jabôt* (frill) on the breast and neck is the most peculiar thing about this pigeon. When it stretches its neck the crop is invisible, as it is hidden behind the so-called *cravatte*. This *cravatte* is formed by several rows of feathers, which stand upwards on the under side of the neck, lying closely to each other from one side to the other. Proceeding from this, the *jabôt* goes downwards to the middle of the breast, forming a rosette. The feathers from this point radiate to all sides, reaching almost over the breast and offering a beautiful sight. This pigeon became known in Germany only a few years ago, and, therefore, the price for a pair is still rather high. It is found in blue with black bars, black, yellow, silver grey, and sometimes white.

"J. Destriveaux, a fancier in Paris, who accidentally came into possession of a pair, originated the name Chinese gulls. There exists a certain obscurity about the descent of these pigeons; however, they probably owe their origin and propagation to chance. Some ships laden with sugar, returning from the East Indies, brought, shortly after 1850, a large number of Chinese gulls to Tilsit and Memel, and that in so excellent a plumage as now-a-days is no more to be seen. From thence these pigeons came into the South of Germany and disappeared from the market for a long time, until later they re-appeared in Paris, from which place the distinguished fencing master, A. Prosche, in Dresden, got possession of some, and he has bred them successfully for years, as well as the Egyptian (Tunis) owl."

From the above it seems that the whiskered owl cannot now be found in such perfection as when first imported. The interesting account of the breed makes one wish to know more about it, and especially as to whence it came. I have seen many varieties and types of fancy pigeons in India, but none of the frilled race, except such as were imported from Europe. There is nothing to connect the re-appearance of the whiskered owl in Paris with the Tilsit and Memel birds. The Paris birds may have been a fresh importation, and the name given them—Chinese pigeons—may not be a mere fanciful one. However good the first arrivals were—and if better than such as I have seen, they must have been very choice birds—there doubtless exists in the hands of fanciers somewhere a race of most extraordinary pigeons, compared to which all other races we know of, are much inferior in *jabôt* or frill.

THE TURBIT.

CHAPTER LXVII.

THE TURBIT PIGEON.

THE origin of the name Turbit seems to have puzzled our old writers on pigeons. It is evidently derived from the Latin, as was first pointed out in the eleventh and last edition of Moubray's Book on Poultry, edited by Méall and Horner, and published in 1854. That the turbit alone, among all the varieties of fancy pigeons known in England 200 years ago, should have had a Latin name, has caused me to think that a frill breasted pigeon of some kind may have been introduced into this country by the Romans as the *Columba turbata*. Willughby appears to have been the first writer to use the word, and though *Turbat* would have been the more correct form, any vowel would have rendered the sound of the name. The name turbit, therefore, signifies a frilled pigeon of any colour, though we now use it only for those that are white with coloured shoulders.

There are differences of opinion regarding the formation of the head of the turbit. I have shewn what the old writers say about it, and that Moore particularly says it should be round; while the earliest picture of a turbit I know of—that in the Treatise of 1765—shows a pigeon rather rounder in head than the owl in the same book. It is a fault too often found in frilled pigeons—the choice African owl included—to be flat on the crown; but although there is no difference specified in any old book between the owl and turbit head, some modern writers have held for the latter being frog-headed. When or how this idea originated I cannot trace, unless it was derived from what was published in Paris by Boitard and Corbie in 1824. They say in their introductory notice of the frilled pigeons: "Their beak is short and head toad-shaped, that is, in the prettiest varieties; the eyes are extremely projecting in the upper part of the skull, where they form two well marked protuberances, as also the bone behind the head, which forms a third, which gives their head a sort of resemblance to that of a toad."

I have seen the frog or toad head even more marked in some birds than this description, the head having a decided hollow between the two rising eyebrows, and this was in the case of some birds bred from a turbit and African owl. I dislike this style of head, and hold with many fanciers, such as Fulton and Caridia, that the nearer the head of a turbit approaches that of the ideal owl, the better it is. The owl type is that most difficult to obtain, for it can seldom be got very good; it is the result of careful breeding, and never comes by chance.

The ideal standard of a turbit, in my opinion, and in that of many more who are devoted to this beautiful pigeon, is therefore exactly the same as that of the African owl, except as to colour and crest.

Size.—The turbit, as it exists, is, even in small specimens, very much larger than the African owl. I prefer it small, but would not have it so at the sacrifice of any property. Generally speaking it is as large as the clean legged flying tumbler. To reduce it materially in size can only be accomplished by crossing with the African owl, its undoubted relative. I have been doing this for several seasons, with much greater success than I had hoped to anticipate, and I believe others are now adopting the same method. Such experiments, however, take long to complete, and as all the frilled pigeons are, with me, more delicate and apt to succumb under that dread disease, inflammation of the bowels, than any other race of pigeons, I have several times been thrown back after making a decided advance. In crossing with the African owl, my object has been both to reduce size and improve the turbit in head and beak; in fact to have a peak-headed, coloured-shouldered African owl, which would be, in my opinion, the perfect turbit.

The Peaked Turbit.—This variety should have a hog mane running up the back of its neck, quite unbroken, and ending in a finely-pointed peak crest. There is much to contend with in getting the right peak and mane. The peak ought to reach higher than the crown of the head; but it is rarely more than level with it, and often set so low down in the neck, that the bird would look better if altogether smooth-headed. As the peak crest is formed by the feathers on the nape and those on each side of it, all drawing to a fine point, the bird cannot look so round-headed as the smooth-headed owl. A very good peak is sometimes seen with no mane on the back of the neck, and this form has generally a deep notch below the peak. Many of the Turkish frilled pigeons are of this style, which is considered very faulty in the English turbit. The peak must not incline to either side of the neck, but rise straight from the middle of the nape.

The Shell Crested Turbit.—This variety, according to Neumeister, is bred largely in the North of Germany. It is not uncommon in this country; but it is not so generally fancied and bred as the peaked. The shell ought to extend quite round the back of the head and be of the cupped form, as in the swallow pigeon. The more extensive, even in outline, and firm in texture, it is the better. There ought to be no mane on the shell crested turbit.

Many turbits are neither peak nor shell crested, but something between the two. Some of these are merely the faulty produce from pure bred birds of either variety; but crossing the two kinds is apt to result in badly crested birds. They ought, therefore, to be kept distinct, for the mane is difficult to maintain in perfection.

Colour.—The turbit should be entirely white with coloured shoulders. The wings, including the scapular feathers, with the exception of the primary flight feathers, ought to be coloured. Nothing is easier to get fairly good, and yet nothing is more difficult to breed to a feather than this beautiful marking. The flight feathers, generally ten a side, though occasionally only nine, may often be got right; but to have freedom from foul thighs, vent feathers, or underbody, on the one hand, and no white feathers on the wings, except the flights, on the other, is the great difficulty. I consider that a bird quite clean below, with white wing butts, looks worse than one free of white on the wings and a little foul below, because bishoped wings are very glaring. With a full set of white flights we almost invariably find the short coverts and adjacent feathers white, thus giving a similar edging to the margin of the wing when closed. To get the spurious wing coloured, which prevents white butts when the wing is closed, is a very difficult matter, if the bird is quite clean below. Formerly black and blue turbits had coloured tails, and they often breed young ones with the tail partly so, but the coloured tail is no longer considered desirable. Reds and yellows do so likewise; but in that case, the tail feathers are usually of a weak half tint only. It is only lately, owing to keen competition at the numerous shows now held, that great attention has been paid to proper marking. Not only in this country, but in others where turbit-marked frilled pigeons are fancied, foul thighs and vents have been very prevalent, simply because these natural faults have not been considered of grave account. It is no easy matter to eradicate such mismarking when breeding from the strains that have it; but once this is got rid of, it is comparatively easy to maintain clean thighs and vents in many of the produce.

The Triganica pigeon, in addition to coloured wings, has the head, tail, and flights coloured, and although it is common enough to find this variety foul below, like the majority of turbits, I found it easy enough to breed many quite clean thighed and vented birds of this breed, by commencing with such as were free from these faults.

I have stated that I have crossed the African owl and turbit, and have mentioned my reasons for doing so. I commenced by matching a very fine green-glossed black turbiteen cock to a pure white African owl hen, and from their young ones I selected a very round headed white cock, with about half of one shoulder black, which was as much colour as any of the produce possessed, some being pure white. I mated this bird, which was smooth headed, like both his parents, to a good peak headed black turbit hen of Mr. Roper's breed. She was not quite clean below, being foul vented. The best of the young ones from this pair was a smooth headed, almost completely turbit-marked cock of small size and good properties all over. I matched him to his mother, and they have bred several very small peak headed birds of first-rate quality, so well marked, that when lifted up by the wings, some of them did not show one foul feather below. I lost some of the best from inflammation of the bowels; but, on the whole, considered my progress encouraging. I have not seen any owl-headed turbits so full of good points as the best of those from the last-mentioned cross. The black turbit hen mentioned above was purchased by me at the celebrated sale of turbits belonging to Mr. George Roper, at Stevens's sale rooms, in September, 1878. She is a sister of the cock sold on that occasion for 24½ guineas, and afterwards re-sold for £40; and she is, like most of the other blacks sold at the same time, descended from the hen of the first pair of black turbiteens which were imported eight or nine years ago, and which were probably superior to any since brought to this country. It was Mr. Fulton who bred the bird which gave all the quality to Mr. Roper's black turbits. This bird was a strawberry cock, and he bred him from a yellow-shouldered cock, imported from Germany, I believe, and the original peak headed black turbiteen hen. There is, therefore, a preponderance of foreign blood in the birds I am writing about.

The turbit is found in all the twelve barred, chequered, and solid colours, mentioned on page 48, but of these only five—the black, red, yellow, blue, and silver, are chiefly bred and shown.

The black colour, when in perfection, is strongly glossed with a green metallic lustre. Even when decidedly bad in colour, a black turbit shows any foul feathers on thighs or vent so glaringly, that they tell strongly against it in competition with others, such as blues and silvers; and I have often seen specimens of the latter colours, which were no better than blacks opposed to them, preferred because they *appeared* cleaner thighed and vented, whereas they were in reality very much fouler. But the inconsistencies of judging at pigeon shows are too well known, and they often arise from too little time being allowed the judge, or from his hurry to leave. The best black turbits I know of, are those of Mr. Roper's strain, now widely distributed. I have stated how those that sold for the highest prices at his sale were bred, and they were probably the best collection of blacks ever seen together. In the production of them he was associated with a reverend gentleman, whose name as joint owner did not appear, and as their sale was consequent on a dissolution of partnership, and each bought back a few in a perfectly *bonâ fide* way, the letters that appeared at the time, on the question of a seller being entitled to buy in his own stock, would not have been written, had all the circumstances been known.

Red and yellow turbits were, at the best, only fair in colour before the introduction of red and yellow turbiteens from Smyrna. A great improvement has been effected by crossing with these beautifully coloured pigeons, and though their feathered legs, head markings, and plain heads, take much careful breeding to eradicate, it has been done. So much has crossing with the turbiteen been resorted to during the past few years, that I imagine few fanciers could say for certain that their red and yellow turbits, if fit to hold their own in strong competition, were of pure English blood. Reds and yellows, when anything like right in colour, show any foulness on their underbody very distinctly; when poor in colour, foul thighs hardly show on them; hence I have known them called clean thighed and vented when so hopelessly foul on these parts that, had their colour been even fair, they would have been unfit to put into a pen. Black, red, and yellow turbits, especially black, when of rich colour, have their eye wattles of a reddish tint.

The blue turbit has not been crossed with foreign blood, at least, to any great extent. The best birds of this colour generally show a sexual difference in colouring, the hens being of a duller and more smoky tint than the cocks. The colour in cocks is sometimes very clear and delicate, so much so that white will hardly show on them, and this light blue is even preferred by some. It is a matter of taste, but I prefer a darker and more vivid blue, like the colour of the wild rock pigeon. The delicate blue is too near an approach to silver, and I think the more pronounced the colours, the better they look from an artistic point of view. Such a beautiful rich blue as I have had in Triganica pigeons would only require to be seen to have its superiority allowed. The wing bars of the blue should be of a deep black, broad and distinct.

The silver turbit should be of a creamy dun, with bars of the darkest glossy dun, merging into black. To have really black bars on the real silver ground is perhaps not an impossibility, but I have never seen them. When I consider that bright red and yellow bars can be seen on rich blue Triganica pigeons, black bars on a silver ground may not be incompatible with nature. So very light in colour are foul thigh and vent feathers on silvers and the light blues, that it is scarcely possible to distinguish them, and so they often pass undetected. I consider that the real silver colour, in a wholly coloured pigeon, ought to have bright golden dun wing bars, with neck and tail to match. In a turbit, this colour, confined to the shoulders, is ineffective, being so light. Darker wing coverts and bars merging into black are, therefore, more effective for a turbit, though this is really half-way between blue and silver.

Red and yellow bar winged turbits, as well as duns, strawberries, and the various chequers, are usually called off-colours, and are not cultivated. The barred colours are, however, very pretty, and if bred for, could be improved by selection. To each of the solid colours, black, red, yellow, and dun, there is a corresponding barred and chequered colour, as referred to on page 48. It is doubtless by the judicious blending of all of them that so many variations are found in the colours of foreign pigeons. But however intricate and effective are chequering, spangling, and breaking up of colour, as in the Smyrna satinettes and Triganica pigeons, they do not fill the eye like black, red, and yellow, when these are in perfection.

There are also pure white turbits, inasmuch as such are occasionally produced by way of albinism from coloured shouldered birds. They might as well be called crested owls, unless they are of the decided frog-headed formation, which no owl ought to be. It is a manifest mistake, however, to allow them to compete with coloured shouldered birds, whether frog or owl headed. The best so-called white turbits I have ever seen were very thick-headed, down-faced ones, of the owl type, with broad shell crests.

Although I have advocated round or owl headed turbits, very few such exist, and when a good one does appear it is generally howled down by certain people as not a real turbit. This is because the great majority of turbits are flat headed, and such would lose value were round heads to be generally recognised. What a good many wish recognised as the turbit standard is the following : A forehead something like that in my illustration, but not rising so high, and running almost in a straight line from the top of the forehead to the bottom of the peak, and bevelled off over the eyes, which should be placed higher in the head than I have shown. There is no doubt this style is very pretty, but there is little difficulty in perpetuating it compared to the other. Many of Mr. Roper's strain are of this kind, though both his blacks and reds descend, I believe, from round headed turbiteens.

CHAPTER LXVIII.

TURKISH FRILLED PIGEONS.

I THINK very highly of these Turkish frilled pigeons, and consider them most valuable additions to our lofts; but it does not appear that they have taken such root in this country as their excellence merits, which may be accounted for in various ways. Though hardy enough when imported of mature age, there is great mortality amongst immature birds, and their produce is equally delicate, I have found, with other varieties of frilled pigeons. Some of them, as the turbiteens and vizors, are of recent production, and their marking by no means fixed, and many are barren or sterile from age, or, if breeders, their young ones often show that they themselves have been strangely bred, so that fanciers find it would necessitate a large expenditure to go thoroughly into any of the varieties. Again, those who might surmount all the difficulties with these fine pigeons, in thoroughly establishing them in this country, have their attention already fixed on our native breeds, and where there are only a few willing to take them up, it becomes no easy matter to establish them, there being work enough in the various kinds to demand the whole attention of many breeders. It requires great perseverance, care, and outlay, to thoroughly transplant any race of domestic animals, and it needs many breeders to accomplish it, more, I believe, than seem willing to attempt it with these birds, so that I fear, were no more importations to be made, there would be few signs of them left in this country after twenty or thirty years. I admire them much, and wish them well, and though they may not increase here there is no fear of them being neglected by the ardent fanciers of the East.

The varieties are the satinette, blondinette, domino, vizor, and turbiteen. The first and third appear to be old breeds; the others more recently established. I am not aware who gave the first three their names; but Mr. Ludlow, of Birmingham, has said he named the last two. The differences between the five kinds consist in colour and marking, in plain or crested heads, and in smooth or feathered legs and feet. They vary a little in size, but for the most part are larger than British turbits. They are generally excellent in carriage, sometimes very round in head, full in gullet, and short and thick in beak, which is generally well boxed and not over-lapping at the point. From a side view their heads are sometimes well arched; but they are often deficient in great breadth of skull and forehead, and, leaving size out of the question, are seldom or never up to the standard of the best Tunisian owls in head properties. When crested, the correct standard for all the varieties is a needle-pointed peak, standing as high as possible; not springing from a mane, as in the turbit, however, but divided from the feathers at the back of the neck by a notch. The peak is sometimes seen very good on these pigeons, though lopsided and half shell crests are common enough. Mr. H. P. Caridia, of Birmingham, considers that "no maned bird can possess a close-fitting well-pointed crest," in which opinion he is certainly mistaken. When feathered on the legs, the correct style is what is sometimes called grouse-legged or stocking-legged, that is, with legs and feet completely covered with rather short feathers, so as to show no bare skin. The feathers on the legs should be long enough to stand out somewhat at the sides of the feet, but the toes ought to be covered with very short feathers.

The great majority of the coloured-shouldered white-bodied varieties are very foul on thighs and underbody. It appears from what Mr. Caridia has written that no attention is paid to this in the East, and that they are allowed to be foul thighed. I have never, however, seen him point out definitely how the colour must be disposed on the underbody, nor can I believe, were competition to arise in Turkey, as it exists here, that foul underbody would be any longer recognised there. With a standard of only seven white flight feathers, and foul thighs allowed, as he says is the case in Turkey, foul wing butts are no difficulty whatever. The Triganica magpie has coloured flights in addition to all the marking of the vizor and domino. Foul underbody is not allowed in Triganicas, according to the Italian writers, and I have both seen and bred them without a foul feather underneath. I think, therefore, that it only requires the attention of Turkish breeders to enable them to eradicate foul underbody in their pigeons, and they certainly require it.

The irides in coloured headed Turkish frilled pigeons should be orange, in white headed ones they should be dark hazel, as in our turbits. Turbiteens, when heavily head marked, have sometimes orange eyes, which look very well. Many, however, have broken irides, which are decidedly faulty.

As regards the frill on the breast, the Turkish varieties are about on a par with our turbits and owls. They are certainly not on an average better than them. In this beautiful and distinctive property, much, therefore, remains to be done for them, if we are to take the frill of the whiskered owl as our standard.

THE SATINETTE.

This beautiful variety is grouse-legged, and usually smooth headed, though a few have lately been imported with peaked crests. It is coloured shouldered and tailed, and the rest of its plumage ought to be white. As for its wing marking, it ought to be similar to that of the turbit, and foul underbody, coloured primary flights, white secondaries, and white wing butts are all as faulty in it as in the turbit. In addition to the colour of the satinette proper, there are several others found in the breed, some of which have received special names, while it would have been less confusing to have retained the generic name for all, prefixing a word to distinguish them, as, for instance, blue satinette, instead of bluette.

The satinette is an old breed, according to Mr. Caridia, who says he has traced it back for 120 years, through three generations of fanciers. When he wrote the account of it in Mr. Fulton's book about five years ago, he said that an aged Presbyter in Smyrna, then upwards of eighty years of age, had bred them all his life, and that his father and grandfather had done so before him. The ground colour of the shoulders of this pigeon, after it has cast its nest feathers, should be of clear pink brown, or nearly of a flesh colour, each feather being laced round with lustrous purple black, or the same with an inner lacing of reddish brown, making the plumage tri-coloured. This is what I consider the most beautiful marking; but it is not the only one. Some of them are chequered at the extremity of each shoulder feather with a triangular or arrow pointed mark, which often runs too large, and which, when blue in colour, as it very often is, considerably spoils the appearance of a bird. Small triangular chequers of purple black are very pleasing on the flesh-coloured ground, and even small blue markings are pretty; but when the general appearance is more blue than flesh coloured the effect is spoiled. The tail and its coverts should be as in a blue chequered pigeon, and on the black bar at the extremity of each primary tail feather there ought to be a large round white spot, which gives a fine effect when the tail is out-spread. The shaft of the tail feather should be dark throughout, and this has also a nice effect, running through the white spot.

The brunette bears the same relation to the satinette as a silver does to a blue pigeon. Its ground colour should be of a silvery dun tint, each feather being laced or chequered with dark dun. Its tail is much the same colour as that of a silver pigeon, and the bar at its extremity should show the same large round white spot as in the satinette. Its more correct name would be dun-laced or spangled satinette, according to the style of its marking.

The bluette, or blue satinette, is of an even clear blue on the shoulders, with white wing bars, which ought to be laced with intense black, and also have an inner lacing of a red or dark flesh colour. The tail is the same as in the satinette, or a shade lighter.

The silverette, or silver satinette, should be of an even clear silvery dun on the shoulders, with white wing bars laced round with dark dun, and if there is an inner lacing of buff or yellow, so much the better. It bears the same relation to the bluette as the brunette does to the satinette. The tail is of the same colour and marking as in the latter, or a shade lighter.

These four varieties may be interbred occasionally, but, if it be intended to follow after the laced marking in the satinette, the bluette and silverette cannot assist it. So many shades of colour appear in the breeding of satinettes, that care must be exercised in the selection of stock. A bird with excessive lacing or spangling must be paired with one too lightly marked. This plan is, however, less likely to produce a large proportion of well coloured young ones, than by pairing two birds which are themselves nearly of the desired colour. I think if the breeding of satinettes were to extend in this country that either the clear flesh tint, evenly laced with black, or, in addition, an inner lacing of red or brown, making three colours in each feather, would come to be regarded as the only standard colour. Besides the foregoing varieties, there are also black laced satinettes whose shoulders are white, each feather being laced with black. Towards the wing butts they appear more black than white. The principal tail feathers and their coverts should also be white, laced round with black.

THE BLONDINETTE.

The blondinette has been produced in recent years, according to Mr. Caridia, who has recorded its history. The blondinettes bear the same relation to the satinettes, in their several varieties, as the *schietti* or whole-coloured Triganicas do to the *gazzi* or pied ones. I am not aware if every variety of colour in the blondinette is represented in the satinette, not having seen so many; but the same natural laws of variation of colour must affect both in course of time.

The satin blondinette is marked on the shoulders and tail exactly the same as the satinette; and where the latter is white the former is of a dark blue, but its primary flights should have large oval spots on their extremities, making them when closed to appear laced. The colour which has gained most acceptance in this country is the clear pinky flesh ground, evenly laced with black, the flight feathers of which, when opened out, are also generally laced all round their edges; but with, usually, a strong brownish cast on their inner webs. There is, however, an immense variety of colour among satin blondinettes, many being heavily marked on the wing coverts with arrow-pointed blue chequers; but the inferiority of these in appearance is at once seen when they are placed alongside the laced kind. The nest plumage of the different kinds of blondinettes is dull and heavy, the intricate markings and clear ground colour only appearing after the first autumnal moult. The bronzy flesh colour of the wing coverts often reaches up the back of the neck, which ought to be dark blue. The blondinettes are grouse-legged and generally peak crested.

Very pretty varieties are the red and yellow laced or spangled ones. The former is reddish brown, and the latter sulphur yellow, where the satin variety is dark blue, and their shoulders are of the same colours, merging into white, each feather being laced, spangled, or chequered at the edge with reddish brown or clear yellow. These varieties fall away in colour in tail and flights. I have not seen similarly shouldered satinettes, but should suppose they could be bred. There are black and white laced blondinettes, in which the head, neck, and underbody are black, the wings, flights, and tail being white, strongly laced with black, dark towards the wing butts, and gradually lighter towards the tail, according to the size of the feathers.

The blue blondinette is of the colour of a blue pigeon, with tricoloured wing bars and white spotted tail, the same as in the blue satinette. Its primary flights ought also to have white oval spots on their extremities.

The silver blondinette differs from the blue exactly the same as these colours differ from each other in the satinettes. There are also whole dark dun blondinettes, with white wing bars, and spotted tail and flight feathers.

I have stated, when writing of the German shield pigeons, that some are spangled, marbled, or chequered on the shoulders, with two or three colours, like some of the Eastern frilled and Modena pigeons. I omitted to state that such pigeons, though classed in Germany, according to Neumeister, among the shields, are generally dark in colour where the turbit marked shields are white. They are known in this country as hyacinths, and may have some connection with the French hyacinth and its sub-varieties; but the pair I have succeeded in obtaining are in no way different in size, form, style of head and beak, and in medium feathered legs and feet, from common Birmingham rollers. In colour they are dark purple blue with black barred tail, their shoulders being of a prevailing flesh-coloured tint, each feather in the cock being laced round with black, while the hen is of the arrow-pointed marking, showing a strong bluish colour on the chequers. Their young ones are of both types and no two are exactly alike. In their nest feathers they look like dull blue chequers with a reddish-brown cast on the shoulders, their bright colour only appearing when they moult. The only difference in colour between these pigeons and the satin blondinettes, is the absence of the white spots or finch marks on the primary flight and tail feathers, which are, however, found on varieties of the German priest pigeon. There is nothing, therefore, in the satinette and its relative, the blondinette, that is not found in other varieties of the domestic pigeon; but they combine in themselves the form of the owl and the feather of other rare pigeons, which makes them very choice examples of the pigeon fancier's skill.

THE DOMINO.

The domino is peak headed, smooth legged, coloured on shoulders and tail, and is marked on the head like a nun. The colour of the head includes the peak crest, and comes low down in front, forming a bib. I have only seen one specimen of this variety, and I believe it is the only one of the pure original race which has appeared in this country. Its marking resembled that of my drawing of the Triganica pigeon, except the flight feathers, which were white. It was imported by Mr. Caridia, and was shown very successfully by Mr. Yardley, of Birmingham. It was blue in colour, with the usual black wing and tail bars. In a letter published in 1879, Mr. Caridia stated that, the dominoes, "though very scarce now, were in colours, blacks, blues, silvers with bars, duns without bars, and chequers of all these colours. There were also a few without the crest, and I possessed there [in Smyrna] some of these which were perfection." The bird I have referred to was of grand owl properties, and its colour and marking were so good, that I venture to think were such birds to be imported, they would take the fancy of pigeon breeders in this country before any of the other Turkish frilled pigeons. They appear, however, to be almost extinct, and it seems to me that it does not say much for those in whose care they were that they are so. A prettier, and, at the same time, very high class pigeon, than the solitary blue domino shown so often during the last few years, never presented itself to my eyesight. I cannot say how it was as regards clean thighs and underbody; but its general appearance was very fine. Minor defects would only be regarded if the breed was plentiful.

THE VIZOR.

This variety was produced by crossing the domino with the satinette tribe, the object being to have coloured headed satinettes. This has been partially accomplished, and I have seen some fairly marked satin and blue vizors. The best of them were, however, somewhat peppered with white about the head, so that much still requires to be done in perfecting them. The vizor should be completely grouse-legged, like the satinette. It may be smooth headed or peak crested—the latter for choice, as it is an additional property. The colour of its head will, of course, be in accordance with that of its shoulders, viz., light blue in the bluette, marked, and dark purple blue in the satin. Black headed visors, with black laced shoulders and tail, would look very well, and will, no doubt, be produced if the Eastern fanciers are successful with the blues and satins.

THE TURBITEEN.

According to Mr. Caridia, it is now about thirty years since this much admired variety was produced. He says it is a composition of the domino, white owl, and Oriental turbit; but I cannot exactly understand the method of breeding which was adopted. I understand from his account that the Oriental turbit was marked as the British kind; and to employ a white owl "to counteract and balance the colour of the black tail" in the domino, appears a very roundabout process when the turbit of Smyrna was itself white tailed. However, it seems a misfortune that Smyrna turbits, marked as we want a turbit, with peak crest and clean legs, and with the blazing colour and grand owl properties of some of the turbiteens, should have been allowed to disappear in the desire for something new. Such pigeons would now be very valuable.

The turbiteen is generally smooth headed, and but very few peak crested ones have been brought to this country. It is grouse-legged and white in colour, marked as follows:—The shoulders should be coloured exactly the same as in the British turbit. The head markings are by no means well fixed in the breed, but are occasionally to be seen very good according to the standard agreed on by fanciers, viz., a round coloured spot on the forehead, commencing at the beak wattle and of about the size of a shilling, and a similar spot on each cheek. There ought to be a distinct white line between the forehead and cheek spots, and the throat should be white dividing the cheek marks. The whole face and throat is sometimes coloured in a heavily marked bird, which is faulty.

The eyes should be orange for choice; they are often broken in colour —a serious fault.

The turbiteen is exceedingly foul thighed in general, the only clean thighed ones I ever saw being a few blacks that I bred myself; but they had white wing butts, which looked very bad. I have seen them with the feathers on the outside of the thighs coloured, and still white vented and white between the thighs. This approached to a specific marking, and may be what is wished for in Smyrna; but I have stated my ideas on this point already. I have seen a few black turbiteens with black tails in addition to the usual marking.

The colour found in some of these birds is superb, and though I have seen it equalled in other pigeons, I have never seen it surpassed. The black, red, and yellow, leave nothing to be desired. There are also duns of various shades, some of them being of a lovely lavender dun, but this colour is apt to fade, and becomes dappled at the moulting season, till all the feathers are renewed. There are blues, silvers, chequers, strawberries, and bar-winged reds and yellows as well, according to Mr. Caridia. Most of these I have seen and bred, but they are of little beauty alongside the glossy artificial colours. The latter are full of the fatty quills about the root of the tail and vent referred to in the Nurnberg Swallows. These feathers only shed, at most, the tips of their fibres, and many of them never break at all.

The standard of a turbiteen, therefore, comprises all that is requisite in a turbit, with the addition of feathered legs and face markings. The feathered legs give little difficulty, but they occasionally come with too little or too much leg and foot covering. The face markings cause much trouble, as they are comparatively new. Out of several scores of these pigeons which I have bred during the past five years, only four were about right in face markings. They may be bred with small cheek marks, about equal on each side; but nothing less than the size of a shilling to that of a florin looks well. The black, red, and yellow may be inter-bred; but the first, with either of the last two, often produces a sandy or strawberry, which, however, frequently throws back to good colour when matched with either a black, red, or yellow. It must not be supposed, however, that it requires no care to keep up colour in this breed. Many of them are bad in that respect when compared with the best; but even the second and third degrees of colour in turbiteens would be highly valued in many varieties of pigeons, which shows how good they are in this feature. I never possessed an imported bird of this breed with a crest; but I bred a peak-headed one from a pair of smooth heads. I consider the peak crest a fine property and difficult to breed right, therefore valuable.

The upper mandible is generally coloured in turbiteens, or at least tipped, according to the feather, white or flesh coloured beaks being exceptional. There ought to be no hard blue however, in the beaks of blacks, reds, and yellows; the black should have a black beak, the red a ruddy brown one, and the yellow just enough colour in the beak to make it show.

I may here mention two other varieties of Turkish pigeons, though they are not of the frill breasted, gulleted tribe. The first, only one pair of which I have seen, were sent to Messrs. Baily and Son, from Smyrna, among a lot of blondinettes and turbiteens. They were smooth headed, grouse-legged, white pigeons, with round heads and short fine beaks like the capuchins. They were marked on the forehead and cheeks somewhat as turbiteens ought to be, and their flight feathers were coloured. These markings were of a bronzed or kite black.

The second variety is what are known as Red Indians. They come from Asia Minor, and have nothing much to distinguish them in size, shape, and form from common skinnums; but their colour, which is of deep glossy blood red, to the ends of the flight and tail feathers, is sometimes as good as can be found in any domestic pigeons. They have been used in dragoon breeding, to give colour to reds and yellows.

CHAPTER LXIX.

THE BARB PIGEON.

THE mention of the Barbary pigeon by Shakspere makes it the earliest noticed variety that I know of in our literature. As Willughby gives a recognisable description of the barb under the same name—Barbary pigeon—within a hundred years of Shakspere's allusion to it, there can be no reasonable doubt that this breed has been cultivated for at least three centuries in our country. Willughby describes it as having a bill like that of a bullfinch, with a circle of naked tuberous white flesh round its eyes, as in the carriers, and with white irides; and adds : "My worthy friend, Mr. Phillip Skippon, in a letter to me concerning tame pigeons, writes that the eyes of this kind are red."

I think it likely enough that Willughby's " worthy friend " was Major-General Phillip Skippon, who was so much associated with Oliver Cromwell in the Civil War, and, if so, he is the earliest English pigeon fancier we know anything of. The part he took in the troubled times in which he lived may be learned from Carlyle's " Letters of Cromwell." He was the author of the following religious books : " A Salve for every Sore " (1643), "Truth's Triumphs " (1648), and " A Pearle of Price " (1649). When Field-Marshal in the army, he was deputed by the Parliament, in conjunction with Cromwell and another, to go to Saffron Walden to allay some discontent that had broken out among the soldiers. He is alluded to in an old ballad :

> Some citizens they say will ride,
> To buy knacks for their wives;
> Let Skippon skip-on as their guide,
> He may protect their lives."

Perhaps Willughby's correspondence is still extant. Skippon's letter about tame pigeons would be interesting to read.

THE BARB OR BARBARY PIGEON.

It is owing to some importations of barbs from the South of France, made by Messrs. John Baily and Son about twenty-five years ago, that this pigeon exists in our country in its present excellence. Its French name is the Polish pigeon (*pigeon Polonais*), and though it is now known in Germany as the Barbary pigeon, from its English name, it was formerly called the Indian pigeon (*Indianische-taube*). Neumeister says, "There is no explanation of the origin of the name 'Indian' and the French designation 'Polish.'" From what we know of modern nomenclature, as applied to new varieties of pigeons and poultry, it would never do to depend on the names of old varieties as being indications of their origin. It is

HEAD OF A BARB.

allowed, both here and in Germany, that the barbs of the South of France are the best, or, at least, were so lately, and though its name in French literature is *pigeon Polonais*, it may have another name in the south. It is evidently an ancient variety, and it is more nearly allied to the highest type of the owl tribe than any other. Both may be from the same stem, and both may have existed from pre-historic times. I have seen a few barbs in Bengal, but was informed that they were the produce of some that had been imported from Europe.

The barb should be smooth-headed and clean-legged; at the same time a crested variety has existed for long, and is mentioned in our old pigeon books. The legs are occasionally slightly feathered, which is so far faulty. A sub-variety is bred in Germany, with frilled breast like an owl.

Size.—There is a certain difference of opinion regarding this, some liking a small bird and others a large one. I think that when the head properties in two birds are equal in proportion to their respective sizes, the larger bird is to be preferred, as being bolder in all its points.

Shape.—The neck short and thin, the breast very broad, the legs short, and the flights rather long and carried neither high nor low, but lying on each side of the tail, is, I think, the correct style for this pigeon, and it is that described by continental writers. Any gullet or fulness of throat takes from the wished-for appearance of a massive head set on a thin stem, which most, though not all, look for in a barb. A gullet, filling up the hollow of the throat, and making a bird broad across the neck in profile, is a grand property in the owl tribe with their sprightly carriage; but the barb has no carriage, properly so called, whatever, and looks much better with a hollow clean run throat.

Skull.—This should be very broad, and is, consequently, rather flat, and generally with a fulness at the back. It should be as much as possible of an equal breadth, and not wedge-shaped. The forehead should be very broad, prominent, and well filled out, and form a curve from the crown to the beak wattle, a straight lined forehead in profile being a bad fault very often seen. The forehead must be well ribbed up with an indented line on each side of it as if carved out, which gives this pigeon a very nice modelled appearance in head, not so marked in any other variety, though seen in a less degree in the owl tribe and ancient German pigeon.

Beak, very short, thick, well boxed, and wide in the gape; the upper mandible in the same curve as the forehead, and the under mandible approaching the upper in massiveness as much as possible, which is hard to get, but which, when got, gives a bird a grand appearance. The beak should be flesh coloured, or no more than tipped with colour.

Eye, as pure white or pearl coloured as possible, though the nearest approach to this is usually a white iris, rather red at its outer edge. Many good barbs have yellow irides, which ought not to disqualify, but be duly allowed for in competition. White barbs have been seen with pearl, but they generally have bull or hazel eyes.

Beak Wattle.—At maturity the beak wattle ought to have filled up all inequality in the curve of the forehead and upper mandible, and it may stand out a little in addition; but it ought to be as free as possible from rough wartiness, and show a clean division in the middle, appearing like a small bean split open and laid across the beak. The jew wattle on the under mandible should not be excessive, but of course grows to a certain extent in such a pigeon as the barb. It should appear as three small warts, one in the middle of the lower mandible, where the feathers finish off, and the others on each side below the opening of the mouth. The beak wattle in a healthy bird is nearly white, the jew wattle and corners of the mouth being of a reddish flesh colour.

Eye Wattle.—This is one of the chief properties of the barb. It continues growing till the bird is from three to four years of age, when it ought to be at its best. It should be of an equal breadth all round, and, consistent with roundness, the larger in diameter the better. It ought to be thickest at its outer edge and of a concave form, or shaped like the outside of a cart wheel, the eye being represented by the nave, which stands out in the centre. The more prominent or less sunken in the head the eye is, the better. The colour of the eye wattle ought to be bright red; with age it often becomes light, sometimes turning almost white.

The hen is generally less developed in all head properties than the cock, though hens have been seen good enough to be mistaken for cocks when exhibited. Before a hen can reach such quality she is generally past breeding. Looked at in front, the barb's head ought to be very square and blunt, the tops of the eye wattles reaching higher than the skull and standing away from it. When they incline towards each other by rolling over the skull, the head appears contracted, which is the opposite of what is wanted.

Colour.—The barb is a self-coloured pigeon, and is found in black, red, yellow, dun, and white. Blue is rare, but is occasionally seen on the continent; in this country I have only heard of one or two of such colour. I think the red eye wattle would harmonise very well with the blue colour. The black is the most usual colour, and it can often be found good, being the easiest of the artificial colours to breed; at the same time, it is not found with such vivid green metallic lustre as in some other varieties. Black may look very well, and yet be far from the best possible tint. What the best barb black is in reality, may be seen by looking at the reds and yellows of the same relationship. The latter colours are not found very good in barbs, the red usually falling off very much in colour towards the rump, flights, tail, and underbody. The yellow may be sometimes seen fairly good, it being a colour which does not look so bad, when a little thin, as the red. Red, well lustred to the ends of the flights and tail, is undoubtedly the most difficult colour to breed and to maintain in fancy pigeons. Where it exists, black and yellow will be found good. Dun in barbs is usually of a deep dark colour, often merging into black. Pure white barbs are scarce; they appear from time to time as albinoes, when breeding from coloured birds. To breed them with coloured ones would certainly result in a pied produce to a great extent, but such are not wished for. By this method, however, some specfic markings would be obtainable in time, if wanted. Black, red, yellow, and dun barbs are so much crossed that, when any two of them are breeding together, there is great uncertainty as to the colour of the produce. Mr. P. H. Jones, in his description of this pigeon in Mr. Fulton's book, mentions having bred from a pair in one season, black, red, yellow, dun, and white young ones. He has given the following measurements, &c., of the barb in the same work: "Weight, 13oz. to 1lb.; length, beak to tip of tail, 12½in. to 14in.; inner edge of eye to tip of beak, ⅞in.; width of skull, a full inch to 1⅛in., measured between, not over the eye wattles; diameter of eye wattle, 1⅛in.; length of limb, measured as pouters, 4¼in. to 4½in. These dimensions would apply to cocks, and would be a little modified for hens, more especially in width of skull." He considers these measurements a fair standard, though a few birds might be found to exceed them.

Formerly, the native breeds of the pouter, carrier, and short-faced tumbler were regarded as the only high class pigeons; the jacobin, fantail, owl, turbit, barb, and trumpeter coming lower in the scale, and being regarded as "toys." Lately, Mr. Fulton, in his book, has removed the barb from the "toy" division, and added it to the "high class" or inner circle, making four varieties of the latter. For my part, I regard the jacobin and all the owl family as much choicer pigeons than the barb and short-faced tumbler; but I dislike placing these various breeds in any order of merit, as they are all very high class pigeons. I daresay the short-faced Antwerp is as difficult to breed to perfection as any, and I have said what I think of it. The barb may be as difficult to breed good in head points as the carrier; but has it the grand lines of the latter? After all, the best criterion to judge by is to note the numbers of fanciers who breed and keep the various varieties, and to take notice of the taste that prevails in other countries as well, otherwise we might come to the conclusion that the dragoon is the choicest pigeon of all.

CHAPTER LXX.

THE ENGLISH CARRIER.

"THIS Bird is esteem'd, by the Gentlemen of the Fancy, as the King of Pigeons, on the Account of its Beauty and great Sagacity." So writes old Moore regarding the English carrier; and, I believe, were a vote of English "gentlemen of the fancy" to be taken to-day, the English carrier would still be found to be considered the king of pigeons. Moore says, "The original of these Pigeons came from *Basora*, in *Persia*, being sometimes brought by shipping, and sometimes in the Carravans; hence by some ignorant People they are call'd *Bussories*. . . . The *Dutch* call this Pigeon *Bagadat*, I suppose, from a Corruption of the Name of the City *Bagdat*, which was formerly old *Babylon*, which *Nimrod* built, because they judge this Pigeon in its Way from *Basora* to be brought thro' that City." I have not met with this account of the origin of the English carrier in any book older than the "Columbarium." It is not to be found in Willughby's "Ornithology," from which Moore has drawn so largely, and, as the breed was well established in England, according to Willughby, sixty years before Moore wrote, it was probably a traditionary account of its origin. I have satisfied myself, however, that Moore's account is a true one, having had many opportunities of seeing the carrier pigeons of Bagdad. In the city of Calcutta, some years since, resided Mr. David J. Ezra, a native of Bagdad, whose business connections extended over all the south of Asia. He had been a carrier fancier in Bagdad in his youth, and at the time referred to, the ships that were consigned to him from Basorah—the Bazora of Moore—often brought him carriers to add to the stock of those birds which he had kept for many years in Calcutta. I shall describe the appearance of these later on. They were kept in an aviary in the courtyard of his house, and shared, with some Arabian gazelles, the care and attention of their owner.

THE CARRIER.

The earliest description of the English carrier known to me is Willughby's. He describes them as "of equal bigness with common pigeons, or somewhat less, of a dark blue or blackish colour; their eyes are compassed about with a broad circle of naked, tuberous, white, furfuraceous skin, the upper chap of the bill is covered above half way from the head with a double crust of the like fungous skin." The beak is described as black in colour, and not short, but of a moderate length. "Of this kind," he says, "we saw in the King's aviary in St. James's Park, and at Mr. Cope's, an embroiderer, in Jewin-street, London." From the repeated mention of him by Willughby, Mr. Cope seems to have been a very prominent fancier in London then; and King Charles II., in addition to his fondness for the breed of spaniels which now bears his name, was evidently a carrier fancier. "Charles was also extremely fond of sauntering in St. James's Park, where he would feed the birds, with which it was well stocked, with his own hands, and on these occasions very much preferred being attended by only one or two of his personal friends rather than by a retinue." This may be found in the short account of the King's personal history in Bohn's edition of Count Grammont's "Memoirs of the Court of Charles II."

It seems strange that among the many admirers of the carrier, no one should have written a treatise on it, which might well have been done, considering how much there is in connection with it worth writing about. Some enthusiastic fancier may yet do as much for this pigeon as Windus and Eaton have done for the almond tumbler. What might have become a monograph on the English carrier was begun in a serial way in the pages of "The Pigeon," by its editor, Mr. Thomas M. Denne, of London, but was never completed, on account of the cessation of that journal through the ill-health of Mr. Denne.

The carrier takes three years and upwards to come to maturity. At some of the principal exhibitions, classes are provided for birds bred during the preceding season; but, generally, the carrier classes are only available for old birds. This pigeon looks particularly well during two periods of its existence, viz., when under a year old, when its noble shape and carriage are at their best, and then again when its head properties are fully developed. A careful study of all that our old books on pigeons contain regarding it, proves that it has steadily advanced in excellence since Moore's time. Like other varieties which take long to mature, good specimens are very valuable, and I believe the sum of £100 has been paid on at least three occasions for a fine specimen of this breed. Its name is, without doubt, derived from the use made of it when first introduced into this country, the same having been retained when it became strictly a fancier's pigeon. Its sub-varieties, the horseman and dragoon—names which also clearly show their origin—were the birds mostly used in Moore's time as homing pigeons, but it was merely because carriers were too valuable " to risque their being lost upon every trifling wager," as he plainly says, and not that they were incapable of homing a good distance, for, says he, "such is the admirable Cunning, or Sagacity of this Bird, that tho' you carry 'em Hood-winkt, twenty or thirty Miles, nay I have known 'em to be carried three-score or a hundred, and there turn'd loose, they will immediately hasten to the Place where they were bred." When Moore has written this regarding the pure carriers of his day, we must come to the conclusion that they were not so developed in fancy points as they now are, or, that such as could fly sixty to a hundred miles were either comparatively young ones, or old ones which had never made up much in beak and eye-wattle. There can be no reasonable doubt that the carrier is descended from the same stock, as has been used for many ages in the East as messenger pigeons, and that whatever it might be capable of doing now, its near relatives, both in this country and on the continent of Europe, are the pigeons capable above all others of homing from great distances. We have no means of knowing when the originals of our fancy carriers were first brought into England. It may have been about the time of the Crusades, but, from Moore's succinct account, it is probable that the breed was of no long standing in London when he wrote, and that his words, already quoted, may have been handed down through only a few generations of fanciers. From the fact of pigeons having been used as messengers from the time of Anacreon, who wrote about 520 B.C., and from the fact of a long-faced, heavily-beak and eye-wattled breed, being the foundation of the highest developed type of homing pigeon, we may assume that such a breed has existed from the time when this country was only inhabited by a race of uncivilised nomads. As, however, ethnologists tell us that the tide of the human race has been ever Westward, our ancestors may have only given up the carrier fancy in the East, to resume it in these later days in the West.

The points of excellence in the fancy carrier are the following:

Size.—The carrier should be a large pigeon, and the larger the better. From the point of the beak to the end of the tail, as fanciers measure a pigeon, it should be from 16in. upwards. I lately measured a blue hen belonging to Mr. G. H. Gillham, of Vauxhall-road, London, and found her 17¾in., and a young blue cock of the same strain was 17¼in. These measurements are strictly correct, and many would have made them greater, for I have generally been unable to make pigeons measure what has been stated to me as their length of limb and feather. This blue hen owed her length as much to neck as to feather, and was not badly proportioned in any way. I should say, then, that a full sized cock carrier should measure 18in. in feather, without having an unduly long tail. Blues are, however, admitted to be very stylish and handsome birds, though not generally up to blacks and duns in head properties. For the latter, 17in. at present is a good measurement.

Shape and Carriage.—In Moore's description of the carrier the following sentence occurs: "Their Flesh is naturally firm, and their Feathers close, when they stand erect upon their Legs, their Necks being usually long, there appears in them a wonderful Symmetry of Shape beyond other Pigeons, which are generally crowded on Heaps." This is so well put that I cannot help quoting it. My drawing of a carrier is entirely ideal, and represents what I consider a model one. It will be seen that the bird stands very erect and firmly on its legs, with a long outstretched neck, and with its beak at right angles to the same. The neck ought to be long and thin, with a clean run under the jaw, showing no gullet or thickness, and with a beautifully arched or rounded-off shape at the back of the head. The neck ought to be as much as possible slender all the way down, till it runs into the body; but this appearance is only seen in young birds. As they mature they naturally get thicker at the junction of neck and body. The wing butts should be well forward and level with the front of the breast, which ought to be broad. The carrier is naturally shy and wild, and this is of advantage to its shape and carriage in the show pen, as any tameness or familiarity is quite at variance with a statuesque appearance. The inflation of the crop and spreading of the tail, which add to the beauty of a good pouter, when seen in a carrier only spoil its fine shape.

The Beak.—This ought to be long, straight, and thick. Moore says:

"As to its Length, an Inch and a half is reckon'd a long Beak, tho' there are very good Carriers that are found not to exceed an Inch and a Quarter." The arguments that have been founded on this statement have evidently been based on the assumption that Moore's measurement was the same as that still known as London measure, viz., from the point of the beak to the inner edge of the eye. I cannot believe that Moore measured as far as the eye, considering the length he gives. He evidently measured from the point of the beak to where the feathers begin to grow, behind the mouth. I think the fairest way to measure is from the point of the beak to the centre of the eye, which is the method now generally adopted and best understood. Measured in this way, therefore, the carrier should be as long as possible; but mere length is of little consequence compared to the style and set of the beak. It ought to be thick, and especially so at the point; and the under mandible ought to approach the upper in consistency as much as possible, fitting closely to it. This is known as a box beak, which is one of the greatest beauties of the bird. The beak ought next to be straight and not inclining downwards, or the bird is downfaced, which takes considerably from its appearance. The division between the mandibles should be exactly straight, and, when the bird is in position, level, or at a right angle with the neck, and should appear as shown in the illustration. As to the length of the beak, measured to the centre of the eye, two inches is about the extreme length ever seen in a box-beaked bird. Thin spindle beaks, and those in which the upper mandible has been allowed to grow out past the under, have been seen exceeding this measurement considerably, but such are of no intrinsic value, a blunt box beak being what is desired.

Beak Wattle.—This being one of the hardest points to breed good, is accordingly a valuable one when anything like perfect. A bird has seldom enough of it, to enable it to be shown with success, till it has moulted four times, and it sometimes continues to grow for five or six years. Many kinds of pigeons get rough in beak and eye wattle with age, but the carrier has an extraordinary developement of these parts. This abnormal growth of wattle round the eyes and on the beak constitutes its chief fancy value, all its other properties being merely adjuncts thereto, calculated to set off these wattle points to the greatest advantage. A good beak wattle must be broad across the beak when seen from the front, short in profile view, so as to show as much of the point of the beak as possible, and rise high above the beak with a forward inclination at its summit, which is called being well tilted. The growth of the beak wattle has been compared to that of the cauliflower, which is a good illustration. It ought to rise in three distinct portions as shown, and be as equal as possible in formation on each of its sides, so as to have their indentations or crevices corresponding and alike. The wattle on the under mandible is called the jew wattle, a term not in use in the old pigeon books, and the origin of which is obscure. Some have considered *jewed* a corruption of *jawed;* but, as it was customary for the Jews, during the last century, to wear their beards when the English did not do so, the word may be no corruption or technicality, but mean, literally, *bearded*. The carrier seems to have had little jew-wattle in Moore's time; he refers to the beak wattle as being "sometimes join'd by two small Excrescences of the same kind on each Side of the under Chap." The picture of a carrier in the Treatise, however, is well jewed. The jew wattle ought to be similarly formed to that on the upper mandible, though less in degree, so that when all is fairly well formed, the beak with its wattles, upper and under, has the shape of a peg top. Sometimes the jew wattle grows very much forward, and is heaviest towards the point of the beak, and this, though not the correct form, is generally found on what are very stout birds. A form of beak wattle, called the walnut wattle, has the three portions on the upper mandible very much in one mass, and not so prominently defined as in the peg top style. This form, when large and well shaped, is also valuable. A full sized beak wattle should measure 4in. in circumference.

The head ought to be long, narrow, and flat on the top. Length is necessary for the growth of eye wattle, and to prevent the crowding together of the beak and eye wattles. Length of head assists what is called the distance, or space dividing the eye-wattle from that of the beak, and this is also improved by the tilting of the latter. However, Moore very truly says, when writing of the distance, "but I cannot allow this to be a Property, because when a Carrier comes to be three or four years old, if the Eye is broad, and the Wattle large, they must of Necessity meet." This is no doubt true; at the same time a clear dividing space or distance between the wattles is admired, and the greater the length of head the more distance there will be. The head ought to be narrow, and as much as possible equally broad over its length; it ought also to be flat across, and it is sometimes depressed on the crown, which is not considered any fault. There is often a protuberance at the back of the skull, but the less of this the better, as it takes from the graceful curve of the head and neck. If the head be arched from side to side, it is barrel-headed, which is a serious defect. In profile view, however, the head ought to be rather rounded from back to forehead, or there is no room for a large eye wattle to spread upwards, in which case it must either grow over the crown, or, if thick and heavy, fall downwards over the eye, which is called being beetle-browed. In the illustration, the eye wattle is supposed to be standing a little higher than the head, the outline of which would run through the first line of eye-wattle lacing from the top.

Eye.—The eye should be large and prominent, or bolting, or staring, as it is called by fanciers. When looked at from above, the pupils should be seen standing quite outside of the eye wattles. The bolt eye always tells well in competition, as it gives an otherwise good bird a fine appearance. The irides of black and blue carriers ought to be, and usually are, of a fiery red; they are lighter in duns and hazel in whites.

Eye Wattle.—This ought to be as large as is consistent with perfect roundness, and consequently the diameter of a perfect eye wattle is limited to an inch or a little more. I have seen a crown piece laid on the eye of a carrier and not cover the wattle. Such enormous eye wattles are generally accompanied by rather small beak wattles, and are of no intrinsic value, as, in their growth, they must depart from the true circular shape. The eye wattle ought to be thin rather than thick in substance, soft yet firm in flesh, of an equal breadth all round the eye, and evenly laced. This is known as a "rose eye," is the most difficult to obtain, and the most esteemed. When the inner edge of the eye wattle takes an angular cornered shape, instead of being round, it is known as a diamond eye; but though many admire this, it is not a form of such true beauty as the rose eye. The eye wattle is a property which is subsidiary to the beak-wattle, which is the most difficult point to get both large and well shaped. Given a good beak wattle, then a distance is necessary between it and the eye wattle to set off both, and, consequently, there is only room for a really round eye wattle of a certain diameter. An eye wattle perfectly circular and more than an inch in diameter must encroach on the beak wattle and decrease the distance.

Colour.—The carrier ought to be self-coloured, and is found black, dun, blue, silver, chequered, and white. Moore says, at p. 28 of his "Columbarium," "Its Feather is chiefly black or dun, tho' there are likewise blues, whites, and pieds of each Feather, but the black and dun answer best the foregoing Properties; yet the blues, and blue pieds are generally esteem'd for their Scarcity, tho' they will not usually come up to the Properties of the foregoing Feathers." This statement remains generally true after a lapse of nearly a century and a half. The black ought to be deep and glossy, showing no dulness on the wing coverts, or with wing bars of a darker colour, as is often the case. A white beak, or the same with a black tip to the upper mandible is admired, as often accompanying lustrous colour, but though a white or flesh coloured beak in a black carrier is allowable, it is not a *sine quâ non.* Strictly speaking, a black pigeon ought to have the beak and toe nails black, just as a white pigeon must have them white. A white pouter without a coloured feather on it would lose all chance in competition if dark beaked; a white beak in a black pouter would be a serious fault; and a black-headed nun with a white beak would have no chance in competition whatever, however good otherwise. How, then, does it come that black pigeons, such as carriers and barbs, are allowed to have white beaks, and are admired with such? The reason is that in breeding the different self colours together in barbs, and the black and light-beaked dun in carriers, the flesh-coloured beak often remains in the best coloured blacks, so that it has come to be considered by many as correct; however, some of the best coloured pigeons I have ever seen—the turbiteens —have generally in black, red, and yellow, beaks coloured according to their feather.

Regarding the colour of the wattles in the carrier, Moore says: "This Flesh is in some Carriers more inclinable to a blackish Colour, which is generally the more valued." At the present time, the whiter they are in the colour of the wattles the better they are liked. Pigeons of brilliant colour are generally inclined to run reddish in the flesh round the eyes, and carriers are occasionally seen so marked in this respect that very good ones have been distinguished as "red eyed." Many have decidedly reddish flesh-coloured wattles.

The usual method in breeding carriers is to freely cross the black and dun colours. By this means the black is more easily kept good than by constantly breeding blacks together. The dun, which is generally considered an off-colour in most fancy pigeons, though not in carriers, is mostly of a soft tint, inclined to fade near the end of the season, and presenting a very dappled appearance during the moult, till all the feathers are renewed. Neither the bright lavender dun seen in some foreign pigeons, nor the deep glossy dun, of the barb, are common in carriers.

Blue carriers are still inferior in average quality of head points to the blacks and duns, but in size and shape they are sometimes excellent. They fail, however, for the most part, in colour, being often of a dull or dusky blue on the wing coverts, with indistinct or half obliterated wing-bars. Blues have of late years risen in favour among fanciers, and some superior ones are occasionally to be seen. Considerable attention is being paid to them, and they will, no doubt, continue to improve.

Silvers are sometimes produced from blues, and have usually the same failing in colour. They are generally hens. The bad colour in blue carriers is often attributed to crossing with blacks, which is sometimes done to obtain stoutness in head points; but I am of opinion that their bad colour is inherent in the breed, and has always existed since it was introduced, as I have observed the same bad blue colour among the carriers of Bagdad, the undoubted originals of our carriers. Black being occasionally bred with blue, and all blacks being full of dun blood, the silver colour, which is the original of the dun, is bred from the black-crossed blue, as a natural consequence.

As the blue and black, and the silver and dun colours exist in the breed, their intermediate or connecting colours, the blue and silver chequers (dun chequers in fanciers' language) are sometimes produced. These colours are not cultivated, however, though they might, if otherwise good, be valuable enough as stock birds. Such blue and dun chequers as are produced in crossing the solid with the barred colours, do not illustrate what might be accomplished were they to be bred for as varieties. A correctly marked chequer must not only be properly dappled on the wing coverts, but show the marking down the rump and on its underbody. To get such marking distinct is a very difficult matter indeed. Red and yellow, the choicest colours in domestic pigeons, do not exist in carriers. I have been told that Mr. Corker, the well known fancier, made considerable progress at one time in breeding yellow carriers, but that he did not persevere in his attempt. There is no doubt that reds and yellows could be produced, but the time and expense requisite for the work would necessarily be very great. Were several breeders to attempt it simultaneously, it is not unlikely that in twenty years, or perhaps even less, both reds and yellows might be bred, fit to show in good company.

White carriers existed from Moore's time, down to about twenty years ago, when the best collection of them belonged to Mr. Potter, a London breeder. His stock was stolen, and it is believed they were destroyed, as none of them were ever recovered. Since then, attempts have been made to resuscitate this variety, and a few fairly good ones have been bred. Although there is no sure way of breeding albinoes from coloured pigeons, we know that they are occasionally so produced, and I know of severa instances. It is not unlikely, therefore, that some one of the many carrier breeders may be fortunate enough to have a pure white young one from his best black or dun birds, and such would be much more valuable than what have been bred from the dragoon cross. When an albino is bred from a pair of coloured pigeons, they ought to be kept breeding together, if albinoes are desired, as they are likely to do the same again, the cause of lack of colour in their produce remaining with them. Ordinary white pigeons are well covered with yellow down when hatched, but an albino from coloured parents is hatched devoid of down, like the majority of pigeons which afterwards prove to be of a poor yellow; for richly coloured yellows have a good covering of down when hatched, though not so much as reds and blacks.

Pied carriers are mentioned by Moore, but how they ought to be pied neither he nor any subsequent writer has set forth. I do not think there is any understanding among fanciers on the question. During the late scarcity of whites, and in the attempts to breed them, parti-coloured birds have been produced, and classes have occasionally been made for "whites or pieds." There is enough in the standard of the carrier, as a self-coloured bird, to require the utmost attention of its breeders, without adding specific white marking, which would have to be done if pieds were to be recognised. There is no doubt the carrier looks best as a whole-coloured pigeon. Blacks and duns have often white vents, and occasionally white feathers at their hocks, or white crutches, as they are called, as well. These faults in the eyes of some judges preclude them being shewn as self-coloured birds, which, with such pigeons as carriers, is carrying the letter of the law too far. A white crutched bird should doubtless lose a point or two in competition, but not be disqualified altogether, unless the white about it is extensive. A merely white vented bird, which does not show it unless when handled, should only lose to an equally good bird free of white. Many good strains of carriers have these small faults, which have not been considered a disqualification hitherto; but the question is one for breeders to settle among themselves.

When the beak wattle of a carrier grows unequally, or when its eye wattles become over-hanging, causing it to be beetle-browed, cutting and carving them into shape is sometimes practised. Pigeons made up or "faked" in this way ought, of course, to be disqualified if exhibited, the object of all shows of fancy stock, such as pigeons, poultry, or dogs, being to encourage natural, not artificial excellence. Carriers cut in the eye wattles for spouts are, however, on a different footing. They have undergone a necessary operation, which should not disqualify them in competition. But, as it is an object to breed the true rose eye which will not spout, one cut for that fault ought to be heavily handicapped in competition, as being a bird likely to perpetuate spouting eyes in its produce, and, therefore, not of a desirable type.

Before concluding my notice of this pigeon, it may be interesting to many to record how some of the best specimens lately seen were bred. About twenty years ago, the London birds, though often well developed in head points, were generally wanting in the style and symmetry necessary to show off these properties. They were short in feather, crouching in attitude, and devoid of the appearance known as "racy." At the same time, the Plymouth strain of carriers, though not generally so heavy in head properties, were upstanding stylish birds, beautifully shaped, and of fine proportions. A well-known Plymouth breeder, Mr. Holman, wishing to part with his stock about the year 1860, they were purchased by two Scotch pouter breeders, Messrs. Ure, of Dundee, and Huie, of Glasgow, the latter making the journey to Plymouth in the middle of winter to secure them. Those gentlemen then commissioned Mr. Fulton, who at that time lived in Deptford, to obtain for them some stout birds of the London strain. The amalgamation of these two strains produced some of the best carriers ever seen, the character and quality of which were quickly recognised, and I believe their blood remains in all the best birds of the day.

CHAPTER LXXI.

THE BAGDAD CARRIER PIGEON.

My acquaintance with the carrier pigeons of Bagdad has been confined to such as were brought to Bengal by Arab ships from Basorah, during my residence in Calcutta. The best I have seen were those I mentioned as belonging to the Jewish merchant, Mr. D. J. Ezra. I occasionally saw an odd pair or two elsewhere, but they were always inferior to his, and would be more correctly described as heavy dragoons than carriers. They went by the name of Bagdadees, from their native place. Mr. Ezra, from his position and influence, would be able to obtain the best birds, and I have no doubt that those in his aviary fairly represented the breed. He had about six or seven pairs, some of which were matured pigeons. They were all blues with black bars, most of them rather dusky in colour. I could see no difference between them and English carriers, as regards size and general characteristics. The old cocks had heavy beak-wattles and fair eye-wattles. Their faults were those of forty-nine out of every fifty English carriers, being inclined to be broad-skulled and rather down-faced or Roman-nosed. I consider them, not only from Moore's account, but from their appearance, as the undoubted originals of our carriers, which have been brought to their present condition by generations of persevering fanciers. And, after all, how many carriers out of the hundreds bred annually in England are fit to be penned at a first class show? The best birds we have produce plenty not nearly so stout as the best of those I have seen from Bagdad. Were any good carrier breeder to visit that city, I believe he might find birds which he would consider well worth bringing home with him, but whether of other colours than blue I am unable to say.

CHAPTER LXXII.

THE DRAGOON PIGEON.

BEFORE touching on the dragoon, it is necessary to say something about the pigeon which our old writers called the horseman, a bird holding a position somewhere between the carrier and dragoon. Although no longer recognised in the fancy, the horseman was distinguished from the carrier in being found in greater variety of colour. It was evidently, when Moore wrote, the pigeon capable of flying the longest distances, and it had then a distinct place in the fancy, as will be seen from the following from Moore's work: "This Pigeon in Shape and Make very much resembles the Carrier, only it is smaller in all its Properties, viz. Somewhat less in Body, shorter neck'd, the protuberant Flesh upon the Beak Smaller, as likewise that round the Eye, so that there remains a larger Space or Distance between the Wattle and the Eye, in this Pigeon than in the Carrier. They are generally more inclin'd to be barrel-headed and their Eye somewhat pinch'd.

"It is to this Day a Matter of Dispute, whether this be an original Pigeon: or whether it be not a bastard strain, bred between a Carrier and a Tumbler, or a Carrier and a Powter, and so bred over again from a Carrier, and the oft'ner it is thus bred, the stouter the Horseman becomes.

"The only thing that seems inclinable to favour the Opinion, that they are original, is a strain of this kind brought over from *Scanderoon*, which will fly very great Lengths and very swift; but still the Answer readily occurs, that they may be bred originally the same way at *Scanderoon* and so transmitted to us, however, *non nostrum est inter vos tantas componere Lites*, that is, we shan't take upon us to determine such Controversies as these.

THE DRAGOON PIGEON.

"There are of this kind, of all Manners of Feathers; but the Blue and Blue-pieds are most noted to be genuine and good, and if flown are very good Breeders.

"These are one of the sorts of Pigeons that are chiefly made Use of in *England*, for the carriage of Letters, or flying of Wagers; because those that are possess'd of the true original Carriers, which are at present very scarce here, pay too dear, and have too great a Value for them, to risque their being lost upon every trifling Wager.

"These Pigeons when regularly flown, twice on a Day, that is, turn'd out alone and put upon wing without any others, will fly very large Circumferences, so that after they have made a Tour or two round your own House, they will fly four or five Miles out at Length and so maintain the Circuit for an Hour or two: This the Fanciers call going an End, and is what *Daniel Moggs*, who was one of the oldest Fanciers, meant, when he jocularly us'd to bid his Pigeons maintain their Length.

"This Practice is of admirable Service to 'em, when they come to be train'd for the homing Part."

And the following is the whole of what Moore says about the Dragoon:

"This Pigeon is absolutely and without dispute a bastard Strain, being bred originally between a Horseman and a Tumbler, and by matching their breed often to the Horseman, they will obtain a tolerable Degree of Stoutness.

"This Pigeon is a very good breeder, and as they are somewhat less than a Horseman, are reckon'd lighter, and more expeditious in their Flight, for ten or twenty Miles, but the Horseman if good, will generally out-do them at a greater Length; they ought to be flown and train'd like the foregoing."

During the last few years, the dragoon has been extensively bred and shown, and its popularity has been so great that, even at first-class shows, it has been encouraged with a classification and an amount of prize money out of all proportion to its merits. This pandering to false taste in pigeon breeding culminated at the Oxford show of 1876, where dragoons had eighteen classes, against sixteen for carriers, pouters, tumblers, and barbs combined. Wearisome discussions have also gone on for years over the standard of a dragoon, and I am not aware if those who have a place in their hearts for fancy pigeons, which the dragoon is capable of filling, have settled the matter amongst themselves yet. Some short time ago the National Peristeronic Society of London appointed a committee of its members to consider the question, and on the 6th January, 1880, this committee, after taking the subject to avizandum, handed in the following report, which it was hoped would have been accepted as the conclusion of the whole matter, but it merely opened up some fresh discussions, so that their deliverance can only be called an interlocutor after all.

"Gentlemen,—Your Committee, appointed to consider and note the points of the Dragon, have the satisfaction of presenting in their Report the following enumeration of properties, which, subject to your approval, will constitute the Standard of the Dragon, as recognised by the Members of the National Peristeronic Society.

"The *Skull* wedge-shaped and broad, yet proportionate to the stoutness and length of the beak, slighty curved when viewed from the side or front, thus showing no angle or extended flat surface.

"The *Beak* thick at its base, and so continuing for about half its length, thence gradually lessening in calibre. Measurement from the termination of the beak horn to the anterior corner of the eye, not less than 1¼ inches. The lower mandible stout and straight; the upper also thick, and terminating in a slight curve.

"The *Beak-wattle* peg-shaped, *i.e.*, broad and perpendicular at its base, narrowing with even sides and longitudinal furrows towards the point of the upper mandible, but not intruding on the lower.

"The *Eye-wattle* small, not fleshy, nearly circular, slightly pinched at the back.

"The *Eye* prominent and watchful. In Blues, Silvers, Chequers, and Grizzles, the irides of a deep rich red colour. In other varieties, an approximation to this colour; except in Whites, in which the iris is dark coloured.

"The *Neck* of medium length, neither thin nor gulleted at the head, and widening boldly at the shoulders.

"The *Breast* broad, the Shoulders prominently defined.

"The *Back* nearly straight, neither hollow nor hogged.

"The *Wings* strong, the Flights carried slightly above the tail.

"The *Tail* running in a line with the back, carried clear of the ground, and extending quite half an inch beyond the tips of the wings.

"*Measurement* of the leg from the hook to the foot, about 1¼ inches. The Thigh stout and muscular. The Whole length of the Dragon, from the point of the beak to the extremity of the tail, about 15 inches.

"*Colour* in *Blues*. — The Neck dark and lustrous; the Body, Rump, and Thighs a leaden blue of uniform shade. Markings — A broad black bar across the end of the tail. Two black bars, about ⅜ of an inch wide, even and distinct, running transversely from top to bottom of each wing, in the form of the letter V inverted. Colour of beak, black. Colour of eye-wattle, a deep blue-grey.

"*Silvers*.—An uniform and bright creamy tint. Neck of a deeper shade. Bars as black as possible. Beak of a dark shade.

"*Grizzles and Chequers*.—Each feather distinctly grizzled or chequered. The Markings, colour of Beaks, and Eye-wattles, same as in blues.

"*Yellows and Reds*.—Colour uniform and bright. Beak of an even flesh colour."

The foregoing scale of points nearly agrees with what was formerly known as the "London style," opposed to which, the "Birmingham School" upheld a more skinnumy kind of dragoon. Both kinds are fully described by their partisans in Mr. Fulton's book, where coloured plates of each are given. I think no one can carefully read Moore's descriptions of the horseman and dragoon without coming to the conclusion that the latter was, in his day, a different bird from the modern London one, which closely approximates to his description of the horseman, with its barrel-head, pinched eye, and various colours, of which, "the blues and blue-pieds are most noted to be genuine and good." I think that, in the course of time, Moore's horseman and dragoon have gradually amalgamated in the present London dragoon, which has become of a somewhat fixed type in the hands of London pigeon keepers, though probably without much design on their part; and now, in these days of pigeon shows, when, in the course of a year, a typical bird, according to the foregoing standard, can win quite a large sum of money in prizes, it is no wonder that what was before show days a pigeon worth only a few shillings, is now very valuable indeed.

On comparing the standards of the carrier and dragoon, it will be seen that much which is faulty in the former becomes positively excellent in the latter. From this, it might be supposed that a very bad carrier would make a very good dragoon, which is by no means the case, for, in practice, it is found no easy matter to breed the latter good according to the standard. About the time of the Oxford show, in 1876, already referred to, Mr. Denne, editor of the *Pigeon*, published an article in that paper on "Exhibiting and Breeding Dragoons," from which I copy the following: "It matters not what interested parties may say, the real value of dragoons is about four or five shillings a pair. Of course, temporary causes, such as this sudden run upon them for exhibition, may cause the price of them to rise to much more than this, but the price we name is the true one, as experienced men know, and we have bought scores of pairs as good as ever have been seen, and could have bought thousands at the price. We have even bought them as late as the early part of this year, and end of last, at an average price of seven shillings a pair, as good as need be wished for, and in some cases good enough to win prizes. The highest price we ever paid for a dragoon in the whole of our experience we paid this year, viz., seven and sixpence for a blue hen, and at the time we did so thought we must have been slightly 'touched' to pay such a price. From these birds we purchased we could, had we been disposed to have gone in for dragoon breeding, have bred as good blues, chequers, and grizzles in the course of one, or, at the most two seasons as the 'next man,' and so can anyone who has a very slight knowledge of breeding, by following the instructions we will give."

Though it is some years since this was written, during the interval, the chief prizes for blue, blue-chequered, and blue-grizzled dragoons, have been won by the birds of Mr. Woods, of Mansfield, Notts, who, for many years, with all colours of dragoons, has kept the premier position against all comers, netting what must have been a respectable annual income from this breed alone. Before the days of pigeon shows, a pair of choice pouters, carriers, or almond tumblers were worth as many sovereigns as the best dragoons were worth fourpenny bits. How is it, therefore, that now a good dragoon is worth, roundly speaking, about as much as a good pigeon of these varieties? Merely because it pays well enough to give as much for a bird as it can win in a season. The dragoon formerly held the present position of the homing Antwerp carrier, and, like it, may have been occasionally worth a large sum for flying purposes. It now holds the same position as the short-faced exhibition Antwerp, and is just about equal to it as a fancy pigeon. Both would go down to their former price of a few shillings a pair but for show encouragement. Real fancy pigeons have undoubtedly risen in value since shows were established; but they were highly valued before, and they would continue to be highly valued were pigeon shows abolished. To establish a breed of exhibition pigeons from the faulty produce of barbs, taking as their standard of perfection a narrow skull, a small pinched eye-wattle, and a run-out face, of a certain length, would be an analogous case to what has been done with the dragoon since pigeon shows were established. Before then, the breed had no fancy value whatever, and as for that, it has no fancy value now out of England, and only there within a limited circle.

The first thing to be observed in the National Peristeronic Society's standard of the dragoon is the name they give it—the "dragon." The analogy between the names carrier, horseman, and dragoon is clear, but at some time before the oldest living fanciers were born it became usual to call the dragoon the dragon. This is noticed in Moubray's Poultry Book, first published in 1815, and which went through five editions in ten years. The author says, "Dragoons (commonly called dragons)." The name would easily become corrupted and more easily pronounceable among illiterate pigeon keepers, who were, doubtless, formerly the chief breeders of dragoons; and, when gentlemen went to buy feeders for their carriers and pouters they would hear them spoken of by shopkeepers and others as dragons, and so gradually come to speak of them by that name among themselves. I have known a similar alteration of the name in my own experience. I can remember when there were very few dragoons, skinnums, or Antwerps in Dundee; nothing but flying tumblers being fancied by the poorer class of pigeon keepers. When homing pigeons became in request, everything with the least beak or eye-wattle more than a tumbler was known in their language as a "draigon." This was afterwards shortened into "draig," and now the word is "drake." I was rather surprised lately to hear a gentleman's son tell me he had some fine "drake" pigeons. I have written *dragon* before now for *dragoon*, but I admit there is no defence for this. However the word may be pronounced in conversation, it ought to be written as of old, because its meaning is clear, and not obscure. There is a quaint note by Eaton, on page 59 of his 1858 book, on this question: "Why do authors on Pigeons spell the Dragon with two 'o's', making the word Dragoon, a kind of soldier, &c. (Walker)? In society we never call it the Dragoon, but the Dragon —Drag-un, a winged serpent (Walker), from which it derives its name. I hope no author who follows me, will be guilty of doing it." This is amusing, and very Eatonesque. Quite a crusade against writing the name "dragon" has in late years been preached from a certain quarter, but whether those who have been lectured consider their would-be instructors' interference obnoxious, or are convinced they are right, is more than I know.

I must next say something about the beak and eye-wattles of the dragoon. What they ought to be in a show bird is clearly stated; but it is quite usual for the best birds, while still in the very prime of life, to put on, with advancing age, more wattle than is allowable for the show pen, or to become "*more than a dragon,*" as it is called. This bird, therefore, occupies a quite unique position among exhibition pigeons. A fantail can never become more than a fantail, nor a jacobin more than a jacobin. I have seen dragoons that could win at from two to three years of age become, when five or six, great coarse-wattled, pinch-eyed horsemen. They are then only fit for stock birds.

The colours of dragoons mentioned in the Peristeronic Society's Report do not include black and dun. This is wisdom itself. It would scarcely do, for reasons good, to have show dragoons of these colours. There was lately an inquiry in *The Bazaar* newspaper on this very subject, and the answer given was this: "They would have no chance in competition whatever." But why not? I would have thought that the more variety of colour in a breed the better. It will be seen from the report that the said society advocates a silver with dark beak and eyes, and with bars as black as possible. There can be no harm in fancying such a colour, but why should the real silver be ignored, and not even be mentioned? As I have said before, what may be called the four primary barred colours of pigeons include the silver with dun bars. There are many variations in the colours of wing bars in pigeons, one of which— the body colour of the silver with the black bar of the blue, or as near it as possible—is what many consider a silver ought to be; but I know this is a mistake. The golden dun barred dragoon, generally called brown barred, is a well known variety which ought to be recognised. It has a yellow iris and light beak.

A well known breeder of blue carriers told me that, having an odd blue carrier cock matched to an Antwerp hen as feeders, he bred a young one from them, which so took the fancy of a dragoon breeder, that he gave him £7 for it. *Verbum sat sapienti.*

The dragoon as a show pigeon is merely an excrescence of the show system. The following is from the "Treatise on Pigeons," 1765, p. 89: "They are very good breeders, and good nurses; and are chiefly kept as feeders for raising of powters, Leghorn runts, &c.

"The following may be depended upon as fact, notwithstanding the appearance of incredibility, as several gentlemen now living can affirm the same if requisite:

"A gentleman of my acquaintance, having a small wager depending, sent a dragoon by the stage coach to his friend at St. Edmond's Bury, together with a note, desiring the Pigeon, two days after his arrival there, might be thrown up precisely when the town clock struck nine in the morning, which was accordingly executed, and the Pigeon arrived in London, and flew to the sign of the Bull Inn in Bishopsgate-Street, into the loft, and was there shewn at half an hour past eleven o'clock the same morning on which he had been thrown up at St. Edmond's Bury, having flown seventy-two miles in two hours and a half; the wager was confirmed by a letter sent by the next post from the person at St. Edmond's Bury.

"I could relate several more exploits of this nature performed by dragoons; particularly of their being thrown up and returning home by moon-light, &c."

In Eaton's 1858 book, p. 59, there is also the following note by Mr. John Boys: "Thirty-six years ago, when my collection of Dragons (about thirty) every morning brought me from London, in slips, the leading article of the *Morning Post* newspaper tied round the leg"—regarding which, Eaton adds, "From London to Margate, seventy-two miles; a decent fly, and proves Dragons can do work."

I think there is no doubt that the Belgian voyageur owes the best part of its homing faculty either to the English dragoon, or to the same oriental pigeon, which I take to be the original of our fancy carrier. I have lately received, through M. V. La Perre de Roo, of Paris, several pairs of these pigeons from the loft of one of the chief amateurs of Paris, regarding which he writes: "They have all been sent this year to Bordeaux (310 miles) and to Bayonne (410 miles), and the oldest of them have been sent last year to Biarritz (420 miles). I know the birds well, as they *all* descend from birds I got myself for him from MM. Georges d'Hanis and Georges Gits, the two most successful fanciers of Antwerp." These birds are all blues, excepting one, which is a light blue chequer. They are so much alike that it is only a fancier who could distinguish the slight differences between them, and then it can only be done after some days' close observation. They appear, whatever their composition may be, to be a mixture of dragoon and tumbler. They have the blue-grey eye-wattles, the red eyes, and short flights of the dragoon. There is a wild look about them, quite different from what pigeons otherwise exactly like them have, and they are always hanging about the bolting wires of their loft, evidently in a hurry to be off.

The following was published in the *Fanciers' Chronicle* of 20th August, 1880, and was noticed also in the *Field* and other papers: "Wonderful performance of a homer.—In February last year I bought from Mr. Mills, Brussels, some homing pigeons. On Sunday, the 8th instant, I gave one of these birds its liberty, and it disappeared. I thought no more of it, but on Thursday last I was surprised to receive from Mr. Mills a letter, saying that the bird reached his loft on Wednesday morning. I send you this information as I consider this a most marvellous performance, the bird having been in confinement many months, and had to travel over about four hundred miles of country which it had never seen. The pigeon in question is a three-year old blue-chequer hen, and will be again in my possession to-night or to-morrow morning, Mr. Mills having sent it off yesterday.—JAMES P. TAYLOR, Moss Croft, Gateshead-on-Tyne."

This is a record of a truly wonderful performance, one similar to that which was accomplished by the birds of Mr. Huie, of Glasgow. Training brings out the natural homing powers of these pigeons, but that they do not fly by sight alone, the above proves. And in training for the long Continental matches the final stages often exceed a hundred miles, over which the best birds fly straight home. What guides them on their way? It is best described poetically in the verse which heads Mr. Huie's paper already transcribed.

Although some of the foregoing ought properly to have appeared under the head of the Antwerp carrier, rather than omit it, I give it here, knowing it will be interesting to many, as the fancy for homing pigeons is daily increasing in this country. For the same reason I give the following interesting account of the origin of the Belgian homing pigeons, only just received by me in a letter from M. V. La Perre de Roo, so well known on the Continent for his researches into the subject, and as the adviser of nearly all the Continental governments in their adoption of these pigeons for war purposes.

"As regards the Belgian homing pigeons, they are very much like our street dogs (*chiens de rue*), they are the result of numerous crossings between the carrier and the different varieties of pigeons which existed in Belgium about a century ago. In other words, *they are degenerated carriers*, as the wattle on the upper mandible of the beak and round the eye shows clearly. Some have thick short beaks, but as a rule they have thin beaks, like those sent you by M. Géré.

"There are some birds with round heads, very short beaks, and frills like owls; but they are very small birds, and are not so much liked in Belgium as the large Antwerp birds, their wings not being so powerful. These birds have undoubtedly been obtained by crossing the degenerated carrier with the owl.

"The carrier was brought to Belgium by Dutch sailors, got neglected, and soon degenerated.

"There are also birds with white eyes, and these are supposed to be a cross between the degenerated carrier and the 'pigeon volant,' or highflier (the cumulet).

"But all these birds have been crossed, as I state in my book '*dans nos fermes et nos basses cours*,' with the *pigeon biset* (the blue rock pigeon) and all the other varieties of pigeons which existed in Belgium a century ago, as is generally the case with pigeons which are kept only for table purposes.

"My father died twenty years ago at the age of seventy-six, and he often told me that the birds he had, when he was a boy, had more wattle on the beak and round the eye than the birds I kept about thirty years ago, but at that time a pigeon which had flown a distance of *twenty-five* miles was looked upon as a very good bird, and the very *few* birds which had been sent to be thrown from Paris, that is about a *hundred and fifty miles* from Brussels, were considered to be most wonderful and exceptional birds.

"Since then you know what regular training has done. During the season about 100,000 to 150,000 pigeons are sent every Saturday from all parts of Belgium, to be thrown from all parts of France, and Auch, Bordeaux, Bayonne, Biarritz, and St. Sebastien (Spain), are now the stations they are generally sent to.

"There are now upwards of 1000 pigeon societies in Belgium."

It is more than a hundred and fifteen years ago since the dragoon referred to flew from Bury St. Edmund's to London. Had English fanciers, since then, cultivated the homing faculty in pigeons on anything like the scale prevailing in Belgium, they would doubtless, long ago, have had their birds coming from all parts of Scotland and Ireland. I think the English societies ought to train north, as well as from the continent, and not remain satisfied till the journey from Wick to London is done with the same ease as from Bordeaux to Brussels. The distance is about the same.

CHAPTER LXXIII.

FOREIGN WATTLED PIGEONS.

THERE are various kinds of beak and eye-wattled pigeons described by continental writers, all of which are called Bagdads or Turks, which serves to show they are considered to be of Eastern origin. Such as seem of distinct breed from our carriers, though undoubtedly belonging to the same family, are described as follows by Boitard and Corbie, whose work on pigeons, it must be remembered, was published in Paris in 1824. Whether or not the varieties mentioned are still in existence is more than I can say.

"*Pigeon Bagadais à Grande Morille* (Great Wattled or Mushroomed Bagdad).—A mushroom, or large fleshy excrescence on the beak; large ribbon round the eyes, forming when the bird is old a second eyelid, fleshy and reddish, which falls over the eyes and prevents it from seeing. These ribbons (eye-wattles) are sometimes so large that they join at the top of the head; beak curved and crooked; eye black. This bird is thick, high on the legs, large, and short in the body, the neck fine and long, wings short, legs bare. Its backmost part is always of an inflamed red. There are several sub-varieties with plumage black, red, black and white, dun, &c. They all produce little and with difficulty; they have also become very rare, and are scarcely preserved, except as a curiosity."

"*Pigeon Bagadais Batave.*—Some authors call it grand Batavian, because the first of them were brought from Batavia; they think also that it, and not the blue rock pigeon, ought to be regarded as the primitive stock of the Bagdads. Larger than the great mushroomed Bagdad, though with less beak and eye wattle; pearled eyes; very long beak, attaining up to *dix-huit lignes de longeur;* neck extremely long; body large, short, and very high on the legs; feet and legs of the colour of blood, often long enough to get a good finger length beyond the tail when stretched out. Its walk is heavy, and its flight laborious, on account of its short wings, which, besides, are sparsely covered with feathers, and the prominent bones of the shoulders appear nearly bare. It produces little, and is not now much sought after by amateurs, who formerly did not grudge to pay up to ten *louis* a pair for them. This is no doubt owing to the little grace of their form, and the destruction they make in the aviary in plucking and killing the young of others with their formidable beak. This bird is the largest of all pigeons. M. Corbie has one large enough to drink out of an ordinary bucket without the least trouble. There has been seen, with a fancier coming from Germany, a bird called a *hen pigeon*" (Leghorn runt, or *hühnertaube*), " in all respects like the Batavian, except having no beak and eye wattle."

The illustration of this curious pigeon has been copied by Brent, on page 21 of his book, and called by him the Scanderoon or great horseman. It has much in common with my drawing of the Leghorn runt, but its very short tail is carried below its flights. I can scarcely believe that it originally belonged to Batavia, though brought thence to France. There has been a trade for centuries between Batavia and the Persian Gulf. It is a question whether the *hühnertauben*, or Leghorn runt race, owe their peculiar form to some cross with such a breed as this, in the remote past, or not. This pigeon is said to be the largest of all, not excepting the runt or pigeon Romain. It is also described by Neumeister, who gives a drawing of it, coloured red, on plate 17 of his book, as the *Französische Bagdette*. He describes it in similar terms to the foregoing, adding, that the tail is sometimes carried upright, but must not be like a swallow's tail, probably meaning that it must be close and not split. He says the plumage is close, fitting the body so tightly that all its parts are sharply prominent, especially the shoulders and the breast bone, the bare skin being often visible on these parts, which is a peculiarity, more or less, of all the carrier race. Brent says: "I have met with very fine specimens in France by the name of Swan-necked Egyptians. They are very large pigeons, almost as large as the best runts. They are thinly covered with feathers, and these lie very close to the body; neither are the tail and pinion feathers remarkable for length. Their beaks are very long and somewhat bent, and they have a moderate wattle, of a whitish colour, and the cere round the eyes is broad and red. The head is flat; the neck long, thin, and much bent; the shoulders are broad, the legs long and large, and they are the most powerful of all pigeons I have met with. They are heavy, clumsy birds, and appear to have great difficulty in rising; but I have found the young, if kept in exercise, and not allowed to get too fat, to be very swift, and excellent homing birds. In the air they reminded me of wild ducks, owing to their scanty plumage and angular form. Many points of the body are left bare, as the front of the neck and the shoulders of the wings, exposing a red skin. Mine were very good breeders, though they are not generally considered so. Their plumage is usually white, black, blue, or pied."

It is worth notice that Brent found these pigeons excellent homing birds.

"*Pigeon Bagadais petit Batave.*—It resembles in general form the Great Batavian, but it differs in its size, being much less. It produces advantageously."

"*Pigeon Bagadais Batave Soie* (lace feathered).—A new variety, quite as rare as singular. It resembles the preceding (petit Batave) in size and general form; but the fibres of its feathers are long and silky, and do not adhere together, which prevents it from flying. This bird, which is not in commerce, no doubt only multiplies in the hands of amateurs, who only consider it an object of curiosity."

I am not aware if this variety still exists, but the fact of a lace-feathered Bagdad having existed, shows that such a natural variation in feathering might occur in any breed.

"*Pigeons Turcs.*—These superb birds make the natural link between the Bagdads and runts. They have, like the first, a large beak and eye-wattle, the latter red in colour, and are of large size; but they come nearer to the runts by their thighs, legs, and neck being shorter, and by their long wings." They are described as of various colours, and both crested and plain headed. I believe most of the fancy runts, such as the one I made my drawing from, have the blood of these *Turcs*, as they have more beak and eye-wattle than the common blue and silver runts. Brent has reproduced the portrait of a *pigeon Turc*, on page 20 of his book.

Coming next to the German varieties of the carrier family, as described by Neumeister, there are the following:

Die Kurzschnäbelige Bagdette, or *Türkischetaube* (short-beaked Bagdad or Turkish pigeon), illustrated on plate 14 of his work on pigeons, and represented as both crested and plain headed, self-coloured black, red, and yellow, rather short in beak, and looking very like English dragoon pigeons.

Die Deutsche Krummschnäbelige Bagdette, or *Nürnberger Bagdette* (the German crooked-beaked or Nuremberg Bagdad). This pigeon is already well known in England as the Scanderoon, and it is well portrayed, by Mr. Ludlow, in Mr. Fulton's book. The German fancier, Führer, has described in Neumeister's work, the history and standard of excellence of this bird, as follows: "This exceedingly interesting pigeon, resembling more a fierce bird of prey than a peaceful graniverous bird, had its home in the Orient, and was probably first brought into commerce from Bagdad. In Germany, it is chiefly at Nuremberg that it is beautifully bred, a town which, hundreds of years ago, was in a lively commercial intercourse with the Levant, and has the merit of having introduced and first bred this stately bird, where it is said to be still the favourite pigeon. The beak must be beautifully bent, long, thick, blunt, and light coloured; the beak-wattle must sit deeply below on the brow, rather flat than high, heart-shaped, and not too broad; the head must be long and narrow, and, seen from the side, must form a semicircle from the nape to the point of the beak; the eye wattle or rose must be large, flat, and regular, bright red in early age, later in life rather white; the neck long and thin, and the chin adorned with a beard; the body must show a broad back and breast; the ridge of the breast bone must spring forth sharply, the pinions must be narrow and short, the tail short, and legs high."

"If the brow and beak form an angle, if the crown has a depression, if the upper mandible is longer than the under, or if they do not fit close, these are faults which are opposed to the beauty of the race."

The only thing obscure in the above is, the chin being adorned with a beard, which word is used in Germany to designate various properties in pigeons. If, in this instance, it means the slight jew-wattle inseparable from all abnormally wattled pigeons, the less of it the better. I should say that a clean cut hollow curve, from the point of the lower mandible down the throat, would look best. The thickenings at the corners of the mouth, connecting beak and eye-wattles, are called the "bridles" or "flies," and are mentioned as points of beauty. It is said that in whole colours this pigeon is only found of the highest type, all white. The pied ones are the most valued, and on the regularity of their markings fanciers set a high value. The chief marking is that shown in the aforesaid drawing by Mr. Ludlow, which may be described as exactly the same as that of the magpie pigeon, except that the head and upper neck are white. From low down on the nape, the white runs down the sides of the neck to a point on the breast, forming a pointed bib. There are also others, coloured, in addition, on lower body from breast to tail, including the thighs; the head and bib, wing coverts and flights, remaining white. The back must always remain coloured, as in the magpie, and forms the figure of a heart, and is known as "the heart." Others, again, are all coloured except the head, upper neck and bib, flight feathers, and butts of the wings, as in the stork pigeon. The quality of colour in this variety is sometimes superb, and I believe it has been made use of in this country to improve colour in red and yellow dragoons.

"Its flight is powerful, quick, and more stormy than dexterous; its voice abrupt and deep. Towards smaller pigeons it is violent, and therefore not suited to live with them, and is best kept alone. It shows mistrust to men, and only gradually becomes accustomed to its feeder." This wild nature is common to all the carrier race and their descendants.

The Himalayan Carrier.—When writing about Indian pigeons, I mentioned some gentlemen named Wood, whom I knew in Calcutta, as enthusiastic pigeon fanciers. There were four brothers of them who bred choice pigeons, and their father had done so before them. The eldest brother had the largest and best collection I knew of in Calcutta, excepting that which belonged to the ex-King of Oude. It was in Mr. Wood's aviaries I first saw the variety which I have named as above, the native name of which I have forgotten, if I ever heard it. This pigeon is about the size of an average dragoon. It is very hard and close feathered, upright in carriage, thin in neck, moderately long in neck and limbs, and inclined to be short in flights and tail. It is short in face, measuring about 1¾in. from centre of eye. The beak is stout and thick at the base, rather sharp than blunt at the point, and straight. The head is angular or wedge-shaped, the brow forming an angle with the crown and beak. It has a smooth beak-wattle, of moderate amount, which never grows quite so large as that considered necessary for a show dragoon. The striking point about this pigeon is its staring or bolting eyes, which stand more out of its head than I have ever seen in other pigeons. They are mostly hazel-coloured, large, bright, and

T

surrounded by a thin, smooth wattle, of about five-eighths of an inch diameter in matured birds. The colours of those I saw were black or blue pied, the white predominating, some being nearly all white. The black and blue patches were disposed without any regularity, no two birds being exactly alike. This pigeon, though a sub-variety of the carrier, has assumed a distinct type of its own, and bears a highly-bred look; and I imagine it is a bird capable of flying long distances.

THE POUTER.

CHAPTER LXXIV.

THE ENGLISH POUTER.

THIS noble pigeon has always been considered one of the finest varieties, sharing, with the carrier, the premier position in the fancy since the time when we have any records on the subject. It is referred to by Willughby as follows: "Croppers, so called because they can, and usually do, by attracting the air, blow up their crops to that strange bigness that they exceed the bulk of the whole body beside. A certain *Hollander* informed *Aldrovandus* that these *Kroppers Duve*, as they call them, are twice as big as the common Domestic Pigeons, which, as they fly, and while they make that murmuring noise, swell their throats to a great bigness, and the bigger the better and more generous they are esteemed. Those that I saw at Mr. Cope's, a citizen of London, living in Jewin-street, seemed to me nothing bigger, but rather less than Runts, and somewhat more slender and long-bodied. These differ no less one from another in colour than the precedent" (*i.e.* runts).

Meagre though this description be, we can learn from it that, 200 years ago, the London pouters were large pigeons, slender and long in body, and with great crops. Sixty years later, however, we have Moore's succinct account of the origin of the English pouter; but whether it was merely a traditionary account, or a narrative of facts within his own knowledge, cannot now, I fancy, be determined. First of all, he describes the Dutch cropper as follows: "This Pigeon seems to be originally *Dutch*, being naturally thick" (this is curious reasoning), "and its Name is derived from a large Bag, or crop of Wind, which they carry under their Beak, and can at Pleasure either raise or depress; they are thick bodied and short, their Legs are likewise thick, short, and feather'd down to their Feet; their Crop is large, but always hangs low; the Feathers on their Thighs hang loose, whereby they are said to be flag-thigh'd; their Legs stand wide and they seldom play upright; they are gravel Ey'd, and generally very bad Feeders, therefore as soon as they have fed off their soft Meat it is proper to put their young ones under a pair of small Runts, Dragoons, or Powting-horsemen, which may be kept as Nurses for that Purpose. There are of all Sorts of Feathers in this Pigeon, and the *Dutch* in breeding it take a very great care; for as soon as they have fed off their soft Meat, they put the young ones under others to nurse, and then separate the old ones, placing them in different Coops, and feeding them high with Hemp or Rape Seed for a Month, then turning them together; and by being very hearty and salacious, they breed Pigeons with very good Properties: from whence we may observe, that wou'd Mankind be like abstemious, their Progeny might be more compleat both in Body and Mind. These are the Pigeons that are most apt to gorge, if not kept constantly supplied with Meat and Water."

Moore next commences his description of the English pouter by saying: "This Pigeon, which was first bred in *England*, and is therefore call'd the *English* Powter, is originally a mixt breed between a Horseman and a Cropper, and by matching their young ones over and over to the Cropper, Experience teaches us, it will add a wonderful Beauty to this Bird, and raise in it the five following Properties." Though Moore does not say what kind of cropper was used for breeding the English pouter, the inference is that he referred to the aforesaid Dutch variety, which is, in fact, the only cropper he describes. His description of what constituted a good English pouter in 1735, is, indeed, excellent, so far as it goes; and though he does not go minutely into the appearance of the bird, his account of it, had nothing been added by the author of the Treatise of 1765, would give those who read his work to-day the idea that our pouter is identical with the one he describes. During the thirty years following the publication of Moore's work, however, a considerable improvement appears to have been made in the breeding of fancy pigeons, as I learn from the following, taken from the preface of the Treatise of 1765, page xiv.: "It is to be observed that the species in general, and the almond tumbler in particular, are, from great care and expence in breeding them, arrived to so great a perfection, and so different from what they were twenty or thirty years past, that if a person who had been a fancier at that period, and had quitted the fancy, and not been conversant therein during the intermediate time, was to give his opinion now, he would be apt to condemn them, for no other reason than because they are not like what used to be thought good when he was in the fancy before; for instance, the powter was formerly bred with thin legs, and void of feathers on them, which by the present fanciers are in no esteem, and called by them, naked and wire-legg'd, who now endeavour to breed them with strong substantial limbs, and well feathered."

One of the set of eight old oil paintings of fancy pigeons which I am fortunate in having lately acquired, and which I have before referred to, represents a magnificent black-pied powter cock, of the kind the above writer describes as having been fancied in Moore's time. Being quite bare in limb, with the exception of a few very short feathers down the outside of the leg, but with none whatever on the toes, I think it, as well as the other pictures, must have been painted about the time Moore wrote his book, for they are all uniform, and evidently the work of the same artist. The pictures representing the pigeons already described being life size, I suppose that of the black-pied cock to be the same, and although I have occasionally seen a bird in life standing as high as he does, it has been but seldom. He is $14\frac{1}{4}$in. from the crown of his head to the soles of his feet, and must have measured about 20in. in feather. He is short of bib, and his rose pinion might have been dressed, had the artist meant to depict a well-marked pigeon. I think, for this reason, the picture is a portrait. I can scarcely believe that such a pigeon could have been produced, in the way Moore says, under half a century at least, for the immense crop and intricate marking would alone take long to fix after a cross with the horseman, and then, Willughby's description of the powter, such as it is, written about sixty years before Moore's, is extant. At the same time, when a drawing of a model powter is made, quite devoid of crop, there can be seen in it much of the shape of the thoroughbred carrier, as anyone may prove for himself, so that it is extremely likely that the union of such a bird as Moore's Dutch cropper and the carrier would result, after a long careful breeding, in such a bird as the English powter. We find that, with age, certain powters develop a good deal of beak and eye-wattle, though birds of the same family vary greatly in this respect. If this be not derived from a remote cross of the carrier, either direct or through some of the long runts which likewise possess it, it must have developed itself in the pouter race in the same way as in that of the carrier. There has arisen quite lately, in Germany, a theory that the English pouter might have been derived from a German variety, the appearance of which I shall describe, and the arguments connected with which I shall discuss, when I come to write about it. In the meantime, I must describe what constitutes a perfect English pouter, which, even on the Continent, where many varieties of the family exist, stands confessedly at the head of them all, and which many in this country consider the finest, noblest, and most beautiful of all pigeons.

As I have already shown, the great run on the almond tumbler, about the middle of last century, was the cause of the pouter being to a great extent neglected in London, and the fancy for it appears to have been languid ever afterwards, till at last the breed nearly disappeared thence. About fifty years ago, Scotch fanciers began to breed this pigeon, and ultimately they got it almost entirely into their own hands. At that time, some of the linen manufacturers of Dundee brought home with them from London, which they were in the habit of visiting annually by way of trade, many fine pouters, which have been described to me, by those who remember them, as stylish birds, good in colour and marking. At the same time, or soon afterwards, fanciers in the West of Scotland also began breeding pouters, and from 1860 to 1870 the fancy for them may be said to have reached its zenith in Scotland. Soon after the Glasgow pigeon shows were established, or about 1860, English fanciers went into pouter breeding, but for some time they were obliged to draw their supplies of stock birds from Scotland, the breed being next to extinct, south of the Border. As records will show, this was so much the case that the pouter was for years often quite unrepresented at the annual exhibitions of metropolitan pigeon societies, the members of which confined themselves to the carrier, short-faced tumbler, dragoon, &c. At the present time, Scotland and England may be said to divide between them the breeding of pouters, but in London, the very home of this variety, where it was undoubtedly produced, so far as I know, there are still few who keep them, with the exception of the great dealers. Irish fanciers have, to some extent, bred these noble pigeons for several years back, and they have had the honour of producing many fine ones, as is well known. Some of the best I have bred myself I can trace back to birds

I bought from the late Mr. Montgomery, of Belfast, whose stock was founded chiefly on Scotch blood.

It has been usual to write of the English pouter as having five properties, viz., crop, length of limb, length of feather, slenderness of girth, and feather. Authorities are divided on the respective value of these properties and on which is the most valuable. It is no use, however, to argue over this, as a pouter must be fairly well up in all points to have any chance of winning at a good show, the bird which fails conspicuously in one of them having little chance in keen competition. In describing the pouter I shall restrict its properties to four, viz., size, shape, carriage, and feather.

Size.—The pouter must be a very large pigeon, very tall and upstanding, the larger the better. It will be found in breeding that the great difficulty is to get it of gigantic proportions, combined with quality in shape, feather, and carriage. Undersized pouters, otherwise very good, are common enough, but as soon as a certain size is reached there is not only a very great difficulty in rearing it, but it almost invariably fails in shape and carriage. It is true that the pouter has not, in late years, reached the value of the carrier; but this is owing to the fact that, at present, it is not so extensively fancied, and not that it is easier to breed. According to what was once told me by Mr. Fulton, whose knowledge of, and experience with carriers is not exceeded by that of any man, six carriers can be bred for one pouter, of the same degrees of quality, according to their respective standards. After size and shape are got, the difficulty of producing good colour and the intricate marking at once decimates the number fit for exhibition. Those whose experience in breeding pigeons has been confined to self-coloured varieties, such as carriers and barbs, know nothing of the difficulty there is in producing colour and marking, combined with size and shape, in the pouter. I believe it was formerly the most valuable variety. Moore says, "I have known eight guineas refused for a single Pigeon of this breed," and the author of the Treatise of 1765 quotes a sale of pouters by auction, two pairs of which realised £13 6s. and £16 16s. respectively. He says two pairs from the same sale were afterwards sold for thirty six guineas by private contract. I believe £60 is the highest price which has been paid for a pouter in late years.

Shape.—My drawing of a pouter represents the shape or outline of a good bird in position. The head and beak do not constitute fancy points, because, *generally*, there is nothing abnormal about them. As I have said, beak and eye-wattle is *sometimes* developed to an abnormal extent; but when it is, it is generally when the bird is past being fit for showing. Allowing for size, the head and beak of the pouter may be said to be of the common type.

The chief and most important part in the shape of a pouter is the crop, towards the setting off of which, to the greatest advantage, all its other parts are designed. By the time a young bird has moulted its nest feathers, the breeder has an idea if it is to be well developed in this respect. The cock is averagely better in crop than the hen, though, as a young bird, she generally shows it sooner. The crop ought to be very large, and as round as possible from every point of view. It ought to be carried with freedom, and fully expanded when the bird is in show.

Slenderness of girth or smallness in waist shows off a good crop to the greatest advantage, and is one of the principal points that contribute to fine shape in a pouter. While most pouters thicken in body after two years of age, I have known some retain their slender girth for six years, and never be shown without winning. Fanciers should strive to obtain birds of the latter type, the only one which a breeder who has passed through his novitiate has any pleasure in keeping.

The limbs are, next to a good crop, the most important points about the shape of the pouter. They ought to be long, properly placed in the body, well shaped, and rightly feathered. Limb is measured from the joint of the thigh, first above the hock, to the point of the nail of the middle toe. A limb measuring in this way 7in. is extra long. A year or two ago, I visited the lofts of more than thirty Scotch and English pouter breeders, and all the real 7in. limbed pouters I saw on my journey could be counted on the fingers of one hand. It is usual, either intentionally or from ignorance of how to measure, to overstate the length of limb in pouters about a quarter of an inch; but this extra quarter sometimes makes a great difference in the value of a bird. A fancier once wrote me that he required his cock pouters to be 7in. in limb and his hens 6¾in.; but when I visited him he could not show me a bird out of thirty measuring so much. Some birds wear down their toenails very much; in others, living under the same conditions, the nails grow out extra long. Neither form is fairly to be taken into account in measuring the limb; the length of an average toenail may only be included, because neither form affects the heighth of a pigeon. The difference in length of limb between the cock and hen pouter is about ¼in., so that 6¾in. in a hen is as good as 7in. in a cock. I have seen, in the whole of my experience, only about a dozen pouters with limbs exceeding 7in. in length, the longest being 7¼in. I have often had birds put into my hands said to measure 7½in. and 7⅜in., but I could never make them so much. I measure the limb of a pouter on a marked board projecting from the wall; placing my left thumb nail in the joint of the thigh, and bringing it exactly to the corner of the board, then stretching out the limb with my right hand, I can find the exact length to 1/16th of an inch. Others, who also measure without assistance, hold the pigeon by the back in the left hand, place the point of the index finger of the right hand on the joint of the thigh, and bringing the limb down the palm of the hand, ascertain the length from the natural marks on their palm. This is a true way if one remembers what signifies such and such lengths on his hand, but not unless, as I have often found. I do not think there ever have been fifty pouters alive at one time measuring truly 7in. or more in limb. Of more importance, however, than actual measurement of limbs, is their position in the body and their shape. They ought to be placed far back, so that there remains a good length of body between them and the crop. It is only birds so formed that can be very tall. They ought next to be placed closely together, and, when viewed from the front, continue to approach each other down as far as the hocks; then, gradually separating, the feet ought to be as far apart as the thighs are at their junction with the body. The hocks must closely approach, but not touch, each other, otherwise the pigeon cannot walk gracefully. In profile view, the limbs must form a very obtuse angle at the hocks, on which, again, depends very much the heighth of a bird. I have shown, in my drawing, as nearly as I can, the correct shape of the limbs from this point of view. While pigeons generally are in-toed, the pouter must turn his feet decidedly out. It is quite unnecessary to describe all the faults in shape of limb usually seen in pouters, every other form from that described being faulty. Limbs, either too straight and stiff, or too much bent and crouching, are frequent faults, as also are those set too far forward in the body, or widely placed, the latter often appearing quite bowed in thigh from a front view. A pouter should show all his limbs as far as the thigh joint, but many have this joint concealed in the feathers of the body, their thighs lying close to their body like a runt's, instead of standing well out. Finally, there is the way the limbs ought to be feathered. The correct style is known as stocking-limbed, or with the legs entirely covered with short, soft, downy feathers. These feathers may overhang at the hocks, as much as shown in the illustration. The feathers on the toes must, however, be very long, spreading out from each toot for three or four inches. For a short time after the annual moult, these toe feathers remain perfect in some birds, if care has been exercised; but they never remain perfect throughout the season, and usually get broken before they are full grown. They give such birds as have them a very fine appearance, but very few are naturally furnished with them in perfection, if the limbs themselves are just completely stockinged, and not overfeathered. Pouters proper, as apart from small croppers, are not now found entirely bare-legged, the least amount of leg-covering being about half of the leg bare, or with short feathers on the outsides of the limbs and on the toes. This is how the portrait of a pouter is represented in the Treatise of 1765, which shows the gradual improvement in this respect from Moore's time. Pouters are now found from half leg-feathered to rough limbed, some of the latter having coarse hook feathers reaching the ground, and toe feathers over six inches long. Such leg-feathering quite impedes graceful movement in a bird; but as it often comes in those otherwise excellent, such are bred with others under-feathered in limb. In matching stocking-legged birds together, the produce is rather inclined to come bare-legged, and it is annoying to find what are otherwise the best young birds so. Rough limbs have, and I fear always must have, a place in every loft; but as a matter of individual taste I dislike them very much, greatly preferring thin limbed birds, as they are infinitely handsomer, more graceful, and have greater freedom in movement. It can be seen what a heavy tax on the pouter breeder this matter of leg-feathering is of itself. All else may be about right, but it is three to one against the limbs being properly feathered.

Length of feather, *i.e.*, the length from the point of the beak to the end of the tail, is next to be considered in the shape of the pouter. This is ascertained by holding the bird in the left hand, then, placing the index finger of the right hand under his beak, and the thumb at the back of his head, he can be stretched out to his natural length and measured against a marked board as before. In this way some birds measure 20in., which is a good length. I once saw one 21in. full, but he had one three-leaved feather in his tail which was an inch longer than the other feathers, and which was accordingly of no value, but rather a fault. I have often measured two pouters and found them the same length, though the flights and tail of one of them were a full inch longer than those of the other. The birds were differently formed, one making up in neck what he lost in feather. I think this is where the carrier cross is proved, in greater length of neck, enabling the bird to stand higher, and giving room for greater developement of crop. Short-necked birds, whose length depends on flights and tail, have little style, and can never have fine carriage. Mere length, from beak to tail, should never have been made a property in the pouter. This has caused much mischief to the bird, by making those who do not understand the design of its originators go no further than the nearest tape line or 2ft. rule when judging them. A pouter may be too long as well as too short. What he ought to be depends entirely on the set and apparent length of his limbs. There are three too long for every one too short. A pouter which has 7in. limbs, of the proper shape and rightly placed, and which has a good long neck, can afford to measure 19½in. from point of beak to tip of tail, and no more. A bird measuring 20in., however long in neck, requires limbs 7⅜in. long, of the very best description, to enable him to stand properly.

The next excellence in shape of a pouter, supposing him to be standing in position in a show-pen or on the ground, is to be hollow-backed, the opposite of which, being hog-backed, is a most serious defect. His wings must be carried close to his body, and well up, so as to show his breast and belly in profile, as I have delineated. Drooping wings, which conceal this outline, are very faulty, and generally hereditary. His flights must always be carried over his tail, and reach nearly to the end of it. They ought to be broad and not narrow. The tail should be carried very near the ground, but not touching it. It ought never to be carried high, which is a great, though common fault. Almost all the best pouters I ever saw were split-tailed, *i.e.*, the tail in two equal divisions, more noticeable when the bird is in the hand than when at liberty. Some of the best old fanciers look upon the split-tail as a mark of high breeding; and they regard long hairs on the breast of a pouter in the same light. Pouters have often extra tail feathers, as many as fifteen primaries being common. Several strains have also an extra primary flight, and I have sometimes had half my stock with eleven flights a side.

Carriage.—Having stated what constitutes good shape in a pouter, as he may be seen standing still in a show-pen, or on the floor of his loft, I now come to describe the way he ought to carry himself when in motion. Regarding carriage, Moore expresses himself as follows:—"Besides the five Properties before mention'd, there is another, which tho' not generally allow'd, will be found to be one of the best—I mean the Carriage." A pouter which is not formed on good lines, and is not well proportioned, can never look well, however he may carry himself; but however well he may be shaped, it does not follow that his carriage will be right. Shape and carriage are, therefore, separate properties, as Moore states. The crop being well filled, the bird may, as he plays up to his hen, begin to "bufle," as Moore describes it, or to choke with wind by overfilling his crop. He then sets up the feathers at the back of his neck, and struggles from side to side, endeavouring to free himself from the encumbrance. Some birds are much addicted to this fault, and will, unless caught up and relieved, by their beaks being opened, and the air being pressed out of their crops, remain choked for half an hour at a time. Some birds, though naturally possessed of capacious crops, never fill them, but allow them to hang down like an empty bag. These are said to be slack-winded, and, as Moore says, "appear not much better than an ill-shap'd Runt." A pouter as he plays must keep himself perfectly upright, so that his head is perpendicular with his feet; he must on no account jump off the ground as he plays, but walk in a very dignified way, and with his tail slightly spread out. A grave fault in carriage is jumping off the ground as he plays, which is generally accompanied by rumping, or setting up the feathers of his back and rump, the tail at the same time being tucked under him and dragged along the ground. All these faults of carriage are often seen in pouters which look well enough when standing still. They ought, therefore, to be always judged in a large show-pen to allow their carriage to be seen, which is now generally done at important shows.

Feather.—The standard colours of the pouter are yellow, red, black, and blue-pied, valuable, both of old and at the present time, in the order named, when equal in all else. Pure white comes next, and then the other colours, pied according to the standard. The way in which a pouter must be pied, or marked with white, is as follows: On his ground colour he must have a crescent or half-moon mark of white on the front of his crop, as shown in the illustration. This half-moon mark looks best when about 2in. wide at its deepest part. It must finish off with fine points a little below the ears, and be set low enough on the crop to leave a large bib of colour between it and the beak. When this bib is wanting the bird is swallow-throated, and then, of course, there is no properly defined crescent at all. The ends of the crescent often reach to the eyes, finishing off too widely, and this is apt to result in broken or bull eyes. All pied pouters should have clear yellow or orange irides, and beaks coloured according to their feather, though it may be mentioned that a flesh-coloured beak is not only allowed, but admired by some in reds and yellows. Serious defects in marking are a blaze of white or snip on the forehead, and a ring neck, which is caused by the crop marking going right round the neck. On the shoulders, and well away from the butts of the wings, there ought to be a mottling of single white feathers, forming what is known as the rose-pinion, which ought to be round, and cover a space of 1¼in. diameter. It is but seldom this beautiful mark is seen well defined; the white feathers forming it are generally more or less in patches, and it is often represented by a single patch of white, which, when it reaches the edge of the wing makes the bird bishop-winged, bishoped, or lawn-sleeved, which is more faulty than being entirely solid winged. The primary flight feathers must be white to the turn of the wing, or a bird is foul-flighted, and, if the outer flight feather alone is foul—a common enough fault—he is sword-flighted. Next, if a pouter be lifted up by the wings, he ought to be entirely white on the lower back, sides, belly, thighs, and legs. The tail with its coverts, upper and under, must be coloured, being cut sharply off the same as in the nun, and the line of demarcation between the belly and breast must be sharply cut, or, as it is called, evenly-belted, as shown in the drawing.

In treating of the various colours found in pouters, the yellow comes first as being the most valuable when all else is equal. Cocks of this colour, really good in properties, are, and always have been scarce, but good yellow hens are common enough. In reds, on the other hand, good cocks are plentiful, and really fine hens scarce. These colours have a great natural affinity, and are to a large extent inter-bred in all varieties of fancy pigeons. The colour of yellow pouters is often pleasing enough, but is not, in reality, any nearer perfection than the majority of reds. The latter were formerly sometimes to be found of a glossy blood-red, but they became very scarce. In late years, attention having been directed to them, much has been done in resuscitating the colour; but, although I have seen in my experience many very *good coloured* reds, I never saw any of these that could compare in general pouter properties with such as were only of a *second* or *third* degree of colour. There is a beauty and richness in the best degree of the red colour, as seen in many foreign pigeons, which makes it universally admired. The best red pouter I ever saw was a cock bred in London, I believe, which was sold by Mr. Fulton to Mr. Ure, of Dundee, about 1870, and from which are descended some of the best coloured reds now in existence. This bird had not a white beak, which many consider essential in a red pouter; his beak was of a dark ruddy hue. His tail was heavily stained with red, and his rump, or upper tail coverts, were as red as his wing coverts. I have always considered that it is owing to the poverty of colour in reds and yellows generally that they are unable to carry colour in the tail; but however white it may appear to be, an examination will always show that the feathers are not really white, like the tail of an all white pouter, the shafts of the primaries being usually dark, and the under coverts grey in the lightest tailed birds. When fine coloured red jacobins, turbiteens, or other red pigeons with white extremities breed young ones with a foul tail feather or two, as they frequently do, these feathers are invariably weak in colour compared with their body feathers. The old breeders, finding it impossible to breed red and yellow pouters with tails as dark as their wing coverts, probably tried to breed them with tails as white as possible, for it cannot be denied that a half coloured or stained tail does not look well. But, then, if the white tail were imperative, it would be necessary to keep reds and yellows entirely distinct from blacks, for how could the black-tailed black, when crossed with the red, be expected to breed reds with pure white tails, and blacks with black tails? As a matter of fact, the best coloured reds and yellows are usually the most heavily stained in tail, therefore, finding that it is natural for them to be so, it should not prejudice them. I do not suppose any intelligent breeder would prefer a brick red with an apparently white tail, to a blood red with a dark rump and stained tail. There is no trouble with the tails of black pouters; however bad their colour, they can always carry it to the end of the tail. In crossing black with blue pouters, smoky blacks, showing wing bars of a darker hue, are a common result. This can be bred out in a series of crosses, but it ruins colour in reds and yellows to breed any such black-bred birds with them. The first cross between black and red, in all varieties of pigeons, however good in colour, often results in a strawberry or sandy. These are of various shades, from such as are very light, looking as if sanded over, to such as are of a reddish strawberry, many of which are ticked with black. It is well known that some of the best black pieds have been bred from a sandy and a black. Blue pied pouters have always been favourites, and their colour being the most natural one is easiest to breed good. Through crossing with artificial colours, blues have certain inherent faults which must be carefully guarded against. Their wing bars ought to be jet black, but frequently come brown, when they are called kite-barred. Their wing coverts ought to be of a sound dark blue, neither smoky nor dusky, nor so light and silvery that the white rose pinions are with difficulty distinguished on them. White pouters ought to have flesh coloured beaks, and they almost invariably have bull or hazel eyes. It may almost be taken for certain that a white pouter, with its beak even slightly stained, has some coloured feathers about its head. A white pouter with a dark, or partly dark beak, cannot rightly be shown in a class for whites, if the strict letter of the law be enforced, but such a bird is in much the same position as a white-vented black carrier, in a class for blacks. The difference between them is that the carrier's fault is hidden, while the pouter's is very glaring. There was once a strain of orange-eyed white pouters, but whether they were free of foul feathers I know not. Pure whites with orange eyes would look very well, and I see no reason why they should not, if ever shown, be allowed to compete with whites, for they would really have an additional property over bull-eyed birds, and one difficult to keep up, as in white jacobins and white tumblers. There would always, however, be a suspicion that they were foul feathered somewhere; but so there is with other pearl or yellow-eyed white pigeons.

The colours of pouters other than yellow, red, black, and blue-pied, and pure white, are generally called off-colours, and are not so valuable, nor are they generally bred for. This would not, however, long continue to be the case if the pouter fancy were to extend greatly over the country, because increasing competition would cause breeders to cultivate some of the so-called off-colours, many of which are very beautiful. Dun, which is a standard colour in carriers, was, till lately, very scarce in pouters. I do not admire it myself, but it could be vastly improved if bred for. Duns are usually hens, and I only know of one good cock at present. I have seen blue, red, yellow, and dun chequers. Of these the blue is the only one which can be said to be common, and it is not so common as formerly. Not being bred for, such chequers as come in crossing the solid with the barred colours do not represent what could be made of them were they to be systematically bred for; but in the present state of the pouter fancy I do not think there is room for them. The blue-chequer is of two kinds, the light and the dark, sometimes called black-chequer. The light blue chequer can be produced by crossing blues with blacks. It is useful for improving colour of wing-coverts and bars in blues, but it must be used with care and with due regard as to how it was produced itself. This colour has always existed in the breed. The black chequer is sometimes so dark that it is apparently black on the wing coverts, but its tail is dark blue with the usual black bar, and any foul feathers on its underbody are greyish blue. This colour is often thrown by a pair of reds which have had a recent cross of black. It is a very good cross for black, and some of the most lustrous black-pieds have been so produced.

The mealy has always been a favourite colour in Scotland, because many of the best pouters ever seen have been mealies. It is of various shades, the correct colour being the same as in the best show Antwerps. The neck and wing-bars ought to be lustrous red, and the wing-coverts of a clear light tint, but still decided enough to show up the rose pinion. The tail should be so light as to appear nearly white. Mealy has been continually bred with blue, and, consequently, most mealies are of a bluish tint, with a hard blue black beak, instead of a soft coloured ruddy one. Mealy could be greatly improved by cultivation, which it is well worth, as are the other bar-winged colours, the silver and yellow-mealy. Silvers are occasionally bred from blues, and are almost invariably, in my experience, hens. It is many years since I heard of a silver cock. The wing-bars and neck of a silver ought to be of a clear bright golden dun, and not as black as possible, which would be a departure from the correct colour, and too near an approach to blue. The wing-coverts should be of a creamy dun, and only dark enough to show up the rose-pinion. The tail is of a medium shade of dun, barred with the same colour as that of the wing-bars. The yellow-mealy ought to have bright yellow neck and wing-bars; but the wing-coverts in this colour are never so decided in colour as to show the rose-pinion without the closest examination. The tail is so light as to appear white. They are usually hens. The four solid colours, black, dun, red, and yellow, have, therefore, their corresponding barred colours, all of which are very beautiful when good, but in the present state of the fancy, I question if there is a sufficiency of breeders to give them the attention they require. In crossing the barred with the solid colours, chequers are produced, which are of great service in breeding back to the barred, but detrimental to the solid colours, which they tend to spoil, which is well known to those who understand breeding for colour.

To give a pouter every chance in competition at a show, it must be carefully tamed and rendered familiar by systematic training. The difficulties which beset the pouter fancier on this account are very graphically described by Eaton, in a note where he compares the ever merry Norwich cropper with the frequently sulky and phlegmatic pouter, which I may give afterwards. Temper and disposition are very variable in pouters, many of the best obstinately refusing to show off what good shape they possess, when penned up. To send the average pouter direct to a show from his loft or aviary, where he has been so far at liberty, without preliminary training, is to lose half the chance he may have of winning. The greater part of the life of some birds, even in the breeding season, is spent closely penned up; but most fanciers have neither accommodation nor inclination to keep them in this way, and only commence to train them after their breeding time. Every bird which is intended to be shown must, therefore, be penned up separately, the cocks out of sight of the hens, and by always talking to them, by using such expressions as "hip, hip, hoo-a, hoo-a," and at the same time snapping the fingers, a good tempered pigeon soon becomes very tame, and shows up whenever called upon. A proud hen that will stand quietly on the hand may also be carried round before the cocks, which soon puts them on their mettle; and it is good to allow all penned-up birds out once a day, so that they may stretch their wings. It is a bad practice to put one's hands in the pens and allow the birds to peck at them, by which they get a habit of always jumping off their blocks and coming to the front of their pens on the approach of anyone. Pouters are naturally familiar birds, few of them refusing to become very tame if any trouble is taken with them; but perseverance and judicious treatment must be exercised, and kindness accorded to such as keep long shy and stubborn, for they will not be driven into showing. The late Mr. Montgomery said, "Pigeons, like other animals, have got tempers; and a sulky, bad-tempered bird will never be a winner in a show-pen, and I question the propriety of breeding from such birds, as they transmit this peculiarity as well as others." As to breeding from such, everyone will, of course, be guided by circumstances. I fear good pouters will never be plentiful enough to allow any hard and fast line to be drawn against breeding from one possessing a particular fault, if good otherwise.

THE NORWICH CROPPERS.

CHAPTER LXXV.

THE NORWICH CROPPER.

The Norwich cropper is a pigeon which is found in its purity in the counties of Norfolk, Suffolk, and Essex. It has hitherto been undescribed by name in any book treating of English pigeons, though quite distinct from the large pouter; but there are some allusions to it by Eaton, who was evidently sensible of its great beauty and fine style. The uploper and pouting-horseman are two varieties of croppers which Moore describes at pp. 37 and 38 of his "Columbarium," as follows: "The Uploper is a Pigeon bred originally in *Holland*, its Make and Shape grees in every respect with the *English* Powter, only it is smaller in every Property. Its Crop is very round in which it generally buries its Bill; its Legs are very small and slender, and its toes are short and close together, on which it treads so nicely, that when moving, you may put anything under the Ball of its Foot; it is close thigh'd, plays very upright, and when it approaches the Hen, generally leaps to her, with its tail spread, which is the reason the Name is given to it, from the *Dutch* Word *Uplopen*, which signifies to leap up. These Pigeons are generally all blue, white, or black, tho' I will not assert that there are no Pieds of this Species. There are but very few of them in *England*, and I have been inform'd that in *Holland* they have ask'd five and twenty *Guineas* for a single Pair of them."

Moore then describes the "Powting Horseman" as follows: "This Pigeon is a bastard Strain between the Cropper and the Horseman, and according to the Number of Times that their young ones are bred over from the Cropper, they are call'd first, second or third bred; and the oftner they are bred over, the larger their Crop proves. The Reason of breeding these Pigeons is to improve the Strain of the Powters, by making them close thigh'd, tho' it is apt to make them rump, from the

Horseman's Blood. They are a very merry Pigeon upon a House, and by often dashing off are good to pitch stray Pigeons, that are at a Loss to find their own Home; they breed often and are good Nurses, generally feeding their young ones well. I have known these Pigeons to be six Inches and six and a half in Legs; they are a hearty Pigeon, and, give 'em but Meat and Water, need very little other Attendance. Some of them will home ten or twenty Miles."

There is certainly much in the description of the uploper which agrees with that of the Norwich cropper, and if Moore had said that they were marked alike, I would consider the breeds identical. The uploper was, however, a self coloured cropper, and Moore could not say positively that there were pieds among the breed. While the shape, carriage, and general characteristics of the Norwich cropper are well described by Moore in his account of the uploper, its merry disposition and peculiar flight is, to a slight extent, mentioned in his description of the Pouting Horseman; but I cannot consider the latter to be the same variety, for it was evidently much nearer the pouter in size, nothing like 6in. to 6¼in. in limb being found in pure croppers, nor have they the slightest indication of ever having been crossed with the Horseman, their heads and beaks being of a pure blue rock pigeon formation. That the Norwich cropper, as it exists, is a much older and more constant breed of pigeon than the English pouter, I am well satisfied of, but I have no means of knowing how long it has existed, or how it was originally produced. Its marking, like the pouter's, is found in several continental breeds of croppers, and the probability is that both our pouter and cropper were gradually bred up from continental varieties, perhaps brought here by immigrants in the middle ages. Gonzales, in his account of Britain (1730), says of Norwich, "the worsted manufacture, for which this city has long been famous, was first brought hither by the Flemings, in the reign of Edward III., and afterwards improved to great perfection by the Dutch, who fled from the Duke d'Alvas' bloody persecutions."

The properties of the Norwich cropper are size, shape, carriage, feather, and flight. The latter is, indeed, the chief point with many, who, though they may admire all the other points, consider them as of little consequence if a bird cannot perform well in the air. The German writers, Neumeister and Prütz, mention certain peculiarities in the flight of some of the continental pigmy pouters; but that similar peculiarities are shared by a pure English variety, the fanciers of which have an old, though unwritten, code of rules to guide them, is not generally known. I learned much of what I know of these rules from Mr. Boreham, of Colchester, who graduated under an old cropper fancier, the late Mr. Perry, of Great Yarmouth, who, I believe, died at an advanced age somewhere about 1871. He was a cropper fancier all his life, always kept up a stock of good birds, and was always willing to buy a good one. I have one old cock which belonged to him, from which the best I have are descended.

Size.—I admire smallness of size in a cropper, though not at any sacrifice of what goes to make up general good shape. Mr. Boreham and others, with whom I have exchanged ideas on the subject, agree with me in this, while many pay no regard to size if a bird flies well. The best croppers I have seen were of a medium size, but there is little difference in size between the largest and smallest birds of the pure breed.

Shape.—While it would take the best parts of several first-class English pouters to make up such a pigeon as my drawing represents, I have seen many croppers quite equal in outline to my illustration. The crop in these pigeons is, for the most part, far better developed than in pouters, their respective sizes considered; indeed, many of these beautiful little pigeons have crops that would be considered *good* in a large pouter. The crop, or *bladder* as it is called in Norwich, is often as round as a ball, even filling out behind the neck, so that a perfectly spherical shape is sometimes attained by it, and in it, as Moore says of the uploper, the bird "generally buries its Bill." The legs should be entirely free of feathers; but about half the number of croppers I have seen and possessed have had some short feathers down the outsides of the legs and on the middle toes, which I consider so far faulty, the bare-legged birds being very much smarter in appearance. However, as some of the best birds are slightly feather-legged, they are not to be discarded on this account. Flight being considered all in all by many cropper fanciers, feathered legs are of little consequence; at the same time, bare legs are allowed to be correct. I have not seen any pure croppers completely stocking-legged, and the more they are so the worse they look. No doubt the pouter is vastly improved with completely feathered stocking limbs; but, as I have shown, it was bare-legged in Moore's time. The little cropper having, however, quite a different carriage from the pouter, feathered legs give it a clumsy appearance, which is a settled question among many of those who keep them. The legs ought to be placed in the body as in the pouter, compared with which the cropper is straighter in limb, not inclining so much at the hocks. Slenderness of girth, or of *waist* as it is termed, is, of course, an admirable property in the cropper, and best seen in young birds, for they naturally thicken as they increase in age.

Regarding length of limb and feather in croppers, I give the following measurements of my own birds, some of which were bred in Norfolk and the adjoining counties, and the others by myself. Ten cocks average 5¼in. in limb, and 15in. in feather; they vary from 5¼in. to 5⅛in. in limb, and from 14½in. to 15¼in. in feather. Nine hens average 5¼in. in limb, and 14½in. in feather; they vary from 5in. to 5⅜in. in limb, and from 14in. to 15in. in feather. There is, therefore, nothing like the variation in length of limb and feather among them that there is in pouters. Their average length of limb, in proportion to their average length of feather, is also equal to what is only rarely attained in pouters, which proves them to be more easily bred good in shape than pouters. This is, indeed, the case, and many perfect models in shape may be found among them, which of course makes them very much less valuable. A good cropper should feel no heavier in the hand than an average sized common flying tumbler. They vary a little in size, like every other variety.

Carriage.—The cropper has the most upright carriage of any variety of pouting pigeon I know of. They occasionally overcharge their crop with wind when young, but generally soon grow out of this habit. Slack-winded birds are almost unknown among them. So long as they keep in health they remain in show, and in this respect present the greatest contrast to large pouters. For the most part they walk perfectly upright, their wings being carried tightly to their sides, and their flights never crossed at the points. They are, however, inclined to carry their wings rather low, thereby not showing so much of their belly and thighs in profile as is desirable. The flights ought not to reach to the end of the tail by nearly an inch, long flighted birds being bad fliers. It is noticeable that the best flying varieties, such as blue rocks, tumblers, dragoons, Antwerps, triganicas, and croppers, are all rather short in flights, long wings being impedimental to pigeons in their flight, whatever they may be to some other kinds of birds. The tail of the cropper is carried as shown in the drawing, and seldom any higher. In stretching itself to its utmost height it often walks only on its front toes, the back ones being off the ground, or just touching it, resembling in this respect the uploper, regarding which, Moore says, " that when moving you may put anything under the Ball of its Foot." Its style of movement so far resembles the pouters ; but it is allowable for the cropper to spring off the ground when playing to another pigeon, and this it often does in leaps of three or four feet across the floor, opening its wings on its way, and quickly closing them as it alights. This leaping, which is so ungainly in the pouter, is executed with such expertness by the cropper that it is pleasant to see them perform it.

Feather.—The cropper is found in eight principal pied colours, all of which are admired, because they are all beautiful. Four of these are solid colours, and the others are their corresponding barred colours. Some of them being known, in the cropper fancy, by different names from what is usual, the following is the Norwich and general nomenclatures :

ENGLISH POUTER.	NORWICH CROPPER.
Black.	Black.
Red.	Cinnamon.
Yellow.	Yellow.
Dun.	Mouse.
Blue.	Blue.
Mealy.	Dun.
Yellow-Mealy.	Cream.
Silver.	Cloth.

Black, owing to the practice of breeding the best flying birds together, regardless of their colour, is seldom seen very glossy in croppers. Some of the best shaped and marked birds I have seen were of this colour. Black pieds are often quite free of objectionable leg feathering, and generally very good fliers. Cinnamons (reds) and yellows are scarce and difficult to get. I have seen and had well marked and fairly coloured birds of both. They are generally somewhat feathered-legged, which makes them valuable to breeders of stocking-legged pied pigmy pouters. Mouse-coloured croppers (*i.e.* dun, as in carriers) are not common. I was told that the late Mr. Perry, of Yarmouth, had a good bird of this colour, and as I bred one myself from the bird which formerly belonged to him, it may have been a descendant of the one he had.

The great proportion of croppers are of the bar-winged colours, blue and dun (*i.e.* mealy) being the commonest. The blue ought, of course, to have black bars, but kite-barred blues are very common. The dun, like all mealy pigeons, has a light tail. Its neck and wing bars ought to be bright red, and its wing coverts of a clear light mealy, when it is called a miller dun. A red dun has the wing coverts of a reddish tinge, and between the miller dun and cinnamon there are many degrees of colour, according to the amount of red in the plumage. Cloth (*i.e.*, silver) is one of the prettiest colours, and is of many shades. Its neck and wing bars vary from a light dove-coloured to a hard blackish dun; a beautiful golden chesnut dun being the most pleasing tint. Its wing coverts ought to be of a soft creamy dun, only dark enough to show up the rose pinion. This colour has, of course, a dun tail, barred to match the neck and wings. Cloths are mostly hens, a really good cloth cock being rather a scarce pigeon. Creams (*i.e.*, yellow mealies) are also usually hens, and very rare. They have, of course, a light tail, and their colour is so delicate that a rose pinion is scarcely distinguishable on their wings. Their necks and wing bars ought to be rich yellow. The barred colours are very much inter-bred, the result being left to chance; in fact, it is usual to breed two good birds together, no matter what colour they are; hence, unless when breeding from a pair of the same colour, and not always then, it is impossible to predict what the young ones will be like. To improve blacks, yellows, and cinnamons, they ought, of course, to be kept distinct from the barred colours. As all the solid and primary barred colours are found in croppers, the intermediate or chequered also exist in great variety of shades, but they are not generally liked or bred for. Pure white birds are occasionally seen, and whites with coloured tails are an old and favourite variety. There are three colours of them, viz., black, blue, and cloth-tailed birds. To be properly marked they ought to be entirely white, with the exception of the tail and its upper and under coverts. Some coloured feathers on the head are often found in them, as well as a white feather or two in the tail or among the under tail coverts, which do not look well when they are flying. Their tail primaries ought to be sound in colour, but are frequently very much grizzled with white. The cropper is very often mismarked in having an excess of white, though I have had a few of them very well marked to the pouter standard. A deficiency or total want of bib, causing the ugly swallow throat, is very common; so is the blaze face, or snip on the forehead. A flesh-coloured beak usually accompanies a large snip; they are then said to be pink-nosed. The whole front of the crop is often white, and ring-necks are sometimes found. The rose pinion is, however, occasionally seen beautifully defined, but a wing free of any white is more seldom seen than a bishop wing. A good flying bird, however ill marked, is bred from, because perfect flight is not easily got, and so bad marking is perpetuated.

Flight.—The cropper is the merriest and liveliest, and can be made the tamest and most familiar, of all pigeons. In the loft, or out of it, he is always on the move, and so long as he remains in health he keeps in show. The rules for good flying are as follow: A good bird should spring up from his trap like an acrobat from a spring board, and go off in a circle, loudly clapping his wings, so that he can be heard from afar. His tail must be carried spread out like a fan, but depressed in the middle, so that it has the shape of a scoop. A well spread scoop tail is valuable, because rare to get. Extra tail feathers are often found in croppers, some having fourteen or more. A well-carried tail is all the better to have these extra feathers. Like other breeds in which more than twelve tail primaries are often seen, croppers generally want the oil gland on the rump. A good cropper must have a rocking action in his flight, his head and tail going up and down like the movement of a rocking horse. Then, as soon as he gets enough way on his flight, he must stop using his wings, and raising them, so that they nearly touch at the points, sail motionless through the air, and the longer he can so sail the more valuable he is. A good bird will sail along for fifty yards, gradually lowering as he goes; then, again using his wings with loud claps, he will rise as much as he has fallen, and go on alternately in this way till he pitches. A cropper ought not to fly far nor long at a time. He may go twice or thrice round his house in a wide circle, then pitch, play up to his hen, and fly off again. The time they fly best is the week or ten days before the hen lays, when their courting is going on; but even when sitting or feeding young ones each will fly well alone, though not in such good style as during the time mentioned. A good way to gain the flight of croppers is to let out a lot of odd cocks and one proud hen, when good sport may be had.

There is certainly nothing in the whole pigeon fancy from which greater pleasure can be derived than a flight of well trained Norwich croppers. Beautiful in shape and feather, grand fliers, ever dashing about with spirit, both in the loft and out of it, the owner possesses in them a source of inexhaustible amusement. I have always kept the noble and majestic pouter, which everyone will allow is one of the choicest pigeons in the fancy, but he sadly wants the spirit and life of the active, merry cropper. The pouter can certainly fly, after a fashion, and if flown from his squeakerhood is fairly able to take care of himself when allowed liberty; but the choicest large birds cannot be said to be at home in the air, which the cropper is, to a much greater extent than most pigeons.

The remarks on pouters by Dixon, in his "Dovecote and Aviary," apply solely to the Norwich cropper, as can be seen by his allusions to its flight, colour, &c. His illustration of it represents a bare-legged blue cropper, and is, perhaps, the best and most life-like picture of a pigeon in his book. I observe from the preface of the work that he was living at Norwich when it was issued. He says, at page 122: "The flight also of the cropper is stately and dignified in its way. The inflated crop is not generally collapsed by the exertion, but is seen to move slowly forward through the air, like a large permanent soap-bubble with a body and wings attached to it. The bird is fond of clapping his wings loudly at first starting to take his few lazy rounds in the air, for he is too much of a fine gentleman to condescend to violent exertion. Other Pigeons will indulge in the same action in a less degree, but Croppers are the *claquers* par excellence; and hence we believe the *Smiters* of Willughby to be only a synonym of the present kind." This description is very true to nature; but, as I have shown, the smiter of Willughby is the bird known in Germany as the ringbeater.

Eaton could appreciate the excellence of the cropper, which he writes of as the Pouting Horseman as follows: "I have seen some of these light-bodied Pouting Horsemen that appeared to me to fly as light as Tumblers, and when flying with the Tumblers, their round globular crops, well filled and up, have a very pleasing effect, owing to the contrast of the Tumblers. With regard to dashing off, they are not only a merry but a spirited Pigeon; not only spirited, but graceful in the extreme; I would rather see an elegant shape, small or narrow-girt Pouting Horseman, 6¼in. in the leg (think of this, Gentlemen of the Pouting Fancy!) than an

English Pouter, even if it would measure 7in. A large English Pouter, with thick girt and hog-backed. Style is a grand thing, and the Pouting Horseman is the English Pouter in miniature, retaining all its properties." As I have explained, croppers are nothing like 6½in. in limb; but Eaton, if he ever measured any, was probably unwilling to write what, at the time, would have been regarded as something very heterodox. How well he goes on to describe what may be seen at any show of pouters: "How often it happens at a grand show of these remarkable, fine, large, English Pouters, after having been previously prepared for showing, that is separating each cock and hen, and not allowing them to see a Pigeon, show well in their own pens; but when put into the show pen, a male bird, expecting it will show, it stretches forth its head and neck, apparently taking a sight of all the Fanciers in the room, almost as much as to say to some of them—you owe me something; some may show to a certain extent. It is very disheartening to Gentlemen Fanciers of the English Pouter when this takes place, after forwarding their birds miles, &c., to give their brother Fanciers a treat, as it was supposed; it does not always turn out to be so, owing to their not showing, as it is called. Nevertheless, it often proves a treat to see what length of body and shape, length in leg and beautiful in feather. It is otherwise with the light (not heavy) merry spirited Pouting Horseman cock, when put into the show pen, always up and ready for his work, not long in stripping himself, putting himself in attitude, and suiting the action to the word, display that fine action of showing which is well understood by the Gentlemen of the Fancy; giving infinite satisfaction with regard to being a merry pigeon, &c. . . . I have this week bought two pretty little Pouting Horseman cocks; I am informed they come from Norwich. I am given to understand they fly tremendously, with very large crops. . . . The Gentlemen Fanciers of the English Pouter may assume that I admire the small Pouting Horseman more than the large English Pouter. The contrary is the fact; I never have and never shall advise the young and inexperienced Fancier to attempt to breed a second-rate bird, while he has the opportunity to breed a first-rate bird, therefore I shall not advise him to breed the Pouting Horseman, while he has the opportunity to attempt to breed the English Pouter, any more than I shall advise him to breed a Skinnum, Dragon, or Horseman, while he has the opportunity to attempt to breed a Carrier, for degeneracy will do that, in spite of the efforts of the experienced Fanciers; but I am desirous you should breed the English Pouter with more style and grace, with a hollow back, smaller in the girt, stout legs, but not like mill-posts, soft downy or snow-like feather legs; but not rushed and sprouted with feathers that almost prevent the bird from walking."

All the foregoing is in a long note to Moore's description of the "Powting Horseman," which I have already given. Eaton took for granted that the Norwich cropper was identical with it, and could evidently not see, though he had had birds direct from Norwich, that they were a pure and distinct breed, having nothing to do with the Horseman. His remarks on their fine style, in comparison with that of the pouter, are, however, well weighed and very conclusive.

CHAPTER LXXVI.

THE PIGMY POUTER.

A FEW years ago, a chapter in a book on pigeons professing to treat of pigmy pouters agreeing in shape, feather, and carriage with the large English pouter, would have been as much out of place as the well-known chapter on snakes in a certain history of Norway. At present, however, there is at least one standard-pied, stocking-legged, pigmy pouter, viz., the black-pied hen bred by Captain Norman Hill, of Ealing, in 1879, a pigeon which has been the admiration of all who have seen it. When in London in December, 1879, I called on Captain Hill to see this pigeon, but it was absent at some show, and since then I have had no opportunity of seeing it; but I have seen its parents and several of its ancestors. Captain Hill, at my request, has kindly furnished me with an account of it, which I will give in his own words. I may say that I had the impression—a wrong one it appears—that this bird had been produced by a mixture of Norwich cropper and Austrian pigmy pouter blood, and thought that a blue-pied cock which I saw at Captain Hill's, and which is an ancestor of his fine bird, was a pure Norwich cropper. It was this idea that caused me to express the opinion referred to by Captain Hill, that his bird was descended from croppers. Captain Hill writes as follows: "Some time ago I saw a letter of yours in the *Fanciers' Chronicle* on the Norwich cropper, which in itself was good, and correctly written; but therein you ventured a remark which I must take exception to, and which, at the time, I fully intended putting you right on, as far as my strain of pied pigmies are concerned. Your opinion then was, as far as I can recollect, that my good pigmy that had been produced lately was a cross between the Norwich cropper and the foreigner. Until I went to Colchester, I had never seen a cropper worth looking at; then I saw one or two in Mr. Boreham's collection, with fair markings and more character than I had before seen. The thought then struck me, had I possessed one of them at the time I began, I might have saved years in the manufacture of my pigmies; but this may be doubtful. However, I never had one in my possession until this season, when I bought three from Mr. Boreham, after he had supplied you with the best specimens he got at Norwich or Yarmouth. I am now giving them up, having no opportunity of witnessing their flying powers, and I cannot agree with you in admiring their other properties in preference to the pigmy.

"In reply to your inquiry how I bred my much admired black-pied pigmy, I may state, briefly, by *in-breeding* and *selection* of the most diminutive and pouter like birds for the last 14 years. Its genealogical family tree, as far as I can trace it, starts from a whole-coloured blue Austrian pouter cock I bought in 1866, from the late Mr. Evans, of the Borough, at that time a good pouter fancier. This bird was quite bare on shanks, and nearly so on toes; but very small and of fine form. I mated him to a blue pouter hen, a weed, small, gay in marking, and well feathered on limbs and toes, determined to try to breed dwarf pouters on the same principle as game bantams were produced. I inbred for five years, and then obtained a whole-coloured, mealy-chequered cock with good limbs and toe feathering, finding it more difficult to obtain the latter points than correct markings. I mated him to my best pied hen, and from them got whole-coloured and foul-marked dun, mealy, satinette, and other nondescript colours. In-breeding then for some years with the blue-pieds, they produced some black and blue splashes, some dark, others nearly white. From two black splashed cocks, mated to a silver and a blue-pied hen, in one season was produced two blacks, a cock and hen, which are the parents of the little black-pied wonder. Its dimensions are, length of limb 5¼in.; length of feather 13¼in. There are bred from it this season, two black-pieds, two blue-pieds, two black and one blue splashes, all small and stylish; but none equal to the parent in markings, or combination of pouter properties; still, I do not despair of producing other equally perfect specimens of the miniature pouter of the period."

With reference to the above, not having seen the bird described, I cannot make any comparison between it and a good cropper; all I can say is that I prefer such croppers as I have to any *foreign* pigmy pouters I have seen. Knowing that a pouter with 7in. limbs, properly shaped and rightly placed in the body, can afford to measure 19¼in. in feather, if such length is made up in a certain way, as described, I at once saw that Captain Hill's pigmy was quite out of this proportion. But even taking 7in. limbs to 18¾in. in feather, this pigmy, being 5⅛in. in limbs, ought to measure 15in. in feather, if formed on the same lines. I pointed this out to Captain Hill, and had the following reply: "In order to satisfy you and myself, I have re-measured my little gem, and find length of feather 13¼in. *full*, or at the outside ¼in. more, limb 5⅛in. These are the same measurements as were taken by Fulten and a crowd of admirers at the Palace, when the bird was first shown there (not for competition) in November, 1879. It appeared there again two months afterwards at the Peristeronic show. Although the above measurements appear out of proportion to those you quote, and are so according to the old rule for the pouter, still no one who has seen this little bird has made the remark that it was not symmetrical; on the contrary, either on or off the block it is considered graceful in form, and walks well, without rumping or jumping. In my opinion, a slender pouter with 7in. limbs, well formed and placed, is much more pleasing to the eye, if under 19in., than one over that length; but such birds are rare. The limbs of this pigmy are not spindly, but well set and stockinged, with the proper curves, not too straight, neither bent, and with perfectly spread toe-feathering. Markings very perfect, good-sized bib, crop and both pinions correct, no approach to bishoping, and a true line at belt; but, like the majority of its larger brethren of same colour, it has a few foul feathers at thigh joints. Flights ample and well carried; colour a deep black; dark orange eye; pout a good size and well shaped; but, as you intend making mention of it, you ought to know what was a great surprise to me and to others, viz., the discovery, when it was about nine months old, that it had deceived us in its sex, as it turned out to be a hen after being matched up to another hen. It is again keeping close company with a large pouter hen. I have known other instances of a similar kind, but never one whose action, voice, and coo were so like to a cock.

"I have given you all these particulars, as I find I cannot bring my mind to risk the journey to and fro of my *wee pet*, much as I would like you to see it at the present time. The mealy-chequer is the only new blood introduced into my strain, with the exception of a yellow Austrian hen, whose young have never lived. The mealy is most unlike the

Norwich cropper, being heavily covered on limb and toes, and the blue cock, wire-legged, is now the oldest bird I bred, and longer in limb than any cropper."

As will be noticed further on, when writing of Brünner croppers, greater disproportion of limb to feather is mentioned by foreign writers than 13¼in. to 5⅜in. Captain Hill's bird must be formed on different lines from the large pouter; but where the difference lies I am unable to say at present. As to the satinette markings he refers to, I think he must mean something else than what I understand by such.

, Properly formed and feathered stocking limbs, with long toe feathers, seem to be the great difficulty with pied pigmy pouters at present. I observe this was mentioned in the reports of the last Crystal Palace show. The *Fanciers' Chronicle* said: "Pigmy Pouters (17). We miss the lovely style and carriage of the birds a very few years back. There is a good opportunity for some breeders to work up this interesting class."

Eaton says, at p. 72 of his 1858 book: "At the sale of Bantams, Pigeons, &c., belonging to the late celebrated and spirited Fancier, Sir John Sebright, I was astonished to see the English Pouters in miniature, possessing the five properties of the English Pouter." Some have supposed these were stocking-legged birds; but no proof of this can be adduced. The above is contained in a note on the pouting horseman, much of which I have already quoted, and my own impression is that they were selected Norwich croppers such as I have myself.

CHAPTER LXXVII.

FOREIGN CROPPER PIGEONS.

ACCORDING to Boitard and Corbie, there are several varieties of pouters bred in France. The writings of these authors evince a personal acquaintance with most of the varieties, but their descriptions are so meagre, and their technical words so impossible to translate, just as the terms used only by pigeon fanciers here would be into any foreign language, that were it not for the illustrations in their books, it would be quite impossible to form any correct idea of the appearance of the birds described.

The largest French pouters are known as *Pigeons Grosses-gorges*, or *Pigeons Boulans*, and are represented as large, thick-bodied, short and bare-legged, clumsy, runtish-looking birds. They appear to be both self-coloured and pied. The latter have white flights and are white in front of the crop, so far approximating in the disposition of their marking to the English pouter and Norwich cropper, which doubtless have some remote connection with them. The crop is well developed. Boitard and Corbie allow that the English pouter attains a greater size than the French. I made an attempt, some time ago, to obtain from France some blood-red pouters of this variety; but my correspondent searched for them in vain. The *Grosse-gorge Bleu*, with white crop and flights, is much spread over Picardy, it is said, where it is much esteemed. Every separate colour seems to constitute a distinct variety with the writers cited, hence nearly twenty kinds are classified, but, except that some are entirely bare-legged while others are somewhat feather-legged, I can find no mention of any difference in form between the various breeds. On page 28 of Brent's pigeon book is an exact copy of Boitard and Corbie's *Pigeon Grosse-gorge Maurin à Bavette*, but entitled by him the "Old German Pouter."

The *Pigeons Lillois* are thus described: "This race of superb pigeons belongs to the pouter division, since, like the preceding, they have the power of inflating the throat,.but in a lesser degree. The crop in the *Boulans* is always of a spherical form, instead of which these have it in the form of a long pear, of which the thinnest part is below and the largest part under the beak. These pigeons take their name from the town of Lille, where they are much bred and esteemed. Their head is small, beak long and slender, and they are not subject to the crop diseases of the large pouters."

The *Pigeon Lillois élégant* is portrayed as a short-legged, thick-bodied, very upright standing pigeon, with a small oval crop, which is white in front, as are the flights. Boitard and Corbié say: "It is very well made, of an elegant and graceful form, body placed almost vertically on the legs in such manner that the head is on the same line as the feet; small head, no cere round the eyes, stockinged legs, only the middle toes covered with feathers—a trait which is only met with in this variety—wings long and crossed. This bird is of light flight, is of great productiveness, and is greatly to be recommended to amateurs who wish to unite the useful with the agreeable."

This pigeon seems to have some resemblance to the Norwich cropper, and from what I can make out its colours are like those of the bar-winged croppers; but to a British pouter fancier nothing more *inelegant* than the shape of it, as pictured, can be imagined, so that I can scarcely believe that it correctly represents the breed.

The next variety has evidently a resemblance to our cropper in flight.

Pigeon Lillois claquart.—"This pigeon, which Buffon has confounded with the *tournant*" (Smiter or Ringbeater), "makes a noise with its wings when commencing to fly like a *claquette*, hence its name. It inflates its throat, has long wings crossed over the tail, a cere round the eyes, and stocking legs. Its plumage is white or chamois, or blue shouldered with white, that is having the upper part of the wing white. It produces well, which makes it much sought after."

For my own part, I have never seen long-flighted pigeons fly so well as the short-flighted.

The *Pigeons Cavaliers* are recommended for their beauty and productiveness. "This race appears to be extracted from runts (*Romains*) and pouters, of which they have the general form, as also the power of inflating the throat more or less according to the variety. Some have thick nostrils, membraneous and fleshy, or even a little mushroomed, but rarely; they have a red cere round the eyes." The *Pigeon Cavalier Faraud* is pictured as a tall, upstanding, shell-crested, long-cropped, and bare-legged pouter. It is said to be a cross between the common *Cavalier* and the *Bagadais Mondain à l'œil*.

Neumeister and Prütz describe several varieties of German croppers (*Kropftauben*), and say, regarding the whole race: "This universally known and favourite kind of pigeon is distinguished from all others by its ability of puffing up the throat to the highest degree, so that it often becomes as large as the remaining body. This is done by drawing in air into the throat, by means of the bill somewhat opened, the throat valve closing; which closing is brought about in a manner which has not yet been thoroughly investigated; but it is likely by a co-operation of the neck muscles. As to the beauty of croppers, it is essential that the neck be long, so that the head does not stick between the shoulders, which gives them an unshapely appearance. Their flight is mostly good, though somewhat heavy, they flap much with their wings, and frequently make playful gyrations with their wings held high. Their propagation is but middling, but they are much liked on account of their cheerful ways and the above described remarkable blowing up of their crops, which gives them peculiarly graceful attitudes and movements. They should never be kept with other pigeons, especially large kinds, as they are helpless when blowing and unable to withdraw from or defend themselves against the attacks of others. The crop loses its feathers by blows from the beak, is even sometimes pierced; when feeding with other nimble kinds they often come short; their pairing is also interfered with, which is telling on the offspring. They are variously marked, of quite different forms, and therefore divided into the following varieties:

"*Der Deutsche Kurz und glattfüssige Kröpfer* (German short and bare-legged cropper) is one of the largest croppers, of considerable height. Its length 55 centimetres" (21¾in., 36in. = 91½ centimetres), "and breadth of outspread wings 105 centimetres." It passes for the original race of all the remaining cropper kinds. The round head is mostly smooth, sometimes with a pointed hood, brow high, bill proportionately short, neck very long, and, along with the crop, strongly hung with hair; breast and back broad, the latter somewhat hollow. The crop always puffed up, hanging somewhat forward, has a diameter of 12½-15 centimetres, and a circumference up to 42½ centimetres. The short, strong legs are

x 2

unfeathered; the wings carelessly hanging down, overreach the tail end by 5 centimetres. This is the characteristic mark of the German cropper, and is not found in any of the following varieties. The usual colour is either white, or blue with white head or tips, yellow with a white tail and head, or black. It is very much to be lamented that this pigeon, in its pure state, seems almost to have disappeared, as it is never represented at the exhibitions. The propagation is extremely poor. The main cause of its disappearance is likely owing to change of fashion, in consequence of which breeders have turned more to the slender, high-legged kinds.

This breed is represented on plate 11. of *Neumeister's Das Ganze der Taubensucht*, in four colours, white, yellow, red, and blue; the two last have turncrowns. The coloured birds have white heads, flights, and tails, but are dark thighed. They are short and bare in limb. It strikes me that, as a cross with the English pouter, to increase its size, they would at least be greatly superior to runts.

"*Der Breslauer Kröpfer* (the Breslau cropper) comes nearest to the preceding, is of stately size, generally speaking is one of the largest croppers, yet not long in body, nor do the pinions reach beyond the tail, so the dimensions are much less. It occurs one-coloured and marked, in the latter case with a white upper head, the yellow marked frequently with white flights and tail."

"*Die Pommersche Kropftaube* (the Pomeranian cropper) has a great resemblance to the English pouter, with which it is unmistakeably connected. It is found in perfect beauty at Stralsund and Greifswald." And then follows a detailed description of it, taken from an article by Dr. Bodinus, published in the year 1858.

In the third edition of *Die Arten der Haustaube*, by Herr Prütz, published in 1878, he states that the Pomeranian cropper "is said to have been imported from England many years ago; but it is without doubt much handsomer than all similar croppers which have lately been brought from England that I have seen. The late Herr Wermann, of Altenburg, an authority on pigeons, was quite delighted when he first saw a pair which I had sent to Herr von Beust." From his description of this variety, it would appear to resemble the English pouter in all respects, except that any white pinion on the wing, which when rightly defined is so valuable in our breed, is a fault in it. It would also appear that the Pomeranian must have much rougher limbs than our pouter.

The principal breeder of Pomeranian croppers, Herr Wilhelm Hevernick, in a lecture delivered in the Ornithological Club of Stralsund, entitled, "The Pomeranian cropper, and its relation to the English one," and published in "Columbia," of February 15th, 1879, a copy of which was very kindly sent to me by its editor, Herr Prütz, says as follows: "If I try in the following paper to establish the relationship of the Pomeranian and English croppers, as well as their descent, to point to the value of a rational breed of Pomeranian croppers, and to warn against crossing with the English, I must preface the plan of my work with this my view, without claiming infallibility, that this subject, so far as I know, has not been handled by anyone before me, excepting Dr. Bodinus. He first described the Pomeranian cropper about 25 years ago, and drew the attention of pigeon lovers to this beautiful bird, at that time not known anywhere beyond Fore-Pomerania. I must remark that only my great love for this race of pigeons induced me to undertake investigations into its descent, developement, and relations, and to communicate the result here, in the hope of giving other breeders a motive, through my views, to consider this circumstance, to make known their views, and to treat this subject further in our club, in order that we may be in a position to breed our beautiful cropper in such quantity and quality that it may equal the English and French breed in beauty. I am persuaded that this is very easily practicable, provided we have the understanding and will necessary for it. To perfect the first, and to aim at the latter, is the plan of my lecture."

He then goes on to describe the peculiarity of all cropper pigeons, argues that the distension of their crops must have proceded from long, careful selective breeding in domesticity, because such pigeons could not naturally exist, as they could never hold their own in a state of nature. Assuming that croppers, as well as all other races, are derived from the blue rock pigeon, he does not think that all the kinds of croppers are necessarily derived from one original race; but that they might have originated from parallel running lines, or, in other words, that the distension of crop in pigeons may have been noticed in different countries and times, and independent races established from them. He does not, however, mean to try to prove which races may be considered originals, but only to express his opinion on the relationship and origin of the Pomeranian and English breeds, as the clearing up of this relationship is necessary for the rational breeding of the former. He evidently did not know that it is on record how our English pouter was produced, which would have materially assisted him in his investigations. He proceeds:

"As I suppose that to all who are interested in our cropper the marks of both races are known, I will omit an exact description of them, yet it appears necessary for my plan to illustrate more nearly the striking peculiarities, as well as the resemblances of both. The English cropper is very large, and very much of the same size as the Pomeranian. The inflated crop is round, and must be intersected by an incision on the breast, so that this incision forms a regular shape; the rump is proportionately thin, the tail long and slender, the legs are very long, possibly equally feathered with downy feathers, only the toes must have standing out feathers so that they quite hide the toes, but at the same time form no shoes, which is a decided defect in the English cropper."

What is meant by "shoes" I do not exactly know, but I learn further on that the Pomeranian breed is much rougher limbed than ours, which, though considered a beauty in them, is a grievous defect in ours.

"The Pomeranian cropper is almost, or quite, of the same size as the English; but its rump is thicker, its crop not inflated so like a ball, on account of which the shape is lost, the tail is shorter and is carried a little more spread out, the legs with good birds are almost as long as with the English. Yet from a distance they do not appear so long, because they are provided with pretty large feathers, which form stockings below the hocks and shoes at the feet; the colours and marks are the same as with the English; pure whites also occur, though they have become rare; and there are whites with black and blue tails. The last mark often occurs, and I have hitherto believed that whites with black tails existed in no other race, especially in the English, for Fulton does not mention them; although he treats his subject very minutely and fully. It is striking that among the Pomeranian croppers there are no whites with red or yellow tails."

I have seen many blue and black-tailed white English pouters, and they can easily be bred by pairing a black or blue pied with a white. The first cross often results in such marking, as I have observed elsewhere, and it can easily be fixed, as in the Norwich croppers. Red and yellow-tailed whites are, however, impossible, or next to it, because, as Herr Hevernick truly observes, the coloured tail is not found in red and yellow pied pouters; at least not dark enough to match the body colour.

"On beard and heart" (*i.e.* bib and half moon) "as it is called, we place the same conditions with Pomeranian as with English croppers; but white feathers on the wings, which with the English are more and more highly prized according to their form, are in all circumstances a defect with the Pomeranian, and a sign of careless breeding or of a bad origin. In consequence of this, these feathers are cut off with a pair of scissors by many breeders. On this occasion, I cannot refrain from blaming this proceeding most decidedly, for there can be no interest, in my opinion, in examining the pigeons of a breeder, of whom we know that he indulges in such rectifications; however, on the other hand, it may perhaps be represented, that someone may say he sells no pigeons, and removes their feathers in order that his pigeons may please him better, no matter to him whether other breeders allow this proceeding or not. But, if anyone sends pigeons to an exhibition, all the same whether for sale or not, I can find no point from which such manipulations can be defended, for they have only impure motives, such as bragging or base dishonesty. The bearing of the Pomeranian must be high and upright, though not so high as with the English. But, if, as Prütz says in his noteworthy book, '*Die Arten der Haustaube*,' the back must be arched a little convexly, he is mistaken; at least I have heard this hog's back, as the English call it, always very expressively blamed.

"Now, if we compare the two races with each other, we find that size and marking are nearly the same, but with the English, the crop is somewhat more inflated, the shape somewhat thinner, the tail more slender and longer, the legs somewhat longer, but less strongly feathered, and the bearing more upright than with the Pomeranian. With both races white feathers occur on the wings, yet this is considered a defect in the Pomeranian, while with the English this mark is highly valued. But this mark is only the result of a careful choice in breeding continued for years, and very difficult to fix; it occurs mostly in England in the wished-for perfection, only very seldom, and is only known to me by description and pictures from English prize birds, while I have never met with this mark in specimens shown in continental exhibitions in anything like such perfection. If we place an English and a Pomeranian pattern bird together, the first must positively please us most, not on account of its beauty, but on account of its peculiarity, which consists therein that the bird with its great length, and upright bearing, shows a very voluminous upper body, and a high, thin underbody, both of which are only joined by the slender figure. Dr. Bodinus says 'the English cropper gives the impression of a large beautiful statue placed on a small pedestal,' and I find this very striking. The Pomeranian cropper, on the other hand, appears very compact, firm, and powerful, yet shows in the parts of its body, and in its whole appearance, such great harmony as I have never seen in any other race of croppers, with the exception of the striped Hollanders " (whole coloured croppers, with white long bars). " If we examine more closely the whole impression of both races, we find that in both the character of the nation is exactly expressed. The Englishman likes the unusual and peculiar, and the Pomeranian (especially the New Fore-Pomeranian) likes the less striking, but compact and strong, and from these motives in the breeding both races have evidently arisen. After having seen that the total impression with each race is quite different, we find that the differences in the single parts of the body are not important. This circumstance lets us know that both races are nearly related, therefore there remains only the question whether one race descends from the other, and which has been the original, or whether both have arisen from some common stock. In my opinion we find the answer to this question very easily, if we look practically into the way and manner of degeneration in both races. That both easily degenerate with careless breeding lets us know that both races are not yet very old, but in this respect we must not think of the generations of man, for, no doubt, both races have existed 200—300 years. If we now examine the degeneracies of English pouters, the shorter legs and less upright carriage show their ancestors must have had these faults. With the degeneration of Pomeranian croppers we find lower and less feathered legs, white spots on the wings and white snips on the forehead, which leads us to suppose that they proceed from a race which had bare legs and white heads. Only the old German croppers are so marked, and I therefore take them to be the original of our croppers."

From the foregoing it is evident that there is enough resemblance between the English and Pomeranian croppers to establish a connection between them. Sailors speak of every northern European who is not a

Frenchman as a Dutchman. Moore's Dutch cropper was evidently a bird with much resemblance to the Pomeranian, so it is not unlikely that this pigeon, "flag thigh'd," as Moore says, was the ancestor of our pouter. The horseman cross would take the feathers from its legs at first, evidence of which I have adduced from the Treatise of 1765, and from the description of my old painting of the time of Moore; but leg feathering, to suit the taste of fanciers, was quickly recovered. As to solid shoulders being infinitely preferable to bishoped wings, there is no doubt; but the Pomeranian breed itself is evidently not altogether free of white " daubs " on the wing, as they call them. As to deducing both varieties from the old bald-headed, long-bodied German cropper, already referred to, I can see nothing in the argument at all. The correct crop marking of the English pouter and similarly marked breeds must necessarily vary very considerably in breeding, there being no certainty in the production of a white mark which has no structural conformation in the bird to guide it, such as a white head, wings, or tail. The rose-pinion for the same reason is a difficult mark to breed. Hence, pouters come, and must always come, more or less close or open-marked. The crop is sometimes seen solid or free of white, and sometimes the bib is wanting; the bird is then swallow-throated, and a white blaze on the forehead often appears. The same may appear on a bird correctly marked on the crop. No one would adduce a white blaze on the forehead of a shortfaced mottled tumbler from baldhead blood. The little Norwich cropper, from careless breeding, is very subject to the blaze face. I have seen runts, imported from abroad, some of which I had, marked exactly as the pouter ought to be marked, except that they had no white feathers on the shoulders. They weighed over 3lb. per pair. It is something for one who admires his own breed so much as Herr Hevernick does, to allow that a pattern English pouter "must positively please" a fancier more than a pattern Pomeranian. It is unlikely that many English pouters of the first quality have been seen in Germany, because they easily sell here for several times the price foreigners will give for them. Were English fanciers to breed for solid shoulders they could very easily accomplish their desire; but they consider the rose-pinion such a set-off to a bird that they will not abandon it; and, although it is rare to see it well defined, it is seen now and then.

Herr Hevernick says that it was Dr. Bodinus who named the

Pomeranian cropper, that it was sometimes known before as the Hollander, and that he has seen some that were brought from Holland very like it. These might have been taken from England, or they might have been of a Dutch breed. He saw some in the market of Rotterdam which were not English, but which resembled the Pomeranian, though not so good. He says the breed has lost quality in late years; that it was better twenty-five years ago; but that, about that time, offers of tempting prices induced breeders to part with their best birds, which were scattered to all places and soon lost sight of. He concludes his lecture by giving much valuable information on the breeding of this variety; observing that of late a great increase in breeding had taken place, and warns breeders against crossing with English blood, which he had found did not improve the Pomeranian cropper. From all I can learn from his lecture, I do not think this variety, though evidently allied to ours, can be of any service to pouter fanciers here, because it seems smaller and rather inferior in all its points of shape in comparison with our best birds; however, if I could see a collection of good Pomeranians, which I may do when I can spare the necessary time, I could at once form an opinion on the subject, more to the point, than can be gathered from any amount of descriptive writing.

Proceeding with the continental croppers, as described by Neumeister and Prütz, the next variety is the "*Die Sächsische Kropftaube*" (the Saxon cropper).—"It is not so large as the German, far quicker and lighter in flight, and of a slimmer shape. The wings lie close to the body and reach to the end of the tail, on which the wing points cross. The beak is longer and thinner than with the German cropper, legs and thighs are high and feathered. It is of a weakly constitution, and propagates poorly. The plumage, generally, is one-coloured blue, black, red, or yellow; frequently, however, bay-coloured with white wing-bars."

"*Die Holländische Kropftaube*" (the Dutch cropper).—I understand that the following description applies to a cropper bred in Germany and known by this name. "The Dutch cropper is distinguished from the Prague cropper by a somewhat larger body, and by a crop more of the shape of a cylinder than a ball. Its legs are high, covered with trousers and feathers. It is always one-coloured, often with white wing-bars. The bay-coloured" (Isabel coloured) "among them are most cultivated, and no other colour is found in the same perfection. In Holland, where this breed is original, it likewise occurs only one-coloured, yet there it has thin legs, less feathered, and short toes, standing close together. The gait of the cock is tripping, and he leaps towards the hen. It is of a very erect bearing, slimly made, and high-legged, because it carries its thighs outside the plumage of the belly. It inflates its crop very well, and it assumes an oval, cylindrical form. The wings do not reach the end of the tail, are narrowly drawn together, and their points cross over the tail. The Dutch cropper in its erect posture, when strongly feathered on the legs, resembles a falcon at rest. It is a very cheerful pigeon, fond of flying, of flapping its wings, and especially of swooping along, floating with high held wings. It is a pretty good breeder."

"*Der Oesterreichische Plätscher* (The Austrian cropper, known as the 'Plätscher).'—It is between the Dutch and German croppers in size, and a powerful pigeon. Compared with the Dutch it is broader built, heavier, has shorter unfeathered legs and feet, does not stand so erect, has longer wings, and inflates its crop in the same way as the German. One might take it for a cross-breed between the German and Dutch croppers; but such is not the case. Its plumage is distinguished by being glossy and glittering; it is entirely self-coloured, and never shows white pinions, or any white on the head, which would be the case if it were a descendant of the German cropper. It is a very good breeder, very lively, and when flying the shortest distance it flaps its wings, so that it is heard from afar, like the ringbeater. It occurs in Switzerland, blue, yellow, and white."

"*Die Prager Elster-Kropftaube* (The Prague magpie cropper).—This cropper, which has become very rare, is of a structure between the German and Dutch breeds, standing higher than the latter, and having well-feathered legs and feet. It is a good pigeon for breeding, very lively, and has the manner of the Dutch cropper." The illustration of this cropper represents an upstanding, rough-legged, magpie-marked bird. The marking is exactly the same as that of the magpie pigeon, except that the head is white. There seems, from what Neumeister says, to have been formerly a similarly marked German cropper. The Prague magpie cropper, though shown with a white head on his coloured plate, has evidently not a pure white head, as he says that from the beak to the middle of the head it is of a "coloured paleness," probably meaning that the head is of a powdered colour.

This concludes the account of the large continental croppers, as gathered from the French and German writers named.

The Indian Cropper.—I have seen, in Bengal, several croppers of a breed which I believe is peculiar to that country. They were of a size between the English pouter and Norwich cropper, feathered on the legs, but not roughly, and by no means very graceful looking pigeons. They were called by a name which signifies *swelled neck*. Such as I saw were either self-coloured blue, or blue-grizzled in colour. They were evidently bred for crop alone, being short in limb and feather. Considering their size, some of them had very large crops. They seemed to me to have no connection with English pouters, several imported specimens of which I have seen in Bengal from time to time. There are probably several other varieties of croppers throughout India and adjacent countries.

Tegetmeier says, at page 71 of his book on pigeons, regarding foreign croppers: "Many of these birds are very prettily marked; a pair, a short time since, came into our possession of a very bright yellow, with pure white wings and flight-feathers, and well-defined white rings round the necks." This marking nearly resembles that of the Prague magpie cropper, already described, to which race they probably belonged.

CHAPTER LXXVIII.

FOREIGN PIGMY CROPPERS.

SOME of the following varieties of continental pigmy croppers have been known in this country for a good many years. The first that were introduced, so far as I know, were self coloured blacks, reds, blues, &c., which went by the name of Austrians. Self colours with white wing bars are also known, the most beautiful being the delicate cream or light dove coloured ones called Isabels. The smallest of these pigmies are now generally known by their German name of Brünners. So far as I can learn from the description of these varieties by Neumeister and Prütz, they ought to have clean legs. I have had them with feathers on the outsides of the legs and middle toes, precisely the same as in many of our Norwich croppers, but prefer bare legs. Tegetmeier figures a pair of pigeons called Isabels very tall and rough legged, but entirely devoid of crop, and with none of the shape of a cropper. He also figures a pair of red Austrians which well represent such as I have seen, except that their limbs are well covered with downy feathers, and their colour is too bright. Such Isabels as I have had were miniature pouters with hardly any leg feathering, more delicate in colour than those Mr. Tegetmeier represents in his book, uplopers in carriage, only medium sized in crop, and they carried their wings crossed at the tips. They were splendid fliers, floating lightly in the air with their wings upheld for great distances, but they did not clap so loudly as Norwich croppers, nor carry their tails so fan-like. They had the ability, mentioned by Neumeister, of bending their hock joints forward, when stretched to their utmost height; but they were not nearly so small as he speaks of, being very little less than average sized Norwich croppers. Mr Tegetmeier gives the following weights and measurements of birds he possessed :

White cock... ... ... 12½in. by 4½in.	Weight	8oz.
Blue hen ... ... 12in. „ 5in.	„	7½oz.
Silver hen ... ... 12in. „ 4½in.	„	8½oz

Neumeister and Prütz describe these miniature croppers as follows:

"*Die Brünner Kropftaube*" (the Brünn cropper).—"It is found particularly beautiful in Prague and Vienna, where it is known by the false name of the 'Dutch' cropper. It is the most elegant and finest of all the croppers. Having been first imported to us from Brünn, it was named Brünner cropper, and it is mostly known by that name. It has the smallest body of all the house pigeons, its whole length amounting to 27¼ centimetres (11in.). Legs very long, the thighs being outside the plumage of the belly, and being so stretched during the act of inflating the crop that they almost form a perpendicular line. The leg measures 14 centimetres (5½in.), the full grown pigeon weighs 200-266⅔ grm. (7 to 9½oz.). Not inflated, it is not much bigger than a blackbird, and so slim that you can draw it through your thumb and fore-finger. When affected, it presses its thighs outwards, to such a degree, that they look like knees which can be moved forward, as it stands almost perpendicularly on the points of its toes. Its smooth, finely shaped head is oval, brow high, neck long, the globular crop is 7¼ centimetres (3in. in diameter), but without hair. The bill is thin, the waist delicate. The wings, fitting closely to the body, reach within an inch of the end of the tail. The tips are strongly drawn together, narrow and long, and much crossed over the rump. Feet and toes are weakly and smooth. On the whole the pigeon has a loose plumage; but, notwithstanding, flies well and perseveringly. The Brünn cropper is mostly coloured like the Saxon. The black with white wing bars, blue, red, and yellow are the most common. The delicate bay with white wing-bars are the rarest. In this colouring the whole plumage, without exception, must be perfectly equally, as it were, breathed upon with the most delicate and aerial bay, not so dark but that the pure white wing-bars can be distinctly seen on it. In connection with this is an unspotted, delicate, flesh-coloured beak, toe-nails, and eye-wattle. The iris is light yellow with an orange border. A dark beak is a chief defect. The Brünn croppers are cheerful and lively, are fond of flying rapidly, and of flapping, but do not like to go near strange dovecoots. It is a worthy parallel to the fine English almond tumbler, and as neat, elegant, and cheerful in its way. Nothing prettier can be imagined than a loftful of these lively, neat, and amorous pigeons, among which there is no end of courting and caressing. The loving cock drives the hen before him, all the while inflating his crop and cooing, while she walks forward in proud decorum. It flies lightly, quickly, and with flapping wings, and is very persevering in its flight; in this the inflated crop helps, for it happens that the Brünn cropper can float for from 50 to 60 steps in the air, holding its spread wings high over its back without moving them. No other pigeon is able to do so for so long a distance. Generally speaking its flight differs from that of other pigeons. If a swarm of these croppers fly, it is clearly seen how fond they are of it. It is for them a pleasure to fly in wide circles around their house for half an hour. The Brünn cropper, when affected, runs on high legs as if on stilts, standing even on its toes, and inflating its round crop so full that it reaches a diameter of 7½ centimetres" (3 inches).

The length of the Brünn cropper, 11in., seems out of all proportion to its limb, and I think, considering the weight of the bird, it is mis-stated. Compared with our Norwich cropper it is doubtless a smaller and more slender pigeon, but those I have had were very little less than my best croppers, which attained a diameter in crop up to 5in., 4¼in. being commonly seen. The Brünn cropper is certainly smaller in girth, and shows its thighs more than the cropper, but its habit of crossing its wings is a bad fault in my opinion. I had one Isabel coloured Brünner hen which did not have this fault, and some who saw her considered her one of the best shaped little pouters they had seen. She was 5¼in. in limb, and 14¼in. in feather, but had only a small crop compared with that of a good Norwich cropper.

"*Die Prager Kropftaube*" (the Prague cropper), "also called the Stork cropper, is not much larger than the Brünner, the legs are of the same height, and, along with the toes, somewhat feathered. It is either one coloured with white wing-bars, or like a stork, white with mottled, mostly reddish-brown breast, flights, and tail. It comes from Bohemia, and frequently very strong blowers are found among them."

This pigeon, of which Neumeister gives a coloured portrait, is represented as a bare-legged, very upstanding cropper, with red crop, flights, and tail. The head and upper neck are light, the colour gradually deepening towards the lower neck.

"*Die Holländische Ballonkropftaube*" (the Dutch Balloon cropper) "is, in the first place, distinguished from all other croppers by its peculiarly short round form, and bent back neck. Its length is 32¼ centimetres (13in.), the length of its leg 14 centimetres (5¼in.), the weight of the body up to 383½grm." (13½oz.).

"The head is smooth, the nape very powerful, the neck bent back as with the fantail, even when not blowing, and this is the first characteristic mark of the balloon cropper. The breast is correspondingly protruding and broad. The crop has, when inflated, a diameter of 12½-15 centimetres" (5in. to 6in.). "The flights do not reach the end of the tail, and are somewhat crossed. The leg is shortly feathered, and the colour and markings vary. It stands with stiff legs and rather low, and walks with dignity, nodding very much. In flying, it holds its head and crop upright, which lends to the pigeon the appearance of a balloon, hence its name. All other pigeons stretch their necks out horizontally when flying, and this deviation from the rule is its second characteristic mark. It propagates badly. In Holland much care is spent on its production, in Germany less, as, on the whole, this pigeon does not make a very fine impression.

CONCLUSION.

A NEW book on fancy pigeons has been lately published in America, a copy of which has been kindly sent to me by Mrs. E. S. Starr, who edits the *Fanciers' Journal*, of Springfield, Massachusetts. It is entitled, "The International Standard of Excellence for Judging Pigeons, with hints to breeders and a chapter on diseases, compiled and illustrated by J. W. Ludlow, president of the Birmingham Columbarian Society. Scale of points and revision by Wm. Simpson junr., president of the National Columbarian Society, New York, 1879." This is a very handsomely got up octavo book of 103 pp., embellished with eight full-page coloured lithographs, each containing the figures of several fancy pigeons, in compartments. The "general points of excellence applicable to each sort" are detailed, and a scale of points, with their numerical value, added; but no discursive writing, on any of the varieties treated of, is indulged in. In addition to the coloured plates there are various woodcuts throughout the work.

M. La Perre de Roo has lately published, in Dutch, a book in octavo on homing pigeons entitled "De Postduif," which is uniform with his French work, "Le Pigeon Voyageur," already referred to. It dates from Thielt, in 1879, is illustrated with engravings, and contains 180 pp., besides an appendix describing, with illustrations, certain rare birds and beasts in the Jardin D'Acclimatation of Paris. Other works by this author, which he has very kindly presented me with, and which are, for the most part, incorporated with the above, are:—

"La Poste par pigeons voyageurs, pendant le Siége de Paris. Extrait du Bulletin de la Société d'Acclimatation (No. d'Octobre, 1872)," 52 pp. In this pamphlet, which is now very rare, is a souvenir of the Siege of Paris—a pellicule, about 1¼in. by 2in., on which is photographed a great number of messages, illustrating the method of communication employed during the siege by the pigeon post. "Les Colombiers Militaires, rapport adressé à M. le Ministre de la Guerre," 28 pp., and 18 engravings. "Les Colombiers Militaires, Paris, 1874," 16 pp., being the author's second pamphlet on this subject.

A translation of M. La Perre de Roo's work on pigeons for military purposes, by M. P. Graells, entitled "Las Palomas en la Guerra," was published in Madrid, in 1873.

M. La Perre de Roo is presently engaged on a general book of pigeons, which he expects to publish in 1881. He has favoured me with an inspection of several of the illustrations, which include some of a new variety produced by himself, and which he obtained by numerous crossings. This variety may be briefly described as a white owl or turbit with the markings of the German spot pigeon. It is either smooth-headed, shell-crested, or peak-headed. It has an oval coloured spot on the forehead, either blue, black, red, or yellow, with a coloured tail and tail coverts to match. He says that they breed true to colour, nine out of eleven young ones bred during the past season being well marked. He has named them *Pigeons cravaté de Sibérie*, the coloured spot on their forehead resembling that of the Himalayan and Siberian rabbits.

The work known as "Girton's Complete Pigeon Fancier," of which I now know of seven editions, was first published in 12mo., as "A Treatise on Domestic Pigeons, containing valuable information, &c., &c. London: Printed for the Proprietors, and sold by all the booksellers in town and country. Price only two shillings and sixpence." The Treatise on Pigeons of 1765, being a book which would likely, from its appearance, cost a good deal, and, therefore, be only available to people of means, as is proved from the number of copies in existence containing bookplates and coats of arms, a cheap edition would soon be necessary, and was brought out as above, without illustrations. However, 2s. 6d. seems to have been too dear for it, and the remainder passed into the possession of A. Hogg and Co., who dealt in remainders, as they afterwards dealt with the remainder of Windus's "Treatise on the Almond Tumbler," as already pointed out. They then printed a new title-page and got a plate engraved containing the figures of twelve pigeons, copied in small from the large Treatise, and sent out the book as "The Complete Pigeon Fancier," price 1s. 6d. This is the history of this manual, which

I have discovered from having found a copy of the first edition, which, I believe, is even rarer than Moore's "Columbarium," of which there are now, at least, six copies known to be extant, i.e., the four in the British Museum, Mr. Esquilant's, and my own.

A curiosity in pigeon literature which remains to be noticed is J. M. Eaton's "Circular," a long rambling notice of his book and portraits of pigeons, which he was in the habit of sending to the committees and secretaries of shows, to induce them to buy copies from him for presentation as prizes. This is closely written on two and a half leaves of paper, about fifteen by six inches, and lithographed from his own handwriting. A space for the date and address in the copy I have has been filled in by him, "Monday, 18th Decr., 1865. To the Right Worshipful the Mayor of Cork. May your show be crowned with success." This is the most amusing production connected with pigeons that has come under my notice, and it would well bear reproduction could space be found for it here; but I fear this is impossible.

I may state that the *Himalayan Carrier* was so named by me because Mr. Wood, of Calcutta, informed me that it was a native of some of the countries north of, and bordering on, the Himalayas.

At page 93 of the Treatise on Pigeons, 1765, "the standard now published and in use among the Columbarians" for judging pouters is mentioned. This is uniform with the "Ordinances" for judging almond tumblers, referred to on page 11. It is a large sheet, headed by the same portrait of a pouter which the Treatise of 1765 contains.

FINIS.

INDEX.

ACCOMMODATION FOR FANCY PIGEONS.

	PAGE
Advantage of several compartments in a pigeonry	30, 40
Description of author's pigeonry	28
Earthenware nest pans	30
Fittings of pigeon houses and lofts	29
Fittings of the aviary or flight	30
Hoppers for grain	26, 38
Nesting places for pigeons	29
Pigeon house, loft, and aviary	23
Sawdust for pigeon houses	31
Wall boxes for pigeons	24
Water fountains for pigeons	27

COLOURS OF FANCY PIGEONS.

	PAGE
Albino pigeons	47, 255
Colour of the Blue Rock pigeon	45
Colour of the dovehouse or field pigeon	45
Gorgeous colours in fancy pigeons	49
Melanoid pigeons	47
Origin of markings in fancy pigeons	47
Variation in colour of field pigeons	46, 48

DISEASES OF FANCY PIGEONS.

	PAGE
Bowels, inflammation of	55
Canker	56
Cold	58
Core, the	58
Diarrhœa	58
Diseases of the joints	59
Egg binding	59
Flesh wen	59
Gizzard fallen	59
Going light	59
Gorging	59
Insects or parasites	60
Leg weakness	61
Moulting	62
Small-pox	62
Spouts	62
Vertigo or megrims	63
Wing disease	63

EXHIBITING PIGEONS.

	PAGE
Exhibition pens	53
Judging pen for pouters	54
Pigeon shows	50
Preparing pigeons for shows	53, 289
Travelling boxes and baskets	51
Value of exhibition pigeons	51, 226, 279

GENERAL MANAGEMENT OF FANCY PIGEONS.

	PAGE
Appearance of good eggs	41
Appearance of young pigeons	42
Assistance in hatching	42
Bathing water	39
Best pigeons for beginners	33
Changing young ones to feeders	44
Chipped eggs, how repaired	41
Elements of success in breeding	44
Evil of overcrowded lofts	43
Fattening young pigeons	67
Feeders for young pigeons	42
Fertile eggs, how told	41
Food suitable for fancy pigeons	36
Gravel for the aviary	32
Green food for pigeons	39
Growth of young pigeons	42
How to match up pigeons	40
How to repair chipped eggs	41
How to tell fertile eggs	41
Incubation of pigeons	41
Lime for pigeons	32
Longevity of pigeons	114
Odd birds in the loft	43
Overcrowded lofts, evil of	43
Pigeons' dung, its value	67
Productiveness of pigeons	43
Rules for breeding good pigeons	39, 44
Salt-cat, the	32
Salt for pigeons	32
Selection of stock	33
Separating the sexes in winter	43
Sex of young pigeons	43
Suitable food for pigeons	36
Use of barren hens	44
Value of pigeons' dung	67

LITERATURE, &C., CONNECTED WITH FANCY PIGEONS.

	PAGE
Akbar's (The Emperor) book on pigeons	1, 18, 123
Aldrovandus on pigeons	8
American standard for judging pigeons	321
Anacreon's ode to the carrier pigeon, B.C. 520	1, 138
Arabic-French book on homing pigeons, 1805	21
Baldamus' (Dr. A. E. E.) book on pigeons, 1878	20
Boitard and Corbie's book on pigeons, 1824	18
Bonizzi's (Prof. P.) book on pigeons, 1872	20
Bonizzi's (Prof. P.) book on pigeons, 1876	21, 134
Boswell (Peter) on pigeons, &c.	14
Brent's (P. B.) "The Pigeon Book"	17
Chapuis (Dr. F.) on homing pigeons	21
Columella on pigeons	8
"De Jure Columbarum," 1706	18
Delamer's (E. S.) "Pigeons and Rabbits," 1854	14
Dixon's (Rev. E. S.) "Dovecote and Aviary," 1851	8, 14
Dutch book on homing pigeons	321
Eaton's (J. M.) Circular	323
Eaton's (J. M.) coloured portraits of pigeons	16

LITERATURE, &C., CONNECTED WITH FANCY PIGEONS—(*continued*).

	PAGE
Eaton's (J. M.) "Treatise on the Almond Tumbler," 1851	15
Eaton's (J. M.) "Treatise on Pigeons," 1852	15
Eaton's (J. M.) "Treatise on Pigeons," 1858	16
English books on homing pigeons	21
French books on homing pigeons	21, 321
Fulton's (R.) "Illustrated Book of Pigeons"	17
German books on homing pigeons	21
Girton's (D.) "Complete Pigeon Fancyer"	12, 322
Harris (E. D.) on pigeons	21
Huie (James) on homing pigeons	140
La Perre de Roo's (Victor) works on pigeons	21, 322, 323
Ludlow and Simpson on fancy pigeons	321
Malmusi's (C.) "Dei Triganieri," 1851	20, 134
Martinelli's (Dr. F.) book on pigeons, 1872	20
Minor works on pigeons	18
Moore's (John) "The Columbarium," 1735	9, 22, 323
Moubray's (B.) "Treatise on Poultry," &c. 1815	16
Neumeister's (G.) "Das Ganze der Taubenzucht," 1839	19

	PAGE
"New Foundling Hospital for Wit," 1784	12
"Ordinances for Judging Almond Tumblers," 1764	11
"Ordinances for Judging Pouters"	323
Pliny's references to fancy pigeons	8
Pope's verses on John Moore	9
Prutz's (G.) "Die Arten der Haustaube," 1878	19
Rarity of Moore's "Columbarium"	10, 323
Reprints of Moore's "Columbarium"	10
Spanish work on homing pigeons	322
Tegetmeier's (W.B.) "Pigeons"	17
Tegetmeier's (W. B.) "The Homing Pigeon"	21
"The Pigeon," 1876-7	13
"The Poultry Chronicle," 1854-5	17
"The Poultry Review," 1873-4	17
"Treatise on Pigeons," 1765	10, 322
Willughby's (F.) "Ornithology," 1676	9
Windus' (W. P.) "Treatise on the Almond Tumbler,"	12, 22, 322
Wolstenholme's (D.) portraits of pigeons	15, 16, 22
Wright's (L.) "Practical Pigeon Keeper"	17

ORIGIN OF FANCY PIGEONS.

	PAGE
Blue Rock pigeon, the original of all fancy pigeons	3
Domestic pigeons derived from a common origin	3
Great variety in domestic pigeons	4
Instance of a new type of fancy pigeon	5, 6

	PAGE
Origin of fancy pigeons	3, 65
Pigeon and canary fancies compared	5
Theory of descent of the various fancy pigeons	4
Variations among wild and domestic animals	4, 46

THE PIGEON FANCY.

Antiquity of the pigeon fancy ... 1, 8, 138
Akbar a pigeon fancier 1, 18, 123
Fancy pigeons among the Romans ... 1, 8
King Charles II. a pigeon fancier ... 1, 247
King of Oude's fancy pigeons 1, 136
Pigeons as messengers 8, 138, 144, 265, 266
Queen Victoria's fancy pigeons 1
Universality of the pigeon fancy 1
Value of fancy pigeons 8, 51, 165, 226, 279

VARIETIES OF FANCY PIGEONS.

The African owl ... 210
,, Almond tumbler ... 154
,, Almond, short-faced ... 164
,, Altenburg trumpeter ... 188
,, Ancient tumbler ... 161
,, Ancient, short-faced ... 180
,, Antwerp carrier 138, 265, 267
,, Antwerp, short-faced ... 148
,, Archangel ... 77
,, Austrian cropper ... 315, 317
,, Azure blue ... 81
,, Badge of honour ... 101
,, Bagdads ... 269—274
,, Bagdad carrier ... 246, 257
,, Baldhead tumbler ... 157
,, Baldhead, short-faced ... 178
,, Balloon cropper ... 319
,, Barb ... 240
,, Batavian Bagdad ... 269
,, Bavette ... 73
,, Beard tumbler ... 157
,, Beard short-faced tumbler 178
,, Belgian voyageur 138, 265, 267
,, Birmingham roller ... 155
,, Black backed gull ... 102
,, Blondinette ... 234
,, Blue Brunswick ... 92
,, Blue Rock ... 3, 5, 45
,, Blue short-faced tumbler 177
,, Bokhara trumpeter ... 182
,, Brander ... 162
,, Breaster ... 74
,, Breslau cropper ... 308
,, Bristle ... 111
,, Broad-tailed shaker ... 189
,, Brünn cropper ... 318
,, Bullfinch ... 77

The Burmese ... 108
,, Calotte ... 71
,, Capuchin ... 129
,, Carmelite ... 87
,, Carrier, Antwerp 138, 265, 267
,, Carrier, English ... 246
,, Carrier, foreign ... 269
,, Cavalier ... 306
,, Coloured headed ... 72
,, Common ... 66
,, Coral eyed ... 128
,, Crescent ... 101
,, Croppers or pouters 275—320
,, Curly moor head ... 76
,, Damascene ... 120
,, Death's head ... 72
,, Dodo ... 108
,, Domino ... 236
,, Dragoon ... 258
,, Drummer ... 186
,, Dutch cropper 275, 314, 318
,, Dutch tumbler ... 155
,, English fire ... 95
,, English owl ... 217
,, English pouter ... 275
,, Fairy swallow ... 88
,, Fantail ... 189
,, Fantail, laced ... 112, 196
,, Finnikin ... 116
,, Fire ... 83
,, Fire, English ... 95
,, Florentine ... 108
,, Foreign croppers ... 305
,, Foreign tumblers ... 160
,, Foreign wattled ... 269
,, Friesland runt ... 110
,, Frillback ... 111, 112

Index.

VARIETIES OF FANCY PIGEONS—(continued).

	PAGE
The Frizzled 110,	112
,, German ancient	180
,, German croppers	307
,, Goolee	127
,, Great Batavian	269
,, Great wattled Bagdad ...	269
,, Helmet	71
,, Hen-speckled	109
,, Himalayan carrier ... 273,	323
,, Horseman	258
,, Hungarian	109
,, Hyacinth...	96
,, Ice	81
,, Indian cropper	316
,, Indian flying	135
,, Isabel	317
,, Jacobin	198
,, Lace	112
,, Lace Bagdad	271
,, Lace fantail	196
,, Lahore	125
,, Latz	75
,, Laugher	130
,, Leghorn runt	107
,, Lille clapper	306
,, Lille cropper	305
,, Lowtan	122
,, Macclesfield tippler ...	154
,, Magpie	89
,, Mahomet	119
,, Maltese	108
,, Mane	76
,, Martin	125
,, Mawmet	119
,, Miroité	82
,, Modena 132,	137
,, Monk	93
,, Montauban	105
,, Mookee	125
,, Moon	101
,, Moor's head	72
,, Mottled tumbler	155
,, Mottle, short-faced ...	175
,, Moulting	93
,, Mourning	98
,, Narrow-tailed shaker ...	125
,, Norwegian	105
,, Norwich cropper	291

	PAGE
The Nun	68
,, Nuremberg Bagdad ...	272
,, Nuremberg swallow ...	86
,, Oriental roller...	162
,, Owl, African	210
,, Owl, English	217
,, Owl, powdered ... 120,	218
,, Owl, whiskered	220
,, Parisian pouter	97
,, Piedmont...	108
,, Pigmy pouter 301,	317
,, Plätscher...	315
,, Pomeranian cropper ...	308
,, Porcelain... ... 81, 97,	100
,, Pouters or croppers 275—	320
,, Pouting horseman ... 291,	298
,, Powdered owl	120
,, Prague cropper	319
,, Prague magpie cropper...	315
,, Priest	91
,, Red Indian	239
,, Riga tumbler	160
,, Ringbeater	116
,, Roller, Birmingham ...	155
,, Roller, Oriental	162
,, Roman runt	106
,, Ruff...	199
,, Runt... 66,	103
,, Satinette	232
,, Saxon cropper...	314
,, Scanderoon	272
,, Shakers ...125, 161, 181,	189
,, Sherajee	123
,, Shield	91
,, Short-faced Ancient ...	180
,, Short-faced Antwerp ...	148
,, Short-faced tumbler ...	164
,, Siberian ice	81
,, Siberian owl	322
,, Silesian swallow	86
,, Silken-haired	112
,, Singing	131
,, Smiter	116
,, Smyrna runt	106
,, Soot	75
,, Spot	73
,, Spot fairy	88
,, Starling	97

VARIETIES OF FANCY PIGEONS—(*continued*).

	PAGE
The Stork	88
,, Stork cropper	319
,, Suabian	99
,, Swallow	85
,, Swallow tailed	115
,, Swift	113
,, Swiss	101
,, Tailor	125
,, Tippler	154
,, Triganica	132
,, Trumpeter	182
,, Tumbler	150
,, Tumbler, shortfaced	164
,, Tunis owl	210

	PAGE
The Turbit	210, 223
,, Turbiteen	237
,, Turkish frilled	230
,, Turkish roller	162
,, Turner	116
,, Uploper	291
,, Ural ice	81
,, Velvet fairy	86
,, Victoria	97
,, Vienna bodice	75
,, Visor	236
,, Whiskered Owl	220
,, Whitehead	93
,, White spot	94

ERRATA.

At pages 15 and 16, *for* Wostenholme, *read* Wolstenholme.

At page 22, eighth line from foot, *for* copy Moore's, *read* copy of Moore's.

At page 76, fourth line from foot, *for* larger hood, *read* large hood.

At page 79, seventh line from foot, *for* two next, *read* two farthest from.

At page 82, title of Chapter XXI., *for* Miroite, *read* Miroité.

At page 106, third line from top, *for* Girtin, *read* Girton.

At page 130, twelfth line from top, *for* similiarly, *read* similarly.

At page 132, tenth line from top, *for* Tasso, *read* Tassoni.

At page 159, eleventh line from foot, *for* beard ought not to be, *read* beard ought to be.

At page 175, fourth line from foot, *for* the remarks, *read* these remarks.

At page 198, fourth line from foot, *for* is all white, *read* in all white.

At page 205, eleventh line from top, *for* divisionof, *read* division of.

At page 212, twenty-second line from top, Only lately, &c., should come in as line 15th.

At page 255, twelfth line from top, *for* severa, *read* several.

At page 281, third line from top, *for* heighth, *read* height.

At page 281, seventh line from foot, *for* heighth, *read* height.

At page 282, tenth line from top, *for* toot, *read* foot.

At page 286, thirteenth line from top, *for* best red pouter, *read* best coloured red pouter.

At page 295, seventh line from top, *for* pouters, *read* pouter's.

At page 300, first line from top, *for* experienced, *read* most experienced.

At page 305, sixth line from top, *for* books, *read* book.

At page 314, sixteenth line from foot, *for* next variety is the, *read* next variety is.

At page 318 eighth line from foot, *for* dark, *read* light.